MR. HALE BRADT, JR.
136 W. 4TH ST.
NEW YORK
N.Y.

WILBER E. BRADT,
HQ 169 FA BN.
A.P.O. #3193, c/o P.M.
SAN FRANCISCO, CAL.
OCT. 8, 1942

Dear Son, — A few minutes ago I was out looking at the stars. The Big Dipper is getting very low in the northern sky so that I cannot see it in the evening. You could see it well because you are farther north than I. Overhead is Vega and in the N.W. is Arcturus which is a bright blue star. In the west is Spica a bright red star and in the south is Fomalhaut which you cannot see at all. You pick out Vega and I will too so we can each look at the same star and know that star carries our greetings to each other. — Today a big turtle like you saw in the Aquarium was swimming in the sea. We soon passed him. I don't believe he was going as far as we are for he had an unambitious look on his face. — The ocean looks as if it were sloping up hill to the horizon and the waves on the [...] make the skyline look wrinkled. Today was [...] — Remember Columbus!
[...] inches long
[...] two inches long.
[...] will be when we
[...] fish are so thick
[...] your school
[...] love you. Wilber

AFTER ___ DAYS RETURN TO
#0982911
W. E. BRADT, MAJ., HQ 169TH FA BN.
A.P.O. #3193, c/o P.M., SAN FRANCISCO

V — MAIL

MR. HALE BRADT, JR.
136 W. 4TH ST.
NEW YORK
N.Y.

PASSED BY
U 19188 S
ARMY EXAMINER

CITIZEN SOLDIER

WILBER'S WAR

WILBER'S WAR TRILOGY
Citizen Soldier (Book 1)
Combat and New Life (Book 2)
Victory and Homecoming (Book 3)

BOOK 1

CITIZEN SOLDIER

WILBER'S WAR

An American Family's Journey
through World War II

Hale Bradt

Citizen Soldier
Book 1 of the *Wilber's War* Trilogy:
An American Family's Journey through World War II
www.wilberswar.com

Copyright © 2016 by Hale Bradt

Van Dorn Books
P.O. Box 8836, Salem, MA 01971
www.vandornbooks.com

All rights reserved. This book may not be reproduced in part or whole without the express written permission of the publisher. For permission to reproduce any material from the book, kindly contact the publisher at the address above or through info@vandornbooks.com

For information about bulk sales,
please contact the publisher at info@vandornbooks.com

Every effort has been made to trace and credit accurate copyright ownership of the visual material used in this book. Errors or omissions will be corrected in subsequent editions provided notification is made in writing to the publisher at the address above.
Book Editor: Frances B. King, HistoryKeep.com
Book design: Lisa Carta Design, lisacartadesign@gmail.com
Typefaces: Minion, Chaparral Pro
Book and case front-cover images: U.S. Army
Back-cover images: Bradt family
Printed by Friesens, Canada, http://www.friesens.com

Wilber's War (the trilogy)
ISBN 978-0-9908544-0-1
Library of Congress Control Number: 2014922173

Limited First Edition

The individual books (if separated from the set)
ISBN (Book 1, Citizen Soldier): 978-0-9908544-1-8
ISBN (Book 2, Combat and New Life): 978-0-9908544-2-5
ISBN (Book 3, Victory and Homecoming): 978-0-9908544-3-2
Library of Congress Control Numbers:
Book 1 (Citizen Soldier): 2014922166
Book 2 (Combat and New Life): 2014922168
Book 3 (Victory and Homecoming): 2014922167

In memory of Wilber and Norma
And for Valerie and Abby
—this is their story too

CONTENTS

Prologue Washington, D.C., December 1, 1945 — xiii
Maps and Charts — xxiii

PART I Farm to academia

1. *I had never seen a newborn baby* — 3
   Nebraska, Indiana, Washington, Ohio, Maine, 1871–1941
2. *Will a duck eat oats?* — 13
   Indiana, 1906–1927
3. *It was one of the perfect days of my life* — 39
   Wilber and Norma, 1927–1930
4. *I'm wondering if Wilber will be called to the Orient* — 57
   Pullman, Washington, 1930–1933
5. *We have a drastic cut in pay* — 69
   The Great Depression, 1933–1936
6. *Our river is still behaving and is fine skating* — 87
   Maine, 1936–1941
7. *I regret very much that you have not appreciated my filial affection* — 107
   Activation of the 43rd Division, 1940–1941

PART II Army camps

8. *Simulated tanks and simulated weapons* — 121
   Florida and New York City, March–July, 1941
9. *I plan to stay on this job until it is finished* — 131
   Florida, August 1941–February 1942
10. *My PhD didn't cut any ice here* — 147
    Mississippi, February–August, 1942
11. *Morale is booming and so are the howitzers* — 165
    California and Greenwich Village, September 1942
12. *There are good times and bad times* — 177
    Fort Ord, California, September 1942

PART III Voyages to war

13 *I will come back to my own, my beloved Nana* 191
    Pacific Ocean, October 1–22, 1942

14 *I'm wearing the St. Christopher medal* 205
    New Zealand, October–November, 1942

15 *The natives here hunt with sling-shots* 213
    New Caledonia, November–December, 1942

16 *So ended Christmas Eve with everyone pretty happy* 229
    Ouenghi, River, New Caledonia, December 1942–January 1943

17 *The silver thread tying all your souls together* 249
    Ouenghi River, January–February, 1943

PART IV Holding the front

18 *You can't tame a machine gun by looking it squarely in the eye* 261
    At sea and Guadalcanal, February 1943

19 *Hail to you, My Nana* 275
    Russell Islands (Pavuvu Island), February–April, 1943

20 *We have ourselves a general now* 289
    Pavuvu, April–May, 1943

21 *Oh! There go 5000 rings* 301
    Pavuvu, May–July, 1943

Acknowledgments 317
Bibliography 321
Index 325

FIGURES

CHARTS
    Chart 1. Bradt, Sparlin, and Bourjaily families xxv
    Chart 2. Organization of 43rd Infantry Division, 1942–1943 xxvi

MAPS
    Map 1. Locations in the United States xviii
    Map 2. Command Areas and Wilber's voyages xxix
    Map 3. Japanese plan for war xxx
    Map 4. Lines of communication to Australia xxxi
    Map 5. Solomon Islands xxxii
    Map 6. New Caledonia xxxiii
    Map 7. Russell Islands xxxiv

ILLUSTRATIONS

PROLOGUE
    Headlines, VJ Day xii
    Wilber on USS Gen. Pope 1945 xiv
    Hale with bicycle, 1946 xvi
    "Fatal Shooting" clipping xix

PART I Farm to academia
    Graves in Humboldt, Nebraska 2
    Isaac and Julia Bradt, 1870 4
    New Marion School, Indiana 6
    Baby Wilber with mother, grandmother 8
    F. Hale Bradt family foursome, 1904 9
    Bradt family outdoors, 1905 11
    Elizabeth and Wilber, 1904 12
    Wilber in rocking chair, 1904 12
    Commonplace, ca. 1930 14
    Commonplace, sketched by Rex 14
    Log house, garage, and barn, 1952 15
    Log house layout 16
    Bradt farm, Versailles, aerial, ca. 1985 17
    Waterloo school, Versailles 18
    "Ducks Damage Oats Field." 20
    F. Hale Bradt in uniform, 1918 25
    USS Zeppelin, ca. 1919 25
    Wilber and friend in SATC uniforms 28

ILLUSTRATIONS Continued

Wilber with mother, 1919 29
Swim team, Indiana U., 1923 31
Chemistry graduates, Indiana U., 1923 31
Auto repair, early 1920s 33
Wilber as second lieutenant 34
Howitzer gun crew 35
Artillery in early 1920s 36
Norma on picnic 38, 39
Andrew Sparlin's wife and children 40
Norma and three siblings, 1909 42
Wilber and Norma engaged 47
Wedding announcement 1927 48
Wilber and Norma, on honeymoon 49
Letter, E. O. Holland to the Bradts 51
Norma's graduation 1929 54
1928 Chevrolet in Calif. on US 80 60
1930 Model A, Texas on US 66 60
Bradt home in Pullman, Washington 61
Baby Hale with great-grandmother 62
1930 Chrysler and family 67
Norma with Hale and baby Valerie 67
Hale and Valerie on steps, ca. 1934 68
Camping in Wash. State, early 1930s 74
Wilber's family, ca. 1935 75
Tacoma strike: soldiers and truck 80
Tacoma strike: Wilber with striker 83
Wilber as professor and officer 85
F. Hale Bradt's family, 1936 90
Norma at her piano, ca. 1937 91
Norma with Valerie, 1937 91
Wilber, Hale and Valerie, ca. 1937 92
Hale and Valerie, Maine beach 93
Aubert Hall, U. of Maine, 1937 94
Officers of 152nd FA Regiment, 1941 117

PART II Army camps

"Captured" soldiers, maneuvers 132
Fifth graders, Grace Church School 135
Letter with signs for truck convoy. 137
Letter during Pearl Harbor attack 139
USS Lafayette (SS Normandie) 146
IOU note Wilber wrote for Valerie 158
Postscript to young Hale's letter. 161
Letter to young Hale before sailing, 1942. 187

PART III Voyages to war

USAT Maui, 1919 193
V-mail, original and reduced 196
V-mail, address side. 197
Shellback certificate. 200
SS Coolidge, soldiers escaping 206
USS American Legion. 214
Nouméa Harbor. 216
Wilber's journal, one page 219
Officers bathing, Ouenghi River 221
Train in New Caldedonia 224
Sketches of switchback trail 235
Monte F. Bourjaily. 243
Sketches of Wilber and ants 250

PART IV Holding the front

USS President Adams 260
Admiral Halsey and General Hester 279
Recital program 315

Front page headlines on August 14, 1945, announcing the end of the war. [FACSIMILE: THE EVENING STAR (WASHINGTON, D.C.)]

Prologue
Washington, D.C., 1945

Joy and optimism were in the air. Germany had capitulated three months before, and on August 14, 1945, Japan had surrendered and accepted the terms of the Potsdam Agreement. People the world over celebrated wildly, while some were quietly relieved they or their loved ones would no longer be in harm's way. One American soldier in the Philippines—who would have faced the Japanese in the forthcoming invasion of the Japanese homeland—was heard to say, "So it's over. Well! I think I'll go sit under that tree."

At the time, I lived in Washington, D.C., with my mother Norma and sister Valerie. I was 14, and they were 39 and 13 respectively (Chart 1). My father Wilber, an army artillery officer, was not with us nor had we seen him for nearly three years. (Charts and Maps follow this Prologue.)

On October 1, 1942, Wilber's division—the 43rd Infantry, a New England outfit (Chart 2)—had shipped out to the Western Pacific where it had fought through three sustained phases of intense combat. Wilber had been wounded twice but had soldiered on, and was honored with several medals. When the atom bomb brought the war to a close, he was a lieutenant colonel and regimental commander of the 172nd Infantry Regiment, the famed Green Mountain Boys of Vermont. If the war had continued, he and they would have crossed the beaches of Kyushu, Japan, under fire on November 1, 1945. All had wondered whether they would have survived that bloodbath, and many would not have.

With the war's end, plans changed, and the 43rd Division was sent into Japan, near Tokyo, as an occupation force. Two weeks after arriving in Japan, the division received orders to return to the United States. I was sitting in a study hall in high school when the school's newscast, read daily

CITIZEN SOLDIER

Lt. Col. Wilber E. Bradt on board the USS General Pope on the day of his return to San Francisco, October 8, 1945, after three full years overseas. He was the senior army officer on board the ship. [PHOTO: BRK00012315_24A CROPPED; SAN FRANCISCO NEWS-CALL BULLETIN, COURTESY BANCROFT LIBRARY, UNIV. OF CALIFORNIA, BERKELEY]

by a student, announced that the 43rd Infantry Division was being shipped home—an item of little direct interest to any other student in that Washington, D.C. school, I would think. But I knew it meant my father would be coming home, and I let out a little "whoop," but nothing more; I did not want to make a scene. The teacher raised her head to look at me curiously and then returned to her work.

My sister Valerie remembers it as a bright, hopeful time; her daddy was coming home at last. Our lives would be happier, even joyous, with him back in our midst. We did not go to the West Coast to meet his ship, on which he was the senior army officer, but a news photographer did and captured him on board the ship in a happy, smiling, perhaps even laughing moment.

Wilber reached our Washington, D.C., home in mid-October to a festive family-only homecoming; he seemed to Valerie and me to be the same daddy we had known so well before. To clear up some seemingly minor issues before separating from the service, he was assigned to the hospital at nearby Fort Meade, Maryland, and would return home weekends. We were becoming accustomed to being a family of four again, when there came a day that was to be—and remains—imprinted on our hearts and minds till the end of our days. Here is my story of that day from my recollected youthful perspective.

x · o · ø · o · x

It is a bright December Saturday morning in 1945 at our Alton Place home in northwest Washington, D.C. I am a lanky 14-year-old boy and I'm off to a downtown violin lesson. My sister Valerie, age 13, accompanies me; she has a dance lesson, also downtown. We leave the house and wave goodbye to our parents. Our father Wilber has recently returned—just six weeks earlier—from three years of overseas duty with the army. Our mother Norma is busy with household chores. We walk the few blocks to Tenley Circle where we catch the trolley with the new streamlined cars that have finally replaced the classic turn-of-the-last-century cars.

My violin teacher, Jan Tomasov, is the concertmaster of the National Symphony Orchestra. My talent and level of accomplishment do not merit such a teacher, but Mother reaches high for her two children. I have been studying with Mr. Tomasov for the last few months. He is a conscientious and demanding teacher with a stern demeanor and is not given to easy praise. At the lesson, I am challenged by new material and incur his occasional displeasure.

After the lesson I head for home, again on the number 30 Wisconsin Avenue trolley to Tenley Circle followed by the walk down Ablemarle and 44th Streets.

CITIZEN SOLDIER

At our front door, I encounter my Aunt Josephine and Uncle Paul, my father's brother. They live across town on First Street, NW; I know them well and have enjoyed extended visits at their home during two school vacations while Dad was overseas. They abruptly tell me I should go to our church (St. Columba's Episcopal) and see the minister because he has something to tell me. And I should do this straight away.

Puzzled but obedient, I go to the back of the house and grab my bike. It's a one-speed, coaster-brake affair with balloon tires, assembled of miscellaneous parts in a Hattiesburg, Mississippi, bicycle shop during our 1942 summer residence near our father's army camp. I walk it out of our back yard into the alley behind the house and bicycle the several blocks and up the final hill to St. Columba's, not a little apprehensive as I pedal those final difficult strokes.

The minister whom I know well through our youth group activities ushers me into his study and asks me to sit down. With little preliminary, he says, "I am sorry to tell you this, but your father is dead."

An accident, he says. I am stunned. I learn little more from him about the circumstances. My father had been in apparent good health, though that day he had had a reoccurrence of malarial symptoms and had decided not to report to

I was 15 in the summer of 1946, and here, I was leaving the back yard of our Alton Place home just as I had done on December 1, 1945, on my way to see the minister who would tell me my father was dead. My right pants leg is rolled up to keep it from getting caught in the chain.
[PHOTO: BRADT FAMILY]

the Fort Meade Army Hospital where he was being treated for other seemingly minor ailments.

Deeply shaken, I go out to the street and get on my bicycle for the downhill ride home. My usual skill and agility fail me as I start down the steep grade. I almost lose control, but don't. In a few minutes I am home.

x·o·ø·o·x

The details of what transpired upon my arrival at the house have faded from my memory. In the subsequent days, we managed to get through the military funeral and burial in Arlington National Cemetery on a dreary rainy day. We were given welcome support by a young half-brother of Mother's, Stonewall Sparlin, a navy medical corpsman who was attending the navy diving school in Washington. (He had served with the Marine Raiders in the Solomons during the war.) He had not realized we had moved to Washington nor had we known he was there. He read of our loss in the Sunday newspaper and promptly contacted us and gave us much needed support in the following days and months.

My violin teacher, upon reading of my father's death and realizing that it had actually occurred before my lesson, called to offer his condolences and to assure himself that I had not known of it during the lesson. When I told him I could not continue lessons, in part because of money, he generously offered lessons at no cost. I demurred, preferring not to continue under his stern critical teaching. I did not resume violin study until college, three years later. I would be a much better fiddler today had I continued with him, I am sure. I am surprised that Mother did not object to my decision, but she was facing much larger issues.

x·o·ø·o·x

My sister Valerie recalls that day, "The Day Daddy Died":

ANNAPOLIS, MARYLAND, 2009
It was a big day. The plan was for me to go downtown with my brother, a year older, for a dance lesson for me and some other appointment for him, but I would come home on the trolley by myself, from Georgetown to Tenley Circle.

I had made it almost home that day, walking from the trolley stop on Wisconsin Avenue down to Alton Place. When I passed the neighbors two doors from our house, they stopped me and insisted I come in for lunch. I did not want to because it was the first day of my first menstrual period and I was afraid to have an "accident."

(Mother had taught me that it was a natural process, but I was still afraid.) They insisted I stay for lunch and even blocked my way, so I gave in and went into their dining room for lunch.

Their three daughters stared at me the whole time. I was uncomfortable, but I did not know what to say to them. Then the rector of St. Columba's Episcopal Church came to the house and I was told to meet him in the living room. He ordered me to sit down.

I did not trust him because he had stood passively by weeks earlier when the boys were tickling me on the floor in the church parish hall and I was almost hysterical. In that small living room, I sensed that something was wrong. He said, "Sit down." I said, "No." He repeated, "Sit down." I said, "No" again. He said, "Okay, your daddy is dead."

I felt a sort of dead anger. I walked out of that house and went down the sidewalk to our house onto the porch and into the dining room to find my mother sitting in a chair crying. There were police and military investigators throughout the small frame building. I asked her what happened. She said there was "a terrible accident." My brother arrived and he was told to go see the minister. He left on his bike for what I knew would be up the long hill to another message of death.

I walked into the kitchen and picked up a paper bag, went upstairs and stuffed my nightgown and a toothbrush into it, walked out and went to Mary Ann Frankenhauser's house. We were not friends, but I did not know where else to go. I said nothing to anyone and stayed there at least a week. I guess her mother called mine and left me alone.

I did not go to the funeral at Arlington National Cemetery. My brother went in the heavy rain with my mother, helping her to accept the folded American flag. I felt terrible about that.

Our daddy had come home after three years overseas and was now gone. I did not know why. I was left in a bleak, dry, empty space that turned into anger. I was driven to get a degree from Columbia University, which led to an extensive career in journalism. The anger finally dissipated, but never my regret for losing those years with my father.

x · o · ø · o · x

I am Hale Van Dorn Bradt, 83 years of age in 2014 and namesake of my grandfather F. Hale Bradt; we pronounce our name closer to "brought," than "brat." I am a retired physicist and professor, and a resident of Salem, Massachusetts, with a wife and two grown daughters. In June of 2012, I made a month-long solo automobile trip of 4700 miles to the Midwest to visit relatives long neglected or never before met. I saw members of my father's

Prologue

Fatal Shooting of Colonel, Pacific Hero, Probed by Army

Officer Is Found Dead in Basement Trophy Room

Washington police and Coroner A. Magruder MacDonald are awaiting completion of an Army investigation of the circumstances surrounding the gunshot death of Lt. Col. Wilber E. Bradt, 45, Pacific war hero and former college professor, who was found in a weapon-filled basement trophy room at his home yesterday morning with a gaping wound in his chest.

Walter Reed Hospital authorities, who assumed charge of the investigation immediately after a neighbor found the often-decorated officer's body in the Bradt home at 4421 Alton place N.W., are expected to conduct an autopsy today. Meanwhile Walter Reed officials have re-

LT. COL. WILBER E. BRADT.

Wilber's death announced in the Washington, D.C., Sunday Star *of December 2, 1945, page A6.* [SOURCE: *WASHINGTON (D.C.) STAR*]

family (the Bradts), my mother's (the Sparlins), and my stepfather's (the Bourjailys). This trip and those families provided me substantial resolution to the dramatic story of my family during World War II, a story that I have spent many years uncovering, and a story that taught me much about my parents and the America of their times.

My search began on the evening of my 50th birthday, December 7, 1980 (Pearl Harbor day!), with a discussion I had with my middle sister, Abigail, then 37, about her uncertain paternity. I was driving her and her husband Tom back from our house in Belmont, Massachusetts, where we had had a small dinner celebration, to their hotel in Cambridge.

The topic was whether Abigail was the daughter of my father, Wilber Bradt, a former university professor and a much decorated army officer who

XIX

had died in 1945, or of Monte Bourjaily, a prominent journalist whom my mother Norma had married in 1947. Abby had been born in 1943, and Monte had subsequently adopted her and given her the Bourjaily name. We knew both men were candidates for the paternal honor, but neither of us knew which one it was. Abigail and I approach our histories from different perspectives, and our discussions could become a little warm. She "felt like a Bradt," and I felt the circumstances favored her being a Bourjaily. However, as on previous occasions, this conversation played out with no resolution. Then, a new thought occurred to me, and I said, "Well, perhaps you really don't want to know, and that is OK too." And, perhaps I did not want to know either. Facing the possibility that your mother had been an adulteress was daunting. We parted at the hotel on that uncertain note.

Upon returning home, I immediately went looking for dated letters from Wilber, my father, that might clarify his whereabouts at the time of Abigail's conception. I knew he wrote many letters to the family during the war and that maybe I had some of them. I rummaged in the old basement file cabinet where I always threw stuff that related to family. Indeed, I found a large manila envelope with about a dozen letters from my father to me. During the war, Mother had gathered them and sent them in that envelope to the *Atlantic Monthly*, which was holding a contest for the best letters written by a serviceman to his children. Our dad's letters did not make the cut and were returned. Decades later she found the same manila envelope in one of her many file folders and sent it with its contents to me. I put it in that basement cabinet and promptly forgot about it.

So, there I was, on the evening of my birthday in 1980, sitting on the cement floor of the unfinished basement reading my father's hand-written letters. The dates and places of their writing shed no light on Abby's paternity, but I found them to be well written, informative, beautifully descriptive, humorous, and self-consciously fatherly. They were also riveting and some brought tears to my eyes. I knew he had written home from overseas profusely and I remembered some of the contents, but I had not appreciated the quality of his writing. I knew, then and there, that I had to find more of them. I had long been interested in the Pacific campaigns of World War II and had collected histories and books about them, but had never delved deeply into the details of my father's involvement. The possibility of retrieving a mother lode of his correspondence that could shed light on his experiences greatly excited me. Abigail's paternity, in that context, became a secondary issue for me.

Prologue

I met Abigail and Tom the next day and described for them the impact on me of Wilber's letters, along with my eagerness to seek out more of them with the aim of learning his entire wartime story. In doing so, I said, I could plausibly discover the truth about Abby's parentage. "Would you mind?" I asked. She responded, "After our conversation last night in the car, Tom and I went to the hotel's rotating sky bar and talked for at least two hours. We realized that you were right, I really didn't want to know, but . . . . yet again, I did." She then gave me her blessing, saying: "Do what you have to do."

That was the launch of my search for people, places, and letters.

I eventually found some 700 highly literate, descriptive letters my father had written during his wartime service. To fill out the story, I interviewed family members, as well as his academic and military associates in the U.S. and elsewhere. I spent one afternoon with a Japanese former colonel who had fought directly opposite my father in the Solomon Islands, ferreted out documents and photographs from the National Archives in Washington and elsewhere, and visited the Pacific areas where Wilber had served: New Zealand, the Solomon Islands, Luzon in the Philippines, and Japan. Much of this I did in the early 1980s. More recently I have delved into letters written by my father's parents and his sister Mary that reveal their profound influences on his life. In recent years, I have found additional fresh material on the Internet.

In all this, I uncovered a fresh and unique view of the Pacific war as experienced by an observant and committed U.S. Army participant, as well as a complex story of an American family during the war. It is time that I shared the story with a wider audience. As my sister Valerie put it, "You must do this, Hale; it is everyone's story." I am motivated to do this by a compulsion to know my parents as real people and also because I alone, at this time, can provide the military and family backstories.

I have chosen to let Wilber and others tell much of the story in their own words, through their letters. They capture, better than I could, the tenor of the times. Theirs is a story of America in the early 20th century, transporting us from the Midwest to the Northwest, and the Northeast to the southern states of Florida and Mississippi, before taking us on an epic three-year tour of the Pacific with its 11 ocean voyages and three phases of combat. Finally, it is the detailed account of my search for the story, including my visits to the Pacific locations where Wilber had been.

Of the approximately 400,000 words in Wilber's extant letters, roughly 150,000 of those words appear in the three volumes of this work. In all they are a remarkably complete record of the Pacific War in both its technical and human aspects. My editing of the letters consisted of omitting letters in their entirety (with no indication) and excising portions of others (always with ellipses). My only modifications to the letters were occasional added punctuation, bracketed clarifications, and a few corrected misspellings and adjusted paragraph breaks. For the most part, however, the inconsistencies of Wilber's impromptu writing, including his casual use of dashes, were left untouched. The remarkable overall clarity and drama of Wilber's writing made unnecessary large scale editing, other than the aforementioned deletions. The work also includes letters by relatives and associates that shed light on the characters and activities of Wilber and Norma.

Wilber consistently dated his letters and, when permitted by censorship rules, gave his location. He wrote often of censorable events, but would delay mailing those letters until it was allowed, typically a month after the action. He clearly was writing for the historical record! Sadly, few of my mother's extensive letters to Wilber survive, but her thoughts and concerns are reflected in his responses. I, as narrator herein, fill in events that Wilber could not or chose not to tell. I also help ground the reader in the local context, the wider events of the war, the activities of our family at home in the United States, and finally my (as Wilber's son) take on the issues at hand. Any material appearing in square brackets [like these] is mine alone.

I relate the story in three phases, or books, that cover the entire Pacific War, including its precursors and aftermath, through the eyes of the participants. Infrequent abbreviated references in brackets provide a sense of my sources, which are more fully described in the bibliography. Photographs of places and people and facsimiles of documents are interspersed throughout the text but frequently referenced material (maps and charts) are placed together following this prologue.

As children we called our parents Daddy and Mommy and later Mom; unfortunately, there was little "later" for my father, although we used Dad on occasion during his life. As narrator of his story, I have chosen for the most part to step back and refer to both parents by their given names, Wilber and Norma.

For me—and hopefully for my readers—Wilber is the hero of this narrative, and Norma is the heroine.

MAPS & CHARTS

Maps and Charts

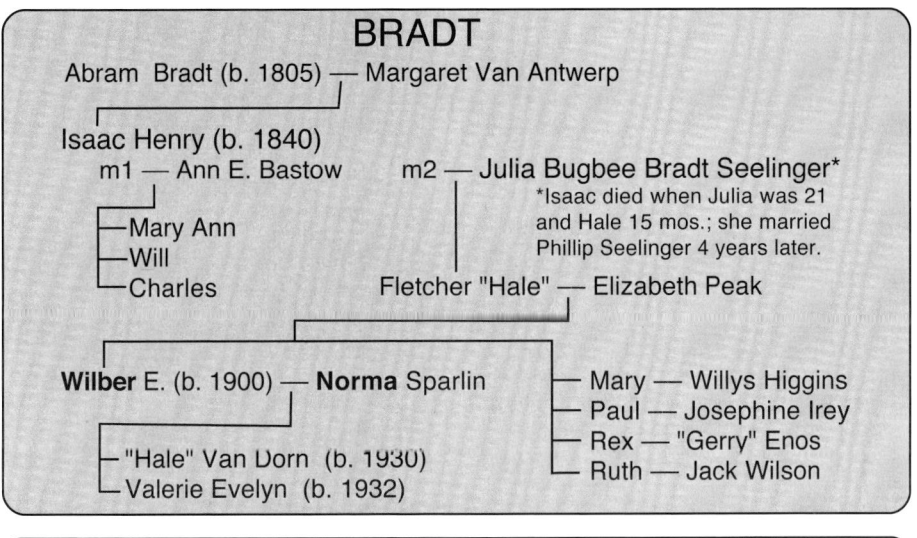

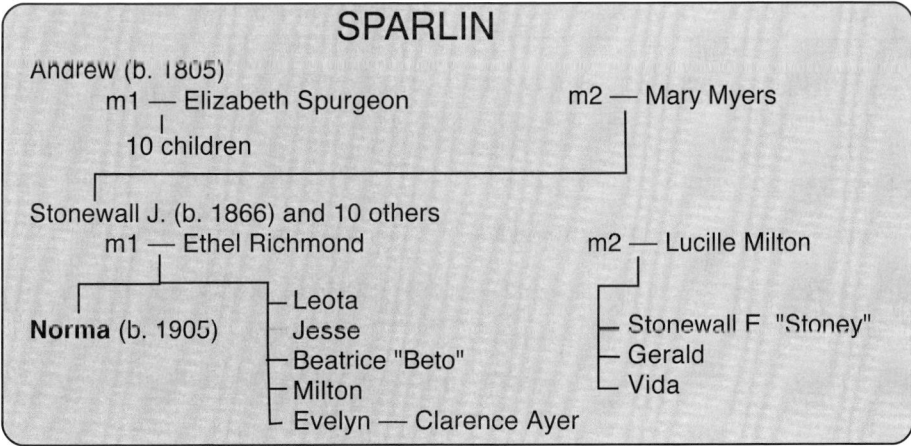

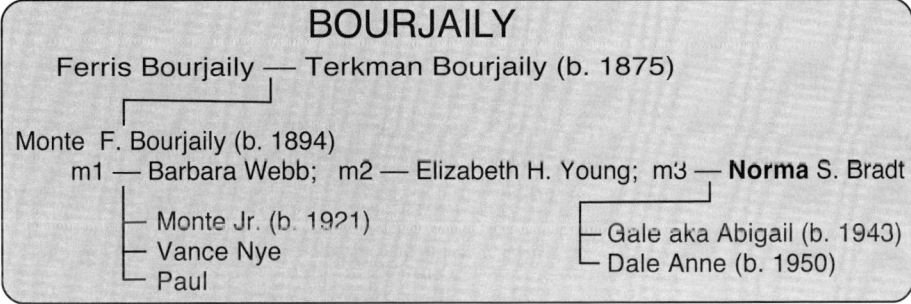

Chart 1. The Bradt, Sparlin, and Bourjaily families.

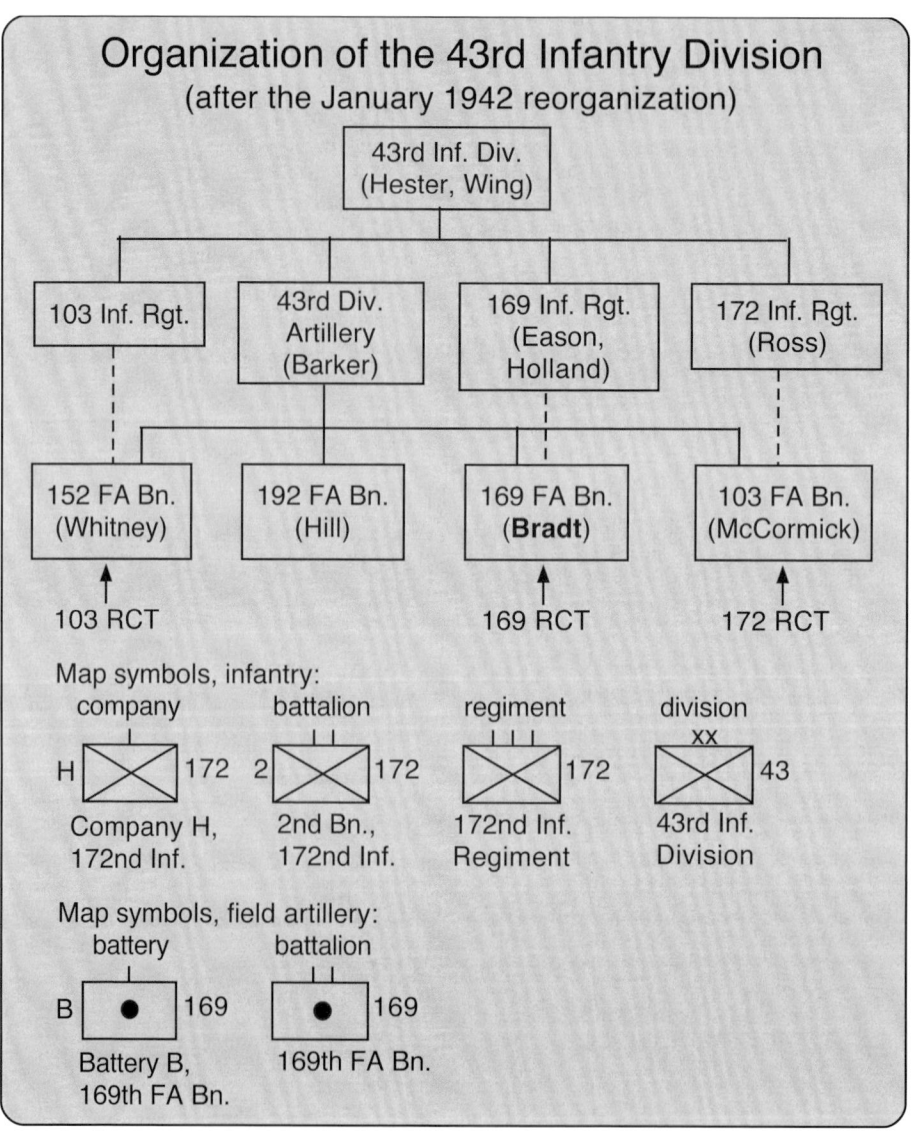

Chart 2. Organization and commanders of the 43rd Infantry Division, 1942–1943.

1. The commanding officers (C.O.) shown are those in command during the Solomon Islands actions who were mentioned in Wilber's letters.

2. The division (Div.) had numerous other supporting elements.

3. The three "light" field artillery (FA) battalions (103rd, 152nd, and 169th) had 105-mm (4-inch) howitzers, which had a range of about five miles. The "medium" battalion (192nd FA) had 155-mm (6-inch) howitzers, which had a greater range.

4. A field artillery battalion consisted of about 500 men and 12 howitzers divided into three batteries (A, B, C) of four howitzers each and a headquarters battery.

5. An infantry regiment (Inf. Rgt.) consisted of three infantry battalions, 1st Bn., 2nd Bn., and 3rd Bn., each with about 500 men in four companies, designated A, B, C, and D in the 1st Bn., E–H in the 2nd Bn., and I, K, L, M in the 3rd Bn.

6. The four artillery battalions were under the command of General Barker, but could be assigned to regimental combat teams (RCT), which could operate independently of one another. The three light artillery battalions were normally assigned to the infantry regiments shown (dashed lines), but assignments could vary. The medium artillery battalion was reserved for general support where needed.

7. The National Guard origins of these units were:
Connecticut: 169 Inf. and 192 FA.
Maine: 152 FA and 103 Inf.
Rhode Island: 103 FA and 169 FA.
Vermont: 172 Inf.

8. Army officer ranks in ascending order in 1943 were: 2nd lieutenant (Lt.), 1st Lt., captain (Capt.), major (Maj.), lieutenant colonel (Lt. Col.), colonel, brigadier general (one-star insignia), major general (two stars), lieutenant general (three stars), and general (four stars). A five star rank, General of the Army, was reactivated in late 1944.

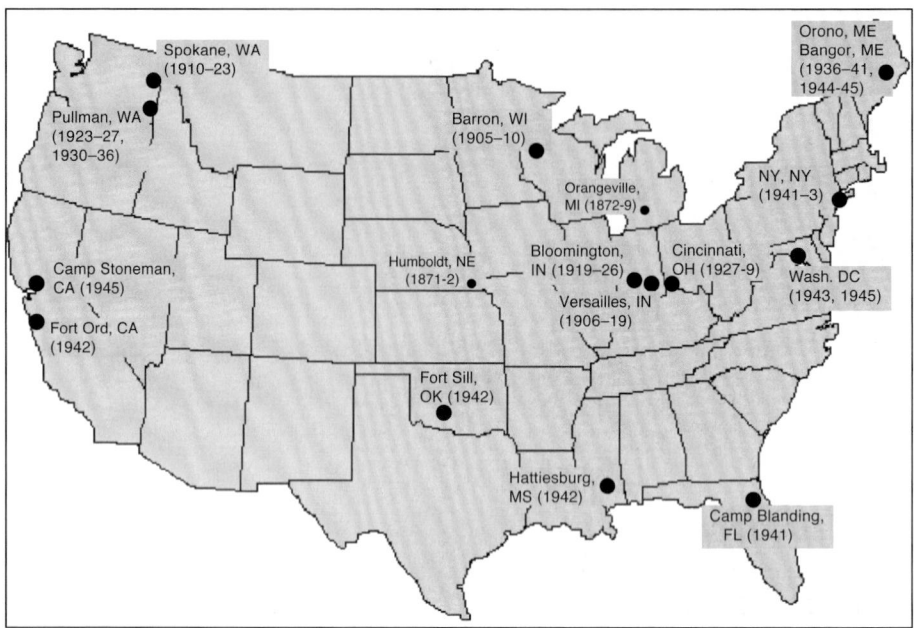

Map 1. Locations where Wilber and Norma lived. The two smaller dots in Nebraska and Michigan are for Wilber's grandmother and father. Wilber and Norma met in Pullman, Washington, in 1927. [UNDERLYING MAP: 50STATES.COM, MARCHEX, INC.; LABELS: HALE BRADT]

Maps and Charts

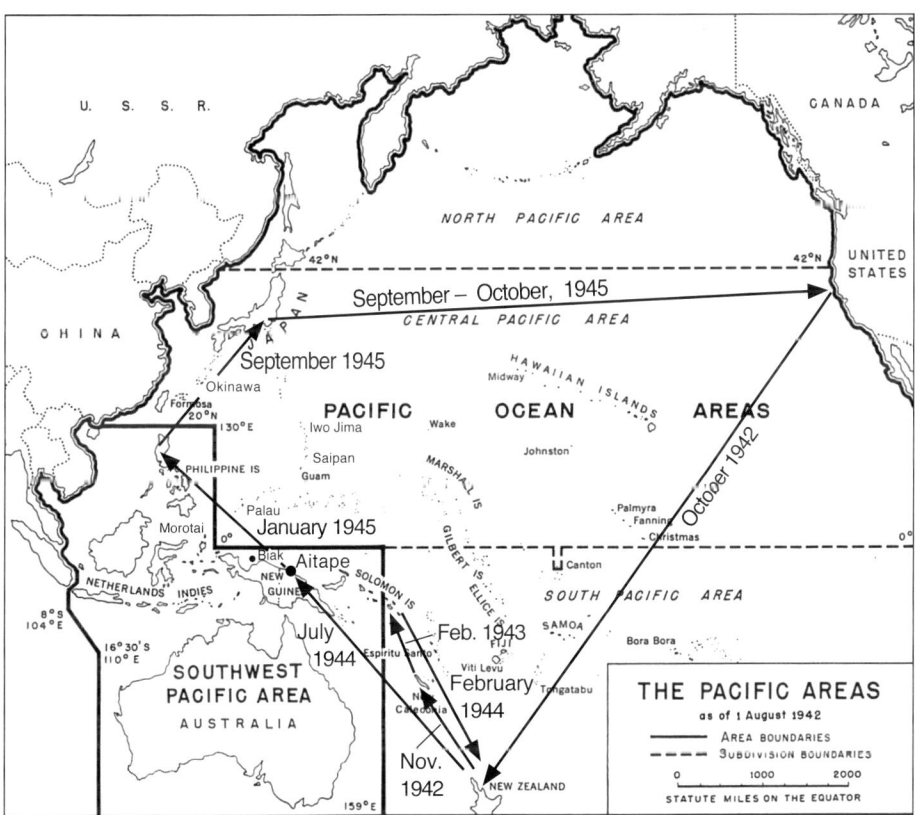

Map 2. Eight sea voyages (black lines with arrowheads and dates) made by the 43rd Division in the Pacific Ocean during its three years overseas. Three additional (overnight) voyages were made within the Solomon Islands. Also delineated are the four military command areas of the Pacific Theater. The North, Central, and South Pacific Areas were the domain of the U.S. Navy (Admiral Chester Nimitz), and the Southwest Pacific Area, the domain of the U.S. Army (General Douglas MacArthur). [UNDERLYING MAP: R. JOHNSTONE, IN MILLER, *CARTWHEEL*, MAP 2, P. 3]

CITIZEN SOLDIER

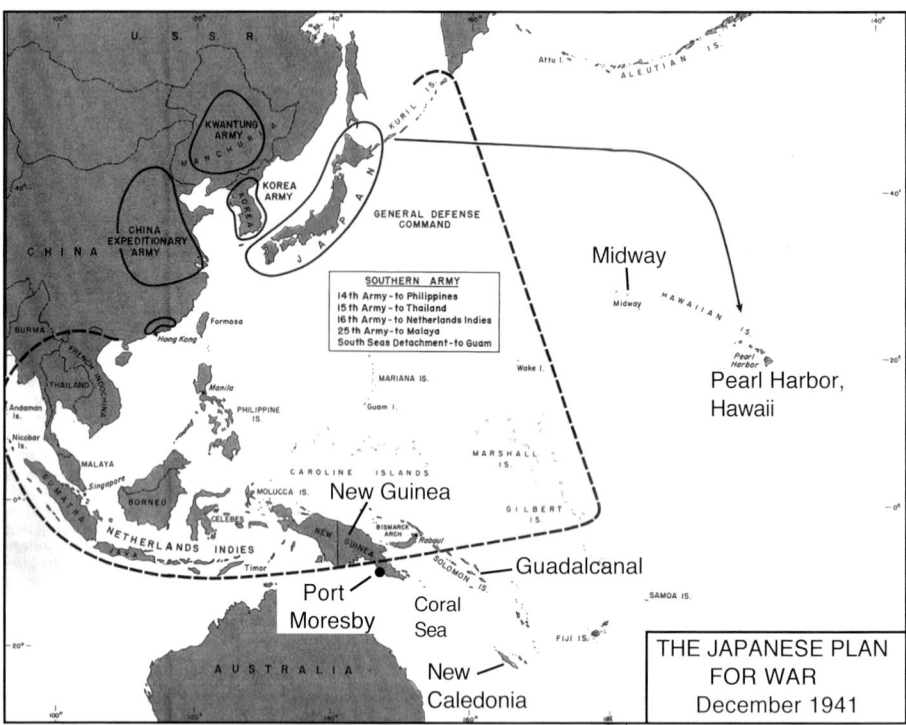

Map 3. Japanese plan for war, December 1941. The dashed line encompasses the planned Japanese sphere of influence, called the East Asia Co-Prosperity Sphere, which was attained in the months following the Pearl Harbor attack of December 7, 1941 (December 8 in Japan). The Japanese drive was halted on the ground at Guadalcanal in the Solomon Islands and at Port Moresby in New Guinea in the fall of 1942. The naval battles of the Coral Sea (May 1942) and Midway (June 1942) blocked planned Japanese attacks on Port Moresby and Midway, respectively. [UNDERLYING MAP: MORTON, *STRATEGY*, MAP 1, P. 106–7]

Maps and Charts

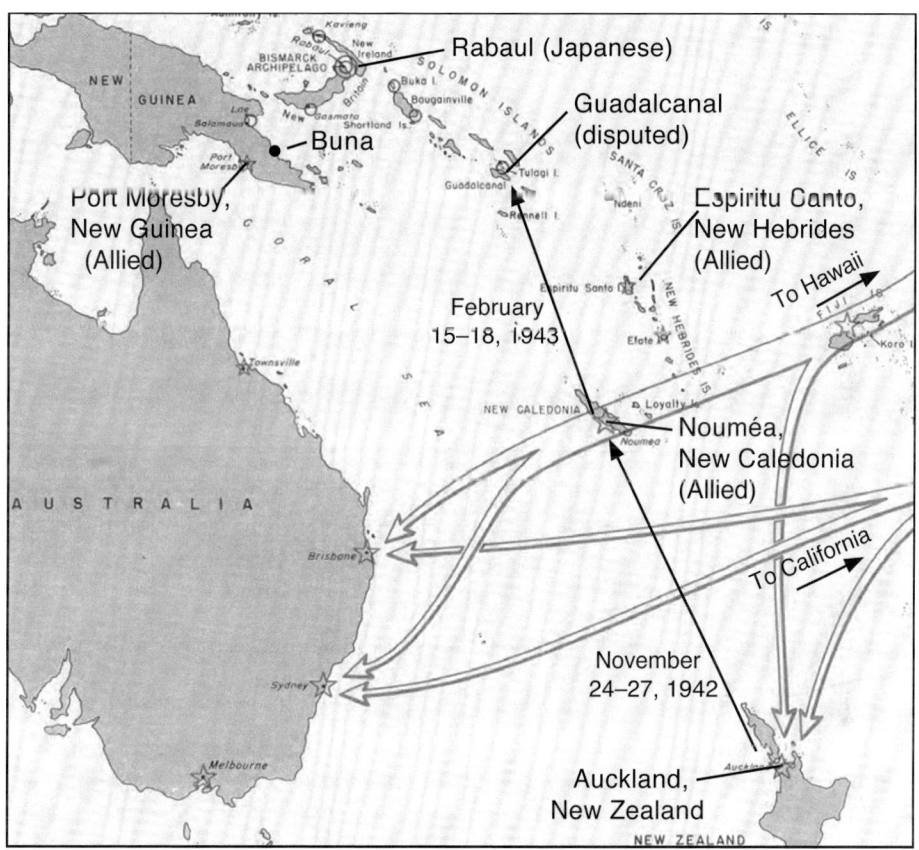

Map 1. Southwest Pacific, July 1942, showing lines of communication (broad double lines) from Hawaii and California, the American bases (stars), and the Japanese bases (circles). The marines were doing battle on Guadalcanal when the 43rd Division arrived in New Zealand in October 1942, less the 172nd Regimental Combat Team, which lost all its equipment in the sinking of the USS Coolidge at Espiritu Santo. In late November 1942, most of the 43rd Division moved from New Zealand to New Caledonia (lower black line with arrowhead); the balance arrived December 29. This released the Americal Division for duty on Guadalcanal. In mid-February 1943, the 43rd moved further north to the front lines in the Solomon Islands (upper black line with arrowhead). The naval battles arising from attempts to reinforce Guadalcanal by both sides were supported from the major naval bases at Rabaul (Japanese, upper left) and at Nouméa, New Caledonia (Allied, center right). [UNDERLYING MAP: MILLER, *GUADALCANAL*, MAP II]

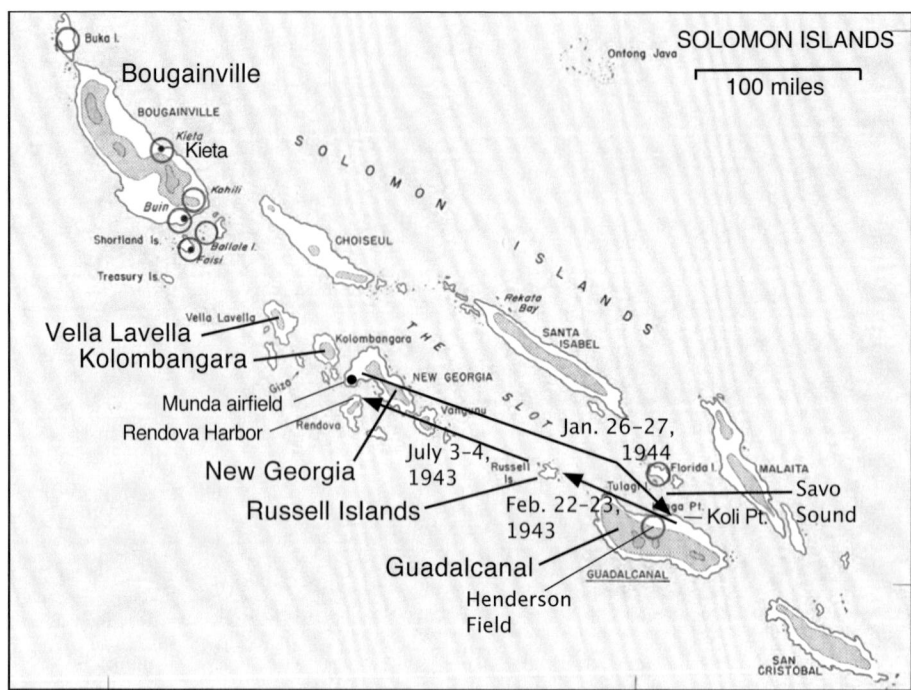

Map 5. Solomon Islands including Guadalcanal, the Russell Islands, and the New Georgia group, all of which are featured in Wilber's story. The circles indicate Japanese bases prior to the marine landings on Guadalcanal in August 1942. The major Japanese stronghold at Rabaul was on New Britain Island, 200 miles farther to the northwest. Another Japanese airfield was built on New Georgia at Munda during the Guadalcanal fighting. The three moves of the 43rd Division during its 11 months in the Solomons are shown.

During the battles over Guadalcanal, Japanese ships would approach Guadalcanal from the northwest through "the Slot," while American ships would approach from the southeast. Both were trying to reinforce and supply their troops on Guadalcanal. Many ships were sunk in Savo Sound ("Ironbottom Sound"), which lies between Florida Island and Guadalcanal. [UNDERLYING MAP: MILLER, *GUADALCANAL*, MAP III, CROPPED]

Maps and Charts

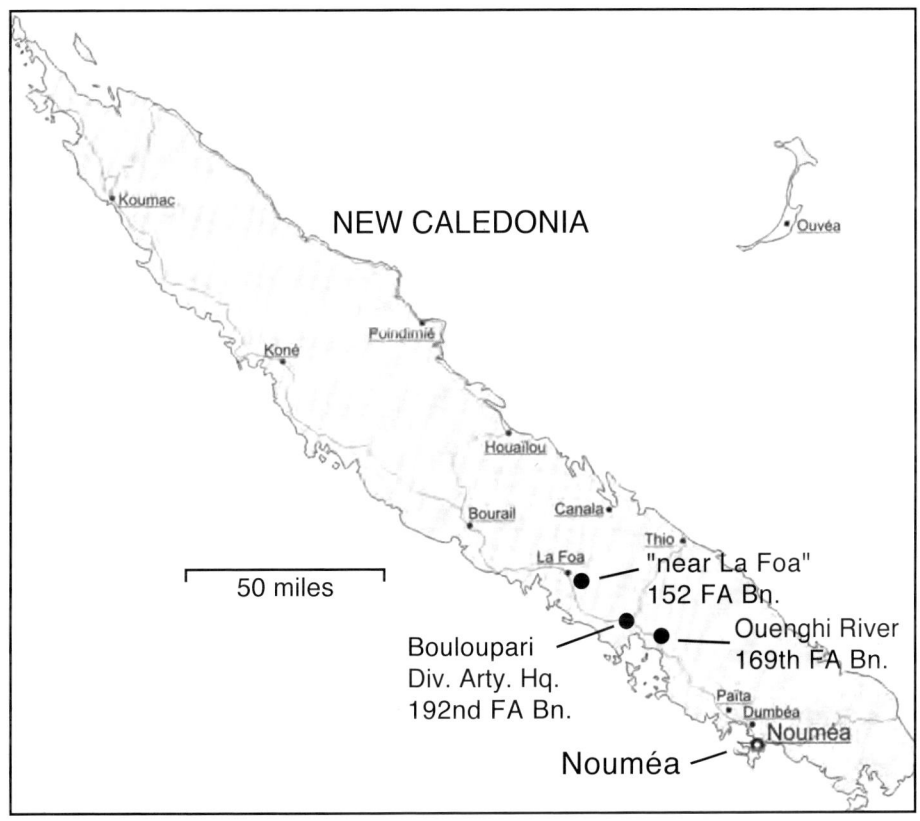

Map 6. New Caledonia with locations mentioned in the text. The location of the 152nd FA Bn. is not known precisely [OUTLINE MAP: D-MAPS.COM]

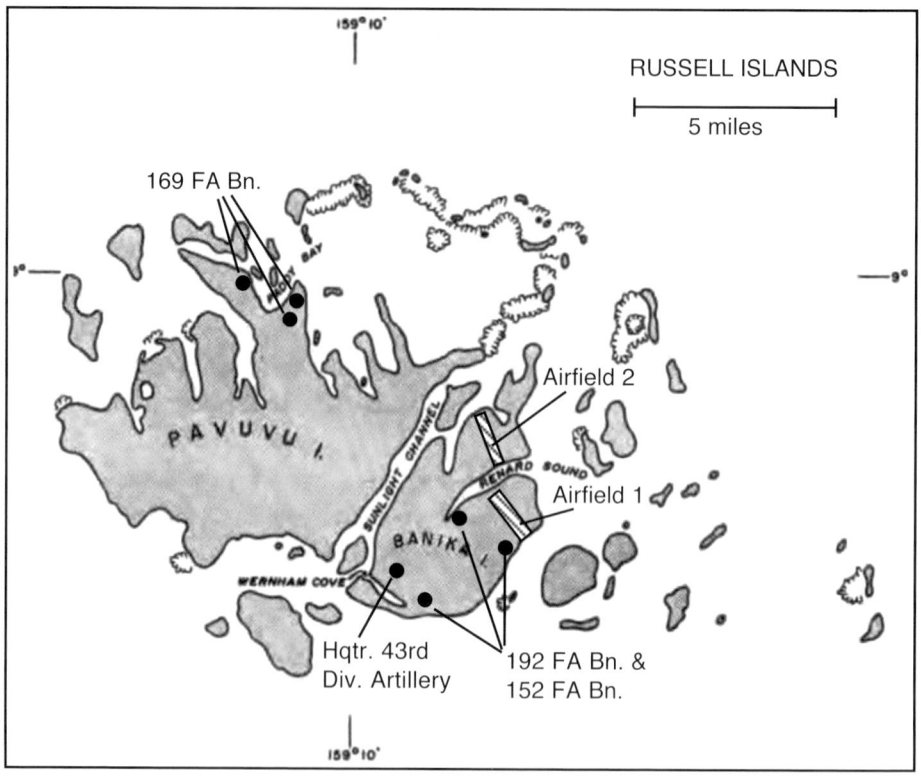

Map 7. Russell Islands showing the locations of Wilber's battalion (169th Field Artillery) on Pavuvu Island, and on Banika Island the division artillery headquarters, the other two field artillery battalions (152nd and 192nd), and the American airfields. Wilber's outfit, the 169th, was quite a long boat ride from the artillery headquarters and Wilber's immediate superior, General Barker. [UNDERLYING MAP: MILLER, *GUADALCANAL*, P. 353, MAP 15; UNIT LOCATIONS: BARKER, MAP P. 30; AIRSTRIP LOCATIONS: SEABEES MAPS, WWW.SEABEES93.NET]

PART I

FARM TO ACADEMIA

NEBRASKA, INDIANA, WASHINGTON, OHIO, MAINE
1871–1941

Graves of Isaac (d. 1872), my great grandfather, left, and his father Abram (d. 1877) in Humboldt, Nebraska, with fields in the distance. [PHOTO: JORENE HERR, 2014]

1

"I had never seen a newborn baby"

Hale and Elizabeth
1870–1906

It was a cloudy day, late on a June afternoon in 2012, when I stood on a hillside in Humboldt, Nebraska, pondering two side-by-side gravestones. One was that of my great-grandfather Isaac Bradt, a Methodist provisional minister, who had died a young man of 32 on November 22, 1872. The other was that of Abram Bradt, Isaac's father, who had died in 1877, five years after his son. On this same hillside on a much earlier cold November day, Isaac's grieving young widow Julia, age 21, would have been holding her 15-month old son, Fletcher Hale Bradt, called Hale. With Julia would have been Isaac's parents, Abram and Margaret Bradt, along with Isaac's three children—Mary, Will, and Charles from his previous marriage, ranging in age from 12 to 9; their mother Ann had died at 30, three years earlier.

Isaac had traveled from Nebraska to Michigan to win Julia's hand and had returned to Nebraska with her via wagon and buggy, accompanied by his own two young sons, Charlie and Will. (Mary stayed in Nebraska with her grandparents.) The thousand-mile journey took a full month, and Julia memorialized it in a diary. Six months before his death, Isaac had taken title to 40 acres of Nebraska farmland near that of his father and brothers. His life was on the rise when he was felled by illness; his death, said to be of "locked bowel," might have been from appendicitis.

As I stood there looking out over the Nebraska farm fields, I imagined that sad day and pondered the outcome. The 15-month-old Hale would

Wilber's grandfather, the Reverend Isaac H. Bradt and his wife Julia A. Bugbee Bradt about 1870. They drove from Michigan to Nebraska in a buggy and/or wagon in August–September, 1870. [PHOTO: BRADT FAMILY]

grow up to become my grandfather, the father of my father Wilber, the soldier who had died so suddenly in our Washington, D.C., home on yet another cold day, this one in December 1945.

x·o·ø·o·x

After burying her husband, Julia had taken her baby son Hale and returned to Michigan—another long wagon, or possibly train, trip—where her brother George Bugbee, a widower with a daughter Grace, worked in a lumber camp. (Julia's three stepchildren remained in Nebraska with their grandparents.) She took care of Grace and little Hale and worked as a cook in the camp. There she met and married, in 1877, another sawmill worker, Philip Seelinger, from Versailles, Indiana, a farming village in southeast Indiana. He had left his hometown suddenly after a confrontation.

My Aunt Mary, daughter of my grandfather Hale and sister of Wilber, told the story of this confrontation in a 1980 letter to me, the younger Hale. The letter revealed the intensity of post-bellum attitudes in Indiana, as well as the source of the Bradt family's strong antislavery views. This was one of several letters that I received from Mary and others in the early 1980s during my quest for information about my parents. At the time, three of Hale's children—my Aunt Mary, Uncle Rex, and Aunt Ruth—were still living, though all are gone now. Each probed their memories for me. But it was my Aunt Mary who excelled at this in her typewritten letters.

24 SEPT, 1980
Dear Hale — ... Father's [Hale's] coming to Indiana goes back to politics following the Civil War. My step-grandfather [Philip Miller Seelinger] had been a soldier in the Civil War as was his father. They felt very strongly about slavery and were strong supporters of Lincoln and the anti-slavery movement. When Grandpa came home [to Indiana] from the war, he went to church one Sunday and while there a pro-slavery man made some statement, which made Grandpa (then in his teens) angry and they started to fight. It was not an ordinary fight, for Grandpa drew a knife on the "copperhead" as Southern sympathizers were then called. Witnesses later told Father that when "Grandpa had cut his abdomen and strung his vitals over the church yard," he left the country, going to Michigan where he worked in a lumber camp....

This was surely an exaggeration because the "copperhead" recovered and Seelinger found it safe to return to Ripley County in 1879 or early 1880 with Julia and Hale, who was then eight or nine years old.

Hale attended school in New Marion and first met his future wife, Elizabeth Peak, age six, when he was ten years old. Elizabeth was apparently quite taken with the handsome new boy in town. The school was new in 1881 and went only through eighth grade. One of the first teachers was Charles Newton Peak, the older brother of Elizabeth by 18 years. He was known as Sonnie to the family and was one of the first in the county to earn a college degree.

Hale lived with his stepfather and mother in Holton, Indiana, a few miles west of Versailles, and worked on the family farm. After eighth grade, he attended "Normal School programs" in New Marion. These were special courses for limited periods, typically in the summer, that prepared graduates for teaching positions. They were offered in New Marion in the summers of 1883 through 1887 under the leadership of Charles Peak and a Mr. Day. Peak may have been grooming Hale for a better future because of his young sister's interest in him.

New Marion, Indiana, schoolhouse where Hale and Elizabeth met as children in 1881. Hale later taught here. [POSTCARD POSTMARKED NOV. 1909; BRADT FAMILY]

Starting at age 17 or 18, Hale taught school for two years in Ripley County, possibly at the New Marion School, and then went to Lincoln, Nebraska, for a university education. There he lived with his half-brother Charles Edwin Bradt (son of Isaac), by then a well-educated Presbyterian minister. Hale attended the preparatory school there in 1891–92 and entered the University of Nebraska in 1892 at age 21. He majored in chemistry, and was on the football team that won the interstate league championships in 1893 and 1895. During summers he worked at a lumber camp in Wyoming to earn funds for his education. After graduation in 1896, he was a detective in the San Francisco area for two years and then returned to Indiana where he taught at the New Marion School where he had first met Elizabeth.

Elizabeth (Mary Elizabeth Peak), who would become Wilber's mother, was born on May 1, 1875. In her youth, she had been known as Lizzie. She received an eighth grade education followed by one year of high school in North Vernon, Indiana (20 miles west of Versailles), and then became a teacher when she was still quite young. In a letter to my sister Abigail, she described a gift she had received from her beau Hale. Elizabeth wrote this

CHAPTER 1   *I had never seen a newborn baby*

on her 86th birthday. She was long widowed and living alone on the Bradt farm in Versailles. The letter shows a rather charming aspect of her complex character. Other less favorable traits came into strong play when her son Wilber chose a bride and later went off to war. My sister Abigail provided me with copies of these wonderful letters to her, one of which is here:

Mon. May 1st, 1961
Dear Abigail — ... When I was in my teens, my sister, Emma, gave my Mother a light-weight silver thimble. Mother had always used an open-end thimble and would not change from her brass lined, steel one, so the silver thimble was given to me. I used it for years, until it was worn thru on the sides and my needle roughened my finger nail. About that time, Hale began holding my hand. – We were engaged. – He inquired about my roughened finger nail and I explained. In about a week he came with a beautiful new thimble. He said a girl who wore holes in her thimble deserved another. That thimble became very dear to me – second only to my wedding ring. I used it for years and always experienced a feeling of pride when I slipped it on my finger.... Lovingly, Elizabeth Bradt

x·o·ø·o·x

On April 3, 1899, after a four-year engagement, Hale married Elizabeth. This was possible because he had obtained a job teaching science and coaching at Bloomington (Indiana) High School where he was one of only six teachers. Their first child, Wilber, the focus of this story, was born there, as described by Elizabeth in another vivid letter to Abigail:

Sunday P.M. Jan. 29, 1961
Dear Abigail — ... Sixty-one years ago at this date, I was expecting [my baby Wilber's birth].... We were living on Hunter Ave. in Bloomington [Indiana]....
Hale stayed with me during the next few days. I don't remember when [Hale's] Mother [Julia] came. I was conscious only part of the time, but I knew another doctor was called. (It was Dr. Ernest Holland's father.) I remember thinking I must be "pretty bad" to have two doctors. I think I thought I might be going to die and I recalled that Hale's Sunday pants had a rip in the stride. I thought "He will want to wear them to the funeral and he will find them ripped. Then he will marry some one who keeps the rips mended and he will love her better than he does me."
The days wore along, until the next Thursday, Feb. 1st [1900]. Wilber was born at 3:20 P.M. I had never seen a newborn baby. My bed had been moved into the living room by the fire and I saw Mother shaking and spanking and blowing her breath

Baby Wilber, about 1900, with his mother, Elizabeth, and paternal grandmother, Julia Seelinger [PHOTO: BRADT FAMILY]

CHAPTER 1   *I had never seen a newborn baby*

Formal portrait of Elizazbeth, Wilber, Mary, and Hale 1904, Portland, Indiana.
[PHOTO: BRADT FAMILY]

into the mouth of six lbs. of baby whose head was elongated, his skin was almost black. I didn't know until later that the long labor had nearly taken the child's life. I like to think Mother saved him.

Hale said, when he went back to school, there was always "Convocation" each morning, with the six H.S. teachers sitting on the platform. When he took his place all the B.H.S. [Bloomington High School] students cheered him and he felt like crying.... Affectionately, Elizabeth Bradt

P.S. Our doctor bill for Wilber's birth was twenty five dollars.

In 1903, Hale became superintendent of the Portland, Indiana, schools and moved his family there. Mary Elizabeth was born in January 1903 and a formal photo portrait of the foursome was taken a year later. The christening of Paul, the next child, born in October 1904, was the occasion of informal photographs Hale took of his growing family. They show the family in a well furnished home with wallpaper, rugs, and quite nice furniture. In one, he catches a serene Elizabeth holding close her elder son, four-year old Wilber, who couldn't quite hold still for the photo. Another shows a thoughtful Wilber in a rocking chair. These photos display Elizabeth's close relationship to her first-born son. They appear to be enjoying their togetherness although, sadly, strains would later develop. In a later outdoor photograph with all three children, their mother, and their maternal grandmother, Hale catches them in a serious mood and then in a (blurred) moment of hilarity. The latter adds an important dimension to family dynamics not often caught in early photography. I learned of these precious intimate moments much later (in 2013) when I belatedly scanned a set of old negatives Mary had sent me late in her life, around 1985.

I also found among family documents in my files a sheet of paper on which the parents of four-year-old Wilber had written down some of the "incidents" of his young life. They clearly doted on their firstborn.

Oct. 21, 1904 [the day Paul was born at home; Wilber is four years eight months] — After hearing Baby's first cry Wilber said: "Papa, Mary [age 17 months] said 'chickie, chickie.' She thought he was a chicken, I guess." Papa: "What did you think it was?" Wilber: "I thought it was a chicken, too."

Nov. 6, 1904 — Wilber: "Mamma, I love you." Mamma: "I hope you will always love me." Wilber: I will 'till I'm not alive any more.

Wilber: "I won't eat your piece of pie, mamma, cause I love you.

Dec. 28, 1904 — Wilber went to visit a primary room in which there was to be a Xmas tree and other exercises. Santa Claus came in and among other things asked all the "good children" to hold up their hands. All hands went up but Wilber's. "Haven't you been good?" asked Santa. "I have been bad sometimes," replied Wilber.

CHAPTER 1   *I had never seen a newborn baby*

Top: informal family photo ca.1905: Grandmother Peak and Elizabeth with children Paul, Wilber, and Mary. Everyone held still except baby Paul. Bottom: A moment later or earlier the camera caught a bit of hilarity, with children in motion and everyone laughing except Grandma—even baby Paul.
[PHOTO: F. HALE BRADT].

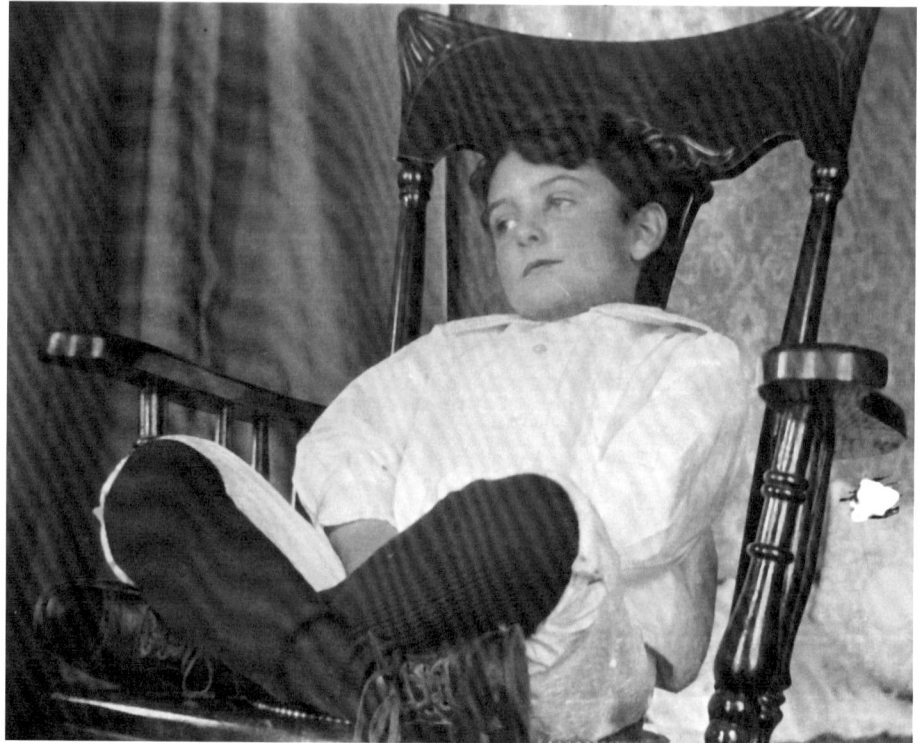

Informal photos taken by Hale in October 1904 of a contemplative Elizabeth (above) and Wilber (below). In the upper photo, four-year-old Wilber could not hold still for the long camera exposure required in those days. [PHOTO: F. HALE BRADT]

2

"Will a duck eat oats?"

Indiana
1906–1927

In 1906, Hale obtained a position as "superintendent of Versailles." This probably meant he was head of the new brick school built in 1903 that included grades one to eight and some high school curriculum. He bought an 80-acre farm three miles east of Versailles and moved the family there. It featured a large barn and a log house, their home for 13 years until 1919. The fourth and fifth of their children, Rex and Ruth, were born there in 1908 and 1916 respectively.

Versailles (pronounced ver-SALES) is 40 miles west of Cincinnati. The farm had a half-mile of frontage on what is now U.S. Highway 50. Today, it is a town of farms with the retail business area concentrated in a classic Midwestern central square of one-story buildings that surround the Ripley County courthouse. Light industrial areas now lie to the west, and immediately east of town lies a deep valley containing Laughery Creek. A three-mile buggy or wagon ride to town would take one down a winding road to the creek, across a covered bridge, and then steeply up into town. The valley and creek are now in Versailles State Park; the covered bridge, newly refurbished, is still there.

The log house on the Bradt farm consisted of a 22-foot-square living room, an upstairs unheated sleeping area, and a kitchen, not used in winter, tacked onto the back. And "yes, of course it had board floors; why would you think dirt?" my Aunt Mary was quick to clarify when I interviewed her in 1987. Toilet facilities were, of course, outside in the outhouse.

Log houses were quite common at that time. According to Mary, children who lived in the newer frame houses would make fun of those who lived in log houses, though the log houses held their heat better. The log

The Bradt log house on the Versailles, Indiana, farm about 1930, when it was not in steady use. It was called Commonplace by Elizabeth Bradt. [PHOTO: F. HALE BRADT]

The Versailles home of the Bradts, drawn and labeled on a brown paper bag by Rex Bradt about 1986 from memories of his boyhood home. It shows the log house and grounds as a well-tended place with fencing, front gate, walkway, mailbox at roadside, outhouse (rear right) and also, from lower left, "Flowering Almond Bush, Garden, Grape arbor, Hollyhocks on East (side of house), Asp., Large Red Cedar Trees, had swing, rose (bush)," and an area for "Basketball, croquet, and skating rink." The rear extension of the home housed the kitchen. The edge of the barn, with water pump, is seen to the far left. [SKETCH: REX BRADT]

CHAPTER 2   *Will a duck eat oats?*

The Versailles log house in 1952 shortly before it was torn down, in a photo taken on my cross-country trip in the 1930 Ford (Model-A). The kitchen addition had been removed from the back of the house. The garage and barn are beyond the house. [PHOTO: HALE BRADT]

house on the Bradt farm was torn down in 1952. Fortunately, during a visit earlier that year, I had taken photos of it. Three and a half decades later, in my 1987 interview with Mary, I queried her in detail about the interior of the house, and together we re-constructed the layout. Prior to that, in 1983, her younger brother Rex had made a pencil sketch of the exterior on a brown paper bag. An aerial photograph taken about 1980 gives a broader view, though long after the log house had been torn down.

In winter, a stove in the center of the living room served heating and cooking needs. There was a hole in the ceiling for the stovepipe, which went up and through the attic, and then through the roof. When the pipe was not in place in the summer, the children in the attic sleeping quarters would remove the covering plate and peek down. Paul was once caught putting his head through the hole when guests were visiting. Mary recalled that on winter mornings "Father was always up early, started the fire, and was always so jubilant when he called [the rest of the family]."

The barn and house were close to one another and right next to the highway. Coins dating from about 1826 were found under the house when it was torn down; the house and barn may both have dated from that time. Elizabeth, Wilber's mother, called it "Commonplace" because she considered it to be quite ordinary.

I came to own the farm in the period 1987–2001, after my aunt died, and am still very attached to Versailles and that land, which is now part of the Versailles (Indiana) State Park. There are no longer any structures on it.

15

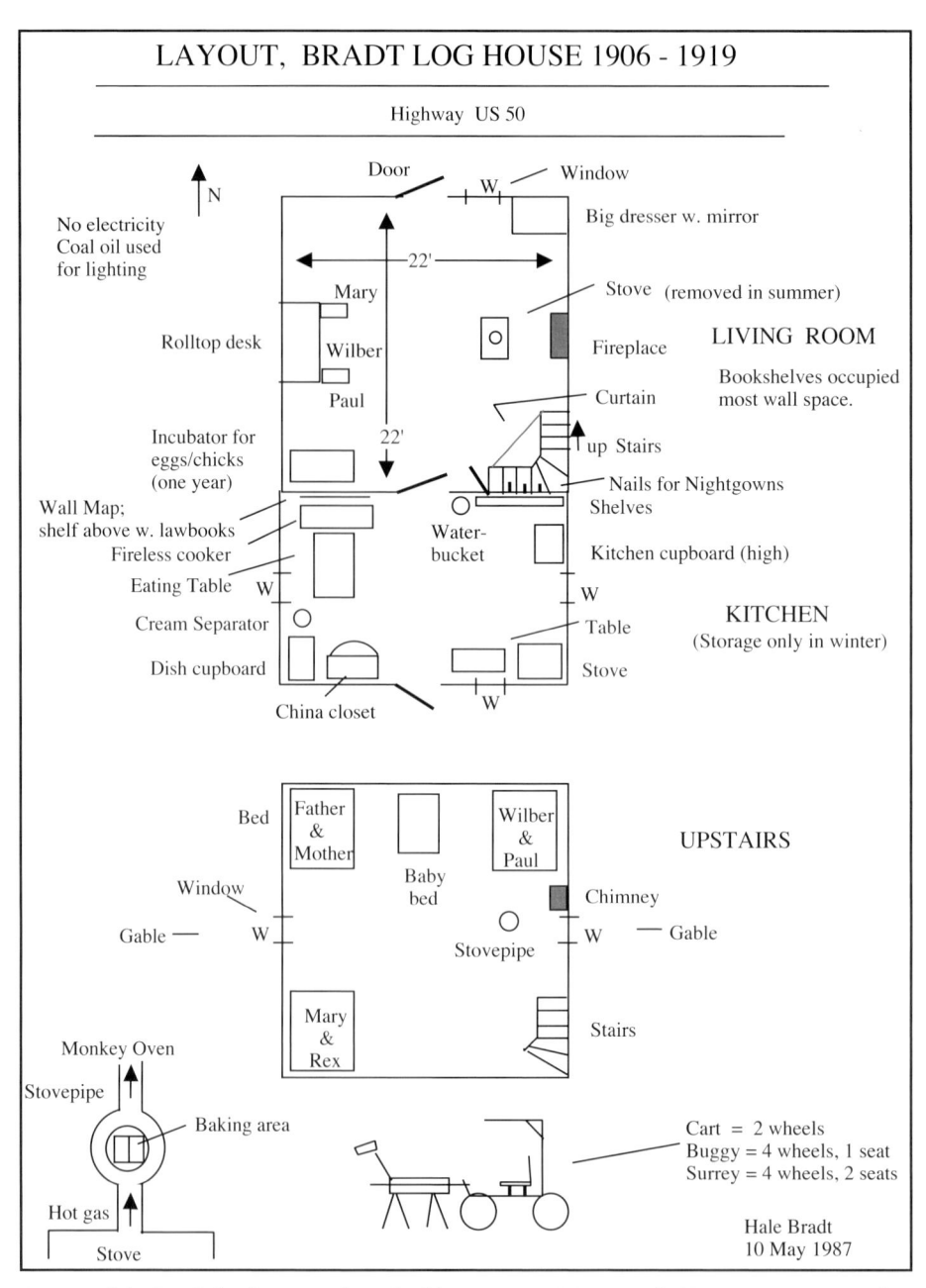

Layout of the Bradt log home as described by my aunt Mary Bradt Higgins in 1987, with additional explanatory sketches. [DRAWING: HALE BRADT]

CHAPTER 2   *Will a duck eat oats?*

Aerial photograph, looking south, of the Bradt Versailles, Indiana, farm taken about 1985. It shows the barn, a garage (white), and the asphalt-shingled house built by Hale about 1939, and the highway, U.S. Route 50. The original log house (long removed) was to the left of the house and closer to the highway. The 80-acre Bradt farm extended about a half mile along the highway and back to the row of trees in the mid distance beyond which is the Henderson farm. [PHOTO: UNKNOWN]

x·o·ø·o·x

In 1907, Hale became county superintendent of schools for Ripley County, Indiana. Five years later, from 1912 to 1914, he took on, at reduced salary, teaching duties at the one-room Waterloo district school just north of the farm. His first three children were students there. The previous teacher had not been able to control the rough-hewn farm-boys, but Hale could. Recall that he had been a football player in college! This sacrifice of status and pay was a measure of the values that were important to him. One son, Paul, wrote many years later (1961), in a personal history, that Hale was

… a wonderful teacher, strict, tactful, encouraging, and sufficiently good judge of interests and abilities to keep most pupils working at top efficiency. He joined in and superintended the [recess] play just enough to enhance the fun and to discourage cheating. After a couple of years we had developed good school spirit and ethics.

The Waterloo one-room schoolhouse near the farm where Hale Bradt (my grandfather) taught 1912–14 so his children would be well educated in a disciplined environment.
[PHOTO: PERHAPS F. HALE BRADT]

The financial needs of their growing family, probably noted most often by Elizabeth, led to Hale taking the position of superintendent of schools in Jackson County, Indiana, 50 miles west of the farm, in 1914–15. From 1915 through 1917, he returned again to teaching in Versailles. During the first semester of the 1917–18 school year, he taught and coached football at Nobelsville (Indiana) High School, 90 miles northwest of Versailles. In the second semester he was principal of the Township School in Westfield, Indiana, just west of Nobelsville.

These distant positions required him to live away from home. His daughter Mary lived with him in Nobelsville and recalled that it was the "nicest place she ever lived." Were these frequent changes of position an indication of difficulties related to Hale's job performance, or simply to his and Elizabeth's searching, year by year, for the best opportunities? I have heard of neither any employment problems, nor any stories of other people's unfair actions, which can often accompany such difficulties. Given Hale's later long stable career at Bloomington High School, however, I believe he was simply going where the best opportunities took him.

During the two years Hale was away, the responsibility for the farm duties and chores fell on Elizabeth and the children. The children said that Elizabeth was the better manager of the two parents. Each child had his/her appointed duties and failure to perform required penance. According to Rex, if the wood box was not brought in, the house stayed cold. If water for cooking was forgotten, then no breakfast. Maybe he exaggerated, but if true, such things probably happened only once or twice; the Bradt kids were not fools!

But Hale's absences, during a total of three years, including his World War I service, loomed large in the children's eyes. Paul wrote in 1961:

When he [Hale] taught away from home, or was in the war, Mother was head of the family. With her, we always worked our hardest, always for the good of the family and the lifting of the mortgage. She was more careful with money than Father and also knew better how and when to break the work with a picnic. Father spent nine months thinking up things that should be done on the farm, and from June to September he set us a grueling pace. It was good for us, but we breathed a sigh of relief when Mother took over again.

Wilber looked up to his father and mother and sought their approval, even into his adult life. His sister Mary helped us understand their parents in a 1980 letter to me:

24 Sept. 1980
… Father was one of the best men I have ever known. In addition to not using profanity he worked hard all his life to keep boys from using tobacco and alcoholic drinks. He was a shy man, but always stood up to be counted for anything which he thought was right. He had a remarkable memory and could remember just what the source was for everything he had ever read as well as the subject matter. He was a remarkable teacher and, being especially interested in scientific subjects, was always in demand.…

This was strong praise coming from Mary, a well-read career librarian and wonderful observer of her surroundings. Mary continued:

Father had a quick temper, but he always kept it under control. Mother angered more slowly, but she boiled inside and never quite forgave anyone whom she considered her enemy. I learned from Father not to judge others.…

These traits came into play in Hale's and Elizabeth's later dealings with their children. Elizabeth's long-lasting anger was apparently rooted in an inner self-doubt that appeared in later letters. Outwardly, though, she was an assured, confident, and highly capable person.

Some contemporary evidence of Hale's character was revealed in a tongue-in-cheek newspaper story that appeared in the North Vernon Sun in January 1913; Hale was 42 at the time. A neighbor sued him because Hale's ducks were getting into the neighbor's field and eating his oats. Hale used his knowledge of the law to turn an adverse ruling into a dismissal. He was an assiduous student of the law and had his own set of Indiana law books so he would not have to hire lawyers. He apparently made good use of them.

x · o · ø · o · x

There was more about life on the farm for Wilber and his siblings in letters written by Mary and Wilber. Here, Mary described a scene that involved her Aunt Mary (half-sister of her father, Hale) who spent the 1911–12 year with Hale's family on the Versailles farm. Wilber was an impressionable 12 at the time.

[ABOUT 1987]
Once while Aunt Mary was with us we had quite a rain after a long hot dry spell. Aunt Mary had a bathing suit, probably the only one in the area. It had pants

Humorous article in the North Vernon (Indiana) Sun, *January 1913, illustrating Hale Bradt's use of the court system. The case was eventually dismissed.* [BRADT FAMILY PAPERS]

that came down nearly to the knees and a skimpy skirt that covered the pants. She donned her bathing suit, took off her shoes, and suggested that my brothers and I put on old clothes and we would go out wading. We did. Mother [Elizabeth] noticed that the buggies went slowly down the road that afternoon and the occupants were interested in a group in the field, slopping along in 12 inches of deep water. Mother was afraid she would be thought to be out in a bathing suit, and so she took her sewing chair out under the cedar trees in the front yard and did her mending.

For Elizabeth, living in a log house did not preclude the need to keep up appearances.

At that time I was under ten years old, and Aunt Mary used to wash my hair, each time reciting a poem about 'Snarley Owl.' She loved to eat a wedge of cabbage with salt sprinkled on it and butter over the salt. Carrots and buttermilk were favorites with her too. I loved my Aunt Mary....

x · o · ø · o · x

In another letter, Mary wrote to my niece, Corinne, who had the same birth date as Mary, January 8. Here, Mary was turning 77 and Corinne 11.

5 Jan. 1980

Dear Corinne — ... As a child there was never any celebration about my birthday, for the family was just beginning to recover from celebrating Christmas, and besides, Mother never made birthday cakes for any of us. She did not have time for that. She did all of her sewing and mine, and made Father's and my brothers' shirts and the pants for my brothers when they were small enough to get pants from the good parts of Father's old ones....

We lived in a log house then.... We all slept in the big upstairs room, with a double bed in three of the four corners of the room, and the stairway in the fourth corner. The logs could not go up to the peak of the roof, for they would roll off if they were not held fast at the corners of the house. During the winter the snow used to blow in under the boards which closed up the space above the logs. As we slept in iron beds, Mother used to tie an umbrella to the head of the bed to keep the snow from falling on our faces.

... It was always my special job to carry in the wood when I was little, smaller than Thomas [Corinne's nine-year-old brother]. And what a big pile of wood would be burned each night and how tired my arms got from carrying it in. Of course, I fell in the snow with those armloads of wood nearly every night.

Have you read the Laura Ingalls Wilder books? Our life was different, but just about as hard. — Best wishes for Jan. 8, Your Aunt Mary

x · o · ø · o · x

In 1981, at my request, Mary wrote me tales of Wilber's childhood.

12 February 1981
Dear Hale — … I shall try to write some of the tales which stand out in my memory. Wilber was a very good older brother to all of us. He was not only older, but was a natural leader and read far more than I (who was 3 years his junior) and so he was always impressing us with his sagacity.

For example, he was always calling himself Dr. Bradt. One case was when he set up a medical office at the far end of one of the big beams near the top of the barn. His drugs were a jar of very salty water and some bran and shorts [products from the milling of wheat], which Father had bought to use as stock feed. Somehow he convinced Paul (and possibly Rex) that we were in need of medication enough that we braved the high climb to get the needed service from "Dr. Bradt." We could have gotten salt and bran and shorts by going into the crib, which was far more accessible than Dr. Bradt's office.

Once, while Father and Mother were away for a trip to town, he decided to become an auctioneer. Our old [corn] crib stood on stone legs to keep out the damaging rodents. Because this was a protected space, it became the dumping area for leaky pots and broken bottles, etc. Wilber decided to auction off this junk to his younger brothers and sister. By the time Father and Mother returned home most of the junk was out from under the crib, and poor Rex, the most unwary one attending the sale, had spent most of his play money and [now] had title to the leaky pots and broken dishes and bottles. When Father drove around the barn and saw the junk out where stock might be injured by it, he demanded an explanation. We all agreed that it all belonged to Rex, who then had to throw his dearly purchased items back under the crib. To this day Rex laughs about that wild experience.…

x · o · ø · o · x

Mary or Rex more than once told me about the time Wilber was throwing stones high up, toward the tall open-topped empty silo and claiming they were going into it. His younger brother Paul did not believe they were and stepped into the silo to check, whereupon the next stone hit him on the head. He could no longer doubt Wilber's throwing ability. This was always told with great amusement. High comedy on the farm!

Wilber himself recalled his farming youth. When I was 13 and he was overseas in the army, he wrote me from New Georgia in the Solomon Islands.

JANUARY 15, 1944
… During one cold winter, I had to cut a hole in the ice on a pond every evening then drive the cows down there. When it was really cold they wouldn't want to go and would break back into the barn. Sometimes the ice would be back over the pool before I could get the cows down there, and I would need to start over again. One day I was very disgusted with cows, so I put some extra salt in their feed. The next night I went down to the pond and cut the ice then back to the barn to open the door of the cow stable. When I opened it that stable seemed to explode cows. They knocked me down and jumped over me and dashed for water. I decided I'd put too much salt in their feed. It probably wasn't very good for the cows either. After that I gave them just enough salt so they had a good healthy interest in water, and we had no more trouble. I'll never forget how surprised I was when they came out of the stable that evening.

Later, he expressed his deep appreciation of natural things in a letter from New Zealand to my sister, 12-year-old Valerie:

JUNE 13, 1944
… Yesterday I went for a walk and saw some of the loveliest geraniums. They practically made a hedge around a yard, and the bright red blossoms spotted in the green were truly beautiful. Did you ever notice that a geranium leaf is perfumed. It is and very pleasing too. For some reason on my walk, I was reminded of some flowers I had when I was eight. I spent about a month plowing a large field, one end of which was near a woods. At that end violets grew wild. I couldn't plow them under so I, whenever I came to a bunch, would dig them up and transplant them to where I had already plowed. Probably Father wondered why I didn't get more plowing done for I'm sure too much time was wasted on the violets. All summer I harrowed and disked and rolled that field and carefully went around my patch of violets. They were the biggest and prettiest violets I ever saw growing wild. I used to think they appreciated not being plowed under.

According to Mary, Wilber loved music, had a good bass singing voice, and took voice lessons. She said their mother and Wilber would sing around the house, songs such as "My Darling Nellie Gray," "A Bird in a Gilded Cage," and Stephen Foster favorites. The family attended the Baptist church in Versailles, three miles west of the farm. Wilber would take Mary to evening services and, on the way home in the buggy with Doc, the old standby horse, Wilber would sing "Love's Old Sweet Song." He sang in the church choir in college and possibly in a choral group.

Wilber and Mary were both baptized by complete immersion in Laughery Creek in 1916. Wilber wore regular clothes. Boys would watch, hoping to see girls' legs and shapes in their wet clothes. Knowing this, Elizabeth made Mary wear many layered petticoats and skirts, in addition to a bathing cap. Mary recalled with a wry grin, "I hardly got wet. And a neighbor commented that 'It [the baptism] probably won't take.'"

Wilber attended Versailles High School where he played basketball and had a front tooth struck and "killed"; it was perpetually dark-colored thereafter. In his senior year, he took an examination—probably sponsored by his congressman—hoping to earn appointment to the U.S. Naval Academy at Annapolis; this proved unsuccessful. According to Mary, he had to learn geometry on his own because the high school did not teach it.

Mary wrote that Wilber dated and was quite sweet on Edna Koehne in high school, but she would not look at him. Years later, after Wilber's death, she asked for a picture of him. She never married.

Wilber graduated from Versailles High School on April 27, 1918, in a class of 13 students. The early-in-the-year graduation date freed the students for work on their family farms during planting season.

We thus learned that Wilber was seriously interested in music, was athletic and ambitious, and had his eye on higher education. He also shared his sister's wry sense of humor.

x·o·ø·o·x

During the Great War (World War I), Wilber's father Hale made several attempts to join the military but was rejected because of his age (45 in early 1917). He then volunteered to serve with the YMCA in a post that provided services to the troops through canteens ("huts") that sold personal supplies (stationery, shaving supplies, etc.) to the soldiers. He entered this service in May 1918, sailed for France the same month, spent more than a year overseas with the 59th Regiment of the 4th Division, and was involved in the battles of Chateau Thierry, St. Mihiel, and Argonne. (Ruth said she had a two-inch piece of shrapnel that had "landed between his feet" in one of

CHAPTER 2   *Will a duck eat oats?*

My grandfather Hale Bradt in uniform, in Germany, 1918. He served with the YMCA, providing services to the soldiers of the 59th Regiment of the 4th Division.
[PHOTO: F. HALE BRADT]

Postcard photo of the USS Zeppelin. Hale Bradt returned to New York from Europe in July 1919 on this ship. The added penned label reads "Ship that brought us home." It appears that "Zeppelin" had also been added; it may have been masked out for security reasons.
[PHOTO: UNKNOWN]

those battles.) The war ended on November 11, 1918 (Armistice Day), and he sailed on the USS Zeppelin for the U.S. in July 1919. He was discharged in New York City that same month.

So what had driven Hale to involve himself in the war despite his age and large familial responsibilities? Surely it was patriotic idealism. In those times, serving your country was held in the highest esteem and those not doing so, if able-bodied, were widely considered cowardly or unpatriotic. The idealism was likely reinforced by the attractiveness of abandoning one's usual civilian work and familial responsibilities, at least temporarily.

Wilber lived on the Versailles farm from age six (1906) until he first entered Indiana University in 1918. His father's absences in Wilber's teens put him in a leadership role in the family, and it undoubtedly created a close camaraderie between him and his mother. His father, though, did not give up his parental role. As he was preparing to leave for France, he wrote Wilber, who, at age 18, would be entering Indiana University in the Fall. Hale was temporarily quartered in Princeton, New Jersey. This, his final letter before shipping overseas, consists of fatherly advice, mostly on moral issues encountered when away from home. The issue he chose to emphasize was, from my perspective, a masterpiece of avoidance!

Princeton, New Jersey, May 12, 1918

Dear Wilber — I am a little anxious to know what is to be the outcome of your Annapolis matter. I am afraid you will not hear until I am on the sea and that I will not be able to get a letter back to you before you will leave home. When you leave home, and the opportunity to talk over with your mother and myself questions that will come up, you will of necessity have to act on your own judgment and there is no long list of rules that can be given which will always guide you aright. There is only the general rule, "Do right," and that leaves a fellow guessing sometimes when right and wrong seem separated by no well defined line.

Take the matter of smoking. I have been very much disappointed at the clear increase in the use of these things in the face of opposition of the best elements in our society – church, schools, and even the law in many cases. It seems to me that practically all the young soldiers here smoke. I would not be surprised to find that your associates at Annapolis are smokers (on the sly). Our Y.M.C.A. people do not support smoking. Practically all of our great leaders are earnestly opposed to it but many, very many of the men here with me do. Mr. Ebersole, the gen. sec. of overseas work and the men associated with him are appealing to the men to quit it.... Several Secretaries have been returned from France after having their uniforms stripped from them because of immoral practices. Others because of profane or vulgar language or drunkenness.

I am sure you see why I am telling you these things. Those men failed when tested not because they failed just at that moment so much as that they had failed to form the right habits in youth. I know you have started right and I believe you will hold firmly to the standard. It is certain that, if you do, you will bless the habit, which has been a help. But should you waver and form other habits, you will regret it many times....

I have walked around some today. More than I have done since coming here. It is an interesting place to wander around. Two presidents of the U.S. have lived here, Cleveland and Wilson, and many other things of interest abound.

We will not be here more than two more days. By the time you receive this, I will have returned to N.Y. and will be hurrying preparations to go overseas.

While I hope you will get the Annapolis position, it may be for the best that you would not. Whether you go or not, I hope you will take time to write to me. If you can't write to both of us, write to your mother first, but I will be anxious to hear from you. — Sincerely, your father, Hale Bradt

The big dirty "s" word was . . . . "smoking"! By contrast years later, Wilber gave me, his son, extended advice on sexual matters when I was 13 and he was overseas [letter 5/3/44, Book 2]. Wilber never took up smoking. (The letter above from Hale brings me back to my first days at Princeton University as a 17-year old freshman in 1948; I had no idea my grandfather had walked those same streets and paths just 30 years earlier.)

Failing to get the Annapolis appointment, Wilber entered Indiana University (IU) as a freshman in the fall of 1918 and was a member of the Student Army Training Corps (SATC). Shortly into the Fall term, he contracted influenza in the great epidemic of 1918–19 that killed millions, but fortunately he recovered. He withdrew from IU in December and returned home to the Versailles farm. The war had ended on November 11, 1918. In March he had his photo taken, in uniform, with his mother. That spring, he tried again for the Naval Academy and again did not receive an appointment.

His father's response to this second attempt was in a letter he wrote to Elizabeth ("Dear Wife") from Vallendar, Germany, as he was about to return home.

MAY 17, 1919
... am sorry Wilber failed again. If he learns the importance of being ready for the opportunity when it comes, his experience may be of great value to him. Let

My father Wilber Bradt (right) and a friend on the Indiana University campus in their Student Army Training Corps (SATC) uniforms in the fall of 1918. [PHOTO: WILBER BRADT]

him make up his mind to make himself so strong he will not fail next time whatever opportunity may come....

Portraying this as a repeated "failure" seems harsh, but his father's attitude may have motivated Wilber to earn a college degree and then master's and doctoral degrees.

x·o·ø·o·x

CHAPTER 2   *Will a duck eat oats?*

Portrait of Wilber Bradt in his SATC uniform with his proud mother, March 10, 1919.
[PHOTO: BRADT FAMILY]

    Hale's return from overseas led to conflict; he and Elizabeth had differing views of their future. He wanted to return to the farm, at age 48, but at her insistence, he took a teaching position at Bloomington Junior High School. Elizabeth probably was ready to return to "city" life after years on the farm, but she could also see the practical advantages of living in a university town (Indiana University) with a college-age son and four others following him. After one year, Hale became a science teacher and sports coach at Bloomington High School. In later years, he was dean of boys, but probably retained teaching duties. This position was a natural for him given his teaching and administrative experience.

29

In 1919, Hale and Elizabeth bought a house in Bloomington, at 527 S. Lincoln Street, on the corner of University Street, which was not yet paved. They made some renovations, moved the family there, and Wilber re-entered the university as a freshman. He and each of his siblings, in turn, attended the university and each successfully completed his or her bachelor's degree; the last child, Ruth, graduated in 1937.

Before the war, Bloomington had experienced a burst of "modern" construction. By 1919, it had shed much of its 19th century clutter, like the hitching rail around the courthouse. Its limestone quarries were a major industry, and it was the home of Indiana University. It boasted two railroad stations, a new city hall, a courthouse and library, five churches, a post office, and a gas and electric plant. (The 1979 bicycling movie "Breaking Away" was set in Bloomington and portrays some of these features.)

For nearly 20 years the Bradt household was a busy student residence. The college students would come home for lunch and supper and return to the college in the evening to study, a distance of about half a mile. Phone calls from the high school for Hale, the dean of boys, were frequent. As the older children left home, available bedrooms were rented to other university students. (In 1987, I took my Aunt Ruth to her 50th reunion at IU and was able to enjoy remembrances of those early days with her and her classmates.)

During the years in Bloomington, Hale and family still owned the Versailles farm and would often return to it for the summer. Other times, Hale taught summer school and Elizabeth and the boys would go there without him. They sometimes had renters on the farm, and several times they attempted to sell it. In one case, the tenant and prospective buyer absconded with seed and equipment that Hale had provided him. Hale never could shake his farming instinct and still owned the farm at his death.

As a student at Indiana University, Wilber was on the swimming team and earned his varsity letter. He told us that his crooked nose was due to his having broken it as he swam along and into the bottom of the pool when it changed slope under the diving board. (I only half-believe this.) His soon-to-be-prominent schoolmates and near contemporaries (within six months) were the wartime journalist Ernie Pyle and singer-song-writer and actor Hoagy Carmichael, both of whom he knew. He earned his bachelor's degree in 1923, his master's degree in 1924, and his PhD in 1926, all in chemistry. Although he was a rather serious and dedicated student, a 1923 photo of the IU chemistry department graduates shows a cheerful Wilber. While in graduate school, he was an assistant instructor in the qualitative

Indiana University swim team in 1923. Wilber is fourth from left in the last row. Varsity letters were awarded to nine of the team including Wilber. [PHOTO: 1923 INDIANA UNIVERSITY *ARBUTUS*]

Indiana University chemistry department bachelor of arts graduates, 1923. Wilber is at far left, third row. Bob Frye, second from left top row, met Wilber in the Pacific. Wilber liked Ruby Bell, third from left, front row, according to his sister Mary. [PHOTO: UNKNOWN]

analysis laboratory for seven semesters. This probably earned him tuition credits and a nominal salary. By agreement between the two, he paid his father $100 a year for room and board during his undergraduate years and $150 a year during his graduate school years.

Collecting such moneys from a student son might seem harsh by today's standards. But in the 1920s, most local 18-year-olds did not attend college and were supporting themselves by working on the family farm or elsewhere. Hale himself had probably paid board and room while staying at his half-brother's home in Lincoln, Nebraska, during his own college days. Wilber never implied that this arrangement was unfair or unreasonable. However, it did get documented when a considerable misunderstanding about it arose 20 years later, in 1941, as the story will show.

x·o·ø·o·x

During the Great Depression of the 1930s, Hale felt it patriotic to borrow money and hire men to do renovations, such as adding a second floor to the Bloomington house, because he had a steady salary as a teacher. However, when teachers' salaries were cut, his financial situation became precarious. Hale was always more of an optimist and spender than Elizabeth, a source of serious conflict between them. Wilber once commented that the strains between his father and mother were sometimes so great that, at times, he thought they would be better off separated. He became very wary of intra-familial bickering.

Wilber revealed much of his parents' characters in a Valentine's Day (1944) letter from New Zealand to his wife Norma:

FEB. 14, 1944

I've just read *O River Remember* [by Mary Ostenso] and it is [the character] Norma Shaleen whom I loved almost as much as my Norma Sparlin. She was (and her aunt too) so like you that I nearly cried several times. Bn. [Battalion] commanders aren't supposed to do that and I just wanted to. The mother in the boys' family was so much like my own, I wouldn't dare send the book home, and the father was much like my father, so you see why the book moved me so.

This novel, popular in the 1940s, portrayed the mother as a strong family leader who exercised excessive, and hence damaging, control over her children and was very conscious of social standing and reputation. The father, by contrast, was more kindly and tolerant, but also rather laid back and impractical.

An assessment of Wilber as a person and student survives in this recommendation letter written in 1936 by a former IU faculty member:

His [Wilber's] speech is essentially correct and his manner pleasant but [he is] inclined to be a bit abrupt. As a student, he presented a decidedly sloppy appearance and poor taste in the matter of dress....

He was not a brilliant student, but he made up at least partially for the lack of brilliancy by his persistence and energy....

The "a bit abrupt" may have derived from Wilber's national guard experience, but that certainly did not account for his "sloppy appearance." (My scoutmaster once pointedly told me, at age 12, that some scouts wore their uniforms as if the wind had blown them helter-skelter onto their bodies. I was slow to get the point.)

Indiana University students fixing a flat tire in the early 1920s. This picture was among Wilber's negatives. It is likely that he was the photographer and these were his friends. Note the inner tube held by the man to the left, the bicycle pump at his feet, the kerosene lantern hanging from the windshield, and the face and wide-brimmed hat of, probably, a state policeman in the background. [PHOTO: WILBER BRADT]

Second Lieutenant Wilber Bradt in his Indiana National Guard uniform, around 1922. The crossed cannon insignia indicated field artillery, and the numerals on it indicated the 150th Field Artillery Regiment. [PHOTO: BRADT FAMILY]

CHAPTER 2   *Will a duck eat oats?*

Indiana National Guard howitzer and gun crew, possibly Wilber's. This photo was most likely taken by Wilber about 1922. Note the wonderful Indiana faces. [PHOTO: WILBER BRADT]

Wilber's sister Mary wrote me in the 1980s that "Wilber was a terribly hard worker, spending 12–15 hours per day in the lab as he worked for his PhD."

The long hours might have seemed natural and not particularly burdensome to him after years of farm work, much of which was repetitious and boring. Think of walking behind a horse plowing a field all day long! Nevertheless, his student days were not all spent in the laboratory. There is, in Wilber's collection of negatives, a wonderful photograph of, I presume, Indiana University students fixing a puncture in the inner tube of a tire on a well used car.

Wilber's long association with the military began during the war, while he was at Indiana University, with his service in the Student Army Training Corps (SATC). As such, he was officially a private in the U.S. Army from October 1 to December 21, 1918. In his sophomore year, he joined the Indiana National Guard as a sergeant, a relatively high enlisted rank. As a college student, he became eligible to be an officer and was appointed a second lieutenant the summer after his junior year. He held that rank until he finished his PhD. His unit was the 150th Field Artillery Regiment. He

Indiana National Guard artillery on a field exercise, early 1920s. The tractor pulled a two-wheeled "limber," which carried an ammunition chest. The two-wheeled howitzer, probably 75-mm and only partly seen here, was hitched to the limber. Note the horses with riders in the background. A caisson (famed in the artillery song) was a two-wheeled cart carrying additional ammunition, which could also be towed by a limber. [PHOTO: WILBER BRADT]

maintained his national guard service, with some breaks, until World War II. His brother Paul wrote in 1961 that

… He [Wilber] was always fun to be with but always serious about important things. I was with him in the Guard for about six years [in the 1920s], and I assure you he regarded it as important even in peacetime.

In 1926, after seven years at IU and with a PhD in hand, Wilber found a position as an instructor in the chemistry department at the State College of Washington in Pullman, Washington. (The college was widely known as Washington State College, or WSC, and since 1959 has been named Washington State University.) Wilber's salary was $2400 per year for an 11-month year, which at that time was the median cost of a house in Washington State; a Ford Model T cost about $260. This position took Wilber away from home for the first time, except for those few months at IU in 1918 when he became ill with influenza. He did not willingly choose to leave his family: university teaching positions were not available in most locales, so one went where the jobs were. He may have sought an academic position, rather than industrial, because his father was a teacher and perhaps also because a professorship might have appeared to be the larger challenge. His destination, Pullman, was (and still is) a small college town in the rolling wheat fields of southeast Washington.

Toward the end of his first year at WSC, he accepted a more lucrative position at the University of Cincinnati for the following year, again as an instructor in chemistry. The summer before leaving for Cincinnati was to be full: he was to teach a chemistry class at the college and was scheduled to serve in August as field assistant to the state geologist of Washington in the western part of the state. He did not anticipate a major, but welcome, perturbation in his life in June of that year, 1927.

Left: Norma on a picnic with Wilber, probably July 4, 1927. Many years later, in a letter to Norma of July 4, 1943, Wilber remembered that picnic and, a week earlier [letter 6/26/43], recalled her black satin pleated skirt. Note the high heels (on a picnic?). Right: close-up of Norma taken that day; Wilber was obviously enamored of her. [PHOTO: WILBER BRADT]

3

"It was one of the perfect days of my life"
Wilber and Norma
1927–1930

On June 26, 1927, a day Wilber would never forget, a vivacious blond 21-year-old student entered his classroom and took his breath away. She was Norma Corinne Sparlin, a music major in her senior year at WSC who needed to fulfill a science requirement. On July 4, one short week later, Wilber and Norma went on a picnic together. Wilber recalled this exactly 16 years later, in a letter. He was on a sea-going landing craft as it awaited a place on the beach of Rendova Island in the Solomon Islands. Here he is writing to Norma:

[JULY 4, 1943]
… I remember too that it was a July 4 in 1927 when I took Nana [Norma] out on a picnic above the Snake R. [River] canyon. We walked a path together over the river and the flowers were lovely and the air was fresh and cool. Later it rained and we sat under a blanket and talked. On the way home Norma sat on my lap and I wished we might never get home. It was one of the perfect days of my life.…

They were probably sharing a seat on a crowded bus.
Who was this attractive young woman who so captivated Wilber? She

Ten of the eleven children of Andrew Sparlin and Mary Frances Myers with Mary (front right) and a younger child of Mary's (front center), circa 1895–1900. Norma's father, Stonewall, is in the center of the back row, with mustache. [PHOTO: COURTESY OF MELANIE POOR COTTAM]

was an accomplished pianist, organist, and writer, and was active on campus in literary and musical circles as well as in her sorority, Alpha Gamma Delta. She was not lacking for beaus and had been elected the "Sweetheart of Sigma Chi" according to her own testimony.

Norma was born in Barron, Wisconsin, on November 30, 1905. Her father, Stonewall Jackson Sparlin, had been born in Missouri in 1866 and named after the famous Confederate general. He was one of 11 children of Andrew Sparlin and Mary Myers Sparlin. Andrew had fathered ten children by a previous wife; today there are Sparlin cousins and half-cousins everywhere! Mary's father, Diedrich Myers, was an immigrant from Hanover, Germany.

Norma's father Stonewall left Missouri as a young man and ran a general merchandise store in Almena, Wisconsin. Later he worked as bookkeeper for the town and then served in the elected position of county clerk. He was a public-spirited man in his community. In 1887, he married Ethel Richmond shortly after she bore a child (Lee Bergen) from an earlier short-lived marriage; her husband had died in a shooting, it was said. She was 17 or even younger when she married Stonewall, who was 21.

Ethel was of early colonial English stock on both sides. Her father, Levi Richmond, raised horses and played the violin and may have been a descendant of the colonist John Richmond who settled in Taunton, Massachusetts. If so, his forbears came to England with William the Conqueror and had resided in the Richmond Castle in North Yorkshire. Ethel's mother, Prudence, was a Scoville, of the colonial Connecticut family. Such connections became important to Norma in her later life.

Ethel and Stonewall had six children before she left him in 1910 when Norma was four. According to Norma, contributing factors to the breakup were their strongly held differing viewpoints on the Civil War—he the Confederate and she the Yankee—as were alcohol and another woman. Ethel took their four youngest children, Beatrice (age ten), Milton (nine), Norma, and Evelyn (six months), to Hillyard, Washington, a suburb of Spokane. Ethel managed to support her four children with her sewing skills, help from an older married daughter, Leota, living in Oregon, and the growing of vegetables that Milton would sell at curbside. It wasn't easy. Ethel was a marked woman: divorces were unusual and frowned upon in those days.

x · o · ø · o · x

Norma, at age 75 and at my behest, typed an eight-page, single-spaced, self-conscious account of her life as she looked back on it. Here she describes her home life in Hillyard:

[1981]
Although money was scarce, there was a close family relationship filled with music. Singing, violin and piano practice, [and] small orchestral rehearsals kept our lives merry and bright. [Norma played the piano; Evelyn and Milton played the violin.] ... Evelyn and I were busy concertizing as early as when she was six years old and myself ten. We played for banquets, lodge parties, weddings, showers, birthday parties, and gave one program at the Natatorium Park band shell.... Evelyn was considered a sensation because she was so young and could play so well.... [Leota] was now a long distance telephone operator and contributed to the family funds. She married young, but did not forget us.

CITIZEN SOLDIER   PART I: FARM TO ACADEMIA

Ethel Richmond Sparlin's four youngest children, Barron, Wisconsin, 1909: Milton (b. 1901), Beatrice (left, b. 1900), Norma (right, b. 1905), and baby Evelyn (b. 1909), possibly taken at Evelyn's christening. They left for Washington State with their mother at about this time. [PHOTO: SPARLIN FAMILY]

CHAPTER 3   *It was one of the perfect days of my life*

Norma's memoir goes on to tell how, as a baby, she nearly died of what was thought to be meningitis, but was revived and was then baptized Catholic with the permission of her parents. Her father was a lapsed Catholic and her mother a Baptist. Norma recalled that "we were always going to church." She became aware of her Catholic baptism in 1951 when the baptismal certificate arrived in a box sent her by her deceased sister's (Leota's) executor. My sister Abigail, who was seven at the time, remembers vividly the arrival and opening of the box and the certificate. This was a joyful discovery for Norma as she had embraced Catholicism after Wilber died in 1945. She and Wilber had previously been regular churchgoing Episcopalians.

Norma's stories could sometimes be rather wishful and hence bore further checking. A recent query to the Superior (Wisconsin) Archdiocese and elsewhere failed to yield a record of her Catholic baptism, though the searches may not have been sufficiently thorough.

Norma enjoyed school in Hillyard where she sang the lead in the eighth-grade musical. At age 12, she entered Hillyard High School, which she was to attend for two years. That summer she traveled by herself to northern Minnesota to spend the summer with her father who had established a successful logging business in the virgin forests there. This entailed a long train trip with one or two transfers and a night alone in the YWCA. Two years later she again traveled there for the summer. I expect that these trips, being rather perilous for a 12- or 14-year-old, were not simply for a vacation or for fulfilling a father's wish to have time with his daughter. More likely they originated in the stresses, financial and personal, in the Hillyard home.

Upon her return, Norma entered North Central High School in Spokane because her mother had moved into Spokane. There, she recalled playing tennis, and was part of the musical crowd of which, she always said, Bob Crosby (Bing's brother) was a member. (Bing was 2 1/2 years older than Norma and went to another high school.) The Crosbys were a Spokane family and Bob did go to North Central, but he was 8 years younger than Norma. Bob did have two sisters who were Norma's close contemporaries, so she may well have known Bob then as a young boy or later in Spokane musical circles. After two years at North Central, she graduated at age 16.

Her expert typing skills landed Norma a job in a law office in Deer Park, some 30 miles from Spokane. On her first day on the job, she discovered that the head of the office and his wife were her godparents and neighbors from Wisconsin. After she had spent some time in that office, they arranged work for her as the secretary of the School of Music and Fine Arts at Washington State College in Pullman, so she could continue her education there. The dean of the school, Herbert Kimbrough, became a mentor. She described her role there in her 1981 memoir:

There I wrote promotions for faculty artists, held art exhibits, arranged for plays, wrote song lyrics of the musicals, traveled with the glee club, [and] promoted everything. All this time I was intensely practicing, taking piano and organ lessons. My sister and I also played Sunday music in the Commons in a trio we organized. We also had the charter for playing between acts for the plays. I played in the student piano recitals, of course, and became accompanist for the chorale for a time.

Norma moved on to other secretarial positions in the architecture department and in the president's office, and began giving piano lessons. She thus came to know President Ernest Holland of the college. She was quite popular and had a circle of close friends. She more than once wore the fraternity pin of a beau, a symbol of "going steady." Over the years she often told us that she sometimes wore several pins at once, but of course, all but one of them were pinned carefully out of sight on her slip. Her sister Beatrice ("Beto"), possibly through jealousy of her younger sister's popularity, thought her behavior was unseemly and flirtatious as it may well have been.

Norma's youngest sister Evelyn, not yet in college, lived with Norma at the sorority house. They slept on the upstairs outdoor porch, even on the coldest winter nights. Norma told us that she had been voted The Best Dressed Girl in Bed by her sorority sisters because of the heavy nightclothes she would wear on that porch. I can see the wool cap now!

A shortage of money was apparently an ever-present concern for the Sparlins. Those many musical jobs at a young age, the secretarial work, piano teaching, caring for her sister, and those long trips alone to Minnesota all suggest that the Sparlin kids had to be quite self-sufficient. Life could not have been easy for Ethel, their single mother. She married several times and the situation at home was probably not consistently secure for the girls.

One of Evelyn's daughters, now deceased, confided in my sister Abigail in the 1990s, while showing her the old Sparlin home in Spokane, that Norma and Evelyn, as young girls, had been subjected to unwelcome advances by one of Ethel's boyfriends. But Evelyn's other daughter, her younger, recalls no such talk or even hints to that effect. However, the first daughter had lived for many decades in the same town with her mother where the events would have taken place. It is not improbable that Evelyn, in a particularly intimate moment, would have confided in her elder daughter. In turn, it is plausible that the daughter, years later, would confide in her cousin and near-twin from the East (far away) as they viewed the site of the putative offenses. Sadly, the story is probably true.

When Norma was ten years old, Ethel gave her to another "family" to care for, a couple claiming to have the resources to do so, whereas Ethel felt that she did not. They lived in a small community some distance from Spokane. In fact, it appeared that they, in Norma's later telling, were involved in a "couple exchange" and needed a child "chaperone," and severely neglected her. After a month or more, on a shopping trip into the town center with that couple, Norma was left to wait on the sidewalk in her dirty dress, messy hair, and possibly dirty bare feet. She was recognized there by a prominent member of her church in Hillyard who rescued her and took her to his home. The parishioner's wife cleaned her up and returned her to Ethel, who, regretting her action, tearfully took her back in. This episode, often recounted by Norma, was a defining experience for her.

The dark sides of Norma's home life were confirmed by Wilber when he wrote to his sister Mary from the Philippines during World War II:

FEBRUARY 18, 1945
[Norma] has been a lonely and fatherless girl who early learned she had to fight her own battles herself.... She and Evelyn have fought since childhood to keep themselves free of the things they found in their own background and as a consequence look on our [the Bradts] home pretty much as their ideal.

These aspects of her home life loomed large in Norma's background, but the strong musical and religious heritage that Ethel managed to give to her children was clearly an important part of their lives. Norma's later memory of "a close family relationship filled with music," even as she suppressed the darker elements, must still have been partly true given the high quality and quantity of musicianship that emerged from that home.

In later life, Norma retained affection for her siblings, but was very sensitive to perceived slights that could result in periods of cut-off communications. Her sister Evelyn came across the country to my graduation from college in 1952. Some misunderstanding during that visit led to no communication between the sisters for several years. Many years later, in Norma's last year of life, 1986, Evelyn visited her in Florida. At the end of the brief visit, I was preparing to take her to the airport and planning to return thereafter. In response to Evelyn's last goodbye, Norma, who was partially disabled by strokes and in a wheelchair, slowly spoke her last sadly confused, cruel words to her beloved little sister, "You always take my children away from me."

Norma seemed to exhibit a need to protect herself. Her striving to excel in music and her later writing, were, at least to me, part of her method of doing so. Her reflexive and unintentionally hurtful last words to Evelyn reflected that need.

x·o·ø·o·x

On July 22, 1927, less than a month after they met, Wilber gave Norma a diamond ring and asked her to marry him that same summer before he left for the University of Cincinnati in late August. Norma was reluctant to get married so soon; she was only a few credits shy of a diploma and had, she wrote, "a super job teaching piano in a nearby high school—private pupils, all day, for two days a week, at an excellent salary."

Wilber pointed out that she could earn credits toward her degree at the University of Cincinnati and at the Cincinnati Conservatory of Music. Despite apparent misgivings, she acquiesced, and they made plans to marry before Wilber moved to his new position. The engagement was formally announced on August 16 at the home of Dean Kimbrough, Norma's mentor at WSC. Wilber left for his geological fieldwork on the west coast of Washington State, "dodging tides" as Norma put it. Upon his return, they would be married.

At the end of his summer chemistry course, Wilber gave his student Norma Sparlin a grade of A. Given the circumstances, and knowing him, I expect that he took great care to ensure and then document that the grade was truly deserved. However, their courtship must have included some coaching in chemistry, which would have been a significant assist. The A in chemistry did not stand out as an anomaly; her record at WSC showed a healthy mixture of As and Bs.

On August 28, a scant two months after meeting, Wilber and Norma were married in Portland, Oregon, where her brother Milton lived. Wilber gave Norma a ring with "Comrades" inscribed on its inner surface. This was not a reference to Communism by any means, but rather to its original meaning of "mates" or "fellow soldiers." Norma described the wedding in her "Bride's Own Book":

CHAPTER 3   *It was one of the perfect days of my life*

Our wedding was solemnized in the dimly lighted Hinson Memorial Baptist Church in Portland Oregon at 10 p.m., Sunday evening, August 28, 1927, after which Wilber tucked me, wedding gown and all, into a taxi and took me to his hotel, the Multonomah. [It was Portland's largest and most elegant hotel; it is now in 2013 the Embassy Suites Downtown.] There were just we two at our wedding party, but red, red roses were in a bowl on the table to greet us. Wilber went out for Silver Spray [a champagne-like non-alcoholic beverage popular during prohibition] and chicken sandwiches and we celebrated hilariously with this bridal fare, eating in bed in great luxury for both of us.

Wilber and Norma exhibiting her engagement ring, 1927. [PHOTO: WILBER BRADT]

It was indeed a small wedding. Eight guests signed or were listed in her bride's book:

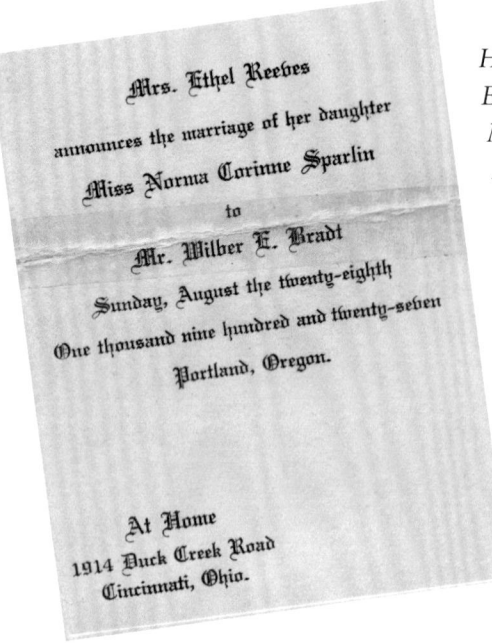

Mrs. Ethel Reeves announces the marriage of her daughter Miss Norma Corinne Sparlin to Mr. Wilber E. Bradt Sunday, August the twenty-eighth One thousand nine hundred and twenty-seven Portland, Oregon.

At Home
1914 Duck Creek Road
Cincinnati, Ohio.

Wedding announcement for Wilber and Norma. It was most likely sent out by Wilber and Norma after they had settled in Cincinnati. [FACSIMILE: BRADT FAMILY PAPERS]

Howard Greer [best man]
Evelyn Sparlin [Norma's sister]
Milton Sparlin [her brother]
Ethel Reeves [her mother]
Mrs. Milton Sparlin
Lillian R. Pettibone [played Scott's "Lotus Land" for them to enter]
Leota Rice [her sister]
Baby Evelyn [Milton's daughter, age 3]

It appeared that Wilber's family in Bloomington, Indiana, were either not notified of the wedding or the notification was lost. (See Paul's letter below.) Wilber's sister Mary, many decades later, recalled that the family first heard of the wedding when notice of it appeared prominently in the Bloomington newspaper, with, as she wrote, surely with exaggeration: "a Pearl Harbor-sized headline, 'Prof. Bradt Takes Bride,'" and with a description of a church wedding, which could be read as being much more elegant than it was in fact. A wedding at 10 p.m. with wedding party and guests totaling eight in a dimly lit church with no following reception was hardly a grand wedding. But being excluded from the wedding was understandably a major insult to Wilber's socially sensitive mother. Wilber was her oldest son and had been her stalwart helper during his father's absences. He surely was very special to her. In her view, she had lost him to this marriage and felt deeply slighted in the process. It created a long-lived bitterness toward both Wilber and his bride that was never completely erased.

Wilber surely understood the inevitability of a strong negative reaction from his parents, Elizabeth and possibly Hale, to his swift marriage to an unknown young woman from a broken home—a woman they had never even met. He rightly sensed, though, that the opportunity to marry the popular Norma could easily pass him by if he did not grasp it immediately.

CHAPTER 3   *It was one of the perfect days of my life*

Norma and Wilber on their honeymoon, possibly at Lake Louise, Canada, 1927. He was wearing his red Indiana University letter sweater. [PHOTO: WILBER BRADT]

Hence, he avoided the inevitable explosion from home and did not notify his parents in advance. Both families would soon have to face up to the situation in person, as Wilber and Norma were to pass through Bloomington on their way to Cincinnati.

The trip to Cincinnati served as a tightly scheduled honeymoon with overnight stops in Seattle and Vancouver, two nights at Sicamous, BC, one night at Chateau Lake Louise, and an overnight in Chicago. They traveled by train, except by boat from Seattle to Vancouver. Nearing the end of the trip they arrived in Bloomington, Indiana, where Wilber's parents would meet the new bride for the first time.

x·o·ø·o·x

There is much to be learned about this and subsequent encounters between the new couple and their respective families from letters written over the years between Wilber's sister Mary and their mother Elizabeth. Mary was single and away from home for much of her working life. They carried on a long and chatty correspondence for more than three decades. When she was living in a Versailles home for the elderly the year (1987) she died, Mary gave me a box of some 500 letters from both her and her mother's collections. I have read these with a focus on the interactions between my parents and the Indiana Bradts. These range from their newlywed days to the events surrounding Wilber's death.

On another occasion, Mary gave me a box of letters between her parents in the years Hale was away teaching or in France (1914–19). The wonderful 1918 letter from Hale to Wilber about smoking was in that collection. All are handwritten. Hale's letters are quite legible, paginated, and dated. Elizabeth's are difficult to read and are neither dated nor paginated. By the time she started writing Mary in the late 1920s, the schoolteacher in her had taken root and her letters became quite accessible.

x · o · ø · o · x

The newlyweds arrived at the Bradt home in Bloomington, Indiana, on September 9, 1927. Just prior to their arrival, Wilber's brother Paul had been writing their sister Mary of the impending visit. Mary was 24 and in library school at the University of Illinois. Paul, almost 23, had just graduated from Indiana University as a physics major and was still living at home. His younger brother Rex, almost 19, and sister Ruth, 11, also lived at home. Wilber, the older brother (at 27) was returning home with his bride (21).

The tension was palpable.

Fri., Sept. 9, 1927
Dear Mary — I am waiting to go downtown with mother and Ruth and to mail this. The newlyweds are to be here tonight, according to a telegram received at noon. It is now 2:20 P.M.

Mother says her knees are wobbly already. She has arranged to slip out after the arrival and write you a note on first impressions, which I am to post before retiring. But they may not get here in time....

Mother wants me to post this now, — Goodby, Paul

[Note from Elizabeth at top of page:] 3:30 and still alive. Wobblier, tho. Mad, too.

CHAPTER 3   *It was one of the perfect days of my life*

Norma was walking into a frosty den! Elizabeth was definitely controlling the action. Wilber and Norma had obviously anticipated this and hoped to calm the waters by asking the president, no less, of Washington State College (Ernest Holland) to write a character reference for Norma, which he dutifully did on September 8. (Recall that Norma had worked as an assistant in his office.) It must have arrived just as Wilber and Norma were leaving. The response to its receipt remains unfortunately unknown to us.

x · o · ∅ · o · x

Sadly, Elizabeth's inevitable detailed report to Mary of the visit is not available, but we have Paul's take on it in a letter written after Wilber and Norma departed.

>
> **STATE COLLEGE OF WASHINGTON**
> OFFICE OF THE PRESIDENT
> PULLMAN, WASHINGTON
>
> September 8, 1927
>
> Mr. and Mrs. Bradt
> Care Bloomington High School
> Bloomington, Indiana
>
> My dear Mr. and Mrs. Bradt:
>
> As you know, your son has recently married a young woman here in the Northwest. His wife, formerly Miss Sparlin, was a student for three or four years here at the State College of Washington and made an unusually good record not only as a student but as a college citizen. Miss Sparlin had to pay nearly all of her own expenses through part time employment. She showed unusual talent as a musician and as a manager of student activities. I may add too that she had the respect both of students and faculty.
>
> It occurred to me that you would like to know something about your daughter-in-law, and it gives me much pleasure to tell you that she is worthy of your highest respect and affection.
>
> Very sincerely yours,
>
> [signature]
>
> EOH:ls

Letter from the president of the State College of Washington (widely known as Washington State College), Ernest O. Holland, to Wilber's parents to assure them of Norma's good character. It was mailed the day before Wilber and Norma arrived at his parents' Bloomington, Indiana, home and might not have arrived before they left. [FACSIMILE: BRADT FAMILY PAPERS]

Sept. 13, 1927
Dear Mary — The couple [Wilber and Norma] has gone long ago. I expect you have heard mother's report. She felt very bitter against him and some against her. Mother says she never wants to see them again. I believe mother would feel better if I denounced him beyond his deserts. This way she keeps expanding on his failures, etc.

(1) Her (Norma's) mother was married to her father. Later they were divorced and she married again. And they were divorced! Not her [Norma's] fault, likely.

(2) Norma is tall and fair, blue (light) eyes, fair skin with a touch of rouge and powder; light brown hair, etc. She is sometimes very pretty, sometimes very plain. She may have a little goiter, and is careless of her English. She probably would not be disgusted by the Baptist Church [attended by the Bradts] for she seems to be a little loud. She is probably a very good girl and as good as he would have gotten if he had spent 10 years in choosing, because of his tastes....

Mother just told me that she is more afraid that the daughter-in-law [Norma] will be a bad influence on Rex's and Ruth's standards. Perhaps this is the reason for her actions. — Your brother, Paul

What "bad influence" had she meant? Coming from a broken family? Getting married without parental involvement? These were not exactly Norma's doing. Elizabeth, in fact, was more upset with Wilber than with Norma. Paul's letter is dominated by his mother's response to the newlyweds; his paragraph (item 2 above) probably reflects her stated views. Elizabeth was the power center in the family, at least on this issue. Wilber reflected on that encounter in his letter of February 18, 1945, to Mary: "You know of the unfortunate introduction she [Norma] received to our family."

Wilber and Norma proceeded on to the University of Cincinnati where Wilber took up his duties as instructor of chemistry and Norma her musical studies. They moved into an apartment in a home at 1914 Duck Creek Road, about two miles east of the University. She studied with the Polish pianist, Dr. Liszniewski, and played for the U.C. Chorale. She prepared and gave her senior recital, which was also given at Washington State College. Her major was music but she also took English and geology courses. Evelyn, aged 19 at the time of their move, lived with Wilber and Norma in Cincinnati for at least part of their time there.

Cincinnati was about four hours by car from the Bloomington home of Wilber's parents. Wilber and Norma did manage several visits there during their two and a half years in Cincinnati. On these trips, they would visit Wilber's grandmother Julia Seelinger and her husband Philip in Holton,

Indiana. Holton is about 60 miles west of Cincinnati and Bloomington 70 miles further west. Julia was very kind to and supportive of Norma.

x·o·ø·o·x

Toward the end of the first academic year, Wilber and Norma made their first visit to his parents since the previous September at the end of their honeymoon. We find a good description of Indiana hospitality. Elizabeth showed little sign of the bitterness she had felt during the earlier visit. Her long letters to Mary during the year were full of details about her daily life and the children still at home. She was able to set aside her grievance toward Wilber, though the hurt undoubtedly was still there. She carefully noted, not altogether uncritically, the details of Wilber's and Norma's appearances and clothing, and revealed her love of natural things.

MAY 23, 1928

Dear Mary: — ... I know you want a report of our Sunday visitors. So here goes: First I washed the dining room woodwork and windows and put up new curtains. That improved matters some. New paper will do the rest. I had a pork roast, mashed potatoes, lima beans, cucumber salad, pickles, jelly, gooseberries, etc. with strawberries and cake for dessert. I wore my black and white flowered dress. The guests arrived at 1:45 P.M. Four of them: Wilber and Norma, Mr. Williams, owner of the car, and a Mr. Arenson. Wilber is still wearing the suit like the sample he sent us. It has felt [been damaged with] acid and is repaired. He is much thinner. His shirt was a bright blue with collar attached and was not very becoming, but it will likely grow dimmer with age. It was like the one you like on Earl. He seemed much more like his former self than he did last Fall.

Norma looked much the same, excepting she has left off the rouge. Maybe only for the occasion. She was wearing a black satin dress, the upper part of which had white figures. Plain and becoming. Her slippers were black patent, trimmed with black and white. They were almost shabby from wear, but she looked nice. I think I shall like her. Her desire to be liked was very apparent and nearly pathetic. She and Wilber have "cut out" the spooning [kissing, I presume] or did for that day....

Our lot looked better than usual. Everything is beautiful now. Norma had never seen lilies of the valley. We have several blooms and the pansies are so pretty.... — Lovingly, Elizabeth Bradt

Elizabeth's "I think I shall like her" was rather provisional!

x·o·ø·o·x

At the end of the summer, Wilber and Norma visited again. They had most likely been to Washington State for the summer and were bringing graduate student Hooper Linford from Pullman to Cincinnati for his doctoral work.

6:50 A.M. SUNDAY, SEPT. 23, 1928
My dear Daughter [Mary] — ... I had just resumed varnishing when we heard someone at the piano. I thought it was Rex but Ruth came and found the tourists had arrived. They said they had been here about fifteen minutes.

Wilber looks very well indeed but Norma looked worn and thinner. She acted as lively as ever tho. We all liked [Hooper] Linford. He is very fair with white eye lashes and brows, fair hair, a good profile, and immense feet....

Wilber in his doctoral robes and Norma in her bachelor's gown at her graduation from Washington State College, June 1929. Wilber's gown indicates that he marched in the academic procession with the WSC faculty as a visiting guest; he was an instructor at the University of Cincinnati at the time.
[PHOTO: WILBER BRADT]

CHAPTER 3   *It was one of the perfect days of my life*

Wednesday A.M., Wilber and Norma went up to the University. She wore a light percale dress and sweater with pockets torn out. Neither you nor I would have been caught up there looking so frowsy [shabby]. Wilber had army shirt and army dress trousers and "yaller" shoes. Not much to brag on for looks either. They left [for Cincinnati] at eleven.… Wilber had to be in the University [U.C.] Thursday A.M.…
— Elizabeth Bradt

Wilber and Norma returned to Washington State again in the summer of 1929. Wilber did geological research in the Cascade Mountains from June to August, as assistant geologist of the Washington State Geological Survey, a higher position than he had held in the summer of 1927. On June 3, 1929, Norma was awarded her Bachelor of Arts in Music with Honors by WSC. There is a photo of her and Wilber both in their academic gowns. It is likely that Wilber marched in the academic procession during her graduation. She visited her family in Oregon and finished the summer in the mountains with Wilber. Decades later, at age 75, Norma wrote,

During the last few weeks of one of those summers, I joined the [geological] expedition, as I had gained some of my UC [Univ. of Cincinnati] credits by taking geology there for two terms. On this mountain location, I took notes on the findings and had other tasks, one of them being left to guard the entire camp when all the men students and profs were drafted to fight a bad forest fire over the ridge. I felt entirely inadequate for this task.

Wilber and Norma did appear to enjoy the outdoors together, though Norma's daughter Abigail in later years sensed that Norma had tolerated it rather than actively enjoying it. I recall no such reluctance, although in my youth, we did more day trips than overnight camping. Norma brought her enthusiasm to any task before her.

On these trips west, Wilber was able to nurture his contacts at WSC to his benefit.

4

"I'm wondering if Wilber will be called to the Orient"

Pullman, Washington
1930–1933

Wilber had not quite completed his three-year stint as instructor at the University of Cincinnati when he was offered an assistant professorship at Washington State College at an annual salary of $3,300, beginning in the spring term of 1930. This position was a major step up in salary and status; recall that his initial salary as an instructor at WSC had been $2,400. The new salary at WSC was raised to $3,500 and then to $3,600 in the subsequent two academic years.

Before leaving Cincinnati, Norma and Wilber visited the Bradts in Bloomington. Thirteen-year-old Ruth wrote about the visit to her older siblings who were in Washington, D.C. She took quick note of Wilber and Norma's public displays of affection.

Jan. 5, 1930
Dear Mary and Paul — … Sunday two weeks ago Wilber and Norma came to see us as you know. The first thing she said to Mother was "You little dickens." And she used large words to express things.… The conversation interrupted about every 5 or 10 minutes by a "smack" [kiss]. Emma Cavin ate dinner the day they left (Thurs. Dec. 26) and they kissed each other two or three times at the table. And actually, Wilber's lips are not as pretty as they use [sic] to be and we wondered if he hadn't caught the thick-lips disease or whatever you call it.

… [On Christmas day], Wilber and Norma gave me a yellow gold or brass necklace with some yellow beads in it. It is very pretty.…

Wilber and Norma took letter paper to Grandmother [Seelinger] for Christmas too. And Paul, the funny little round thing is called a Yo-Yo. In Bloomington last fall, nearly everyone had one. Haven't they had them in Washington yet? They still have them here too.…

With much love and a happy New Year, — Your sister, Ruth

At the risk of over-interpreting the "thick-lips disease" comment, I will note that Norma had somewhat pronounced lips that became more so as she aged, as did at least one of her sisters. Thirteen-year-old Ruth was most likely repeating a phrase used by her elders.

x·o·ø·o·x

On the same day, Elizabeth wrote Mary about the visit. She revealed a pragmatic side, a willingness to accept Norma at some level and to reduce her bitterness toward Wilber. She told of Wilber's and Norma's plans, was critical of the Sparlin family's finances, and expressed pride in Wilber's new position.

Sunday P.M. Jan. 5, 1930
Dear Mary — Here goes my first epistle of the year.… Wilber is fatter than ever, was wearing a plaid cap and is inclined to talk out of the right side of his mouth. I wondered if it is because of that black front tooth.

She [Norma] looked about as I had seen her. I tried and tried, but I can't see any beauty in her. They seem very happy. Wilber doesn't take the initiative in spooning like he did, but there is plenty of it done, yet. I was thankful I could say [that] Ruth didn't like oysters [a favorite of Wilber's] when she began looking too sick at the table. It really wasn't the oysters at all, but they served their purpose.

I hurried up my meal and we settled down to visiting. Wilber will never be renowned for his modesty. Guess I'll have to take the blame there – if blame it be. Of course, we are proud he can go back where he has been [Washington State College]. Norma is thrilled to go back as a faculty man's wife. Evelyn [Norma's younger sister] is going back with them. Her mother is to go to Pullman and have her and Evelyn's rooms ready when they reach Pullman. Wilber and Norma plan to rent rooms for a while. Suspect they will all be living together before long. Wilber is sending Norma's mother $25 per month now, and they have been keeping Evelyn for nothing. I mean she doesn't pay board and room.… — All well, Elizabeth Bradt

CHAPTER 4   *I'm wondering if Wilber will be called to the Orient*

Evelyn was just 20 years old. Her staying with Norma and Wilber evidently was the best available solution to getting Evelyn some college education with acceptable and economical living arrangements. Evelyn eventually earned her BA at WSC in 1934 at age 24.

x·o·ø·o·x

For the January 1930 trip to Washington State, Wilber and Norma avoided the snow-blocked passes over the Rocky Mountains and traveled southwest in their 1928 Chevrolet roadster. They entered California on US 80, which terminated in San Diego. Their route and mode of transportation to Washington State was unknown to me until August 2012. Among Wilber's photographic negatives, there was a photograph of a 1928 Chevrolet roadster beside a California US 80 road sign. It has a "193?" Ohio license plate, consistent with their recent Cincinnati residence. I do remember talk of a roadster being their first car. It had a luggage trunk but no rumble seat. Did they really squeeze Evelyn into that narrow front seat with them, as Elizabeth's letter suggested? Before the days of mandatory seat belts, if you fit you could ride. It must have been a cramped yet interesting trip with nights spent at campgrounds. It was the economical way to get a family of three to Washington!

This is wonderfully reminiscent of the trip I took across the country for navy duty in 1952; I was 21. I had bought a 1930 Ford Model A Roadster very similar to theirs for the trip, and I would stop beside highway signs for photos, as they did. I traveled with a college classmate, a Dutch exchange student; we entered California on US 66, not US 80; our track must have crossed my parents'. I find it remarkable that Norma never mentioned their earlier similar trip as I took off on my own adventure. She was probably more worried about my safety because a cousin of Wilber's had died at 18 when his roadster overturned on a cross-country trip in 1918. She, wisely, did not mention that either.

Wilber and Norma moved into a small duplex in Pullman and later into a small house at 403 Side Street. (The street has since been renumbered.) During their residence in Pullman, Norma played organ at St. James Episcopal Church, and accompanied the WSC concert band on a tour as the married chaperone for the woman dancer in the group. Edward R. Murrow (of future radio broadcast fame) was on the tour as a WSC spokesman, and as Norma later wrote, he sought her out as a sympathetic ear for his romantic troubles. Murrow was a prominent student leader at WSC and graduated in June 1930.

CITIZEN SOLDIER   PART I: FARM TO ACADEMIA

Top: 1928 Chevrolet roadster in which Wilber, Norma, and Evelyn made their way from Cincinnati to Pullman, Washington. It was winter (January 1930) so they avoided the snowbound Rocky Mountains and took the long southern route through California on U.S. Route 80. Bottom: my Model A 1930 Ford roadster in Texas in June 1952, en route from Princeton, New Jersey, to Long Beach, California, for navy duty. The rumble seat was full of luggage. I was 21 and my companion was Toby Swelheim of The Netherlands. I must have crossed my parents' 1930 track twice on that trip. I had no inkling at the time that I was mirroring their adventure. [PHOTOS: TOP, WILBER BRADT; BOTTOM, HALE BRADT]

CHAPTER 4   *I'm wondering if Wilber will be called to the Orient*

The house in Pullman, Washington, on Side Street that Wilber and Norma bought after I was born in 1930. That was probably me on the swing, which consisted of a rope tied to the house and run over a high tree limb, a Wilber creation. [PHOTO: WILBER BRADT]

On December 7, 1930, I, Hale Van Dorn Bradt, was born at the Catholic hospital in nearby Colfax, Washington. Wilber gave Norma a Bulova wristwatch inscribed with "Comrades Three 12·7·30" to honor the event [letter 4/2/44, Book 2]. I still have this watch. My earliest memories are of the Side Street house.

In those days, help with home, kitchen, and nursery was affordable for middle class families. For help with baby Hale, Wilber and Norma enlisted a young newly married woman, Frances Burtsch, from nearby Moscow, Idaho. She and her husband Stanton became life-long friends of our family. Easter egg hunts and horseback riding in the yard of their home at their "ranch" are among my earliest memories, as is a drive in Stanton's car to the ranch in the rainy season. When we left the highway, the dirt road soon became deep soft mud. We would have been badly mired had we been without chains. I found that road rather scary.

I visited Frances some years ago, perhaps around 2000, in Moscow. She was around 90 and I about 70. It was a touching encounter; she had known me since I was an infant, and we both knew it would probably be the last time we would see each other. It was.

CITIZEN SOLDIER   PART I: FARM TO ACADEMIA

x·o·ø·o·x

At WSC, Wilber's academic activities and connections broadened. He not only taught and supervised research students, but also attended meetings of the American Chemical Society and The Electrochemical Society to present research results; he also served as the primary organizer of an American Association for the Advancement of Science (AAAS) meeting at Pullman. He was active in Phi Beta Kappa affairs, serving as secretary of the WSC chapter. These connections led to trips east from time to time, and he would try to fit in visits to his Indiana family. On some trips, he took his own family along.

One such trip took place in August and September, 1931. It was a six-week trip in our quite new large four-door 1930 Chrysler automobile to a meeting in Buffalo, New York, and for other business in Providence, Rhode Island. I was a mere nine months old and rested in a hammock strung across the car just behind the front seat. In a sixth-grade essay, obviously coached by Norma, I wrote: "While we were traveling I seemed to be most amused by looking out of the window when we were driving through cities."

En route to Providence, we stopped in Bloomington, Indiana, to see Wilber's folks and in Holton, Indiana, to see his grandmother, Julia Seelinger.

My great-grandmother, Julia Bradt Seelinger, holding me in late summer 1931, Holton, Indiana. This was taken during our family's cross-country trip from Washington State to the East Coast and back in our 1930 Chrysler. [PHOTO: WILBER BRADT]

62

CHAPTER 4   *I'm wondering if Wilber will be called to the Orient*

After Providence, we visited Washington, D.C., to see Wilber's siblings, Mary and Paul. We have a photo of Julia holding me and letters from Elizabeth and Mary describing these visits.

From these letters, it is clear that Wilber and Norma were traveling not only with me, but with Norma's sister Evelyn (then just 22) and Marie, another young woman. Taking on two extra people (and Evelyn's violin) might have seemed a huge extra burden, but to Wilber and Norma it was likely quite natural to take along two young women to help with the baby. In return, they would get to see many parts of the country, and camping out kept expenses under control. Not a bad deal all around, but one that could lead to conflicts in the confines of automobile and campgrounds. Mary, and to some extent her mother Elizabeth, were quick to ferret out discontent!

This trip was quite a bold undertaking at the time and was probably viewed as a great adventure. Elizabeth's letter, written after the Bloomington visit, contained a few afterthoughts (an earlier letter describing the visit in detail has been lost). This letter expressed some understanding of Wilber and Norma, but also gave a chilling glimpse of how Elizabeth handled her own husband when she was displeased with him.

Friday night, Sept. 11, 1931
Dear Mary [from Elizabeth] — ... The main reason I have for writing this letter is to tell you to be very kind to Evelyn. She and Marie were charming to me. Evelyn told me many things that would have cleared matters a lot at the beginning if I had only known. She apologized to me for some of the things Norma did. I hope she plays [violin] for you.

Wilber and Norma were not very kind to the girls sometimes, and they (the girls) were not happy when they were here. I couldn't help them much for there was nothing I could do. My heart aches for Wilber because I'm afraid he isn't very happy I really cannot bring myself to write any criticism of Norma or feel any for her because in some way it would not seem loyal to him....

The baby [Hale] is a bright happy little fellow you will both love. He isn't pretty. Even Grandma Seelinger says he isn't. Wilber and Norma are not friendly – not even on speaking terms – with Norma's mother. The girls told me this. Evelyn says Wilber tells her [Norma's] mother [that] he has no divorces in his family. But we have only one side [of the story], of course. She may be a disagreeable woman, but she and Evelyn like cats [so she cannot be all bad]....

Hale and I had one quarrel. I said the porch foundation was not well made and he sat on me hard right before [in front of] the workmen who had all agreed there was a weak place in the wall. I resented the publicity and tried to make life as miserable for him as possible. I think I was fairly successful, although I'll admit I wasn't ladylike as you and Miss Fallon were [at Mary's workplace]. That was a masterstroke, but rough stuff is more along my line.... — Love, Elizabeth

x·o·ø·o·x

Ten days later, the group had just departed from Washington, D.C. The tension-laden visit was well described by Mary who had a good eye for detail. She lived with her brother Paul in an apartment in downtown Washington. Touring the nation's capital city was far easier in 1931 than it is now.

SEPT. 21, 1931
Dear Mother [to Elizabeth from Mary] — ... Then, they [Wilber and Norma] insisted that we go out riding with them while the other girl who was in the apartment, which they had taken for the night, [and who] mixed the baby's "formula" and did the washing. I suggested that we go by [to] pick her up and leave me there to care for the baby and mix his food or drinks. Norma said that she wouldn't trust me to do it! And so we rode out Sixteenth St. and back through Rock Creek Park. Paul and I were saving the most interesting part of the city until the second girl could be along....

Later, they set off again to see the city with, it appears, all six adults and the baby in the car. It was a Sunday evening at about 8 p.m., rather late for starting a tour, though the important monuments and buildings may have been lighted and quite beautiful. Surprising to me, they were able to enter the Library of Congress and the Smithsonian. Note that they drove through the "front yard" of the White House! The public was not excluded from the White House grounds until World War II.

We drove up 17th [St.] past the Pan American Union, the Red Cross, and the D.A.R. headquarters, then around through the front yard of the White House, and down through town past the Patent Office to the Capitol and Library of Congress. We suggested that they get out and go in to see the Constitution and Declaration of Independence. Neither Wilber nor Norma cared to, and the girls said, "if they don't want to go, we won't either." Paul and I insisted and gained consent to go provided we would be back out in front in ten minutes. When we went in, you should have heard them gasp. Evelyn was walking with me and she kept squeezing my arm and commenting upon how beautiful and spotlessly clean it was. She said it [the Library of Congress] was the most beautiful building that she had ever seen. We showed them the Constitution and D. of I., the reading room, and looked out the porch at the Capitol. Then, it was time to go.

They told us over and over how glad they were to have gone in. Wilber and N. had driven on and so we left Paul at the trysting [meeting] place, and we went across toward the Capitol, climbed the [East] steps, and stood "just where the president stands during inauguration ceremonies." Marie said, "Now, when I see pictures of that I can think I've stood there myself." Poor little girl, seeing so little and so happy over that little! Then we rode down through the Mall and Paul, Evelyn, and Marie got out to peep in at the "Spirit of St. Louis" [in the Smithsonian]. I was [seated] under the baby's hammock and Wilber and Norma didn't care to see it.

So often, Norma would say, "Oh, we won't bother to go see that now, sometime Wilber and I will come back and really see things in Washington." They didn't care whether Evelyn and Marie saw them or not, in fact didn't seem to want them to have a good time. It was awful. I don't mean that there were any cross words between Norma and us, she was visibly trying to act nice. Wilber seemed worried and none too happy, but he is taking out his spleen on the wrong person in my opinion.

It was late and the Washington residents probably had had much too much to say and show for Wilber's and Norma's patience at that time. The air of disapproval emanating from at least three of their four adult passengers and possibly also from me in the hammock (!) could have been difficult for the new parents.

Then we drove past the [Washington] Monument, around the tidal basin past the Lincoln Memorial.… Evelyn said that is just the way they are, don't seem to care about anything, wouldn't even go a mile out of the way to see West Point, and always drive through "the nigger part [the poorest part] of all the big cities." …

I think that I acted the lady, though at times rather a militant lady, and I'm quite sure that Paul was quite a gentleman. Paul told me that he thought that a man should know a girl for at least four years before marrying her. If he continues thinking that he will probably wind up with Irene ___ or someone from Bloomington.… — Good night, Mary

According to this account, my parents, Wilber and Norma, were really ogres on that trip and the two "nurses" were sorely put upon. Were they really? The complaints of the girls could have been significantly encouraged and amplified by hosts who were instinctively critical of Wilber and Norma. As lovable as she was in her later years, Mary, in our family, was said to have been rather difficult to get along with in her younger years. It was easily possible, though, that Norma overemphasized the servant roles of the girls on the trip, and their grievances therefore had some merit.

x·o·ø·o·x

Wilber had joined the Washington State National Guard in October 1930. He had not been affiliated with a unit since separating from the Indiana Guard in April 1927. The appeal of military life, a strong sense of patriotism, and the steady stipend all might have contributed to his rejoining. The Washington unit was the 161st Infantry Regiment. They met for weekly drills and summer encampments. The infantry was a change from the artillery expertise Wilber had developed in the Indiana Guard, requiring some make-up study and training. He soon regained his second lieutenant rank and was promoted to first lieutenant in June 1933.

Wilber was in Company E and became very close to its men and officers. After the weekly guard meetings, some of them would drop into the local Chinese restaurant, Charlie's Place, in Pullman for food and talk of "fighting the Japs" [letter 2/22/43] should it become necessary. Aggressive Japanese moves in China made this a real possibility, as Elizabeth noted:

Feb. 7, 1932
Dear Mary — … I wrote Wilber a letter for his birthday – a long one. Hoped Norma was well and would be well throughout her [second] pregnancy, which is true. Then I told him I had a nice letter from Evelyn [at] Christmas in which Evelyn's mother sent her love. I said I was glad she did. I wondered just how it [my letter] would be received but could see nothing in it to make trouble for Evelyn or her mother. I wouldn't want to do that. I'm wondering if Wilber will be called to the Orient. The western troops would likely be the first to go in case we get into the mix-up over there.… — I love you very dearly, Elizabeth Bradt

Elizabeth was on tenterhooks in her communications, afraid her words would be taken wrongly and cause more hard feelings.

Our family became a foursome with the arrival of Valerie Evelyn Bradt on April 18, 1932. To commemorate it, Norma gave Wilber a Scabbard & Blade key with the inscription: "Comrades IV 4·18·32" [letter 4/2/44, Book 2]. Scabbard & Blade was a military society to which Wilber belonged. This was to be their last child. Thereafter Norma suffered three or four miscarriages, possibly from an Rh-factor incompatibility. And life was soon to offer further hurdles to this young family.

In the following section and occasionally later on, I step back and apprise the reader of war-related events that have taken place elsewhere in the world.

CHAPTER 4   *I'm wondering if Wilber will be called to the Orient*

The 1930 Chrysler with Norma, Valerie, and me on the front seat, June 1933. Wilber held the door. [PHOTO: WILBER BRADT]

Valerie at eight months, Norma, and me just after I turned two, Christmas 1932. [PHOTO: WILBER BRADT]

Valerie and me on the steps of our home, dressed up for church or for Valerie's second birthday, impatiently tolerating the photography session, about 1934.
[PHOTO: WILBER BRADT]

On September 18, 1931, across the Pacific in Northeast China (Manchuria), the Japanese Army set off an explosion at an isolated railroad station. This event, called the Mukden Incident, was a provocative act blamed on the Chinese. It was used as justification for the Japanese invasion and occupation of Manchuria. The Japanese established the "independent" state of Manchukuo (Manchuria). There was wide international outrage at these actions and the Japanese withdrew from the League of Nations. This was the beginning of tensions between the U.S. and Japan that would break out in war ten years later. The following winter, on January 28, 1932, the Japanese attacked Shanghai and took the last major Manchurian city, Harbin, on February 4. The United States issued strongly worded objections to these actions.

In January 1933, President Hindenburg of Germany appointed Adolf Hitler as Chancellor of Germany. In July, Hitler proclaimed the Nazi party to be the only legal party; all others were banned. Germany was in the depths of a depression with huge unemployment.

5

"We have a drastic cut in pay"

The Great Depression
1933–1936

My sister Valerie was born into a world sliding into the Great Depression. In the fall of 1932, industrial production and farm prices in the U.S. were at their lowest point. In response to budget pressures, faculty salaries at Washington State College were cut by ten percent. Wilber's went from $3,700 to $3,330 per annum. This wasn't the only problem the young couple with two children faced, as Elizabeth explained to her daughter.

WED. P.M., JAN 18, 1933
Dear Mary — … Ruth had a letter from Wilber Monday. It had been started several days ago but on last Thursday, he had added a hasty few lines in which he said,
  "Norma fell on the sidewalk yesterday and broke both bones in her leg, one bone protruding through the flesh. She is in St. Ignatius Hospital in Colfax, nineteen miles from Pullman. The car is out of commission, so I can't see her often. She is suffering intensely. We are praying no infection sets in."
  We have not heard from him since. I wish I knew how she is. I've written to Wilber but was afraid I might make her worse if I were to write to her. I'm so sorry for both of them. Wilber said they had been having the flu about Christmas time….
  My eyes hurt. I do love you. — *Elizabeth Bradt*

x·o·ø·o·x

Valerie was an infant of nine months, and I was just two when Norma broke her leg. Wilber had his hands full. He wrote to his brother Rex and wife Gerry.

2-10-33
Dear Gerry and Rex — Just a note to report Norma's progress. Estimates by doctors indicate that she may be in the hospital for from 6 mo. to a year. The bones aren't knitting. I hope they are wrong and am sending over special diets and dopes that a chemist suspects might be helpful.

Hope this letter finds you both well + happy. The babies are still OK tho Hale calls for "Mama" each morning. Rather pitiful. — Love from Wilber, WB

x·o·ø·o·x

The elder Bradts did pay some attention to Norma, who responded with great care from the hospital.

February [1933, Hospital, Colfax, Washington]
Dear Bloomington Folks (Mother, Father, Ruth, Mary, Paul, Gerry, Rex) — This must necessarily be a "round Robin" letter because I get so tired writing and yet I want all of you to know how I appreciate your sympathy as expressed in your letters and flowers. I believe that the tenderness and solicitude of those we love has a definite healing effect. Each letter, as it came, brought additional encouragement and made the outlook brighter. The night that Mary's and Paul's roses came I was especially low in spirits and tired from pain. The nurse brought them in all beautifully arranged in a vase and they were the crispest, loveliest roses ever. They were all damp and dewy, as though they had just been picked from a moonlit garden.…

Another joy is that my babies are having good care. Wilber is so concerned with them and makes every detail of their diet, etc. his duty. I have such pleasant things to remember about him – only pleasant things. He has proved to be such an ideal husband from the first, and has improved on his own perfection each year. I will be so glad to return and manage his household affairs. — With love to all, Norma.

Norma felt the Bradts needed the strong plug for Wilber and acknowledged her role as "manager" of his household. She was a woman of her times despite her professional aspirations.

x·o·ø·o·x

CHAPTER 5   *We have a drastic cut in pay*

But things got worse after Norma's return home:

3-27-33, 11 A.M.
Dear Mother, Ruth + Father — Norma's crutch slipped on the linoleum this morning. She fell and re-fractured her leg. She is in the hospital again. Her leg had been out of the cast for three weeks and was progressing even better than we had hoped. The doctor said she could begin to put her weight on it by the middle of July and we were so encouraged.

Now she cannot have it really set because of the cartilage growth, so it is in a cast. This is supposed to straighten it but will not prevent shortening of the leg. We hope it will not shorten since the bones did not seem to slip past each other. They twisted and the leg bent again.

Please forward this to Rex, then to Paul. I have much to do today, for Nana + the babies. — Love, Wilber

x · o · ø · o · x

And worse.

3-28-33
Dear Gerry and Rex — Enclosed is your card for Mother's flowers. I am also attaching a photograph of George Washington [a dollar bill], which you may either use to get the flowers or insert into the card envelope depending on who is collecting antiques. They [dollar bills] are quite rare out here now. We have a drastic cut in pay and personnel of the faculty coming up next month. Hoping for the best.… — Class coming up, Wilber

The pay cut for the forthcoming academic year was probably announced that spring. It was an additional 15 percent, which lowered Wilber's 1933–34 salary to $2,830. Fortunately, Wilber kept his faculty position. In April 1934, his pay was raised to $3,265 and remained there until his departure from WSC in 1936.

x · o · ø · o · x

Here, Wilber's father Hale described the negative impact of the Depression on his extended family and their relatively good fortune before that. More important, he revealed a warm concern for the well being of his grown children and their families in those trying times.

71

BLOOMINGTON, IND., MAY 16, 1933

Dear Daughter Mary — … I have been expecting something like this – the loss of the job I mean – for some time, but had thought Paul would be more likely to lose his than you.

Our family has been very fortunate during this depression up until recently. The last week however has been full of bad news. About a week ago we had a letter from Rex that he had lost his job, … and now you are out. Wilber has had a cut in his salary tho I do not know how much, and the misfortunes that have come to him are equivalent to another cut.

But, all in all, I think we have much to be thankful for and much to be hopeful for. I am very thankful that we have a home to which you and Paul and Rex can come in an emergency like this. Even if there were no other consideration, you and Paul have a real share in this house because of the financial contributions you have made. If this terrible crisis brings on still greater suffering and loss, I hope we can draw together and fight it out together either here or on the farm.

I spend as much time each day as my urgent duties will permit endeavoring to read the future of my country and the civilized world through the fog of kaleidoscopic changes which each day's news brings to our homes. But the future is hidden from me as it is from everyone else. So "What is the use of worrying." We will do our best to meet each problem as it comes. I hope and believe all will come out well in the end.

Bring home the car. It may help you get a job. At any rate your mother will be more inclined to ride in it than in my Ford.… — Much Love, Hale Bradt

x·o·ø·o·x

At the end of the 1932–33 academic year, Wilber wrote to his younger sister Ruth. At age 17, she was graduating from high school and was about to enter Indiana University. Wilber commented on the value of doing well in school, but mostly gave an update on his own challenges. He was preparing to take his annual two-week national guard training in western Washington. The mood was grim, and Norma's morale was low.

JUNE 7, 1933

Dear Ruth — You are probably a graduate now, wondering why I have not at least written congratulating you. The fact that we didn't know the exact date of your Commencement was discouraging so time has passed. Norma has suggested my writing several times.…

Norma + I hope your graduation exercises were fun and that you were thrilled. We wished we could surprise you and be there. We went to the Colfax, Wash. H.S. commencement last week and watched one of our friends (a previous hired girl) graduate. Her folks did not want to come and she was quite broken hearted. Norma got so tired she could hardly sit in her chair and I finally had to carry her out.

She is improving steadily and can look forward to taking her cast off in September. She is getting pretty tired of it and worries more than she did. The weather too has been depressing. We have built a fire in the furnace almost daily to date. The children cannot play out of doors and they fret and worry Norma because she can't be a real mother to them. I am taking her to Fort Lewis with me next week to be an army officer's wife for 2 weeks. I hope she's improved by the change.

You don't realize what a change it will be. Compared to this side of the state, the west side is a green garden. The air is cool, fresh, there are deciduous + evergreen trees, rivers, and lakes. Over here the higher elevation cuts the deciduous trees out, and the dry climate thins the forests. We have lakes, and rivers but of altogether different types. There is dry sage brush + cactus are common. Norma will stay in a house on Puget Sound with trees all around and a big lawn for the babies. We still have 2 girls to help care for her and the babies so she can't worry too much....

> Wilber hoped the two weeks on Puget Sound would brighten the situation. His professional duties on top of his familial responsibilities were a heavy load. I find it commendable that he took time to reach out to his much younger sister. Two weeks later, he continued his letter, noting that Norma could not make the trip after all:

June 20, 1933 — I am at Camp now and have just returned from two days' maneuver. Norma could not come so I am pretty lonesome.... I am a First Lieutenant now. Am sending you a piece of wooden money in use in a town out here....

Must write to Norma so will close soon. I am glad you have done so well in High School. Your record is what I am congratulating you for. The graduation is a routine incident. I see all the time people who have affected to be "above making grades," who were having a "well balanced" college life and who were satisfied with a "good" record instead of a superior one. Most of them are either out of a job, losing a job, or afraid of losing one. They blame conditions and do not consider themselves responsible.

I know you will continue your fine record in college. Love to you and to Mother + Father from — The Washington Outpost, Wilber

Camping in the rolling hills of eastern Washington State, early 1930s. Note the Chrysler, the tent, all the equipment, and the mountains in the background. That was probably Norma on the right, with her back to the camera. Another photo of this outing showed a playpen for Valerie or me. [PHOTO: WILBER BRADT]

Wilber was critical of those who did not take maximum advantage of their educational opportunities. I can only surmise that he retained empathy for those who did not have opportunities. At times, a hobo (a homeless person) would come to our back door looking for a meal and would be politely accommodated with a meal handed out the back door.

Our life in Washington State included outdoor activities for the whole family. Camping trips in the rolling fields of eastern Washington State and daytime picnics were extensions of Wilber's and Norma's previous participation in such activities. With small children and much impedimenta, these outings were rather civilized.

In addition to family and teaching, Wilber as an academic had to be active in research. His work in the electro-deposition of manganese attracted the attention of the Vanadium Corporation in Pennsylvania, which established a research fellowship for a graduate student to work under Wilber at WSC. Wilber was also gaining visibility in other scientific venues. He was elected fellow of the American Association for the Advancement of Science (AAAS) in 1933 and elected as executive secretary of the western division of Phi Beta Kappa in 1934. He was appointed to the PBK national committee for the revision of the PBK constitution and bylaws that same year. These associations and presentations at meetings of the chemical societies continued to require travel to the eastern states.

The world of trains, written mail, postcards, and ten-word telegrams when long-distance telephoning was expensive and inconvenient was revealed in this very brief letter to his brother Rex and his wife.

CHAPTER 5   *We have a drastic cut in pay*

Our family around 1935 on another outing in Washington State with an unidentified friend on the left. [PHOTO: WILBER BRADT]

SPOKANE, 9-5-34, 11:30 P.M.
Dear Gerry and Rex — I will reach Racine [Wisconsin] sometime Saturday AM. I must leave for Bloomington the evening of the same day. May I come out to see you + Rex? — Your brother, Wilber

x·o·ø·o·x

The national guard was on its 1935 summer duty in western Washington when Wilber's battalion was called to extended "strike duty" to control crowds and strikers in Tacoma, Washington, during a bitter strike of timber and sawmill workers that shut down operations and sawmills across the Northwest. The strike began officially on May 6 and extended to mid-August. It was motivated by the poor and dangerous working conditions in the industry and also by a successful (from the workers' viewpoint) strike of longshoremen and dockworkers the previous summer. It took place in the context of major Federal "New Deal" legislation in 1933 and 1935 giving rights to unions and workers, including the right to strike. The latter, the National Labor Relations Act, was signed into law on July 5, 1935, as the timber workers' strike was sputtering to a conclusion.

Public opinion was generally supportive of the strikers at first, but as the economic effects of the strike began to be felt more broadly, it turned more negative. In June the state moved to help reopen the mills. Workers willing to work were threatened and beaten by strikers and strike sympathizers, and the local and state police were unable to control the violence. Hence, on June 23, the governor called for one battalion (about 500 men) of the Washington National Guard, then concluding its two-week summer encampment in nearby Camp Murray, to assist the state police in Tacoma.

Although the guard unit was there simply to preserve order and keep streets open, these actions de facto were most helpful to the mill owners. The national guard used tear gas and limited picketing by union members to groups of no more than three. Mills were thus able to open in Tacoma with non-striking workers ("scabs"). In Tacoma, the situation remained unsettled until union members ratified, in early August, an agreement that provided for higher wages, better conditions, and local union recognition. Independent agreements in other communities gradually allowed the industry to regain functionality. The national guard was not released from duty until early August. Wilber spent the later part of his duty in Aberdeen, one of the last communities to reach an agreement.

Wilber wrote his parents a dramatic and vivid account of his involvement as a first lieutenant of the national guard, which Norma typed up. Her forwarding letter and Wilber's account revealed, in part, their feelings about these events and his concern about his own leadership skills. It can be read for hints of Wilber's attitude toward the strikers or the mill owners, but his focus was mostly on keeping order and performing well as an officer. This strike duty was the precursor to the actual combat Wilber would encounter eight years later. His account is one of the most extended and coherent of all his letters. It enlivens an important event in America's history.

During this period, Norma, Valerie, and I vacationed in a cabin at Pacific Beach, not far from Tacoma. "Little Evelyn" (my first cousin, Milton Sparlin's daughter) spent time with us. At age 11, she was like a big sister to Valerie (age three) and me (age four). I remember her carrying us one at a time across a log used to bridge a small brook; I found that rather scary. Another memory is of a big army truck stuck in the wet sand in a rising tide. I was fascinated by the eventually successful efforts to retrieve it. (Little Evelyn had a long fruitful life and died in 2013 at age 89.)

Here is Norma's forwarding letter to her mother-in-law.

August 13, 1935, Pullman, Washington

Dear Mother Elizabeth [from Norma] — Wilber gave me these notes to copy shortly after the first of August. I purposely held them up for a time because he was still on duty and, if I had read that letter and been so far away from the scene of action as you are, I would have worried myself distracted thinking of the huge bloodthirsty mobs he was running into. I have not edited the notes because in so doing I might have destroyed some of the drama, which the original words carry.

We returned home here last Thursday [August 8]. Weeds were waist high in the flower beds; a large stack of office correspondence and a move into the new Chemistry Building awaited Wilber. Consequently, we are very much rushed at present. The babies enjoyed their stay at the beach and are as brown as Indians. They have each gained about six pounds weight. They have each bought a picture postcard to send to "Gran'fowder." Very soon I shall have them initial the cards and mail them. Wilber has some more typing for me to do, so must say goodbye for the present. Hope you are well and that the weather is not too warm there. — Love, Norma, Wilber, Hale II, Valerie

Norma's "huge bloodthirsty mobs" arose from a valid fear for Wilber's safety and also from her own ability to dramatize any scene, but it also revealed her serious lack of appreciation of the strikers' needs. Wilber's views were more moderate.

Note that Norma was functioning, without complaint, as Wilber's typist. Men, for the most part, did not type in those days, and wives catered to their secretarial needs. Secretaries typed their bosses' letters from dictation or hand-written drafts. Norma was a superb typist and her letters were often typed rather than handwritten. In contrast, Wilber's personal letters were always handwritten, unless typed by Norma or a secretary. Here is Wilber's story:

July 26, 1935, Armory, Aberdeen, Wash.

Dear Mother, Father, and Ruth — It is about time that I told you something about the strike duty I have been engaged in during the last seven weeks. Company E went to the annual encampment June tenth. The last Sunday of camp is a holiday affair. In the morning there is a band concert in which the three regimental bands compete for a prize. In the middle of the day we form for and carry out a divisional review before the governors of Wash., Ore., and Ida. After returning to the regimental area many guests are present for dinner, then another band concert, and finally a competition to select the best enlisted man.

During the last band concert and competition our battalion (the 2nd) received confidential orders to be prepared to move out at a moment's notice. We quietly went about picking men away from groups of visitors, out of the competition, and out of the many groups celebrating the end of camp. It was rather dramatic to be assembling equipment, issuing ammunition, loading rifles and pistols in the company streets while around the regimental area only 30 yards away was the happy-go-lucky crowd of guests and men and officers of the N.G. [National Guard] who were in the 1st and 3rd battalions.

Within an hour we had loaded rifles, rolled packs, packed kitchen equipment, etc., and were ready to move out. An officer of the division was present and told me afterward that he saw nothing to suggest an unusual situation.

At midnight June 23 [Sunday night] we arrived by truck in Tacoma, unloaded at the Armory and slept on the floor until about 3:00 A.M. The trucks were busy all this time bringing in kitchen equipment and cots. At 4:00 a.m. we breakfasted and were on the bridge at the foot of 11th St. in Tacoma. This was called the 11th St. Bridge and connected the city with the lumber mill and factory area.

We found about 1000 striking men on the bridge blocking traffic to the lumber mills. They were mostly unarmed but very antagonistic toward us and determined to block the bridge, which is about 400 yards long.

I was quite complimented to have the first assignment of the day – to clear the bridge. The men [in my platoon] were mostly of high school age with a few of college standing. None had ever had any experience of this type. Most men were armed with loaded rifles and a few with pistols. Bayonets were fixed on all rifles and men armed with pistols carried no other weapon. Later they received policeman's nightsticks. The main point of course was to accomplish the mission without bloodshed. I had 12 men. We placed about eight on the most crowded side of the bridge, using the others to clear the other side. I walked up the center of the street somewhat ahead of the line of soldiers, urging the strikers to move on. Those who did so kept ahead of me, and those who refused were about alongside of me, most of them on one side. These were shoved along by the soldiers. The push of a rifle at high port was usually sufficient, for anyone who insisted on his rights the boys applied strokes with the butt, the piece against the body or of the rifle proper or barrel about the striker's head. None of them would face the soldiers. By eight A.M.

the bridge was cleared, my boys had gained considerably in self-confidence, and the strikers had stopped calling the boys tin soldiers and boy scouts and had started calling them more manly but less courteous names.

> At "high port," the rifle is held in front of the chest and head at a 45° angle from the vertical. Either end (butt or barrel) or the entire "piece" can be used to control individuals in a crowd.

About 11:00 a.m. the crowd had about doubled and had begun to get behind us by filtering thru on various pretexts. But orders were still to permit traffic. I took six men to the other end of the bridge to block other entrances to the bridge. Before I could get back to the original position I received word from my sergeant that he needed more men. I came back with one man and found that the crowd had decided we were afraid to do anything and were crowding me badly.

I sent this extra man back for my other five and instructed them to bring all men [presumed strikers] loafing [loitering] on the bridge to my end. With the six others we went to work on the crowd [with] the gun butts and fists (I was afraid of the consequences of drawing pistols) and moved them back to the end of the fill leading to the bridge. During this rather critical time the other troops were off to parts unknown on other missions. It was not a case of my men getting hurt for we could always use bayonets or fire on them, but rather was it important for my boys to get the feel of the situation. They did. One said, "I didn't know there was a strike yesterday. I wasn't mad at anyone when I came down here, but if the ///???? [epithet] gets in my way again I'm going to knock him cold." They had found that they were the authority there, and they were no longer impressed by 2000 strikers.[1] I was proud of them.

About that time twelve more men were sent down as reinforcements in a truck. They didn't dismount, but their presence had considerable effect on all present. We then really went to work and [tear] gassed the crowd, then chased them back to the end of the city block beyond the bridge.

The gas was a new experience for most of the boys. We had no masks. When the crowd was gassed we went in and worked on them while they were confused. Tear gas was the only gas used then. I never cried so much in my life. However I would not want a mask under such circumstances because of the temporary character of the situation. The gas dispersed in a matter of two minutes due to a gusty wind.

We held the bridgehead until 4:00, then were relieved for mess [supper]. My Captain replaced me. At 4:30, we were called back by a tense situation at the bridge and found about 5000 people there (No Food eaten yet). This time the crowd was chiefly strikers but they all had their families along. There were small children, cripples, school girls, old women and men and mothers with babies. This

National guard truck and troops of Wilber's unit on strike duty in Takoma, Washington, about June 24, 1935. They are on the approach to the 11th Street Bridge, possibly just east of A Street, which gave access to the lumber mills. A police wagon is seen to the right. [PHOTO: *POST-INTELLIGENCER* COLLECTION, MUSEUM OF HISTORY & INDUSTRY, SEATTLE, WASHINGTON, PHOTO PI 24042]

complicated things considerably for us. In the back of the crowd were the agitators. A continuous torrent of abus[ive] ridicule was hurled at the boys all the time. They are veterans by this time and paid only slight attention. Major Hand ordered the crowd to disperse and received only more abuse.

We drove a wedge deep into the mob and stood put watching to locate the instigators of trouble. There were as many women as men and the women were far more active in stirring up trouble. They felt that they could not be handled physically. We were somewhat leary of starting something violent by giving one of them a chance to start screaming. However, it soon became obvious that if a woman wanted to take the man's part we would have to treat her as a man. From this wedge we officers and members of the state patrol would wade into the crowd and [pick] out the trouble makers. Incidentally the Washington State Patrol consists of only 70 men, but they are selected from a waiting list of over 2000. One man whom I arrested tried to resist by getting behind one of the large steel street mail boxes. I started to follow him around behind the box and a Patrolman reached over with one hand, grabbed the poor fish by the collar and pulled him right over the top of the box, which was shoulder high to me. If one of the Washington State Patrol ever tells me to come along I'll be the picture of cooperation. After about an hour of picking out the trouble makers, the crowd was gassed with tear gas and smoke, but they did not disperse, due to the fact that the streets were solidly packed with people for five [or] six blocks. Those in back continually pushed forward to see better.

During this period the scabs [workers who chose not to strike] had been coming across the bridge and were shunted up a cross street we had kept clear. About 5:30 p.m. we received word that all workers were in the clear. Major Hand ordered the troops to withdraw to the trucks at the other end of the bridge. I was in charge of the last platoon to move out. We had been farthest forward in the wedge. As we withdrew I saw that Major Hand and a Lieutenant Davisson (?) and two Patrolmen were still in contact with the crowd. Just as I went over the arch of the bridge, I saw fighting again. I yelled at the column and about one company, Co. E., heard me and we went back on the double. The rest of the battalion followed shortly. One worker had decided to come through late and the mob was beating him.

While we were coming back one Patrolman waded into the middle of the fight and really went into action. I saw part of it. It seemed that he was using both hands and each time a hand moved a man went down. He reached the beaten man, was knocked down, and came up with a man in his hands and threw him into the mob, knocking several down, grabbed another and threw him clear over the top of a sedan which was parked there.

The boys were mad then clear thru. The Major gave his orders as we passed and we certainly cleared that mob out. There were no shots fired and no bayonets used, but plenty of butt strikes were used. I think the sight of us coming back on the run satisfied the sightseers clear up to the fourth street above. At least they moved out all the way up the street. The Major and the gas officer threw gas bombs into the crowd and finally drove a car which had tear gas dissolved in carbon tetrachloride connected to the exhaust pipe, up the street. Everyone cleared out permanently and we retired about 7:00 p.m. to the armory, TO EAT.

That night the streets were patrolled by National Guardsmen in cars all night. My Captain was sick and we were short a 2nd Lt. so I was carrying a pretty heavy load. As a result I was only assigned one [night?] patrol during the entire two weeks.

The next morning we occupied the bridgehead at 6:00 A.M. There were about 1000 strikers in the street at the bridge: no women and no children. These men were here to fight and we gave them exactly that. First gas, then rifle butts and night sticks. Further, we arrested all men we recognized as having made trouble the previous day. One man who had thrown a gas bomb back at the Major was in the street I cleared with part of Co. E. I said, "I want that man" and pointed at him. He could not have seen me point but he started on the run. I grabbed his collar and he came back with both fists flying. He swung at me four times and each time I cracked him on the head with my night stick. The first time I eased up quite a bit and it didn't even phase him. I doubled the force of the blow next time and the last two times I was too busy to even worry about hitting him too hard. We fought all over the sidewalk, out to the middle of the street and back to the sidewalk where I threw him down against the wall of a building.

I didn't do all this by myself, but that is all I was conscious of at the time. Later I found that one of my boys [had] hold of him for a while. When I threw him down about four bayonets poised over him. The boys were berserk. They hoped he would try to get up. That was my high point in notoriety. The Seattle P.I. [Post Intelligencer] published a picture of me marching him to the patrol wagon with my hand on his collar in a most melodramatic manner and three or four of my boys with bayonets poised eagerly in case he tried to get away. It wasn't posed because none of us knew it was taken until the next day.

My Captain, being sick, was not able to be very aggressive in these affairs. I tried to show that I would go with my boys. As a result my status has changed considerably in the battalion. Formerly I was the college professor. Now I am the Lieutenant that they want to go out on duty with. It keeps me worried all the time for fear I'll do something to fall down on my reputation. I was described recently by a prisoner brought in by my detail as "That hard-faced Lieutenant." So just now among the officers, I am "hard-faced Bill."

During the next few days our regular routine was to get out at four A.M., eat at 4:30, go downtown at 5:30 and occupy the strategic corners. My post was the "hot" one where we had had our battles. This was accomplished by placing men in pairs on each of the four corners of a street intersection. The remaining four men were usually placed on moving patrols which covered any parts of the four adjacent blocks which might collect crowds. Our chief troubles here were with the "taxpayers." It seems that a taxpayer feels that he has the privilege of standing for any length of time at any place he desires. It doesn't matter if he is collecting a crowd and the trouble will develop because of the crowd. He is a taxpayer. The latest one we have encountered announced that he was not only a taxpayer but he had a baby and consequently he would not move on. They will admit that they have no business in the "hot" area but that they stand on their rights and no National Guard is going to keep them out.

Incidentally, during the little personal battle that I described above, about 150 strikers started after me on the run to rescue the man I was fighting with. All but one of my men were occupied. He, a sergeant, was [there] and started on the run for them, yelling like an Indian. The mob melted away and he chased them out of the area.

CHAPTER 5   *We have a drastic cut in pay*

Four national guardsmen escorting a demonstrator to the patrol wagon in Tacoma during the 1935 lumber mill strike, published in the Seattle Post-Intelligencer *on June 26, 1935. Lt. Wilber E. Bradt of Co. E, 161st Infantry, second soldier from the left, had his hand on the striker's shoulder.* [PHOTO: *POST-INTELLIGENCER* COLLECTION, MUSEUM OF HISTORY AND INDUSTRY, SEATTLE, WASHINGTON, PHOTO PI-24063]

CITIZEN SOLDIER   PART I: FARM TO ACADEMIA

August 1, 1935 — During the last few days I have been in charge of M.P.s [Military Police] in Aberdeen with resulting lack of sleep. Consequently, this [letter] is indefinitely postponed. I have maintained the direction by weekly mail of 4 graduate students all summer. — Love, Wilber, 1st Lt. 161st Inf. [Infantry Regiment]

Monitoring graduate students in the midst of all the military activity! Wilber gained in leadership experience and showed that he could manage himself in tense and physically difficult circumstances. He took pride in that and wanted his parents to know. He showed little empathy toward either the strikers or the employers, though his actions necessarily supported management by keeping the streets open for workers to pass through to the factories. His job was to keep the bridge open and to maintain order, and he addressed himself to those tasks. Nevertheless, I found it discomfiting that he nowhere expressed any concern about the poor working conditions that led to the strike. He and Norma were sensitive and educated enough to appreciate those issues and were surely sympathetic to the strikers' plight, but probably at a more theoretical than gut level and not at the cost of a breakdown of "law and order."

It is amazing to me that the confrontations with troops untrained in crowd control and carrying loaded firearms did not result in accidental shootings. I credit Wilber's guidance and control of his men for that restraint.

Sometime after our return to Pullman, Wilber had a commercial photographer take his portrait in both civilian and military apparel: the professor and the lieutenant. They were posted side by side in the window of the photographer's shop. Valerie and I were quite impressed to see our dad's photos displayed there in public.

x·o·ø·o·x

How did I come to possess the above letter and others that Wilber had sent to his parents? On that cold December morning of 1980, when my sister Abigail gave me her blessing to pursue the story, I asked her what she remembered about the existence of Wilber's letters. She replied that Mother (Norma) always claimed she had burned them, and this was consistent with my memory of Mother's rather vague responses to my occasional queries.

I then asked Abigail about the letters he had written to his parents in Indiana. She reminded me that they were at our cousin Alan's log home in the hills behind Luray, Virginia. His parents had built the house and had lived there. At the funeral of Alan's father Paul (Wilber's brother), in

CHAPTER 5   *We have a drastic cut in pay*

Wilber, the chemistry professor and the national guard officer, Washington State, 1936. Note the crossed rifles of the 161th Infantry Regiment on his lapel. [PHOTOGRAPHER: UNKNOWN, PULLMAN, WASHINGTON]

1978, she had spotted them in an old desk and recognized the handwriting. She told me that Alan had asked me if I was interested in them, and that I had casually replied, "Not really, but I know where they are if I ever am." I had totally forgotten this exchange in the intervening two and a half years! I then asked Alan for the letters and he shipped them to me, but not until he had copied some of the passages that interested him; he was a veteran of Vietnam combat.

Alan at first withheld some of the more "sensitive" letters, but I prevailed upon him to send those as well. He apparently thought they reflected poorly on the family and in particular on our grandparents, Hale and Elizabeth, of whom we have many fond memories. These turned out to be arguments about finances in February 1941, presented below. I told him that presenting the complete picture shows the humanity of the participants and would not detract from their many fine qualities. Alan then relinquished the remaining letters.

These letters were mostly from Wilber to his father. Wilber, in large part, took on the role of a reporter of events around him, from family to academia to the Pacific war. They were written by a mature son to his father, a retired Indiana high school teacher. The son, as always, strove to do well in his father's eyes. It is a rich trove, only surpassed later on by the discovery of Wilber's letters to Norma.

In his three years as head of state, Hitler had solidified his power as fuhrer and had restored Germany to relative prosperity with deficit spending on public works, industrial rejuvenation, and military equipment. On March 7, 1936, he ordered three battalions of German troops into the long disputed industrial Rhineland, which had been demilitarized by the Treaty of Versailles in 1919. It was a test of French diplomatic will; the French did not respond.

6

"Our river is still behaving and is fine skating"

Maine

1936–1941

The fortunes of Wilber and Norma's family depended on Wilber's work. The economic climate remained grim, salaries had been lowered at Washington State College, and tenure was not certain. Wilber thus enlisted Norma in a campaign of letter writing to universities across the United States. The following letter was sent to the president of the University of Maine in Orono.

FEBRUARY 3, 1936
Dear Sir: — Dr. Colin G. Fink, Head of the Division of Electrochemistry at Columbia University, has suggested that I write you regarding a position in your Department of Chemical Engineering.

My qualifications include a Ph.D. degree, membership in Phi Beta Kappa and Sigma Xi; teaching experience at the University of Indiana, the University of Cincinnati, and the State College of Washington.

During the past 10 years, since I have received my doctorate at the University of Indiana, I have published in scientific journals twenty-two articles, dealing with organic chemistry and electrochemistry. The D. Appleton-Century Company is publishing this month my book entitled "Study Units in General Chemistry." At the next meeting of The Electrochemical Society, there will be presented three or four articles outlining results of research work completed under my direction. During the past five years, work in my laboratory has included research in applied phases of organic and electrochemistry. As electrochemical advisor to the Planning Council of the State of Washington, I have presented by request two papers dealing with the electrochemical possibilities for utilizing power in the Inland Empire [region of Eastern Washington and North Idaho].…

Although conditions here are quite satisfactory locally, I am interested in a position at an institution nearer the industrial centers of the country.… I assume you will not jeopardize my present position by writing at this time to the State College of Washington regarding this application. — Respectfully, W. E. Bradt

x·o·ø·o·x

Conversations with the University of Maine went forward and letters of recommendation were sought. Most were quite positive about Wilber's research, his ability to motivate students, and his organizational abilities as demonstrated by his work on the Phi Beta Kappa committees and as organizer of the AAAS meeting at the Pullman campus.

One academic colleague at Carnegie Institute of Technology, who knew Wilber when he was a student at Indiana and whose quote about Wilber's "sloppy" appearance as a student is noted above, gave a rather mixed review of Wilber's credentials. He wrote to Maine's dean of technology.

February 21, 1936
My Dear Dean Cloke — … His disposition is in general optimistic and I believe that he works and lives harmoniously with his superiors and associates. He might be inclined to be a bit arbitrary in handling subordinates and students. However, I believe he would be patient with students in difficulty. I have no basis for passing judgment on his administrative or executive ability. He was very trustworthy and capable as an assistant some time ago and I believe that he has been very successful as a teacher in undergraduate courses at the University of Cincinnati and at the State College of Washington.

… He has published some ten or twelve research papers since 1930. In my opinion, the investigations he has reported were worth doing but they do not impress one as being especially important.… — Sincerely yours, [name withheld], Assoc. Prof. Theoretical Chemistry

These last few words, in a more competitive environment, would have been disastrous. In the absence of very strong counter evidence, they would kill any potential appointment at most universities today.

CHAPTER 6   *Our river is still behaving and is fine skating*

x · o · ø · o · x

The dean of the Episcopal Cathedral in Spokane, Washington, painted a broadly positive picture of Wilber's non-academic life, including a 1930s perspective of a wife's role. Wilber and Norma had affiliated themselves with the Episcopal Church; recall that Norma was the organist at the Episcopal Church in Pullman.

MARCH 16, 1936
My Dear Dean Cloke   … In addition to his ability as a member of the College of Science and Arts, Dr. Bradt is the sort of person who inspires confidence, and suggests a strength of character which is invaluable in college work. He is the type of administrator and executive who goes about his work quietly and manages to achieve good results without undue excitement or confusion. He devotes considerable attention to detail, but never at the expense of greater objectives. As a member of the faculty and the Episcopal Church, he commands the respect of those with whom he is associated.

He is a lover of outdoor life and although thoroughly scientific in his approach he has a keen appreciation for cultural values. Incidentally, he was appointed a member of one of the most important committees of Phi Beta Kappa.…

His home life is desirable in every sense and his wife is a person who has the faculty of minding her own business, and is possessed of more than ordinary attractiveness. She is a graduate of Washington State College, I believe, and is very much interested in music, being an organist of some ability.… — Yours sincerely,
Chas. E. McAllister

The chemistry department at the University of Maine was at the time primarily a teaching department. The university president and dean wanted it to develop a research program. A strong head was required to change the habits of senior faculty members. A 36-year-old outsider with a credible but not outstanding research record, good teaching credentials, and demonstrated leadership skills in the national guard may have been just what Maine's Dean of Technology Paul Cloke felt he needed.

It was not until early in July that an offer was tendered to Wilber as full professor and head of the Department of Chemistry and Chemical Engineering. Another person had been chosen for the position, but that had not worked out. The appointment was for the nine-month academic year with a salary of $4,000 to be paid in 12 equal monthly installments. At that time Wilber was an assistant professor of chemistry at WSC with a

The entire F. Hale Bradt family (Wilber, his siblings, and his parents) with our 1936 Plymouth, July 1936, Bloomington, Indiana, during our visit en route from Washington State to Maine. From left: Wilber, Mary, Hale, Elizabeth, Rex, Ruth, and Paul. This was probably the last time they were all together. Wilber was the only one married or with children at that time. Norma, Valerie and I were all present, but I have found no photo that shows us at this gathering. [PHOTO: WILBER BRADT]

salary of $3,265. The offer occasioned queries by Wilber and Norma about conditions in Maine, particularly those pertinent to the children: schools, reduced sunlight, tuberculosis rates, and so on. But of course, such a position could not be refused and wasn't.

Wilber purchased a new 1936 Plymouth, which I at age five thought was absolutely terrific. That summer, the family headed east for Maine, stopping at national parks (Yellowstone and Glacier). Valerie and I danced with Native Americans at a show in a park lodge, I was treated for sunstroke with cold cloths and lots of ice in a Kansas City hotel, and we saw our grandparents in Bloomington, Indiana. A photo of Hale, Elizabeth, and all five of their children in front of the new Plymouth is a favorite of mine. This may have been the last time the Bradt siblings and their parents were all together.

We settled in Orono, Maine, in an apartment building across a small park from the Stillwater River, a tributary of the Penobscot River. I began my schooling as a kindergartener in the nearby Webster Street School and Norma delved into her music. I played with Valerie outdoors in the large cardboard box in which Norma's new Vose & Sons grand piano had arrived. She gave Valerie and me piano lessons on it. Almost 70 years later, it is still well used by my nephew, Scott Hymes, a talented jazz pianist.

CHAPTER 6   *Our river is still behaving and is fine skating*

Norma at her new grand piano in Orono Maine, about 1937. [PHOTO: WILBER BRADT]

Valerie and Norma after church, Orono, Maine, 1937. [PHOTO: WILBER BRADT]

CITIZEN SOLDIER   PART I: FARM TO ACADEMIA

Wilber with Valerie and me, 1937, Orono, Maine. [PHOTO: WILBER BRADT]

CHAPTER 6   *Our river is still behaving and is fine skating*

Proud possessors of several small fish (held by me) and sailboat (held by Valerie), Maine, about 1938. [PHOTOS: WILBER BRADT]

    Sunday trips to Sandy Beach on Mt. Desert Island in the summer were welcome diversions; Valerie and I were not put off by the cold water and relished playing in the breakers. We would stop for fried clams on the way. Norma often told of my comment upon first viewing the Atlantic Ocean. I was five. When asked what I thought of it, I thought awhile and then responded, "It's OK, but it's not as big as the Pacific."

    In January of our first winter in Maine, Wilber joined the local unit of the Maine National Guard. The guard provided him with exposure to the outdoors and the camaraderie of fellow soldiers who were of a different social set than his academic colleagues. It gave him breaks from his academic duties, and there was, of course, the patriotic incentive. The Maine guard unit was artillery. Wilber had thus gone from artillery in Indiana to infantry in Washington and then back to artillery. Upon leaving Washington, his guard friends there gave him a .45 caliber Colt pistol for his personal use. His notebook carefully carried its civilian serial number, C17943, which distinguished it from identical government-issued pistols.

x · o · ø · o · x

That first winter, Wilber was very busy professionally but he also found time for recreation with all of us. A postcard to his parents two days after his 37th birthday gave them a glimpse of our lives in Maine.

2/3/37

Dear "folk" — Just a note to let you know we are still OK. The weather here is still mild but about 4 inches of snow. Hale and Valerie spend most of their time outdoors. Our river is still behaving and is fine skating except when the snow is on the ice. My friends in Wash. [State] are having 37° below zero [temperature] now with "several" feet of snow. Over [on this postcard] is a picture of Aubert Hall, the chem. bldg. here. My office is at other end.…

Thanks for the birthday [greetings]. The first 37 years are pleasant to recall so I really mean Thanks. — Love, Wilber, Norma

x·o·ø·o·x

Six weeks later, he wrote his parents again, but with a broader picture of his and our lives in Maine. The letter exhibits the intertwining of his professional and personal lives. He was very busy, with many balls in the air.

Aubert Hall, home of the chemistry and chemical engineering departments, University of Maine, as it appeared in 1937 on a postcard Wilber sent to his parents on February 2, 1937. The building has since been expanded and renovated. [PHOTO: CABEEN]

CHAPTER 6   *Our river is still behaving and is fine skating*

3-15-37

Dear Father, Mother and Ruth — Last week I wrote you a letter but never finished it and now it is lost. It was typed [by me] and was worse than my handwriting so I am not very sorry.

It is snowing here now. The natives are quite hopeful. They have predicted a terrible winter ever since I came, with no results. With the end of winter in sight they have become almost desperate. The winter here has been very mild with only occasional snow, at least three days of sunshine a week and warmer than Washington winters. Last week Norma + I went out in the woods on a south slope, built a fire and cooked steaks on sticks. What a treat!

People here are ice fishing a lot. They cut holes in the ice (30 inches thick in some of the northern lakes) and fish thru the ice. For salmon the baited hook is hung two or three feet above the lake bottom and tied to a willow or other timber wand, which is frozen into a hole in the ice. A red rag is tied to the stick so the fish will make it bob up + down. The general plan is to have about 30 holes and to spend the day running from fish to fish. What seems to happen is that one runs all day keeping the 30 holes from blowing full of snow or freezing solid. So far I haven't tried it out.

Today Prof. [Walter Gordon] Whitman, Head of the Dept. of Chem. Eng. at Mass. Inst. of Technology visited me. He talked with me about some of our men as chemical engineers. He seemed in general accord with my own ideas and policies and since M.I.T. probably has the best Chem. Eng. Department in the world, that means something.

Whitman has been proving himself a real friend. This is the second conference this year in which he has been very helpful.

I have been spending all my spare time on a reorganization of our curriculum to bring it more in agreement with modern policies and needs. One thing has been to definitely separate the chemists from the chemical engineering students and to give each a training more pertinent to their career. Another situation: one of my staff is a firm believer in asking examination questions which were not covered by previous assignments. "It develops reasoning power." I hope to tell you it does. The student reasons that he didn't have a fair deal with pretty good logic. This has existed for several years. I have been pretty careful but am gradually solving this – I hope.

Tonight   in 5 minutes in fact, Norma + I are taking Dean Stevens (retired dean of Arts + Sci. here) to hear a string quartet in Bangor.

… I go to Philadelphia next month … I present two papers there before the Electrochemical Society. One paper is on manganese plating and the other is on the oxidation of lactic acid.

The Vanadium Corporation of America is interested in my work on manganese and may develop the commercial aspects of it. Their lawyers are working on a patent application now. Someone else is also submitting another application on the same thing. I don't know how it will come out. It's a good thing Paul [Wilber's brother] wouldn't pass on it. I would expect him to be so sure he didn't favor me that I would be left out in the cold. If the patent goes thru, the Vanadium Corp. will want me to consult with them on commercial uses for pure manganese.

They aren't buying my rights but are offering to go into the development on a royalty basis with the reminder that there now is no market and maybe no longer [time]scale possibilities. It will be fun anyway. Going now. — Wilber

Wilber's brother Paul worked in the U.S. Patent Office in Washington, D.C. Wilber's association with Vanadium Corporation continued well into the next decade. His Patent #2,398,614, "Electro-deposition of Manganese," was filed in March 1938 on behalf of Wilber E. Bradt and Harold H. Oaks, a graduate student at WSC whose 1933 master's thesis was on this topic. It was assigned to the Vanadium Corporation and was finally issued in April 1946 four and a half months after Wilber's death. The corporation never developed it, and to my knowledge, there never was any financial return from it for our family.

x · o · ø · o · x

In April, Wilber wrote his parents and sister again. Wilber and Norma strove to get themselves and their children out into natural surroundings. Wilber's spectrum of academically related activities was daunting and revealed an ambition to excel. He was proud of being a demanding supervisor of his graduate students.

4-5-37
Dear Mother, Father + Ruth — This is the last day of spring vacation. During the past week I worked for the first five days, then we took the children on an all day "pin-pic" [picnic]. The south slopes are clear of snow and wooded. We drove out to within a half mile of the hills and hiked in thru the woods and climbed Little Chick [aka Little Peaked Mountain, 18 miles east of Bangor]. It was only about 1200 ft. [actually 800 ft.] high but was steep and in some places rocky. The children had a grand time. The top gave a fine view of the surrounding country and Bangor, Orono, Old Town, Mt. Katahdin 100 miles to the north, and several lakes. Most of the country is timbered (small second growth).

While on top, the children played in some deep snowdrifts. Next we climbed down and built a fire alongside a little stream and cooked bacon, steaks and baked potatoes in the fire. The children drank milk and we made tea in the fire.

CHAPTER 6   *Our river is still behaving and is fine skating*

Valerie especially is absolutely in love with water. She + Hale hung over a big boulder and threw egg-shells and sticks into the creek. By four P.M. the children had had a nap and were ready to start home. The sun was warm and in the woods there was no wind so we were very comfortable. We were home early and in bed by 8:00 and did the bed feel good. No trouble about getting the children to bed either.

4-14-37 — … This Saturday Dr. Glasstone of the University of Sheffield, England will talk [to] the Amer.[ican] Chem[ical]. Soc[iety] [Maine] members at Bowdoin College. I expect to go down [120 miles] to hear him.… The following weekend the various Chem. faculties of the state meet at Colby College [70 miles distant] … and I will give a talk on the teaching of chemistry there. The following week I go with a graduate student to Philadelphia to a meeting of the Electrochemical Soc. People tell us that here the month of May is a mad-house. If it is worse than April, I'll leave the state.…

It is only fair for [a potential student] to know that I am a slave driver when it comes to research. I won't waste time and apparatus on a man who works only for the credit. I want men who are interested enough that I have to watch them to see that they don't miss too much sleep or too many meals. Each year there are students who prefer not to work with me – for good reasons – and I am content to have it that way.

We are making progress with our manganese plating and have solved a couple of important points. Columbia Univ. and also the U.S. Bureau of Mines are taking up the work too. We are well in the lead but may lose it due to lack of time and money. Anyway I showed them it could be done. — Love, Wilber

x · o · ø · o · x

Norma was in good health in Orono even though she had suffered multiple miscarriages after coping with the multiple fractures of her leg in 1933, her gait showed no sign of any disability from the fractures. She entered the music scene at the University of Maine and in nearby Bangor with gusto. Valerie and I were long used to going to sleep with her playing her repertoire; Beethoven's Waldstein sonata would resonate through our home as we fell off to sleep. That music has been with me ever since. She played with and for friends but had few opportunities for formal concertizing. She did not take on pupils other than Valerie and me. In Bangor, she stood out as a highly accomplished musician.

She was a writer too. In those years, beginning in Washington State, she wrote a novel, *Grand Coulee*, named after the huge hydroelectric dam built from 1933 to 1942 in eastern Washington State. The novel was never published but attempts to get it published led to many revisions over the years.

Norma took seriously her roles as homemaker, mother to Valerie and me, cook for the family, and hostess to academic colleagues. She was the parent who was always home for us, getting us off to school and being there when we returned for lunch and at the end of school. It was she who got us off to bed on time so we would be fresh in the morning. Sunday afternoons were the occasions for family outings, perhaps to the beach, and Norma would organize sandwiches and children's bathing suits for the trip. I never heard her voice any frustration at not having more time for her musical and literary interests, though she may well have felt it.

The family went to Sunday services at St. James Episcopal Church in nearby Old Town, Maine; it was a "high" church with rites similar to the Roman Catholic Church. I was impressed by the incense and services performed by three priests at the altar.

At the end of our second winter in Orono, Norma was the piano soloist with the Bangor Symphony Orchestra in a performance of Paderewski's Polish Fantasy, Opus 19. The concert was in Bangor's city hall on May 5, 1938, and was repeated the next morning in the Memorial Gymnasium at the University of Maine in Orono. This was the high point for her on the local music scene.

x·o·ø·o·x

In a letter to his sister Ruth, Wilber took stock of the past two years in Maine and offered her employment advice. Ruth had graduated from Indiana University the previous year. Wilber played the professorial role as well as that of big brother. Wilber's family debt was worrisome, but a successful fishing trip earned bragging rights.

6/8/38

Dear Ruth — Final examinations are now over and the last grades are in the Registrar's Office. Since my own classes totaled over 350 students, that means a lot of grades besides the ones I must check as head of dept.…

Some facts I have established this year with reference to my own graduates are outstanding: 1. There is much more unemployment this year than last. 2. Positions in chemistry are paying less and are less common than last. 3. This is the best time to be in school.

CHAPTER 6   *Our river is still behaving and is fine skating*

Altho we have been pretty successful in placing our seniors, I am pointing out to them that the "hard times" are the times when a year of college is cheap. I believe you should seriously consider getting your M.A. next year before trying for a position.… If you want to teach Botany in college, go after it and get outstanding qualifications. Schools like Maine, Smith, Barnard and Prep. Schools would really be interested in a good M.A. You could do well and would like it if you tried. The Ph.D. and better positions could come later. You would probably go nuts in a museum or greenhouse.…

I was unable to go to the Electro-Chem. meeting – am not able to come to Indiana this spring but still wish I could. I may make it in Sept. if I go to the Milwaukee meeting of A.C.S. We are making every effort to clear off our debts next year. Our move [from Washington] has sunk us for three years.… These "opportunities" have quite a backlash.

We are well. I went deep sea fishing 3 weeks ago – brought home a wash boiler full of codfish. Some weighed 8 pounds. It is mosquito time in Maine. The Dean told me I had done a good year's work so I feel pretty good – but tired. I expect to do research this summer. — Love to you + Father + Mother, from Wilber

That summer (1938), Wilber and Norma bought a house at 204 Broadway in Bangor, a Penobscot River city of about 30,000, eight miles from Orono. The purchase price was $4,200. The large Victorian house featured big picture windows in both front and back, creating sunny living and music rooms. It had roofed porches on both sides, which have since been removed. The rear bathroom had a pull-chain toilet with a high raised tank. We had kittens that loved to chase one another down the long hallway; when they tried to change direction, they would skid sideways on the smooth hardwood floors, to our great amusement. Our new furniture was in the very modern (late 1930s) "art-deco" style. Some of it is still in the family

We had a vegetable garden in the large rear yard that produced rhubarb, radishes, corn, beans, and more. This was my first touch of "farming." I did not care much for it, especially the laborious weeding. One year, Wilber thought it quite clever to plant corn and climbing beans together—the corn stalks provided the poles needed by the beans. Weeding this when the corn was tall was, for a small boy, like moving through a jungle. Wilber created a small swimming, or "dipping," pool (about eight feet by five feet and two feet deep) by digging a hole and lining it with cement and mortar. We enjoyed it greatly. In reviewing old photos recently, I note that we had such a pool, though much smaller, in Pullman.

In Bangor, we attended St. John's Episcopal Church on French Street.

(Wilber's name is now in one of the stained glass windows as one of the church's war dead.) Valerie and I entered the Mary Snow public elementary school a half-mile down Broadway, she in first grade and I in second. It was a long walk for little kids but we did it every day through the Maine winter. I think we returned home for lunch also. Norma repaid my resistance to her piano instruction by offering me violin lessons with a local teacher, Mr. Cayting, and I eagerly took her up on this.

In our new school, I was immediately in trouble in arithmetic; everyone seemed to know the multiplication tables. They were new to me, and I was terribly confused by them. Dad solved that efficiently. He declared that each day after school I would learn one of the "tables" prior to going out to play. The first assigned was the "sevens" because they were the hardest. I did learn them and successfully passed his verbal test. After learning several others over the next few days, I remember being happily surprised at how easy the "fives" were. I was soon back on track in arithmetic.

Wilber also attended to my mechanical education. In the kitchen one day during breakfast, I inadvertently stepped on and crushed the electric plug for the hand iron. Wilber told me I would have to fix it, handing me a screwdriver and a new plug. When I asked him how to do it, he said that I should be able to figure it out by studying the broken one without help from him. That gave me pause, but I managed to do it. I have liked working with mechanical and electrical things ever since.

Our clear western accent was in sharp contrast to the "down-east" twang of our Maine schoolmates. Valerie and I were occasionally called upon to pronounce a word for the class. However, we were also occasionally corrupted. After school, I was describing to my parents plans for a school play and used the word "audience," pronouncing it "ordience." When corrected by my parents, I vociferously insisted that my pronunciation was correct because our teacher had pronounced it that way.

Our life in Maine was further described in four brief essays I wrote several years later, in 1942, for school in New York City. I was in sixth grade and just turning 12. Norma had sent these little essays overseas to Wilber who then sent them on to his parents. They survived among Wilber's letters to his parents. These vignettes illustrate my focus on activities with my father (Wilber) and the type of family activities Wilber and Norma arranged. At the time, Wilber had been away from home almost two years, albeit with visits home, and had sailed overseas only a month before I wrote the first of these letters. He was obviously on my mind.

CHAPTER 6   *Our river is still behaving and is fine skating*

Nov. 2, 1942
Fun at Sandy Beach
Sandy Beach is on the coast of Maine on Mt. Desert Island. One day when my Sister, Mother, Father, and I went there, we took the air-mattress with us. When we arrived we ate lunch and Daddy blew up the mattress.

After about an hour, we went in swimming where the big waves rolled upon the beach. As the tide was coming in, we took the mattress out with my Sister on it, and let the waves bring her in. Then it would be my turn. Sometimes we would turn all the way over.

Once Valerie was right under a big breaker, which, of course, would roll her right over. She fortunately got on the end of the mattress, so the front stuck up. The result was that the breaker landed just under it. I hope I can go to the beach again.

x·o·ø·o·x

Nov. 5, 1942
A Fishing Incident
Bar Harbor is on Mt. Desert Island as Sandy Beach is. This time we went there to fish with Dr. and Mrs. Klein. We were fishing off the rocks when Daddy moved to a shallower place. Mrs. Klein said, "If you catch anything there, you are a better fisherman than I am," and as if in response Daddy pulled out a fish.

x·o·ø·o·x

Grade 6, Dec. 4, 1942
A Lumber Camp
While we were living in Maine, Captain Buzzell [sic, Stephen Bussell] invited the National Guard to go to his lumber camp. He also invited me.

We got up early that morning, and drove to Old Town. This was in late fall, so it was cold and crispy. After about an hour we drove to the camp in army trucks. The road was very rough, and in places very muddy.

When we reached the camp we ate breakfast in a small building, which had beds, a place to eat, and a place to cook. After that we explored the camp which was very interesting. Later we ate a big dinner.

After dinner there was some pistol practise [sic]. First, there was some instruction, and later each man fired about six shots at a target, while I collected the shells *[shell casings]. When it was my turn to shoot, I shot only once. This shot missed the [entire] target, which wasn't a small one. — Bradt, Hale*

x · o · ø · o · x

Grade 6 [1942–43]
Deep Sea Fishing
One Saturday Daddy woke me up early, and told me that we were going deep sea fishing. After breakfast we met Daddy's friends. Then we drove to Bar Harbor, which is forty-eight miles away. When we reached Bar Harbor we rented a fishing boat, which was run by a motor. We rode for about an hour, till we came to a good fishing spot.

I just sat holding my line while one line after another was coming up with a fish on it [but not mine]. I finally caught one. This fish was the biggest one there was. After that I just sat some more [with the line, catching no more fish] till we went home.

(This happened to me again in my fifties! I went on a fishing charter with my brother-in-law in New Jersey and caught only one fish all day, but it was the boat winner, weight-wise!)

As Valerie and I grew in independence, it was believed in some quarters that corporal punishment, judiciously applied, would benefit young children. Wilber was a fair but stern disciplinarian. He never slapped or hit us in anger, but when he deemed it needed, would apply measured strokes to our behinds, sometimes bare and sometimes not, with his hand, a belt or switch, as we lay facedown on a bed. On one occasion, for a short period, he put Valerie and me in the enclosed space beneath the double bed, which sat quite high off the floor; it was a mini prison. Were these punishments too harsh? Were they an element in creating my fear of schoolyard bullies in my early school years and a moderate level of insecurity that persists to this day? Perhaps so.

Our sex education was also attended to. We knew where babies came from, but not all the details of conception and delivery. Most children in those days learned from other children, not their parents. Wilber had once told us that he grew up not having any idea what a woman's body looked like; for all he knew her torso was boxlike under her clothes. (I don't really believe this.) Although I had seen my sister naked numerous times, he had Mother lie down face up with legs apart in order to expose her genitalia to

CHAPTER 6 *Our river is still behaving and is fine skating*

Valerie and me. The various parts were pointed out—where babies came out, and more—but, in my haste to have this embarrassing display over with, I did not care to distinguish the various parts. This display was not repeated for the male genitalia, thank goodness.

Wilber's duties as teacher and department head were not always without conflict. He worked hard at getting the chemistry faculty to do research. One faculty member was neglectful of his duties, which led to detailed record-keeping and unhappy recriminations on both sides. In contrast, Wilber developed close relations with other colleagues, many of whom became close family friends. He spearheaded and brought about a major expansion of the chemistry building, Aubert Hall, doubling its size. He also remained active in research, in the teaching of graduate students and undergraduates, and in the national guard.

It was in Maine that Wilber's weight had escalated to 240 pounds. At an even six feet, he had become quite overweight, a hurdle he would have to overcome before embarking on the military life that the growing threat of fascism foretold.

After years of skirmishes between Japanese and Chinese forces in China, full-fledged war broke out on July 7, 1937 with an exchange of gunfire near the Marco Polo bridge in the outskirts of Beijing. By the end of 1937, the Japanese had captured Shanghai and Nanking. Two Chinese victories in 1939 brought the fighting to a stalemate, but skirmishes continued.

In November 1937, Italy joined the Germany-Japan Anti-Comintern Pact against the Soviet Union. Hitler then felt free to move against Austria. On March 12, 1938, German troops marched into Austria, and made a triumphal entry into Vienna two days later. Britain and France protested and did nothing more.

Hitler's troops had hardly arrived in Vienna when he began a diplomatic offensive against Czechoslovakia. Under threat of war, he demanded that portions of western Czechoslovakia heavily populated by ethnic Germans, namely the Sudetenland, be annexed to Germany, and this was acquiesced to by the English and French leaders, Chamberlain and Daladier, in negotiations leading up to the famous Munich Agreement of Sept. 29, 1938. "Peace for our Time" was Chamberlain's phrase for the Agreement upon returning to London. German troops occupied the Sudetenland in the next days, and later, in March 1939, the western (Czech) portion of Czechoslovakia, which included Prague. Romania and Poland annexed portions of the eastern (Slovak) portion. This "rape of Czechoslovakia" was so blatant that finally, the spines of France and England were stiffened; it was to be their final appeasement of Hitler. If Hitler moved again, war was inevitable.

Hitler's next target was Poland, but Russian interests had to be taken into account. On August 22, the foreign ministers of Germany and Russia signed a non-aggression pact in which it was agreed that Poland could be divided between them in the event of a German-Polish war. This pact between two countries of ideologically opposed philosophies, fascism and communism, shocked the world. The ink on the pact was hardly dry when Germany attacked Poland with airplanes and fast moving tanks (blitzkrieg) on September 1, 1939. Two days later, Britain and France declared war against Germany. Poland was in German and Russian hands by the end of the month.

World War II had begun.

In the following eight months, all was quiet on the German-French border despite the state of war. However, further north, in November 1939, Russia attacked Finland and—after huge losses imposed by the well-trained Finns—succeeded in obtaining basing rights in Finland and large strips of Finnish territory near the Russian city of Leningrad. Russia also moved to annex Lithuania, Latvia, and Estonia, which it eventually accomplished in June 1940.

The quiet on the western front ended dramatically on May 10, 1940, with a fast-moving German blitzkrieg attack on the Netherlands, Belgium and Luxembourg. It carried on into France, making an end run around the heavily fortified Maginot Line. By mid-June, Germany occupied the heartland of northern France, and a humiliating treaty was signed between the two countries on June 20. With the fall of France, Germany acquired French ports, which increased the effectiveness of German wolf-pack tactics against Allied convoys. A total blockade of Britain by Germany was reportedly Churchill's greatest fear.

Germany's next target was England. Hitler's plans for crossing the English Channel to invade England in the favorable fall weather of 1940 were stymied because the German air force failed to win control of the skies in the Battle of Britain during August and September. Over 20,000 British civilians were killed in German bombing raids on English cities from July to December, but in the end, the British aviators, with the aid of newly developed radar, fended off the German air force.

CHAPTER 6   *Our river is still behaving and is fine skating*

In September 1940, Italy began the war in North Africa by entering Egypt from Libya and gaining control of the Suez Canal. That same month, Japanese troops marched into French Indochina, and a Tripartite Pact between Germany, Italy, and Japan (the "Axis") was signed. Meanwhile, the United States was actively aiding England by providing destroyers in exchange for bases on British territory. The Italian Army attacked Greece on October 28 but was repelled by Greek forces. Also British forces were able to drive the Italians out of Egypt by December. German forces would soon come to the aid of Italy and set back these advances.

As 1940 came to an end, Europe had become an Axis fortress. England remained as an isolated outpost of democracy, but it was in great danger of being starved into submission. Large areas of China were occupied by Japan. American involvement in the war was becoming more and more likely. President Roosevelt proclaimed the U.S. to be the "Arsenal of Democracy," but politically he was unable to bring the country directly into the war due to strong isolationist sentiment. National guard divisions were activated on a "temporary" basis beginning in September 1940 and conscription of individuals into the armed forces began in October.

The tension between interventionists and isolationists in America was bitterly divisive; such divisiveness would not be seen again until the Vietnam era three decades later. The interventionists believed that America could not survive a Nazi Europe and giving aid to Britain was essential to our future. The isolationists believed America could thrive on its own and should not be pulled into yet another European conflict. President Roosevelt was a committed interventionist, but he could not afford to get too far ahead of public opinion, especially with the 1940 election approaching; isolationists could easily defeat him if he angered the country by moving too aggressively toward war. That could lead to Britain's defeat and eventually the isolation and defeat of America by the Axis. The call-ups and draft were accepted by the public as necessary steps for "keeping the peace," given the growing distaste for Adolf Hitler's actions.

7

"I regret very much that you have not appreciated my filial affection"

Activation of the 43rd Division
1940–1941

Anticipating that his guard unit could be called to active duty, Wilber had begun in July 1940 to provide instructions to Norma should she have to run our home by herself. Six pages of handwritten notes were in his indestructible leather-bound seven-ring notebook. It is likely that they were written at different times in the months leading up to his departure. The closing is quite ominous.

7/4/40
Darling Norma:
— Care of furnace and oil burner…
— In case of electrical trouble…
— In case of gas trouble…
— For [furnace] oil [leak] trouble…
— For personal and important messages which a censor might delete, use the Bible. I will understand that the month* word of each verse to be a message word. Obviously only very short messages would escape suspicion and they should be well buried in discussion. Verses could be quoted or referred to.
*The month word would be the first [word of the verse] for all letters dated January, the second for letters dated February, … If this code becomes important, destroy this sheet. Wilber loves Norma + Hale + Valerie and doesn't expect to lose them. [Norma never used this coding scheme.]
— For general repair work around the house, check with …

— Remember, if I am in the army during war *not* to pay my accident insurance since it does not cover war accidents. However, be sure to notify Dan Downen [insurance agent] and the company to cancel it.

— The important documents are ...

— The car radiator must be drained ...

— If the heat is turned off in the bathroom, ...

— Roof. Allow only reliable firms ...

— Finances on house. In case of difficulty with Jewett, check with Mr. Newman.

— In case of catastrophe, I will look for you first in this vicinity [Maine], next in Indiana, and third in the Spokane area, and 4th in Portland, Ore. In case of bombing raids, get away from town and main highways. I'll be looking for you afterward. The safe place is usually where you are known.

Wilber was imagining the worst based on the newscasts from European countries showing refugees fleeing with their belongings on crowded roads. He and Norma had no idea how their futures would evolve.

In the fall of 1940, the New England 43rd National Guard Division received notice that it would be activated in February 1941. Wilber was low in rank (a captain) for his age (40) and considerably overweight. The latter disqualified him for active duty. This was unacceptable to him. He had been in guard units for most of the years since his student days, and believed he should serve his country in a time of crisis. He began a regimen of severe dieting: salads, no carbohydrates, and lots of exercise with handball. He successfully brought his weight down to below 200 pounds, which qualified him for active duty. He was a driven, disciplined person when sufficiently motivated. Because of his weight, he did not have to go to war, but his entire national guard experience, including remuneration, had been based on a readiness to serve his country when it needed him. And, it was an adventure in historic times that he was not about to miss.

Christmas of 1940 was a somber occasion. The family was being broken up and America was on the verge of war. The future was unknown. Roosevelt had just defeated Wendell Wilkie to earn a third term as President (Wilber and Norma had voted for Wilkie). For gifts, Wilber gave Norma 78-RPM recordings of piano concertos performed by the renowned pianist, Walter Gieseking, whom Wilber and Norma admired. That may also have been the Christmas I received a new violin of the next higher size, three-quarter size. I played a simple tune on it early that Christmas morning. I was just ten.

Upon activation, the 43rd Division would move to a Florida training camp. Norma chose neither to remain in Bangor nor to take us to Florida.

CHAPTER 7   *I regret very much that you have not appreciated my filial affection*

Instead she and Wilber decided that she and the children would move to New York where she could study piano and pursue her writing. Much later in her 1981 memoir, she took great pains to deny that this was mostly her own idea:

Bill [Wilber] discouraged me not to go [to Florida] as the unit's training was to be very intensive, and he would have little time for us. We decided that I should go to New York City to study piano, and that the children of course would stay with me there.... It sounds as though I was trying to be one of these liberated women, but no, Bill decided on his own that I should advance in my profession so that I could take care of the children financially should the need arise. [i.e., if Wilber did not survive the war.]

Heaven forbid that people should consider her a liberated woman! At least that was her view, looking back at age 75 in 1981. Her 1941 frame of reference was different. Her close friend in Washington State, Gladys Anderson, had moved to New York City in 1927 to study violin at the Juilliard School of Music, as had a character, a dancer, in Norma's unpublished novel. The seeds had been planted and when the opportunity presented itself, she grabbed it. The prospect of moving to New York City must have energized her.

I asked Norma years later if she had felt embittered by Wilber's decision to go to war, effectively abandoning the family. She replied, harking back to her youth, that no, she was used to picking up and moving on when her support structure fell away. Not only was Wilber leaving, but her father had died in Minnesota 18 months earlier and her mother in 1935. Her children at ages eight and ten were becoming thinking self-sufficient beings. Her life was approaching a new liberated phase with wonderful possibilities. However, she was not free of responsibility and worries. She was becoming the prime manager of the family and would have to attend to the needs of the children and Wilber (at long distance), as well as her own. Then there was concern for Wilber's safety in a deteriorating world situation.

We rented our Broadway home in Bangor to another family on February 1, 1941, and moved into a small, depressing apartment above a grocery store a few blocks away at 169 Center Street for the few weeks until our departure for New York City at the end of the month.

Just as we moved into that little apartment, Wilber received letters from his parents with requests for financial help. This was far from the optimum time to place a new burden on Wilber and Norma, but the Indiana Bradts seemed to have missed that point altogether. There is a remarkable quartet of letters, from Hale, Elizabeth, Norma, and Wilber, in which each provides a perspective on this request as well as on past events in their lives. Sadly, this exchange strained relations between the two families for many months, if not years.

It appears that an earlier letter from Hale requesting money did not yield a positive response. He then wrote in his scrawling but comfortably legible hand.

1-29-1941, Bloomington, Ind.
Dear Wilber [from his father] — … Wilber, I regretted very much the sentence in your letter in which you said "I cannot help you." I judge that you meant by that that you will not send me the money I need to finish my payments on the Retirement Fund.

This is a matter of great importance to you and to your Mother and me. I cannot release you from your promise … to pay your share of the debt incurred in your education …

… Therefore I am asking you to send me the $1500.00 and take a non-interest bearing note for that amount to be collected when the estate is settled. Since I have paid the interest on this money all these years it is only fair you should do so from now on. If you will send it to us now, I can use it to complete the payments on the retirement fund and our income will be $960 [per year] instead of $772, which it will be unless I make this arrearage payment – about $1850.00 now.…

Unless you do your duty to us, Wilber, we will be obliged to change our plan to treat all our children the same and will reward those who have been true to the teachings we tried to instill in them of honesty and filial duty.

I need to have your answer to these questions in a comparatively short time. I must make the payment of $1850.00 on or before May 25 or settle for the $772.00 annuity. — Yours truly, Hale Bradt

The $1,500 was a huge sum. Perhaps it would be $25,000 in today's dollars. It was equivalent to four or five months of Wilber's salary as department head. His army base pay as a captain was to be only about $200 per month with additional allowances for dependents and time served. In aggregate it was unlikely to reach the level of his academic salary. Accusing a son of lacking "honesty and filial duty" was a severe indictment. These values clearly meant a lot to Hale, and he knew they would be important to Wilber.

x · o · ø · o · x

CHAPTER 7   *I regret very much that you have not appreciated my filial affection*

The laying on of guilt by Wilber's father was apparently deemed insufficient by his mother. Two days later, she added her bit, admitting that she and Hale did not always spend money wisely. Again, a penalty for Wilber's noncompliance—a loss of faith—is slipped in.

Jan. 31, 1941
Dear Wilber — You have repeatedly told me you intended to pay what you owe for your education when you could be sure your father would not waste the money. The Teachers' Retirement Fund furnishes exactly this condition. The money is allotted to him for so long as he lives. He has saved for himself much more than he is suggesting you pay. He isn't asking that you "help" him. He is asking you to keep your word. You may say you worked. So did we all. Happily for each other's mutual good. Maybe as parents we didn't always spend wisely but no one can truthfully say we spent selfishly.
When Hale applied at the Bl. Nat. [Bloomington National Bank] for a loan before you had your A.B., Mr. Adams asked him how he intended paying. Hale replied the children planned to help when they were thru. Mr. Adams said, "But will they?" Hale assured him they would. Mr. Adams knows which ones did. Hale still has faith in you. I hope – Mail's here [i.e., must quit to give this to mailman]. — Mother

x·o·ø·o·x

My parents' prompt responses to this request would not be what Hale and Elizabeth hoped for. First was Norma's reply. She eloquently revealed the hurts she had endured upon entering the Bradt family and the effect of their monetary requests over the past years. She underestimated the pain her eloquence would cause. Her appeal, late in the letter, that they appreciate Wilber's goodness and sense of filial duty was compelling, but was likely lost in the hurt of the earlier paragraphs. She was an excellent, rapid typist, and this, unfortunately, fostered neither brevity nor tact.

This letter gives insight into the stresses a family encounters when a member enters the military and the importance of family support. It exhibited the prevailing attitudes about military service, which, unfortunately, Norma used as a weapon. She began with a rather cold salutation; in contrast, her 1937 note began with "Dear Mother Elizabeth."

Feb. 3, 1941
Dear Mr. and Mrs. Bradt — You can't imagine what your letter has done to us – indeed you have never seemed to consider our feelings and states of mind at very

crucial times. So many times I have written letters trying to tell you this and have burned them, but I feel I should not burn this one.

This very unfortunate demand came at the time when Wilber is most deeply troubled, when he most needs sustenance and affection and uplift. He is doing what he thinks is right for his country at great personal sacrifice, leaving a position he has dreamed of and worked for all his life. He is only condemned by you for doing so. He is the only one of your three sons who is doing so, no matter what excellent reasons they may have for not entering into preparation for the coming conflict.

> Playing the patriotism card was not very kind. It was widely believed at the time that not serving in the military, if qualified, was shameful; it was one's patriotic duty to serve. Although Wilber's brothers were too old to be drafted, they too could also have felt some guilt.

We have just left the home for which we have worked and dreamed so long, left all the little things which mean so much to a family and moved into a bare and unfurnished apartment, doing with a minimum of comfort and convenience, in order to make this change which seems right to us. We are trying to make the children feel right about it, that we are keeping them "cozy" but Valerie said tonight that she likes her own home so much better.

This has been a time of tension for everyone. Wilber has been doing double work at the University all the time, trying to do a year's work in half time, he has been carrying heavy Guard responsibilities. You should see what your letter has done to him, when he was trying so desperately to keep up his strength and courage. Your lack of faith and your importunate commercial demands seemed to crumple him.

I am reminded of what Troy Daniels said when he found we were married. He said I should "keep his chin up," that Wilber had suffered so much from his family, had repeatedly been made terribly despondent from their letters and that their financial demands upon him during his first year of teaching had been heavy. He said this not because Wilber had him read your letters, but because he lived with him and could observe the effects and note the financial sacrifices he made to fulfill what you constantly and un-parent-like urged as his responsibilities, with compounded interest and all the rest of it.

Anyone out there or anywhere who heard of it was astounded that a father and mother could keep such books and send out like bombs such wild figures, with interest calculations, about sums a son had no idea were charged against him. Good heavens, this world would be a terrible place if such things were true generally.

CHAPTER 7   *I regret very much that you have not appreciated my filial affection*

Troy Daniels was a young academic in pharmacy at Washington State College who shared living quarters with Wilber during his first year in Washington (1926–27). He was almost exactly Wilber's age. I had heard from Norma of Daniels's admonition to her about Wilber's morning despondency—rising to face the day was sometimes difficult for him. It is only in this letter that I see such "despondency" attributed almost solely to his parents. It was likely more generic to Wilber's makeup.

… I certainly believe Wilber when he tells me that he never promised any such thing as you mentioned. I have watched him searching his memory sincerely and honestly to try to discover how you arrived at any such conclusion. I believe he will try to help you all he can, but it is really most unkind of you to put this strain of such a demand upon him in the face of what he has just done, remained with the Guard when he could have resigned …

It is only by dint of unceasing and unremitting effort and hours of extra work that he has been able to keep ahead of things in this Depression, with no help from outside and with many serious setbacks.… The children and I are giving [up] our daddy and husband, and there is not much more that we can do. We shall all or any of us be lucky to have food and shelter if things go on as they are. I had thought the children and I might come to you for refuge if things grew desperate, but I can see now that this would not be possible.…

If you would only realize it, he is a son a father and mother should be proud of in all circumstances. He has been a wonderful husband, whom I could respect in all circumstances, and whose love goes beyond any financial arrangements we might make between us.

I know you will be very upset by this letter and I am very sorry, but Wilber has endured so much silently, it is time you knew the way your actions have seemed to us, on this side. — Very sincerely, Norma Sparlin Bradt

Again, the closing was quite formal. Norma was undoubtedly under severe tension at this time and, indeed, had been mistreated by the Bradts. Nevertheless, there had been warm feelings and approaches on both sides in the intervening years. Unfortunately, this letter undid all that. In turn, Elizabeth, Wilber's mother, also greatly overreacted. Both women were fine people in their own right and I loved them both. But it saddens me to think about the unnecessary pain they caused each other and themselves.

x · o · ø · o · x

Wilber's letter was somewhat more measured and much more in control of the facts than his father's. It was dated the same day as Norma's and may have been sent in the same envelope. Like Norma's, it was a letter of offense and self-defense. It was here that I learned of the familial financial arrangements during Wilber's college years. Though addressed to both his father and mother, he was clearly communicating with his father.

169 CENTER ST. BANGOR, MAINE, FEB. 3, 1941
Dear Father and Mother — I shall endeavor to make clear in this letter some facts, which are apparently not yet clear in your mind. You suggest in your letter that I take my pencil and do some calculations. I have done so with the following result.

During my undergraduate years, I paid you $100 a year, and during the graduate years of my study I paid you $150 a year. According to your statements, the following year I paid you an additional $100. This figure totals $950. According to my understanding, during my undergraduate degree, in return for my services on the farm you were willing to pay for my books, clothing and tuition. This you did in part. Tuition varied from $18.00 a semester to something less than $30. We are each aware that the other items were quite reasonable. I notice that the University of Maine estimate of the cost of room and board this year is $161.00 per year. This figure of course includes profits and a retirement fund for the dormitory construction. Consequently I am convinced that your statement at the time that $100 and later $150 a year was a reasonable, non-profit estimate of my room and board cost to you.

You state that some time, during the time that we were in Bloomington, you went to the bank and borrowed an indefinitely large amount of money and that you informed the bank that your children would pay this amount. I am reminded that your statement some years ago was that my share of this indebtedness was $3000. Some months ago you asked for a promise that I would be responsible for a much more nominal amount, $300.00....

You seem to be under the impression that I could go to a bank and borrow $1850!!! [actually $1500] by some means. This is not the case. My bank where I have, as a professor at the University of Maine, very high personal credit rating, has repeatedly been willing to lend me $200 or $300 as emergencies required. The same bank has informed me and the other officers of this regiment that they are not willing to make loans to army officers leaving this region. It is the feeling in this part of the country that this regiment will be in active service in battle before six months have passed....

CHAPTER 7   *I regret very much that you have not appreciated my filial affection*

... Except for this military emergency, my finances are in such condition that Norma and I had definitely planned to be of regular monthly assistance at the time when your regular school salary would terminate. This arrangement of course would have depended upon the continuance of my own income. At present, and facing actual facts, I have only a very vague conception of what my living costs will be during the next months. Neither have I any assurance as to the certainty of my returning to my family after this emergency, nor of my having employment after my return, if that return is delayed over twelve months.

It is probably your privilege to do so, but you have consistently tried to specify in what way and to what extent your children will assist in your finances. I am not concerned about obtaining a share of your estate....

Although I have consistently objected to and denied any financial obligation or indebtedness, I of course recognize the responsibility of a son to his parents. I regret very much that you have not appreciated my filial affection. It is my plan that beginning next June [when Hale will retire] to send you twenty dollars a month as my finances permit. This is not a promise to pay. This is a plan I hope to maintain, which will be cancelled automatically in the event of a cess[at]ion of my income. In consideration of these circumstances, and in spite of my frank and honest statements, I close by sending my real love. — Wilber

> The $20 per month ($300/month in today's dollars) that Wilber proposed to send his parents would have netted them $240 a year which was more than the $188 pension increase Hale was seeking, though the pension would be much more secure in the long term. Although reverberations of this conflict continued, this letter was sufficiently reasonable in tone that it left the door open for an ongoing relationship between Wilber and his father in the subsequent months and years; that with his mother was more problematical.

x · o · ø · o · x

After several months of preparation, the 43rd Infantry Division was formally inducted into Federal service on February 24, 1941, for a period of one year, a period that was to be extended to over four and a half years. The next day, Wilber submitted a request for a one-year leave of absence from the university. Undoubtedly, the dean and president had advance notice that this was coming, but Wilber cautiously waited until the induction was an accomplished fact to give formal notice. His very carefully worded letter to Dean Cloke protected his options and closed on a foreboding note.

FEBRUARY 25, 1941

Dear Dean Cloke — In view of the fact that I have been inducted into Federal Military Service as a captain in the 152nd Field Artillery [Regiment] and have passed the physical examination, I hereby request leave of absence from the University of Maine without pay for one year, effective March 1, 1941. My actual contact with my classes ended on February 19, but I shall remain in daily contact with my office until March 15.

Although my induction into military service is for a period of one year, there is the remote possibility that my absence might be for a shorter time, in which event I should want to terminate my leave and return to active teaching and administrative status. If my military duties require that I be absent from the University of Maine longer than one year, I shall ask that you consider an extension of my leave period.

In accordance with our conversation on the matter, I shall appreciate receiving on March first any portion of my summer salary, which might be considered as due me.

I should like to state further that I am looking forward to an early return to this college, but if, due to international developments, my return is delayed or permanently cancelled, you should know that I appreciate very much working under your supervision. I shall look back during the next year on our association as having been the most pleasant and happy years of my life. It is with the greatest regret that I interrupt this association. — Sincerely yours, Wilber Bradt, Head, Department of Chemistry and Chemical Engineering

> Over the next several weeks, the 152nd Field Artillery Regiment left towns across Maine, including Bangor where we lived, to travel to Camp Blanding in Starke, Florida, near Jacksonville. Convoys of military trucks and trains full of soldiers left the snowy streets of Bangor to join other elements of the 43rd Infantry Division in sunny Florida. Wilber was on the staff organizing the move, and thus did not leave until March 15.
>
> On about March 1, 1941, Norma (age 35), young Hale (age ten) and Valerie (age eight) left by train for New York City. Our good friends the Butlers came to see us off; Jean had been in my fourth-grade class and I was rather sweet on her. They brought flowers for Mom and Val, but not for me. I understood that flowers were not for men, but was surprised at my quietly tearful disappointment.
>
> The two parts of Wilber's family were now off on their own separate but still entwined adventures in a rapidly changing world.

CHAPTER 7   *I regret very much that you have not appreciated my filial affection*

Are To Leave Bangor Today
Will Direct 152nd on Year of Service

News photo of the staff officers of the 152nd Artillery Regiment before they left Bangor, Maine, on March 15, 1941, for active duty training in Florida. These officers had been managing the departure of the various units of the regiment since its induction into Federal service on February 24, 1941. Seated from left: Colonel John F. Choate, commander, and Lt. Col. Frank Silliman, 3rd, executive. Standing from left: Capt. Wilber E. Bradt, Capt. Joseph S. Dinsmore, Capt. Corwin H. Olds, Lt. Milton E. Lepage, Lt. James Ruhlin, and Lt. Walter I. Ireland. Choate and Ruhlin appear in Wilber's story; he admired them both. [PHOTO: *BANGOR DAILY NEWS*, MARCH 15, 1941.]

PART II

ARMY CAMPS

MARCH 1941–SEPTEMBER 1942

8

"Simulated tanks and simulated weapons"
Florida and New York City
MARCH–JULY, 1941

In New York, we settled into a large one-room apartment on the ground floor of a small three-story building at 310 West 73rd Street, which Norma's college friend Gladys Anderson Gingold had found for us. Directly across the street was the magnificent Charles Schwab mansion, which occupied two city blocks. It has since been razed and replaced by the 17-story Schwab House, now a cooperative.

Norma commenced piano studies with the world famous Casadeus family. Her studies were mostly with Robert Casadeus's wife Gaby, with lessons in New York, at the Casadeus home in Princeton, New Jersey, or on one occasion at their summer residence in Rhode Island. Gladys Gingold's husband, Joseph Gingold, was a first violinist in the NBC Symphony Orchestra led by Arturo Toscanini. He was also the second violinist in the eminent Primrose String Quartet. Performances by both the orchestra and the quartet were broadcast regularly over NBC radio. Norma quickly entered the social life of the Gingolds' musical circle. She recounted in her memoir:

Evenings at their [the Gingolds'] home, where the quartet rehearsed, were pure heaven. I did not ever play with the quartet, but at various times I accompanied individual members of that musical circle, composed of quartet wives and others, or practiced a sonata with someone. Earl Wild was the official pianist of the quartet.

As a ten-year-old, I was promptly signed up to continue my violin studies with a Mrs. Irma Zacharias, an elderly widow and friend of the

Gingolds; she lived in the same West 71st Street building. I studied with her off and on through my early 20s.

Valerie and I attended a rather depressing public school the rest of that 1941 spring term. It was PS 87 on West 79th Street at Amsterdam Avenue. The classes were large and unruly, the teachers harassed, and my fellow students rough and intimidating. Fortunately, we only had to endure this until the end of the academic year. The school has since been rebuilt, and is now, I gather, a much friendlier place.

New York was not yet a wartime city; America did not enter the war until the following December (1941). Rationing of tires, gasoline, meats, and more were in the future as were the infamous blackout drills to protect against air raids and dim-outs to reduce lighting that made offshore ships visible to marauding submarines. Nevertheless, the fear of enemy sabotage was rampant; people were well aware that war was not far away.

x·o·ø·o·x

Camp Blanding, 30 miles southwest of Jacksonville, Florida, had been newly created in 1939 as a military reserve. It bordered the east and south shores of the 1.8-mile-diameter circular Kingsley Lake. It had (and does to this day) a varied topography of pine plantations, oak clusters, and desert-like terrain. It was rather harsh territory with extreme temperatures and biting insects; Army Rangers trained there in later years. The construction of camp buildings, streets, and facilities was still in process, and the soldiers of Wilber's division were recruited to assist the contractors [Fushak, p. 13]. The division was housed, at least in part, in a city of tents on wooden platforms.

The entire U.S. Army was woefully deficient in equipment, training, and manpower due to parsimonious funding in earlier years, and the 43rd Division was similarly lacking. It initially had only 11,000 men of its full 20,000. Its ranks were supplemented with men from the first pools of those drafted in the newly authorized Selective Service. They joined the 43rd Division immediately after completing basic training. Many of them were, fortuitously or possibly by arrangement, from New England.

Unfortunately, the letters written by Wilber to Norma during his stateside training have been lost. Nevertheless, letters to his parents, children, and siblings do survive and give a flavor of his and our lives in this period.

After Wilber arrived at Camp Blanding, the monetary dispute with his parents continued, though Wilber made a real effort to normalize relationships. The New York branch of the family was having its own difficulties.

CHAPTER 8 *Simulated tanks and simulated weapons*

MARCH 23, 1941 [CAMP BLANDING, FLORIDA]

Dear Father and Mother — This is the last day of [my first] month in the Army. I have thought several times that it might be possible to write to you. However … continuing obligations at the University and the re-organization [of] our family as well as learning a new job myself have kept me busy. In fact I have never worked so continuously before.

Tomorrow formal training begins. We have spent about 20 days in Bangor [Maine], sending detachments to Camp [Blanding] as fast as division schedules permitted, then we have spent about ten days making camp and getting organized. The whole schedule has been very interesting.

I am the Regimental S-3, or Plans and Training Officer, and as such am in charge of training for the Reg[iment]. I write programs, schedules, issue training orders, correlate the work of subordinate units and pass information pertaining to training to the Battalions.

Father & Mother I hope you have not misunderstood my letter [about money] of a few weeks ago. I do want you to know that your son is going to stand by you. It will not be with any reservations that I send you what I can. I do love both of you very much and want you to know it.…

Valerie has been suffering from a "strep" infection in her ear. The doctor gave her Sulfanilamide for four days, and Norma I guess got about 4 hours sleep during that time. Valerie seems out of danger now, but things were pretty bad for a while. It is pretty hard for the rest of the family just now. They are in New York City and will probably stay there for most of the time. Norma is trying to prepare herself to support the children in case I return unable to do it or in case I am eliminated. We aren't insisting on being pessimistic but are trying to be in the best situation possible when the readjustment comes. Our house is rented so the taxes and a little more are covered but not enough to make the payments. In case this lasts over a year, I'll probably let the mortgage holder take the house.

I am sending Mother's birthday present early because I have it now. [Elizabeth, his mother, would turn 66 on May 1.] Later it might be absorbed. This check is for three days pay for a Capt. not including allowances for rental and subsistence, which would increase it somewhat. I hope it is accepted with my love, Mother, and I also hope you may have many more and happy birthdays.

Taps has just blown and I must go to bed. Tomorrow inspectors will be following us around all day. I'll try to look more efficient than I am. This camp is very sandy and is on a lake shore. The other day a crocodile came up on shore, walked down the Battery Street, decided the confusion was annoying and went back to his lake. He was about 3 feet long and is reported to be about 12 years old with a very respectable record. — Good Night, Your Son, Wilber Bradt

Wilber's mother Elizabeth wrote on this letter that the check Wilber had enclosed was for $17.78 and that on April 7 she returned it "without comment." Elizabeth really did play rough; recall her comment a decade earlier [letter 9/11/31] that "rough stuff is more along my line."

x·o·ø·o·x

Six weeks later, it appeared that Wilber had received no letters from his parents other than the returned $17.78 check. He wrote again two days before his mother's 66th birthday. He was walking on eggshells.

APRIL 29, 1941
Dear Mother — Happy Birthday to you. I hope it is really a happy day and the beginning of a happy year. That means that I love you and that I will be loving you a long time to come. Please don't be angry with me. I am sorry you didn't keep the present I sent last month. If anything I said was the reason for your returning it, I am sorry I said it.
[Note in margin:] The paper [this stationery] is a present from the children. Don't you like it?

As I said in my letter last Jan. or Feb., I had planned to help out with the family finances beginning this June. I am sorry it cannot be more than twenty dollars a month but that is equivalent to the income increase, which would have resulted if I could have paid the larger lump sum. My finances have fairly well stabilized now so I can plan on the new basis. Please remember that both Norma + I are anxious and glad to help out your readjustment and new arrangement for living.

After seeing Florida, I can appreciate even more the advantages of a northern home. It is late spring now and the thermometer in my tent reached 94° F. the other day. We have a good camp but are in a rather dreary part of Florida. Palm trees, southern pine, scrub oak and everywhere running loose are pigs and cows, all half starved. They belong to the State and people fence them out, not in.

I have been working hard. It is a pretty serious Army this time. From the top to bottom every soldier expects to face a hard job soon and we are trying to train men before it is too late. Now is the time the U.S. people pay for pacifist attitudes.

I love you and Father both and hope I have said no wrong thing here. — Wilber B.

[Note in margin:] Norma + the children are well. Valerie had a bad time with an infected ear but is OK now. Norma is studying hard and trying to be ready if she must support the children later. — WB.

CHAPTER 8   *Simulated tanks and simulated weapons*

Wilber was 41 years old when he wrote this but was responding to his parents as a youthful offender. Nevertheless, he did not shrink from reminding his mother of the coming cataclysm.

x · o · ø · o · x

The response two weeks later from Elizabeth could not have been colder. It simply quoted verbatim the two paragraphs of Norma's letter about how their letters had upset Wilber.

MAY 16TH, 1941
Dear Wilber — I quote: "I am reminded of what Troy Daniels said when he found we were married. He said I should "keep his chin up," that Wilber has suffered so much from his family, … Anyone out there or anywhere who heard of it was astounded that a father and mother could keep such books … Etc., etc., etc. Norma Sparlin Bradt 169 Center St., Bangor Feb. 3, 1941" — Elizabeth Bradt

I am appalled that my grandmother could have been so coldly cruel and so unlike the person I knew and respected. This letter survived as a copy in Elizabeth's handwriting that she kept with the letters from Wilber. The original could have contained other paragraphs but the completeness of the copy with date, salutation, and signature suggests otherwise.

x · o · ø · o · x

Wilber arranged for Norma to send Hale and Elizabeth $20 monthly in case circumstances interfered with his ability to do so reliably. The first such check, signed by Norma, arrived in early June, anticipating Hale's retirement, with the notation, "monthly payment (from Wilber's army check)." On June 4, Elizabeth refused it, sending it on to Wilber, possibly again without comment. She was not about to accept a check signed by Norma. Wilber's response upon receiving it was brief and anguished.

JUNE 8, 1941
Dear Father and Mother — Please forgive the things that have been said in the past. I am sorry they were ever said.

Believe me, please, when I say it. I do love you both and cannot bear to let this misunderstanding last.

Although it was impossible for me to raise the large sum of money you asked, I did assure you to the best of my ability of a larger annual income than you asked. I am returning the check for twenty dollars to you and hope you will accept it.

From a practical viewpoint you should accept it even if only to relieve yourselves and the rest of the family of that much.

It is very hot in Florida now but not unpleasant. We leave here in another month for Louisiana [for maneuvers]. I hope you are well and happy. — I love you, Wilber Bradt

Typically, Wilber used the weather to break away from an emotional topic, as did his father; see below. Weather, of course, was (and is) all-important to farmers.

x·o·ø·o·x

Later that month, Wilber's father replied much more warmly, but with the check returned yet again, forced most likely by Elizabeth's continued intransigence. She was apparently expecting an apology from Norma.

6-22-1941
Dear Wilber — Your letter of 6-8 and the check received. Since we have had no word from Norma, I am forced to return the check. The $20.00 per mo. is very satisfactory for me.

After over a year of much below average rainfall and just when everyone was crying "What will we do when the well goes dry?" (Headline of article in Farmer's Guide) we had three weeks of almost constant and very copious rains. Now the corn fields and gardens are covered with grass and weeds and many wheat fields – dead ripe – are so soft harvesting machinery mires down....

Wilber, I am proud of your achievements as a teacher and as a scientist and of the fact that you did not resign from the Guard but are doing your "bit" when duty called. — Sincerely, Hale Bradt

Hale had apparently come to realize that $20 a month was a substantial contribution, and was finally ready to admit that he was pleased Wilber was doing his patriotic duty. He was trying to mend the family rift.

Hale retired from Bloomington High School in June 1941 after 22 years of service; he was just turning 70. He and Elizabeth moved to the new frame, asphalt-shingled house that Hale had been building since 1939 on their Versailles farm. To supplement his income, he served as a truant officer for the Versailles school system.

CHAPTER 8   *Simulated tanks and simulated weapons*

Wilber's monthly letters to his parents continued but after a series addressed to "Mother and Father," he began to address them only to his Father as it was only his father who wrote back to him. Recall Mary's comment quoted above [letter 9/24/80] that "Mother … never quite forgave anyone whom she considered her enemy." Mary, when queried about this, discounted any such boycott by Elizabeth, saying that her parents divided up the correspondence, Hale to Wilber and Elizabeth to the stateside children. The evidence, to my mind, argues otherwise.

Despite this apparent estrangement, my grandparents were portrayed to Valerie and me as benevolent. I caught no inkling of this rift. Wilber, and from time to time Norma, would apprise Hale and Elizabeth via letters of our progress and activities.

Wilber responded to his father's overture and used news of his unit's training activity to reestablish a "normal" relationship. The international situation was not good.

JULY 18, 1941
Dear Father — It was good to get your letter of June 22 and I must apologize for not answering it sooner. I am sorry you returned the check and am sending you one with this letter. It seems rather working at cross purposes to be going through a "No you take it" routine, but this is what I have planned for with Norma for a good many years. You will understand, I hope, when I say that I never dictate to Norma what she shall say. I know she has real affection for you and that there will probably always be a lack of confidence between her and Mother. I, knowing and loving both, can see why this is true, and no one regrets it more than I. You should know however that Norma has worked hard and deprived herself toward the plan of helping on your finances during these years and that she still wants to do it as a privilege only open to sons and daughters.

In order to spare any further embarrassment to Mother and you, I tried to have part of my pay allotted to you by the government. They won't do that this year or this war, so I'll send the check hereafter [rather than Norma]….

The $20 check was eventually accepted, as were subsequent checks. Later, the government permitted such allotments and Wilber set one up for his parents.

Training is slow with shortages of equipment still the normal thing. It is hard to simulate fighting simulated tanks and simulated planes with simulated weapons. Some of the men know that "there warn't nothing there." I am more pessimistic than I want to admit. If the American people still think they can have their cake and eat it too, I believe they are ripe for a real fall. The enlisted men of the army and navy are way ahead of some of our congressional leaders who visited us here this week in realizing the gravity of the situation and in being willing to do the job. I am not worried about the enlisted men. Whether the officers can keep their jobs done [do their jobs] as well may be harder. I am wearing a major's leaves [insignia] for the first time today so I mean me too. We are trying hard though. I love you. — Your son, Wilber

Wilber had been promoted and was now a major. This good news was offset by the woeful lack of equipment provided to his troops. His comments about America's preparedness reflected the bitter divisiveness in America between the isolationists and the interventionists. Wilber's statements would have evoked strong feelings among the former.

x · o · ø · o · x

In their ongoing communications, Wilber's sister Mary takes on the role of her mother's therapist and vice versa. In this revealing letter, Elizabeth divulges her innermost thoughts and anxieties, mostly focused on her relations with her children and their spouses.

Bloomington Ind., July 23, 1941
My dear Daughter [Mary] — … I'm beginning to think Gerry [Rex's wife] dislikes me very much. I am beginning to think something else, too, and that is that before long you will be the only child I have who feels kindly to me. Wilber plainly doesn't. Paul thinks Hale and I are too hard on Wilber and Norma. I had thought they were hard on us. Ruth told me she and John [Wilson] are to marry. That is alright [sic] and I'm not going to object, but Ruth will become critical of us just as Wilber did. I was not prepared for her announcement and couldn't quite get control of myself.

I could remember how much faith I had in Wilber's love for me when he went away. When he broke that faith it hurt and I am not quite so sure I'll not be hurt again by another child.…

In every letter, Wilber writes to Hale [his father], he "lambastes" you and me, for he never fails to tell what he thinks of Americans who "still think they can have their cake and eat it too. I believe they are ripe for a real fall." I may be wrong to think he means me and you, but I do think so. He always says something like that. He said too that he knew Norma has a "real affection" for Hale. Didn't that letter sound like it!! He can't wave a check for $20 under my nose and make me forget.

CHAPTER 8 *Simulated tanks and simulated weapons*

Mary and Elizabeth apparently were committed isolationists. I don't believe Wilber was consciously thinking of them when expressing his interventionist leanings.

Hale sent the check back twice when it was signed by Norma. I don't know whether Wilber returned it again or not. Hale didn't say.... Sometimes Wilber seems like he didn't have good sense. There was no occasion for his saying any of the above only to be insulting. But I'll not let him know it hurts....

I'm all crossways tonight, but, don't worry. I'll get over it. Just thank your stars I'm not cross at you. In fact, I am so happy to have you and I do love you dearly. — Sincerely, Elizabeth Bradt

It is sad to contemplate how Elizabeth nurtured her grievances and took offense at statements not intended as criticisms. She was a suffering lady. On the other hand, she could snap right out of it. The excised portions of this letter (about one half of it) were chatty descriptions about other routine events in her life. She did not obsess about family all the time.

Wilber was not focused solely on his parents as the letters here might suggest. In fact, these months were full of army activity. The division was preparing for large-scale maneuvers in Louisiana in August, and this would have generated a myriad of tasks in training, supply, transportation, and other requirements. Wilber wrote in March, "I have never worked so continuously before," and the pressure surely continued. In addition, he was presumably writing almost daily or every other day to Norma in New York and she was reciprocating. His attention to his parents was limited, at least outwardly, to a letter every month or so.

As the U.S. was mobilizing its military forces during 1941, the Axis powers made additional advances, and the one-year activations of national guard units were extended in September. Yugoslavia and Greece had been overrun in April 1941. Crete, the Greek Mediterranean island, was captured by German paratroopers and airborne troops in May. In North Africa British forces were doing battle with Germany's Africa Korps under Gen. Field Marshall Erwin Rommel. In epic desert tank battles, Rommel advanced eastward from Libya toward Egypt in April, and the British drove him back in November and December. Rommel than retook the offensive in January 1942 and by June 30 was approaching El Alamein deep into Egypt. Control of the Mediterranean was contested with fierce air and sea battles for the island of Malta, an important British military and naval fortress—battles that continued until November 1942. In the end, the Allies successfully held Malta.

Bombing raids by British and German aircraft on their opponents' home cities continued. In March 1941, President Roosevelt signed the Lend-lease Act, which permitted China, Britain and other allies to purchase, but delay payment for, U.S. military supplies.

On June 22, 1941, Germany invaded its ally the Soviet Union, with an overwhelming three-pronged attack. This was a shocking but well-received (by the Allies) surprise—their two enemies turning on each other. Moscow and Leningrad were soon under threat of capture. This automatically made the Soviet Union one of the Allied nations. The imperative of stopping Hitler led the U.S. President, in October, to authorize lend-lease aid to Russia. As November ended, the Battle for Moscow was in full force. Growing Russian resistance together with freezing weather brought the German offensive to a halt and reversed some its gains. But the Germans did not retreat from Moscow, as Napoleon had done in 1812. Both sides dug in for the winter as they awaited the summer campaign season.

9

"I plan to stay on this job until it is finished"
Florida
August 1941–February 1942

The 43rd Division participated in maneuvers in Louisiana in August and September. These were large-scale war games involving some 400,000 men in 19 army divisions. Two armies were formed (Red and Blue) which "fought" to defend or capture key positions over 3,400 square miles of the Louisiana countryside. Anti-tank defenses against German blitzkrieg tactics were tested. Two generals who later rose to great fame, Dwight Eisenhower and George Patton, were participants. Much later, on November 14, 1942, shortly after the Allies landed in North Africa, Wilber wrote: "We claim we taught Patton in maneuvers what he knows. Anyway, we taught him what FA [Field Artillery] could do to tanks in Louisiana to his sorrow."

During the Louisiana maneuvers, Wilber wrote a letter directly to me, his ten-year old son, rather than to the family as a group. He was consciously working at developing a long-distance relationship with me. He harked back to our common experiences but also gave us glimpses of his boyhood and his immediate situation in Louisiana.

RAGLEY, LA., AUGUST 5, 1941
Dear Son Hale — Your very good letter came the first day our regiment had in this area. It was really a big help to me to hear from you so soon; sort of made this camp a little more like home to me. I would hate to have to go somewhere where I would never hear from you. It is pretty lonesome now sometimes.

You seem to have had a pretty sore time with sore toes. Maybe you could write

"Captured" soldiers (with tags) of the Blue (3rd) Army, at Louisiana maneuvers, September 1941, Winnfield, Louisiana. The sergeant at the desk was in the Red (2nd) Army. [PHOTO: US ARMY SIGNAL CORPS, SC 123563.]

a song about it. There is a song called "Blossom Time." You could call your song "Sore Toe Time." A poet named Riley who used to live in Indiana wrote a poem about a boy who had a sore toe. Nana [Norma] could probably tell it to you. When I was your age, it seemed to me I always had at least one sore toe – sometimes two or three. Another thing I used to do too often was to step between two boards in the barn and scrape the skin off both sides of my leg.

A lot of people keep talking about the "good old days" when everything was OK. I think every year of my life has been better than the one before. This year has been pretty bad in some ways, but I never got so many nice letters from my children or presents from them before. You never took me on a hike before, and Valerie never took me to the theatre before, and I never had a happy home in New York, and I never had a year before when I was an officer that America needed. I am pretty proud to be that just now.

> Wilber stressed the positive aspects of our separation and wanted me
> to think likewise. This attitude contrasted to the darker, bluer moods we

CHAPTER 9   *I plan to stay on this job until it is finished*

sometimes saw in him. Was he trying to convince himself as well as me? Perhaps.

The reference to a hike and theater outings indicated that he had been home to New York on leave sometime in the spring or early summer. This would have been the visit when he took Valerie and me to the New York Museum of Science and Industry and to the aquarium. In the former, I was impressed by bouncing ball bearings and push-button exhibits, and in the latter, by swimming sea horses that resembled—amazingly—horseheads.

You must be learning a lot about the Army and the Navy from the library. I know you will be a good soldier when your country needs you. Don't forget that only strong and husky boys make good soldiers. You need to play outdoors good and hard for a while everyday so you will be a strong man....

It was the expectation of that era that the next generation would also serve—and indeed it did, in Korea and Vietnam.

... I am sitting at my chair and table now and Little Joe [the gasoline generator] is furnishing the light, for it is dark outside. I have to stop now because several officers are coming in with some work for me. The tax tokens are for you and Valerie, and the Alabama one is extra for you because I know you are being helpful to Norma. I love you son and hope we will be together again when the war is over.
— Your Father, Wilber

x · o · ø · o · x

Three weeks later, still in Louisiana, he turned a simple hickory stick into a complete sermon.

IN BIVOUAC [LOUISIANA], AUGUST 28, 1941

My Dear Son — Today I mailed you a stick. It is a very particular one and I have been looking for it for over a week all along the roads in Louisiana. This is a hickory stick and should be very good for various play games....

When you play with this stick I hope you will notice how reliable and capable this stick is and will remember that I sent it to you because it was a message to you. You are also tall and straight and honest and strong. I hope you aren't too brittle and easily broken or discouraged by hard knocks. They make you bend a little but won't stop you from still trying to do your job. This stick wouldn't have come to you if you hadn't been the kind of boy I wanted. It is a great comfort to know you are my boy. I love you a whole lot.

… Sunday we start a CPX (Command Post Exercise) where the staff officers in all the Third Army go out and carry on a practice war except the soldiers all stay home. Sounds silly doesn't it. — Love from Daddy

Although he was well satisfied with me, he set a high standard for the future. The stick was about five feet long, an inch thick, and very straight. I had it for quite awhile. I used it for hiking and became expert at balancing it upright on a finger, and on my nose and chin.

Several days later, on September 2, the 43rd Division began motoring back to Camp Blanding. In early October, it was assigned a new commander, Maj. Gen. John H. Hester, a regular army officer. He would command the Division for almost two years.

x · o · ø · o · x

During that summer of 1941, the New York branch of the family stayed in the city. Valerie and I entertained ourselves with books, music lessons and practicing, piano and violin respectively, and other indoor and outdoor activities. Our apartment was near Riverside Park. On many days, I would accompany Gladys Gingold on her walks to the park with her two-year old son Georgie. I enjoyed their company.

Norma was as concerned about our schooling as were we. In the fall, she enrolled Valerie at Blessed Sacrament School on West 70th Street. Valerie remembers that she was, quite conspicuously, the only non-Catholic in her class. Also that fall, I was accepted into the choir of Grace Church on East Tenth Street, which provided me with a salary of a couple of dollars per week and, much more valuable, free tuition at Grace Church School. The choir of men and boys was "professional" with afternoon rehearsals three or four days a week for the boys. The school was a new scene for me; it was "Yes Sir" and "No Sir" to the teachers, and we studied Latin the two years (fifth and sixth grades) I was there; amo, amas, ... amant is still implanted in my brain.

I rapidly became expert on the Fifth Avenue #5 bus or the IRT subway traveling the several miles from West 73rd Street to Grace Church. I liked to stand in the front of the subway's first car looking out the front window with my hands on the brake wheel there, making believe I was driving the train as it rushed through the dark tunnels. On the way to services early Sunday mornings on the double-decker Fifth Avenue bus, I would ride in the front seat of the closed upper deck as we careened and swayed at high speed down deserted Fifth Avenue.

CHAPTER 9 *I plan to stay on this job until it is finished*

Five of the ten fifth-graders in my class at Grace Church School at Broadway and East 10th Street, 1941–1942. From left front: Peter Blaxill, Gerry Iannelli, Rocky Martino. In rear, from left: Philip Davis and me. I kept in touch with Peter and Gerry over the years; Gerry died in 2011. [PHOTO: GRACE CHURCH SCHOOL]

x·o·ø·o·x

Three months later, the 43rd Division participated in another session of maneuvers, this time in South Carolina. It was a large-scale war game with two armies consisting of some 300,000 troops with armor, cavalry, and aircraft. Again this was in part a test of tank and anti-tank tactics. Horse cavalry, used in these maneuvers, was judged to be relatively ineffective and was thereafter phased out as a combat force. These war games revealed effective strategies and distinguished effective from ineffective commanders. It also exposed large deficiencies in training, strategy, communications, supplies, and other areas. These became the basis of corrective actions.

UNDER A TREE NEAR CAMDEN, S.C., NOV. 27, 1941
Dear Father and Mother — This is a short lull in the program of Gen. Drum chasing the IV Corps around the Carolinas. During the last maneuver, we were saved by the bell. It was freely admitted by the bigwigs that the stubborn fighting of the 43rd

Div. saved the day for the IV Corps. All in all we seem to have gotten out of the dog house and are now a well esteemed outfit.

Just now we (the Hq. 152nd FA) are alerted for a move. The firing is getting pretty close on the front and on one flank. One of our Battalions was badly disorganized by an attack while they were marching. We have been finding pieces ever since. One thing about Maine soldiers, they do well in the woods. A whole battalion with 12 guns and 75 trucks did that during an attack by the Blues. Apparently none were captured, but we are still collecting them. It was rather funny because each fragment reported that all the rest were captured. The Bn. Commander reported to me that the whole Bn. was gone. Two Battery commanders claimed to be the sole saved. Now it looks as if the 152nd was still in the fight.

Hale has been having an attack similar to appendicitis. We have checked closely and it is definitely not app. He was in the Fort Jay Army Hospital and very thrilled because he shared a bathroom with a Colonel. The final diagnosis was essentially that he recovered before the doctors found what caused the trouble. They said he was not underweight, was in good physical condition and that his blood count had not gone down. They suggested a serious allergic attack but generally were sure he was OK now.

Must stop now, we are on the move. I love you — Wilber

> The military took good care of its dependents. The hospital was on New York's Governor's Island. I had a stomachache, and Norma was quick with her fertile imagination to call it appendicitis and have it attended to, though it turned out to be nothing (I still have my appendix). I do not remember "the colonel," but do know that I was well treated and that for some reason a plethora of comic books was available to me there. I read so many that I became satiated and was much less interested in them thereafter.

x·o·ø·o·x

In the collection of letters from Wilber, I noted a paucity of letters to my sister Valerie and guessed that they might also have been sent off by Norma to the same *Atlantic Monthly* contest as had mine. I thought it likely that Valerie would also have a brown envelope with letters to her similar to the one Norma had sent me. Valerie and her husband are journalists with a Maryland home full of files and papers. She had previously looked for the letters, without success. On one of my trips to the nearby Goddard Space Flight Center, I had met with her and urged her to try again. We went to her home and, with her son's help, did find the brown envelope.

CHAPTER 9 *I plan to stay on this job until it is finished*

The delightful letters therein to Valerie, or "Tumblebug" revealed a gentle side of Wilber's personality.

In this letter to her, Wilber provided glimpses into the Carolina maneuvers and the practicalities of directing large numbers of men during a long-distance move. He wrote to Valerie alone, not to the family group. He wanted to stay close to his nine-year-old daughter.

DECEMBER 2, 1941
My Darling Valerie — We are getting the 152nd FA ready to march back to Camp Blanding. Today I inspected several Batteries to see if their trucks were ready. The boys have cleaned up the trucks and have loaded them very well. All day tomorrow the boys will clean up and get haircuts and wash clothes. They will take down their tents and sleep on the ground without tents tomorrow.

The maneuvers are over and General [Oscar] Griswold [corps commander] said that the 43rd Div. and 31st Div. were OK, that he wouldn't trade them for any other divisions in the Army. We all worked very hard and were supposed to defend Camden [South Carolina] and did defend it. Gen. Drum's army never got near Camden so he didn't defeat us even [though] he had twice as many men as we did. Ha Ha Joke on him!

Day after tomorrow, I will start for Savannah. Col. [John F.] Choate and Sgt. Cook and I will ride in the first car and the others [in the regiment] will be stretched along the road for ten miles. Whenever the road turns or comes to a Y [fork in the road], we put a man there with a small blackboard like this [sketch]. When Col. Choate and I pass that place we give him a note saying when we passed and he takes a piece of chalk and changes the board to look like this [sketch].

In this letter to Valerie of December 2, 1941, Wilber explained how a convoy of army trucks was managed.

When the batteries come along the road they look on the board at the arrow and say to their drivers, "go that way." They look at the time on the board and say "go a little faster" or "a little slower" depending on whether they are too many minutes behind the Col. or not. Each battery is allowed to be five minutes behind the head of the one in front of it, so they can figure just how many minutes they are supposed to be behind by the time on the board. Sometimes when we want a short column we allow them only 2 minutes for each battery. That keeps them all close together and we get past towns in a hurry.

It has been good weather lately and since you sent the comfort[er] [quilt], I have been very comfortable at night. It was good to have it.

I am counting the days until I come home. I'll have to start back to Blanding on Dec. 27 so some other officer can get home on New Year's Day. Only half of us can get away at one time. — [no closing]

> Wilber planned to be home for Christmas, but did not know, as he wrote this, that Japanese aircraft carriers were steaming toward the U.S. Naval Base at Pearl Harbor in Hawaii.

x · o · ø · o · x

The Japanese air attack on Pearl Harbor began shortly before 8 a.m. in Hawaii. Wilber heard the reports on the radio as it occurred. He was back in Camp Blanding in Florida.

DECEMBER 7, 1941, 3:00 P.M. [9 A.M. IN HAWAII]

Dearest Wife and My Darling Children — I am just hearing newscasts of Japan [sic] attacks on Hawaii and Manila. We have expected war to come to us for a long time. It is here and I want you to know I love you. That seems to be all there is in my heart. This may and probably will mean, "all leaves cancelled." If so, I am content until I can come back to you to stay. The American people have given us a lot better chance to train than the soldiers of the last war. We are approaching a state of being well equipped. I am not worried.

Beloved, do not be afraid. This time of trial can only hurt you if you are afraid. Bad times are ahead, but we will come through them together. I am counting on you to be my reserves. Goodbye now. "So sorry" will say Japan. He [Japan] will be sorry too. — Wilber

> Wilber's mention of an attack on Manila was incorrect. He wrote this when it was 4 a.m. in Manila on December 8; the first air attacks on U.S. airfields in the Philippines occurred many hours later at about noon.

CHAPTER 9   *I plan to stay on this job until it is finished*

Letter written by Wilber during broadcasts of Pearl Harbor attack, December 7, 1941. The letter is transcribed in the main text of this book.

Perhaps the newscasters were anticipating these raids because U.S. forces in the Philippines were so much more accessible to the Japanese than those in Hawaii; it was a foregone conclusion that they would be attacked. Unfortunately, despite the long forewarning, U.S. airplanes on Luzon in the Philippines were caught on the ground and largely destroyed.

The next day, after an inspiring address by President Roosevelt ("a date which will live in infamy"), the U.S. Congress declared war on Japan. On December 11, Germany and Italy declared war on the U.S., and the U.S. Congress responded in kind.

The United States was now a belligerent in the war.

x·o·ø·o·x

Wilber's first extant letter during wartime was to his father.

DECEMBER 17, 1941
Dear Father — I am expressing [mailing] to you a worn pair of shoes, boots and some other things that are no longer quite up to the level expected of an officer – a wool shirt and wool breeches that can be burned if you don't find them useful. I've had the shoes repaired but don't have any chances to repair one of the boots. I believe, if you get it fixed, they will be good for a lot of wear....

> In those days, shoes were not discarded when "worn out"; they were taken to the shoemaker for new soles and/or new heels. A well-made shoe would be good for at least a half dozen new soles.

We are very busy getting ready for [a] possible move. Officers are required to always be on call and within two hours of duty. My leave was cancelled, so I'm hoping Norma and the children can come down for a week. [We did.] ... Tonight we are anticipating an "Alert" under black-out conditions. I am pretty tired these days and regret not having a little leave but am well and feeling OK. The general attitude here is pretty good with the higher commanders determined not to have any Pearl Harbors on their record. It is late. — I love you, Wilber

> After Wilber's leave was cancelled, Norma, Valerie, and I made a hastily arranged trip to Florida to join Wilber for Christmas week. The bus ride down was long and depressing. Some drunks were aboard and one had urinated into the depressed aisle well, and there was no hurry to clean it up as we motored uncomfortably through the night.
>
> Florida still brings pleasant memories. Immediately upon arriving at our

beachside cabin in Ponte Vedra, Valerie and I went out to play in the surf while our parents stayed in the cabin. The tide gradually pushed us down the beach, so that after awhile we were quite far from our cabin and quite unsure which cabin was ours. As we walked back, hoping we would recognize our cabin, our very worried folks came down the beach looking for us. (Fifteen months later, Wilber recalled his afternoon lovemaking there with Norma [letter 3/27/43], undoubtedly while we were playing in the surf).

As a northern boy, I was amazed and delighted to be walking around in short sleeves and shorts at Camp Blanding on Christmas Eve. On one occasion, Wilber had a serious talk with me about the war. I found it deeply disconcerting to learn that the Germans had many, many more divisions than the Americans.

On our return to New York, I was severely chastised by the choir director for skipping out on choir obligations for the Christmas festivities at Grace Church; as a paid choir boy, I was a professional and should have known better! Needless to say, Norma's view of priorities differed radically from his. She probably made that very clear to him.

x · o · ø · o · x

At the end of the month, Wilber dutifully wrote to his parents.

DECEMBER 29, 1941
Dear Father and Mother — Enclosed is the usual check. I hope you had a Merry Christmas and that the next year is a happy one for both of you. Norma and the children came down for a week and return in a day or two. The children look well and seem very well adjusted in spite of the absence of their father. Maybe it's an asset.

Business here is on the move and slightly more serious now than before Pearl Harbor. We the 152nd have sent one unit to coastal defense, and I may lose others to the same mission. Weather here is cool but very pleasant today.… — I love you, Wilber

Was an absent father an asset? For me, possibly so. I found myself growing in confidence among my peers, and I voluntarily took on responsibility for family matters—for example, seeing that all items of the family luggage stayed with us when we traveled. I have attributed this improved confidence to the absence of my father's strong disciplinary hand, though it may have been simply growing up. Valerie, on the other hand, would never have dreamed of calling her father's absence an asset!

CITIZEN SOLDIER   PART 11: ARMY CAMPS

x · o · ø · o · x

By January, the 43rd Division was approaching the one-year anniversary of its activation; its service had been extended beyond that date three months prior to the Pearl Harbor attack. Realizing that the war was not going to be a short one, Wilber wrote to his protégé, Prof. Irwin Douglass. During Wilber's absence, Douglass held Wilber's former position as department head at the University of Maine.

JAN. 23, 1942
Dear Doug — In answer to your letter about the date of my return, there is no likelihood of my being released by the Army during the next year. You know the international situation as well as I, and you also know that I plan to stay on this job until it is finished. Therefore I would like to ask that my leave be extended to July 1943. That date will be most useful to you and is as good a guess for me as any....

Norma and the children are well. We spent Christmas Day in my tent. Later, I had 6 days in New York with them. Please give my best regards to each of the staff. I think of them often but as you know send most of my letters home. — Your friend, Wilber

x · o · ø · o · x

In the aftermath of Pearl Harbor, Wilber wrote his father with portraits of life in New York and in Florida.

JAN. 25, 1942
Dear Father — Your letter of Jan. 11th came just after I returned from ten days leave. The Army got over the Pearl Harbor hysteria eventually, and I was able to spend about six days at home. The children are well and it was great to be with them again. We bought Hale his first long trousers. He looked quite the young man in his blue suit.

Hale is doing well in the Grace Episcopal Boys Choir School and is now allowed to sing regularly in the choir. He is getting wonderful training in their small group classes [at the school] and is very serious about staying in the honor group.

Valerie goes to another school nearer home and has a "Sister." Her teacher is a Catholic Sister whom I met on a tour of the school. Both the Principal and teacher were very loud in their praise of Valerie. I'm afraid she would not make such high grades if she did not so early captivate her teachers. Her grades are all superior too.

As a regiment we have been pretty busy. Our officer strength is reduced to about

CHAPTER 9   I plan to stay on this job until it is finished

50% now. They have gone on all types of missions. Some will return, but most are away for good. Several are at technical schools, others have gone to the air force because they were too old for combat, and we did not promote them to [a] rank that would make their age OK.... Others of our officers have gone to the Tank Destroyer Units. Still others have fallen by the wayside [with] physical breakdowns.

> The constant turnover of personnel was due in part to the huge ongoing expansion of the U.S. Army. New units required cadres of experienced men and officers and these would be extracted from existing units. Unfortunately, this resulted in constant turmoil within the units and also hindered the development of unit cohesion, which is so important in battle. Soldiers under fire will stay in the line to protect their fellow soldiers as much as, or more than, they do to protect a country or a principle.

The last loss was Lt. Col. Silliman who was promoted from the position of Executive [second in command] in our regiment to that of Commander of the 192nd F.A. He will eventually be promoted to Col. because of this. I have been promoted to fill his place, and in my case a promotion in rank may also follow. I was quite pleased because I am the junior and not the senior major in the regiment. Result – I am working at both the new and old job. In fact for a week I filled the positions of S-2 [Intelligence], S-3 [Operations], Assist S-3 and Executive. The only other staff officer with us was the Adjutant. We were certainly busy. Last Thursday we were inspected by Ordnance, Signal, our Brigade for training, and our Division Commander for the condition of our motor equipment. The Division Commander is still talking about the fine condition of our equipment. Mostly eye wash though.

It is warm here. I wish you could spend a winter here. It is amazingly pleasant. The sun seems to shine with more regularity than anywhere else. I don't know what the plans are for this Division. We are prepared to move without warning. All personal affairs are supposedly arranged....

If I leave the country it will be hard to get my check to you on a schedule. Will it be satisfactory for Norma to mail it? — Love, Wilber

> Wilber's appointment to executive officer of the 152nd Field Artillery regiment was a significant step up for him. Wilber had been a major only since July, and this position would normally be held by the next higher rank, lieutenant colonel. The executive officer was second in command of the regiment with the job of relieving the commander of all administrative tasks, thus leaving him free to concentrate on strategic or other global issues. It is interesting that Wilber, with a PhD and five years experience running a university department, was pleased and almost grateful that he was chosen to do this essentially administrative job for which it seems he

was eminently qualified, if not overqualified. He might rightly have felt that it should have come much earlier. His ego was certainly not in the forefront here. However, his industriousness and desire to do well certainly were.

In January, the 43rd Division was reorganized from a so-called "square" division (four infantry regiments and three artillery regiments), into a "triangular" division (three infantry regiments and four artillery battalions). The artillery regiments were broken up into their constituent battalions, three of which were assigned to the infantry regiments, which could then operate with greater mobility as independent regimental combat teams (RCT). The four battalions of artillery were to be commanded by Brig. Gen. Harold R. Barker, a national guardsman from Rhode Island. The three "light" battalions assigned to the three regiments each carried twelve 105-mm (4-inch) howitzers, while a "medium" battalion (for general support) carried four longer-range 155-mm (6-inch) howitzers. (Chart 2.)

With the old artillery regiments disbanded, Wilber's new position as regimental executive officer vanished. He was appointed as the executive officer (second in command) of one of the division's light battalions, the newly named 169th Field Artillery Battalion (often written as 169th FA Bn.). This was a position for a major, his current rank. His opportunity for a promotion was thus temporarily lost. The 169th Field Artillery Battalion was the former 2nd Battalion of the disbanded 103rd Field Artillery Regiment, a Rhode Island outfit with a long history dating back to 1801. Wilber would later become its commander and lead it into combat. It would take many steps to get there though, and the first of these, a move to Mississippi, took place two months after Pearl Harbor.

Looking back on the origins of the Pearl Harbor attack, one finds that diplomatic relations between Japan and the U.S. had become critical due to Japanese expansion into China, French Indochina, and Vietnam. Retaliatory embargos, especially on oil, put in place by the U.S. and its allies, greatly increased tensions. The Japanese, to protect their economic interests in these materials-rich regions, decided to go to war to create an expansive sphere of influence called the "Greater East Asia Co-Prosperity Sphere" in East Asia and the Western Pacific (Map 3). It initiated the conflict with the infamous preemptive strike on Pearl Harbor on December 7, 1941.

With the U.S. in the war, the belligerents had devolved into two camps: The Axis powers—Germany, Japan, and Italy—and the Allies, the major powers of which were the United States, England, China, and Russia. Other substantial allied forces were the Free French, the British Commonwealth nations of Canada, Australia, New Zealand, and South Africa, and the British Crown Colony of India.

In the next few days, Japanese forces swept into the Philippines, attacked Hong Kong, which fell on December 25, and the American Pacific outpost islands of Guam and Wake. Guam fell immediately on December 10 and Wake on December 23. They also moved into resource-rich Southeast Asia. The Malay Peninsula was invaded on December 10, which led to the catastrophic surrender of the British fortified naval base at Singapore on its southern tip on Feb. 15. This capitulation of 130,000 troops, together with the loss of the battleship *Prince of Wales* and battle cruiser *Repulse* to Japanese land-based planes, was "Britain's greatest military disaster" according to one historian [Basil Collier; see Keegan, p. 261]. American resistance on Luzon Island in the Philippines was centered on the Bataan peninsula until its surrender on April 9, after a courageous and extended defense. This was followed by the tragic and cruel Bataan Death March, during which many American and Filipino prisoners died. The Manila Harbor island of Corregidor held on until May 6. General MacArthur had left there for Australia the previous month. He would be a leader of Allied forces in the Pacific for the rest of the war.

Borneo was attacked by the Japanese on January 1, as were Sumatra, Java, and the Dutch East Indies in February and March. Japanese troops pushed back British and Indian troops in Burma toward India. Farther to the southeast, on March 8 and 10, Japanese landings were made on the northeast coast of eastern New Guinea in a first move toward isolating Australia. The Japanese were aided by the long-standing resentment of British, Dutch, and French colonial rule in these areas.

The first months of 1942 were deeply discouraging for the Allies. The good news, though, was that the U.S. was finally in the war. The long-term outlook was in favor of the Allies if England and Russia could hold off Germany until America's huge industrial and human resources could be brought to bear.

The USS Lafayette—formerly the French luxury liner, the SS Normandie—on its side at its pier in New York after capsizing on February 9, 1942, due to water taken on during firefighting. Wilber and I walked down the pier to the left where we could see up close the bottom of the stern and the huge screws. [PHOTO: U.S. NAVY]

10

"My PhD didn't cut any ice here"

Mississippi
February–August, 1942

The 43rd Infantry Division was ordered to Camp Shelby in Mississippi on February 8, 1942, and was in place there by February 19.

On February 9, 1942, a Monday afternoon, as I walked down 71st Street in New York City after a violin lesson, someone pointed out smoke rising into the sky from a distant fire. It was from the burning SS Normandie, the former French ocean liner. It had been in New York since the war began in Europe, and was seized by the U.S. in May 1941. It was being converted to a U.S. troopship under the name USS Lafayette. A carelessly used welding torch caused the fire, though there was much speculation about sabotage. The ship capsized onto its side at its Hudson River Pier 88, near West 50th Street, due to taking on large amounts of water from the fire-fighting efforts. It lay there for all to see for many months.

Meanwhile, as Norma continued work on her novel and her piano skills, she found herself reaching out for non-threatening social connections. She was active in the nearby Episcopalian Church, and a young (thirtyish) red-haired man in the choir became a friend of the family. From superficial impressions, particularly his focus on the family and not Norma, I have wondered if he was gay. He was around enough that I found myself inadvertently calling him "Daddy" once or twice, which must have been disconcerting to Norma. On one occasion, he took us to either the arrival or departure (I can't remember which) of an ocean liner, possibly the Swedish Gripsholm, a festive occasion.

As for Wilber, his thoughts about the reorganization, the move to Mississippi, his survival odds, and more were revealed in his monthly letter to Indiana. It was addressed solely to his father.

[ABOUT FEBRUARY 25, 1942]

Dear Father — Your good letter of some time ago came while we were in the midst of preparations to move the 43d to Camp Shelby. We are now in Shelby and the 43d has been reorganized into a triangular division.… The "square" division is … unwieldy and organized for strong defense. The "Triangular" division is organized for mobility.… I am now Executive temporarily in command of the 169th FA Bn.

I'm content to do any job that's pushed my way so shan't worry. It was too bad to leave some fellow officers who have become very dear friends, but we all knew it could happen. I asked Gen. Barker if he has called me up [to see him] to discuss the advisability of my transfer or to discuss the consequences of the transfer. He said it was all settled but that he regretted breaking up the Damon + Pythias [close friends in Greek mythology] relationship of Col. Choate and myself. My answer was that he couldn't do that [break up the friendship] and that my only question was if he were sure I could do the work he wanted. He said he was sure and began to talk about future promotions. I told him I preferred not to plan on the future until I had made good on the present assignment. He seemed a bit surprised by that.

> Wilber had his priorities straight, but I also think he enjoyed confronting the general with them. Colonel Choate had been the commanding officer of the 152nd Field Artillery Regiment and had been a close friend of Wilber's since their national guard days in Bangor, Maine. They had similar interests, including classical music, and got on well together. Choate was transferred out of the division and never went overseas. Wilber had little or no further contact with him.

The one thing I fear is too much advancement until I am beyond my depth and then a blunder in combat. I suppose each officer feels the same way.…

The experience of commanding a battalion is proving interesting. Of course, I had done the same thing for a regiment only always in the Col's name. My officers seem a solid, and capable, and clean group. They take pride in being a working crowd, and I like that. When the regular commander [Lt. Col. Chester Files] returns from school, I expect to learn a lot for he is considered the most capable in the 43d. This takes me out of the "staff only" group and puts me in the "fighting" troops again.…

Norma is studying hard on the piano. Her teacher [Gaby Casadeus] reports outstanding progress.… It is just the old game of investing in ourselves rather than

CHAPTER 10   *My PhD didn't cut any ice here*

putting the investment in a bank account. I have urged this plan mainly because I have had a pretty definite and persistent feeling that I won't be back. I never told Norma or anyone else because I feel a bit silly about it and have a very healthy desire to be pleasantly surprised in the matter.... She wrote recently that children will soon be evacuated from the city and that she may move to Princeton, N.J., where her teacher lives....

Col. Choate's wife is dying tonight unless she has already done so. He was called home yesterday. She has been getting worse for a year with an incurable cancer. He has 5 children age 12 to 18. I'm sorry not to be with him now.

Will send checks as usual. Before we embark, we will need 105 Howitzers. If I can, I'll notify you by the word "The 105's came." — Love Wilber

[Marginal note:] I was invited to accept a commission as Major in the Chemical Warfare Service the other day by the head of Offensive Warfare Research at Wash D.C. I refused, admitting [to myself] I'd probably regret it in some swamp later.

>   This letter was loaded with insight into Wilber and war. First there was his concern about his abilities in his new position. I do not think this was false modesty; I too would have been worried about my performance in combat. Second, his practicality about his possible death illustrated what every soldier in a shooting war faces. It is still chilling for me to read this. Third, the Colonel Choate story revealed starkly the conflict between military and familial duties. How was Choate to care for his children? Fourth, Wilber was deliberately planning to bypass the censors with a coded message. This surprised me because Wilber was very much a by-the-book person. He did practice such deception at least once early in the war, a practice that I believe was nearly universal. Later in the war, he carefully followed the regulations. And, finally, he refused a prestigious non-combat position in Washington, D.C.

x · o · ø · o · x

At about this time, Wilber was ordered to the Field Artillery School at Fort Sill, Oklahoma, for an eight-week course beginning March 3. He became a student again. In the civilian population, fear and hysteria regarding German and Japanese agents or spies was rampant. During January and February, German submarines were sinking ship after ship off the East Coast and President Roosevelt ordered the internment of Japanese Americans on the West Coast in February. In this letter, it is clear that the war directly affected our family in New York.

FORT SILL, OKLA. [ABOUT MARCH 25, 1942]

Dear Father and Mother — Again my address has changed, this time temporarily. Gen Barker has sent me to the above course [Field Officers' Course No. 5]. It will last until Apr. 29. Fort Sill is the intellectual center of the Artillery in the U.S. I have as S-3 been sending officers here for the last year but couldn't have the chance myself. Now with a changed assignment, I have the privilege. Our classes are very interesting, and the material most valuable. We attend class continuously for 8 hours a day for six days a week and study all other possible hours. The students are Artillery Majors, Lt. Cols, and Colonels. Three of the last have been made Brigadier General since we arrived March 3.

Some of the instructors are just back from Europe, and others are using the latest information from MacArthur's experiences. Exams are graded U or S [Unsatisfactory or Satisfactory] So far I am specializing in the latter, but some officers I consider my betters haven't had such good luck. Anyway I'm primarily interested in the practical application of this course and seem to be very little concerned in what my teachers think of me.

I want to thank you both again for the field glasses you gave me years ago. They are 8 power while those issued by the Army are only 6 power. Last week I spent $5.00 to have an artillery scale put in them and $3.00 for a new case. That extra power may help me "see the snakes first" as the schoolgirl in Louisiana said to one of our officers who asked her about going barefoot. Thank you again....

Norma and the FBI are in some espionage business together. She is reporting [to them about] a radio station that is supposed to be [a] secret and is to everybody but the FBI and Hitler's agents. Hale and Valerie read the dots and dashes, but of course the messages are in code. She is under orders (direct) of the FBI and reports daily to an address she is not to write. Her information probably coupled to the reports from others has led to the arrest of 26 people and the seizure of "numerous" safes full of diamonds and stamp collections. That is the way these agents transport funds – say the FBI. The Army and FBI both moved into her apartment one day and brought all their prisoners in there for questioning. She was sent out to the bathroom each time, so she would not be seen by them, but Hale was kept in during the cross-examinations. He was very impressed.

This week the radio started again after being silent for four months. It had been removed (?) before the search for it was not found. Apparently it is being allowed to continue for the time being, for Norma is required to make daily reports of the messages and was told to make a complete report to [J. Edgar] Hoover [head of FBI], which she did. They said there was some danger in what she was doing and they could not furnish continuous protection but would do their best. I asked if she wanted to move away. She considered it and decided she was too mad. That "no foreigner was going to make her move out of her home."

She isn't allowed to keep my letters there because this [German] agent was going thru her desk one day. She chased him out and I guess told him what she thought about his coming in. He said the neighbors' little girl asked him, but that sounded pretty weak. The reason all this happened to Norma is that the key tone of the radio, or the spark sound, travels down the heating or water pipes to the bathroom. I'm worried, but have decided we all may be called on to do any job that comes along, and no one has the right to be safe now. The children know how to find you if anything does happen so [that] they are on their own, and [they] know to go either to the Police or Army for help.

Hale reports his team "beat 14 to 7" in the [Central?] Park the other day. It seems he "put somebody out on 2d [base]." If true he must be better than I ever was.… It's late (11:00 P.M.) and I need sleep so good night. — I love you, Wilber Bradt

In today's terms all of this sounds rather extraordinary, but I think Norma's concerns were very real; the "radio station" was, she believed, a transmitter in the apartment above us. I remember her telling us repeatedly that the man living upstairs was a spy, and that the building superintendent was his associate. Both of their names are imprinted on my mind to this day. The superintendent would carry a package or case containing, she believed, the transmitter from his apartment in the next building into our building, and she would hear the sounds of Morse code from above. The FBI was watching the building on some days, she said. One Sunday morning, Norma woke me to the sound of Morse code and asked me to transcribe it, but it was much too fast for my scout-level ability. I do find the bits about the man going through her desk, interviews in our apartment, safes, and large-scale arrests to be quite implausible on the face of it and also because I remember nothing of those particular aspects.

Several years after the war, as a college student I visited the building and found a levelheaded former neighbor (a former WWI army captain) who still lived there. He told me in some detail of a 1942 raid by either the FBI or Army Intelligence on that upstairs apartment. I am thus convinced that *something* was transpiring in that building. My searches in the 1980s and more recently, including Freedom of Information (FOI) requests to the FBI, have yet to turn up any indication of spy activity in that building or of the letters Norma surely wrote to the FBI.

The fear of sabotage gripped many otherwise reasonable people, as did the Communist scares of the 1950s. In both cases, Norma took a strong protective stance "for America," finding subversives where there may have been none. Yet, in 1942, she may indeed have been on to something real. She was far from a shy letter writer and I have no doubt that she deluged the FBI with reports. Her letters about suspect "commie" activity in the 1950s did turn up in FOI searches by the FBI! Until I find some evidence of this 1942 correspondence and the FBI reaction to it, I hesitate to declare the entire affair a figment of her imagination.

x·o·ø·o·x

In a letter to Valerie, Wilber exploits their mutual experience in chemistry and slips in a bit of moralizing about kissing.

APRIL FOOL'S DAY [APRIL 1] 1942
Dear Daughter Valerie — I'm certainly glad you are my daughter. Every time I think of it I am happy. Your picture is on the wall in front of me and you are smiling at me. I wonder if you are smiling when you read this letter.... I notice you know your chemistry OK. Do you know the formula for salt and the name of the acid in vinegar?

Such a lot of kisses and hugs in your letters. I have noticed how easy it is to keep on kissing and hugging when you get started. This is one reason it is so important to start on the right person. I started with Nana and it is still a lot of fun. Good night Darling I must go to bed. I love you. Give Hale a big hair-rumple for me and mother a big smack. — I love you very much, Wilber, XXX OOO

Wilber often closed his letters with multiple Xs for kisses and Os for hugs. He sometimes crosses the O like this: Ø, the significance of which escapes me.

x·o·ø·o·x

There is more about Wilber's life at artillery school in an undated letter to Valerie written around the time of her tenth birthday on April 18.

[APRIL 1942] FORT SILL, OKLAHOMA
My Dear Daughter [to Valerie] — It is five minutes until eleven o'clock but I promised myself the pleasure of writing to you today so I'll not go to bed quite now.... The other day I saw a blue-bird. He was so pretty and he reminded me of you and I thought maybe you were going to have a birthday....

CHAPTER 10   *My PhD didn't cut any ice here*

This is a pretty hard school. We listen to the teachers from 8:00 to 12:00 then from 1:00 to 5:00 then study for all 8 classes during the evening. There are no study periods. We had an exam the other day. My paper was ok except for one mistake.

This country is a lot like Pullman [Washington]. It has bare plains with small mountains sticking up here and there. It is pretty cold out of doors yet. Saturday we were in outdoor classes all day. I wore some wool long legged underwear, and a wool shirt and trousers, some long grey wool stockings over my sox, leggings, my scarf that you all gave me, my field jacket with the extra lining inside it, gloves, overcoat and fur cap. I remembered how my family had gotten me the fur cap, the scarf and the gloves, too.

We stood on top of Signal Mt. all afternoon and sometimes the wind blew so hard it would make you walk a few steps. We watched some Infantry from the 2d Division attack across the country while the 18th Field Artillery fired over their heads at targets. The Artillery just about blew some of the fields, where the targets were, to pieces. There was a lot of noise, and dirt and rocks flew into the air, and the enemy would have had a pretty hard time if he had been there. I am studying hard and learning a lot. I hope it will make me a better officer so I can get this war over with sooner.

Good Night Sweetheart, I love you. Take care of Valerie for me and Nana and Hale, too. Good night my little Sunshine Girl. — This is Pop signing off, Wilber (sleepy)

> We would not have this vivid letter today had Norma not sent our letters off to the *Atlantic Monthly* for publication. Otherwise they would have been lost with all those others to Norma. Note the depersonalization of "the enemy," as if it were a child's game.

x · o · ∅ · o · x

Wilber liked doing well in "school" and especially wanted his father, the schoolteacher, to know it.

APRIL 25, 1942
Dear Father — My "School Days" are almost over and I am content....

You would have been interested in the way we had to work. My Phi Beta Kappa key and my PhD didn't cut any ice here, and weren't mentioned by me either.

I was pretty discouraged for a while but finally hit the scholastic level at which I thought I belonged by getting a little more sleep. That doesn't mean I was as good as I would have liked to be. However my never having any military school before had to be overcome; the class was about 30% Regulars [members of the Regular U.S. Army] and some were pretty good.

I did achieve some publicity the other day by getting a public commendation from the most hard-boiled umpire on my ability to conduct fire. He had given me an assignment he thought I couldn't do and set another umpire on me to see [that] I got no information from anyone else. It just worked out that I got a target hit on about the 8th round. He thought it was a fluke and gave me another target and watched me himself. It was my day for I landed four shells on the target at the second volley. I tried to act nonchalant, but I really was surprised. I know it should have taken at least twice that many. Consequently, I'm not so much impressed, but the gunnery department has claimed I am just the result of their fine teaching and is endorsing me with enthusiasm. You see, it was the Tactics Department that put me on the spot, and the Gunnery Dept. that watched me save their reputation. Lots of fun in practice. I hope my luck holds when we play for keeps. By the way, the only instruments I was allowed were none, so I used those binoculars again. The scale I had just put in was just what I needed.

The weather has been changeable. I wore a fur cap once last week and rubber boots twice this week, and I was comfortable in a shirt on Wednesday.

The General granted me 10 days leave, so I will go to Pittsburgh to give the Manganese Patent Application a little help. I had hoped to stop a day in Indiana but am afraid it will be impossible. I have to be in Pittsburgh the morning of May First (Happy Birthday to Mother). Finances will force me to travel by bus, if it will go fast enough. If I do pass [the farm] on Highway 50 and if it is day and if another bus will follow in an hour or two, I'll try to stop. I would like to see both of you again even if for only a short time. I won't know any schedules until I get to Oklahoma City next Tuesday.

> Visits to the Versailles farm were usually a matter of asking the Greyhound bus driver to stop at the farmhouse, which was directly on U.S. 50. After the visit, you could flag down the next bus going your way.

I appreciate your writing to Norma and the children. It means a lot to me. I seem to have spoiled things pretty badly in a good many ways and it is fine of you to be willing to not blame them. Anyway I've been consistent.

> Hale, by writing to Norma, is acting on his better instincts but is risking the displeasure of his wife.

If you won't be home on the 29th or 30th (A.M.) please send me a wire before the 28th so I'll know not to stop.

I hope this Spring is a good [one] on the farm for you. — Your son, Wilber

CHAPTER 10   *My PhD didn't cut any ice here*

Wilber did not visit his parents. They must have waited anxiously those two days, hoping each passing bus would stop.

x · o · ø · o · x

Wilber next wrote from New York.

310 WEST 73, NEW YORK CITY, MAY 10, 1942
Dear Father — I hope that my card from St. Louis arrived explaining why I was unable to stop in Indiana.… The most immediate and severe consequence of all this was that I spent only four days – two badly interrupted – with the family. It was a wonderful four days, as you can appreciate.

> Sadly, Wilber was not aware that he would never see his parents again. Given his fatalism about surviving the war—and with more thought—he might have reordered his priorities. I cringe at this story, as I myself once skipped visiting the farm and my then elderly grandmother Elizabeth on my return from California in 1952, when I had said I would. She was very disappointed, and I still regret it.

The children are well and doing unusually good work in school. Valerie had been suffering with a little indigestion but the army medicos had her in good shape by the time I arrived. She and I had a "special date" having lunch together and going to the show, while Hale and I the next day spent our time visiting the over-turned Normandie. With my uniform we were able to be admitted for close inspection. The guard searched Hale on leaving, which impressed him considerably.…

I wish you both a happy Mother's Day. I'm leaving for camp in ten minutes. — Love, Wilber

> Wilber, in his uniform, gained us entry into the pier building alongside the Normandie. We could see up close its huge bottom and gigantic screws (propellers). I was mightily impressed with the Normandie's underside and also with my father's uniform and his way with the military guards.

x · o · ø · o · x

HQ. 43D DIV. ARTILLERY, MAY 20, 1942
Dear Father — … I am back on the job again and am Plans + Training Officer for all the 43d Division Artillery for the next few weeks.… This is the reason General

Barker gave me for taking me away from Col. Choate and the staff of what was then the 152d F.A. [Regiment].... I returned on a Monday and slept out in the field with the general that night. We are firing over the heads of our Infantry now so cannot allow any slips. That means close supervision, as you know.

I enjoy visualizing your crops and work on the farm. If I would let myself, I could be pretty homesick about it sometimes. That is undoubtedly the just desserts of the wanderer. I had chosen that role knowing some of its drawbacks but I have about decided one is unable to forget or outgrow the tie to the scene of his childhood.... — Love, Wilber

> Wilber viewed himself as a "wanderer," perhaps referring to the Old English poem by that name wherein a solitary exile meditates "on his past glories as a warrior ... his present hardships, and the values of forbearance and faith ..." [author and date unknown; possibly around 600 CE]
>
> Wilber had suggested to his parents that Valerie and I spend the coming summer on the Indiana farm while Norma spent the summer with him in Hattiesburg, Mississippi, but they did not take him up on it. Our spending a summer on the farm in Indiana would have broadened our worldviews, but Hattiesburg served that purpose quite well. We were exposed to the cultural environment of the Deep South at a time when segregation was still in full bloom and Civil War veterans were still around.

x · o · ∅ · o · x

The German-spy scare made Norma quite uncomfortable in our 73rd Street apartment building in New York, and its location had also forced me to make that rather long commute to Grace Church School each day. Hence, she found an apartment in Greenwich Village (136 West 4th Street) just off Washington Square. We would be away in Mississippi for the summer and would move there upon our return. Norma may have arranged for the storage of our furniture and her grand piano for the summer in order to avoid paying rent while we were away.

Train tickets for our trip to Hattiesburg were not easily obtained; much of the country was traveling by train and bus in war related activities, like ours. Norma commissioned Valerie and me to wait near the ticket windows in Pennsylvania Station one afternoon in order to be present when a cancellation presented itself. At ages 10 and 11, we were considered to be up to the task. She had prepped the ticket agent on our needs. We finally secured the tickets and departed on June 25 for Hattiesburg on an express streamliner train, called the Southerner. I tell about the trip in a brief school essay written after our return to New York:

Grade 6 [Fall 1942]
The Southerner
[by Hale Bradt]
The Southerner is a stream-lined [sic] train that travels between New York and New Orleans. We got on the train at 4:30 P.M. [in New York, June 25]. There was one thing that puzzled [sic] me, and that was that we were not on the Southerner. I found out later that we had to change to the Southerner at Washington.

We arrived at Washington [D.C.] about 6 P.M. [actually about 8:30 according to the train schedule]. Here we changed trains. The train left about an hour later.

Since it was getting dark I tried to go to sleep but found it very hard, although I slept some. We woke up in South Carolina. After awhile we ate breakfast. During the rest of the day we slept, read, and walked through the train. We arrived in Hattiesburg at 8:00 P.M. that evening.

A streamliner was a train with engine and cars contoured to reduce resistance through the air, in this case with a stainless-steel exterior of sculpted lengthwise ridges. The Southerner was an "all reserved" train featuring comfortable "latest type reclining ... seats."

Our summer in Hattiesburg was memorable. Valerie and I attended a day camp for part of the summer where we learned that "Yankee" was not a complimentary term. We found that we were not like other people, even those with the same skin color.

I have retained few explicit memories of segregated facilities or segregation in action. We accepted segregated seating, waiting rooms, rest rooms, and so on as the way of the South. Being from the unsegregated North, we surely disagreed with such policies. However, having negligible experience with blacks, our mantra of "equality for all" was in large part theoretical. The often-unconscious belief that "blacks are inferior" permeated the North as well as the South. Such inherent (and unquestioned) racism was then a deeply unfortunate fact of life.

The irony and unfairness of segregation did penetrate my 11-year-old mind one day on a city bus ride from our day camp across town to our home. Valerie and I hopped on an empty bus headed for home, paid our fare, and sat down about half way back. The white driver beckoned us to the front and in no uncertain terms told us to sit at the very front, next to the front door. This was treatment we had experienced in our classrooms when we were too talkative, but how had we transgressed here? Nevertheless, we obeyed and soon understood. As the bus crossed town, it filled up to standing room only with blacks who by law had to sit or stand further back in the bus than the whites. If we had remained in our original seats, the blacks would have had to crowd in behind us to the back half of the bus. The irony was that Valerie and I were more restricted in our seating than the blacks were. As in the South generally, the segregators only served to constrict their own choices and opportunities.

Since leaving Bangor, our family had relied solely on public transportation. In New York City, Valerie and I traveled on foot, subway, or bus. Owning bicycles was our unfulfilled dream, as bikes would have been impractical for safety reasons in NYC. The quiet residential streets of Hattiesburg were another story. I was 11 that summer and Valerie 10. At some point in the past, Wilber had rashly told us that we could each have a bicycle if we could each come up with half the cost of one—he would cover the other halves. Since we were returning to NYC at the end of the summer where we would not ride bicycles and where storage space was limited, such purchases seemed foolhardy to our parents, though not to us.

We found that we could buy mongrel bicycles assembled from spare parts from a local bike shop for $26 each. Because of the war, new bicycles were unavailable. I had managed to save $13 from my weekly earnings, and

IOU written by Wilber and signed by ten-year-old Valerie for the loan to cover her share of the bicycle purchase. I had forgotten that she did not pay her full share and laughed long and hard upon discovering this in Wilber's papers. Little girls can easily manipulate their fathers and Valerie was no exception. I'm sure Wilber never saw the $11.75. It reads: "July 22, 1942 Memo: Today I bought a bike for Valerie with the understanding that she will repay me $13.00. She has today paid $1.25 leaving a debt of $11.75. She agreed to pay me the balance as soon as possible after returning to New York. Wilber E. Bradt. Agreed — Valerie Evelyn Bradt" was thus determined to have a bike, and so was Valerie. To counter our determination, Wilber had carefully assembled his share of the cost for both bikes ($26) in quarters, 104 of them piled in 26 stacks of four each, so as to make it look like a lot of money. He told us we could have his share for some other use or for our savings if we would forgo the bicycles. His ploy did not work; we insisted on and got our bicycles. They were old-fashioned coaster-brake bikes with heavy frames, large balloon tires, and no gears. Valerie, who had not actually saved her share, had convinced our father to float her a loan for most of her share.

We loved those bikes; the mobility gave us great freedom that summer. At the end of the summer, we took them to NYC on the train but did not use them until we returned to Bangor two years later. Their transport and storage must have been a great nuisance for Norma.

x · o · ø · o · x

Wilber's monthly letters to his father were sometimes quite cryptic. He was incredibly busy, serving as temporary S-3 (Training and Plans Officer) of the divisional artillery. Training was intense due to the anticipated shipment of the division overseas.

[CAMP SHELBY, MISS.] JUNE 30, 1942
Dear Father — I started this letter two days ago and wrote only two lines. Gen. Barker has kept me on the jump [as S-3 of Div. Arty.] and I've tried to see a little of Norma and the children.

They came last week [to Hattiesburg, Miss.] and are in a tourist cabin until next Thursday. It is surely grand to be able to see them occasionally.

Training continues to be dominated by the expansion of the Army. We develop the men for certain positions and lose them to new divisions that are being organized. It's discouraging work, but I suppose necessary.

It's late 11:30 P.M. and I must get to bed. I marched 14 miles the other day – pretty fair for the F.A. — I love you, Your Son Wilber

x · o · ø · o · x

One month later, Wilber was back to his "permanent" assignment as executive officer of the 169th Field Artillery Battalion. Shortages of officers remained a severe problem.

JULY 30, 1942

Dear Father — I've been trying to write this letter for several days but no luck.... Recently the division has been advanced along the "priority" list, and equipment is beginning to come our way.

I am back in the Bn. acting in my assigned capacity as Executive. While the C.O. (Lt. Colonel Files) was away recently, I was in command. We have had a good group to work with in the 169th, and Col. Files is a very fine gentleman. I enjoy working with him very much....

It is terribly warm here, and I'm doing a lot of puffing all over this part of the state. The other night I marched with a 35 pound pack 25 miles. No foot trouble and no after-effects except for loss of sleep and some new muscles in my legs. I think I can outwalk the Japs if necessary.

Must get to sleep. It's nearly 11:00 P.M. The children have had a series of colds and [have] not been very well here. I don't know why. — I love you, Wilber

> These training marches were usually done at night to avoid the summer heat and to toughen up the men before they went overseas. They culminated in the particularly long one mentioned here (25 miles). This was definitely a challenge to all. After the hike, Wilber told us of a dog who was in the habit of accompanying the troops on their hikes but who had "forgotten to ask" how long this final hike was to be. At first the dog took enthusiastic excursions into the countryside chasing chickens and so forth, as was his usual habit, but his excursions became shorter and shorter as the miles wore on. Eventually, he simply walked on the dirt road in front of Wilber who was leading half the battalion in a single-file column on one side of the road. Apparently the dog's feet were getting a bit sore for he wandered back and forth carefully avoiding rocks and stones. Wilber simply followed the dog, also avoiding the stones, which he could not see in the dark, and the entire column quietly followed Wilber. On the other side of the road, the colonel and the men following him were continuously kicking and stumbling on the stones. Wilber felt that his column had a much easier time of it, thanks to the exhausted dog. This story definitely had a tongue-in-cheek quality.

x·o·ø·o·x

Hattiesburg, Miss., August 22, 1942

Dear Grandfather "HAPPY BIRTHDAY" [from Hale at age 11] — I hope it is a good day in Indiana. The rainy season is just starting in Mississippi.

CHAPTER 10   *My PhD didn't cut any ice here*

A few days ago I went out on the field with Daddy, and stayed all night. I saw the big 105 M.M. How [105-mm howitzers] fire. I also saw two shooting stars while lying in bed [on a cot under the stars] as it was a clear night.

Give my love to Grandmother. Valerie sends her love. — Congratulations and Love, Hale

P.S. We are going home Sept. 11 in a train which leaves Hattiesburg at about 10:30 A.M. [This postscript was presented via sketches that substituted for some words.]

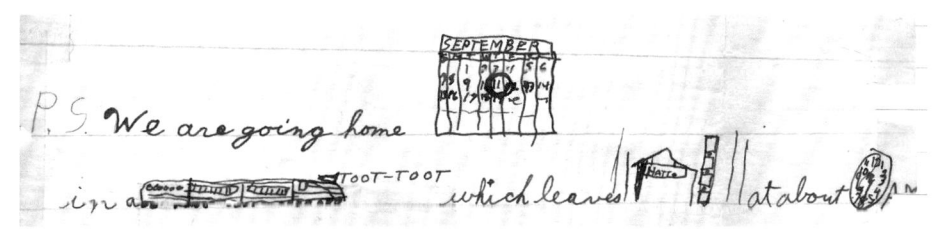

Postscript to my letter of August 22, 1942, from me to my grandfather Hale, explaining our departure from Hattiesburg. "P.S. We are going home [September 11] in a [train] which leaves [Hattiesburg] at about [10:30 A.M.]"

This overnight encampment with Wilber remains a highlight of my memories; it was a real Wilber & Son event and quite special in that I was allowed to be present on an actual army encampment—the sole family member there to my knowledge. Wilber showed me that you could actually see the shell as it left the 105-mm howitzer—an instantaneous dark spot—if you stood directly behind the gun. The "shooting stars" were part of the traditional and prolific Perseid meteor shower, which still peaks about August 12 and extends until about August 25.

x·o·ø·o·x

CAMP SHELBY, MISS., AUG. 23, 1942

Dear Father — Your Birthday [Aug. 22] was not forgotten. I'll just put a note in Hale's letter. It was a pretty rushed time for me. Eight of us are running a battalion, which is supposed to have 28 officers. We were out on an exercise the night before and ended it by firing some ammunition [shells] over the heads of several generals who had, in my opinion, an exaggerated trust in the eight of us.

I was at the C.P. [command post] doing the fire direction. Three officers were acting as safety officers at the guns. The "Col" and 4 others were observing the fire and entertaining the generals with explanations and demonstrations.

I hope this is a happy birthday for you and I wish I could be with you. Please take care of yourself and Mother till I can. — Love, Wilber

> The battalion was to leave for overseas in five weeks, and they did not have two-thirds of their officers! Some were likely on leave or away at schools.

The spring of 1942 brought some long awaited encouragement to the Pacific theater. In April, the American aircraft carrier, USS Hornet, launched 16 B-25 bombers, which then bombed targets in Tokyo, Japan, and other cities. It was a largely symbolic raid led by Col. James Doolittle. In early May, a Japanese attempt to capture Port Moresby, the port on the south coast of New Guinea—which would have been a direct threat to Australia—was foiled in the naval battle of the Coral Sea, which was more or less a draw. In early June, the Japanese attempted the capture of Midway Island, a scant thousand miles northwest of Oahu, Hawaii. In a battle of carrier aircraft, the Japanese suffered devastating losses; all four of their attacking carriers were sunk along with their planes and many of their experienced pilots. The Japanese and American carrier forces in the Pacific were now more or less evenly matched, but the industrial might of America would eventually overwhelm that of Japan.

The Japanese then decided to strike at Port Moresby overland; this involved landings at Buna and Gona on the north coast and a march over the Owen Stanley mountain range on the Kokoda Trail to Port Moresby on the south coast (Map 4). In the mountains, the trail was only a footpath; vehicles could not traverse it. From July to November the battle between the Australians and Japanese raged up and down those mountains. Finally, after having come within sight of Port Moresby and facing American as well as Australian troops, the Japanese, exhausted, withdrew to their bases on the north coast.

The news from Russia was less encouraging. The Germans, in their summer of 1942 offensive, did not renew their drive toward Moscow, but rather drove deeply southward into the Caucasus oil fields. They were approaching the major city of Stalingrad on the River Volga by mid-July

1942. This presaged an extended battle for the city that began with German air attacks on August 23 and lasted through January 1943.

The Japanese advance continued into the Solomon Islands, which extend southeastward from New Guinea, against little or no resistance. They occupied the island of Tulagi in May 1942 and began construction of a large airfield on Guadalcanal in early July. This was a direct threat to the shipping lanes for Australia, and the Navy argued strongly that the U.S. Marines should quickly capture the field before it was completed and fortified, which they did on August 7, 1942, against negligible opposition. Their toehold, though, was in great jeopardy from Japanese forces at nearby Rabaul on the island of New Britain. This led to a series of massive land and sea battles as both sides attempted to reinforce their troops on Guadalcanal. The Marines were very hard-pressed at times but were able to hold onto the airfield, which was named Henderson Field after the first marine aviator lost in the Battle of Midway. The island was not completely secured until February 1943. The critical situation on Guadalcanal in the late summer of 1942 determined the immediate future of the 43rd Division.

11

"Morale is booming and so are the howitzers"
California and Greenwich Village
September 1942

Shortly after the Marine landings on Guadalcanal, in early August 1942, the commanders in the area argued vociferously for more forces in the Pacific. Without them, Guadalcanal could be lost, and Japanese planes there could strike as far south as New Caledonia and could support Japanese landings in the New Hebrides, jeopardizing shipping lanes to Australia (Map 4). Such pleas had previously gone unanswered by Army Chief of Staff Gen. George Marshall. The U.S. had agreed to a Europe-first policy, and it was preparing for amphibious landings in North Africa in November. Nevertheless, the situation in Guadalcanal was deemed to be so desperate that arrangements were made to ship one army division to the Pacific—the 43rd [Morton, p. 328].

Two of the regimental combat teams of the 43rd Division would ship to New Zealand and then to New Caledonia for its defense. The third combat team, the 172nd, which included the 103rd Field Artillery Battalion, would sail directly to Espiritu Santo in the New Hebrides (now Vanuatu) to either defend the Allied air base there, the next obvious Japanese objective beyond the Solomons, or to assist the marines on Guadalcanal.

The 43rd Division was sent to California in early September 1942 for shipment to the South Pacific. Norma, Valerie, and I were still in Hattiesburg when Wilber left on September 3. We would not see him again for three long years.

Here we begin to see Wilber's letters to Norma. On a series of postcards mailed on September 8, he announced his arrival at Fort Ord, California, near Monterey, 100 miles south of San Francisco.

FORT ORD, CALIF. SEPT. 8, 1942 [POSTCARD]

Hello Dearest [Norma] — Arrived OK. Pleasant trip. Remembered our drive over the same route every hour. Have ocean view from my tent and ants in my bedroll. Wonders of Calif. I love you. — Hub. Wilber

SEPT. 8, 1942 [POSTCARD]

Dear Valerie — The mountains were beautiful. If you and Nana and Hale had been along [on this trip] we would have had fun. I hope you are helping to keep the morale up at home. — I love you. Wilber

x · o · ø · o · x

In one of her rare surviving letters, Norma told Wilber's father of Wilber's departure, at the same time providing some insight into our summer activities. Wilber's leave-taking, presumably for overseas duty, was a memorable moment for us.

SEPT. 8, 1942, 801 CAMP ST., HATTIESBURG, MISS.

Dear Father — In case you have not had word from Wilber by this time, he wanted me to tell you that he has been moved to Fort Ord, California. He left last Thursday [Sept. 3] and we received a wire last night that he had arrived safely. His address there is A.P.O. 43, Fort Ord, Calif. I suppose this is a "temporary station." I could not write you until he had arrived. He was in good spirits when he left, and all were relieved to be leaving the tedium of camp training.

The children and I have had our [train] tickets for some time for the return to New York on September 11, so we almost left at the same time as Wilber. It was difficult to see him go and to know we may not see him for some time, and we are glad we have our work to turn to. Your grandchildren have grown in wisdom and stature this summer. They were ill at first, but all this past month have been riding bicycles in the sun and are deeply tanned. Hale has gained about six pounds and Valerie has lost eight, both of which were my objectives in their diets....

… This summer I have been revising my book [novel] on the Grand Coulee. I have rewritten (practically all new writing) fifteen large chapters. I have also practiced [piano] a good deal. Valerie [age 10] has sewed a little, made mud pies, dressed

CHAPTER 11   *Morale is booming and so are the howitzers*

and dressed again her rag doll, and been a regular little girl for which I am glad. She was beginning to feel too old for dolls, but the summer relaxed her spirit....

Since you will want to hurry and write to Wilber I will say goodbye, but I want you to know he was in wonderful condition physically, spiritually, and mentally when he left. Everyone who knows him agrees there is no finer man or officer to be found anywhere. Everything he does, says, or thinks, is a credit to you. He is always fair and just – he is never mean or selfish – and is "absolutely tireless on behalf of his Battalion" (the Colonel). The men under him say he knows how to make them do their best work without rancor, and I do believe this Arty. Bn. is the best trained in the whole U.S. Wilber has used his inventive genius on them and their training, and he is so noble and strong and good. With such a leader (Executive) they cannot help but be excellent.... — With love, Norma Bradt

> Norma's eloquence was put to good use here as she so effectively reassured the father about the son's development as a person and soldier. I, Wilber's son, do not think it exaggerated. Wilber indeed was a fine man and an extremely effective officer.

x · o · ø · o · x

> Three days later Wilber got a postcard off to Norma, sent to our New York address; he knew we were to leave Hattiesburg that day.

SEPT. 11, 1942 [POSTCARD]

Dear Wife — Maybe I'll have time to write tomorrow. We are firing steadily and training is going ahead by leaps + bounds. We are on the ocean. I can see it now thru my windows. Notice the fact that we have a window. Our home is a luxurious barracks bldg. Have received a grand lot of wonderful letters from you. I love you and hope to be on Pacific Beach [Washington] with you and the children for a summer some time soon (?). I had forgotten how nice Old H.E. [His Excellency] Pacific was. — Love Wilber

> The question mark after "some time soon" was ominous; the future was so uncertain. Norma was writing Wilber frequently, as she undoubtedly had been doing for the previous 19 months. Wilber's letters typically acknowledged Norma's letters (now lost) to him, so we often learn indirectly what concerned her.

x · o · ø · o · x

We returned to New York on the Southerner again. It left about 10:30 a.m. on September 11 and was scheduled to arrive in New York at 1:50 p.m. the following day. As the train glided out of the Hattiesburg station, I resolved to, and did, fully enjoy every minute of the relaxing luxurious trip.

In New York, we moved into our fifth-floor apartment on West 4th Street, and I began my second year at Grace Church School, only a half-mile distant. Valerie attended nearby public school PS 41 on West 11th Street. During recesses on the playground, she could hear the women prisoners calling out of the windows of the adjacent New York Women's House of Detention. We did not ride bicycles and gravitated to sidewalk games or indoor activities. A friend and I, on the way home from school, sometimes made a game of proceeding an entire block down one side of the street without touching the sidewalk by clinging to the brick facings of the street's row houses.

Our apartment was in Little Italy in Greenwich Village. Communication among the relatives who lived in different apartments would be carried out via loud yelling from window to window across the central courtyard. One of my games was to play elevator operator in our building. I would press the button for the floor above mine and then would stop the cage-like elevator at our floor by opening the inner door at just the right moment.

The Waverly Theatre around the corner on Sixth Avenue was a favorite of mine. The tragic plot of the film "King's Row" (with actor Ronald Reagan) affected me deeply as I watched it alone one afternoon; I absorbed every bit of it as absolutely real. Upon exiting the theater, I was shocked back to reality by the bright afternoon sunlight and the noisy Sixth-Avenue traffic.

x·o·ø·o·x

In his letters to Norma, Wilber shared the happenings of his life. She was his long-distance morale booster and lover and his helper and aide who could send him items he needed and also sign legal documents for him; she had his power of attorney. The following letter, along with telling Norma about his train trip and arrival in California, included a list of routine items, typical of those I have excised (for brevity) from other letters. His artillery was at long last getting some real practice and their ranks were being replenished. His long-distance courtship of Norma surfaced here. It would intensify as he approached embarkation.

CHAPTER 11   *Morale is booming and so are the howitzers*

SEPT. [12?], 1942
Darling Wife — I have felt badly that I could not write you sooner about our move. Your letters have been sweet. It is lovely of you to try to write so much but I know you need to do other things too. I won't worry if you don't write so much because I know all the demands the children make on you. One letter a week [from you] will probably be more than I can write [respond to] and could be a little longer than these daily ones with less burden on you and Hale & Valerie. Business:

a. Enclosed is a special rule for Hale. [It was a drawing rule or ruler, triangular in cross section, with different scales on each of its 6 edges.]

b. Thanks for the "Spirit of Man." [an anthology of poems and philosophical writings by Robert Bridges]....

c. For X-mas I'd like a transformer that would let my Remington shaver work on a 6-volt car battery. The shaver is "110 A.C.–D.C." Incidentally it doesn't work well and I am trying to get it repaired. If it can't be done, then I'll send it to you to keep for after the war for me. In case I send it to you I won't want a transformer.

d. I love the pictures of Valerie, Hale & Nana. Cute!

e. Thank you for writing Father. Here is a letter for Hale and Valerie from him.

Our trip out [from Hattiesburg to Fort Ord] was very pleasant. René & I had a [train sleeping] compartment and each of us would have gladly tossed the other out in favor of our wives. All the way across, we kept instruction going and held two inspections daily. The RR [railroad] commended the men for their conduct and care of train equipment....

> Major René DeBlois (to whom Wilber referred), from Rhode Island, was the training and plans officer (the S-3) of the 169th Field Artillery Battalion, the third most senior officer of the battalion; Wilber as executive officer was second. DeBlois figures prominently in Wilber's story. He was a superb officer whom Wilber greatly admired.

We arrived here [on Sept. 7, 169 FA Journal] at the auspicious hour of 2:30 A.M. in a black out [lights out or covered] and detrained and unloaded at once. At 4:30 A.M. we went to bed in a field until about 7:30 A.M. We woke to find we had been the first train to arrive. In fact our train had passed the five first trains to leave Shelby. We even beat the General here. Everybody [the Fort Ord staff] seemed to be quite upset about us [being here], but we insisted we were here and asked & got action on tents and vehicles. By night we were in tents and pretty well organized for training. The 3d Div. from Wash. State had been here and was supposed to leave before we arrived. We came early so were sent to a field outside of camp.

Now the 3d is gone and we have moved into barracks. The 3d must have expected to stay here for the duration for the barracks were luxurious. The boys were a bit dazed and still explain that it is just because we won't stay long. When we arrived in the field at 2:30 A.M. of a cold foggy night, one Buck Soldier [Buck Private was a colloquialism for the lowest enlisted rank, Private.] was heard to say, "We built Blanding, we cleaned up Shelby and By ___ we'll make something out of this dump."

The 3d had a lot of 105 ammunition saved up and we inherited it. No one will inherit it after us. We have accomplished more instruction in firing since coming here than during all our 18 months before. The morale is booming and so are the howitzers. We fired over 230 rounds yesterday and 180 today.

The situation here is confusion completely permeated with rumors and counter-rumors. My estimate is now that we aren't staying here long but when & where [we go] is not concerning me much. We are getting equipment and men & officers as I expected. Three new (very new!) 2d Lts in the last 2 days. [Second Lieutenant was the most junior officer rank.]

Dearest don't worry about my thinking you should be with me. I may [have] want[ed] you at Blanding and Shelby, but I know you helped me by letting me dig in. That may save my life some day …

Things are progressing about as you & I expected at about normal speed. It is impossible to foresee any dates but your Old Man was always partial to the Pacific. Don't be fretted by my absence, Darling. It is so nice to come back to you. I count as precious memories each minute spent with you. My family is such a joy to me. The children are such a comfort to me. I would be so worried if you were alone but I feel the family is our strength. So you are my 15-year Bride. I remember your coming down the aisle in 1927 to be my wife. You were so lovely and clean and dear.

You have always remained so to me. I love the look of you, the perfume of you and the sweet touch of you. When this war is over I'll stay so close to you that you'll have two shadows. You had better get all the freedom and self determination out of your system by that time for I'll be wanting just a wife who looks, acts and is just like you. All you'll have on your mind is worry half the time that you are pregnant and the other half that you aren't going to be pregnant.

Don't worry about anyone seeing your letters. They are just for me and I save your thoughts for just Wilber....

It's late here – you have been in bed 4 hours — Lover of my Dreams. Wilber

> Wilber was realizing that he would be leaving his family and bride for a long, long time and perhaps forever. He also referred to the difficult choice made by many wives: whether or not to travel to California in the hope of obtaining a few more hours with their spouses.

CHAPTER 11   *Morale is booming and so are the howitzers*

x·o·ø·o·x

SEPT. 16, 1942 [POSTCARD]
Dear Son — I am changing my "Dog Tags" [metal nametags worn around neck] so they will carry your 136 [NYC] address. I have been studying about photos taken out of airplanes so the picture is oblique. Now I know how to use them to figure fire commands. Too bad for the Japs I hope. — I love you Hale and hope your school is fine this year.

x·o·ø·o·x

SEPT. 17, 1942
Dearest [Norma] — … The latest impression I have is that the next move is still not to combat but to an island base. So don't imagine too vivid pictures. I'm sorry to be so slow about getting into this war but I really am trying.

Speaking of trying, the 3d Div. formerly of Fort Lewis [near Tacoma, Washington] was here until a week ago. They were Regular Army. The barracks were surrounded by carefully tended flower beds, the furniture was elaborate and Day Rooms and Rec. Halls had plaques and carved wooden decorations in them. The 3d is continuing its training in the U.S. at another post now. We are also deriving pleasure from the fact that the very superior 31st Div. is being pared to fill our ranks. We have received a good number of their men. Also some other divisions that are chronologically senior to us are contributing. It is more wonderful to receive than to give.…

> The 3rd Infantry Division was deployed to the East Coast in preparation for the amphibious landings in North Africa (Operation Torch) scheduled for November 8. In its infinite wisdom, the army chose a division located in the eastern U.S. (the 43rd) for deployment to the Pacific, and one located in the west (the 3rd) for Africa. Politics surely played a role here; the 3rd was regular army and the 43rd, national guard. The European war had primacy in policy and the public eye. The 3rd probably had better connections with the decision-makers; it may also have been considered the better trained division.

Do you remember the mornings on the porch [in Hattiesburg]? Imagine us as "Porch Sitters!" I never really thought we could. It has been great to be with you and to feel your presence near. And such lovely nights in your arms. No one could love a man so marvelously, so sweetly, so passionately or so thoroughly. It is sweet to remember you didn't begrudge me any part of you the last night. I know you would have done anything I asked then without regret. I would never want to do anything to affront or offend you, my little white skinned slave. It is so wonderful to remember my hands on your hips and to feel the clinging folds of you caress me. It is so precious to recall my lips on your lovely breasts, to hold your soft body in my arms. I am in love with you Nana. The joy of your presence in my home can carry me thru this war and back home and it will, I know. — Wilber

> The long-distance courtship of Norma was heating up, as was the prospect of overseas combat for the 43rd Division.

x · o · ø · o · x

> Now, we begin to see some of the activities involved in getting an entire infantry division and its equipment aboard ships for a long voyage. It was only 13 days till embarkation. Wilber ruminated about what was going on around him.

SEPT. 18, 1942
Hello Better Half [Norma] — Did I tell you this camp is still full of Washington [State] cars [3rd Division families]. The Bulletin is full of advs. wanting a "companion" for the trip back to Wash. State. A lot of these Wash. girls have that breezy wide-open-spaces look and the hint of a bit of Palouse dust in their hair that reminds me of the AGD House [Alpha Gamma Delta, Norma's sorority at WSC]. If I write you next from Wenatchee [Washington], come to the rescue. Don't be worried; I haven't even gone to the "What Part [of Wash. State]?" stage so no beautiful friendships are developing. If I stayed around one, I'd probably say something [insulting] about the zinnia-growing of the 3d [Div.] and start a riot.

> Wilber was teasing Norma by the mere mention of the possibility of his straying, but quickly backed off. In later life, she would not have passed this off at all easily, and might not have been able to even at this time.

Just now I have both feet on my desk – a symbol of independence on my part. Feet under the desk for me means efficiency and servitude to work. Feet on the table indicates inefficiency and irresponsibility that no schedule can depress – How I love it! The phone just rang twice on my desk but I didn't even interrupt my beautiful (?) penmanship. Why should I? If my feet had been under the desk I would have grabbed the phone before the first ring had stopped. It was probably a wrong number anyway. Tomorrow I'll answer it. Today there are two sergeants with nothing to do except answer it and worry. It was a wrong number.

It is just the kind of a day for me to come home and say to my family, "Let's go for a hike in the country." The sun is warm, there is a soft breeze, and everything seems calm. Nothing on my mind except the three men AWOL [Absent Without Leave], the two drunks, the two who tried to fight the MPs [military police], the three who argued with the MPs, and the one who stole a cuspidor from the hotel; except the team of inspectors (officers) from the Port of Embarkation who are inspecting individual equipment, and the P. of E. inspectors who are inspecting instruments and guns, and the P. of E. inspection of chemical warfare equipment, all of which inspections are now in progress.

We could put on bathing suits and lie in the sand on the beach until the sand fleas made us move except the beach isn't safe for swimmers so we would have to mostly just lie. However I remember how well you do that so I still like the idea.

Just back after a shot in the arm for tetanus.... — Wilber XXXOOO

> Wilber cleverly juxtaposed his duty-free fantasies and the real-life activities going on around him.

x · o · ø · o · x

> Four days later, the pace of preparations for embarkation had picked up, and Norma was flooding Wilber with letters, as he acknowledged.

SEPT. 22, 1942
Hello Some More [to Norma] — It's the next A.M. and I have a few minutes to write. Today it is foggy. Usually the fog goes away by 9:00 A.M. Our howitzers are gone now [to be loaded aboard ship] so the firing has been interrupted. Today we receive 60 trucks (2-1/2 ton) full of clothing and men's equipment. All that is worn has to be replaced.

You are sweet to write so often. Imagine 16 letters already – you must stop soon and take care of Nana. It is so comforting to know the children are trying to be helpful. I do so much want to know my home is OK. I do think they are such good children that it grieves me to have them quarrel or fight.... Good Bye Sweet. It's time to go to work again. I love you. I love you. — Wilber. A Big Hug for Sister [Valerie] and a special pat for Hale — WB

x · o · ø · o · x

At the end of the day, he wrote again. He was in a sentimental mood. He recalled their lovemaking and revealed his fantasies. Was he courting Norma or just unburdening himself? Did this represent an underlying fear of the unknown? Few men, I think, would have revealed their thoughts so frankly; I doubt that I would have.

SEPT. 22, 1942

Little Flower of Mine [Norma] — Another day is passed and I am in my PJs that you bought on my cot in my room alone with my thoughts of you. It is so clubby to be alone with dreams of you. I have stopped and dreamed a bit of your loveliness. You are a beautiful girl. I'll never forget the curves of your throat, the glory of your hair, the sympathy in your touch or the understanding and love in your eyes.

You have built a wonderful thing for me with your dear fingers, sweet helpfulness and beautiful guidance. My life is divided into two parts: one empty and B.N. (Before Nana) and the other W.N. (With Nana). The B.N. was barren and cold and comfortless. The W.N. has been the ringing of bells in the country in May; the light of the moon on the Ohio River; the waves on an ocean beach; the caress of a girl beside a Palouse road; everything a man could wish and more. The perfume of your hair, the music of your words, "Wilber I love you. Wilber I want to be the mother of your babies." Darling Mine you are my beloved mate. No soldier ever went to war with more reason.

I will be yearning for your arms until I come back. No man was so fortunate – so many letters, so much love in them. You give me of yourself in each one. I just stopped and read a couple again. I'm saving the last one from #9 on to read and reread on the boat. No one can see them so don't worry. Also I disposed of the one [that] mentioned one of the fellow wives. I saw the one signed with the V again too.

I was all thrilled again too. I can see that sweet V now. Lovely knees up and apart to make it and such sweet joy inside. My eyes peep in deep and Nana I love you – I'm glad I've peeked and kissed and played and loved in that V. You have been grand to let me love you all the ways I know. It seems so amazing to me that I am permitted to possess you, that you don't mind, that you will come to my arms to be loved. I never get used to your cuddling close and reminding me of your joys by caressing and fondling me until I am all aflame.

It is a shame I was so sleepy that I only loved you in the mirror once this summer. You were a sight I'll never forget tho, so white, so utterly seductive, so completely clinging, so satisfying. I never can realize the completeness of your response to me except by looking back and remembering your hands, your arms, your lips.

[Note in left margin:] This is the scandal sheet. I suppose you will be shocked and get rid of it as soon as possible. [She didn't!] OK. But I love talking to you about the real you and this is part of your life with me. However the censor will be on the job soon, and I can't write about you and our personal practices. — WB....

> For some time, I was puzzled about what the "V" symbol meant for Wilber and Norma, but this particular letter made it abundantly clear. It was clearly unconnected to the widely popular V sign, in use since early 1941 (both the letter itself and its Morse code, dot-dot-dot-dash) as a symbol for Allied "Victory." This letter got a bit too explicit for my comfort. Were these really my parents?!
>
> The next news directly affected Wilber. The executive officer of division artillery (Col. Francis Rollins) was being appointed to a higher position and Lt. Col. Chester Files, the commander of the 169th Field Artillery Battalion (Wilber's unit) was to replace him, thus opening up the battalion commander's position.

Col. Rollins is being promoted to Gen. Rollins and Lt. Col. Files is to be Col. Files unless some outsider is put in Rollins' place. I don't know who will command this Bn. However the rumors are floating about and most of the majors are considering themselves as very promising possibilities. I don't know who is senior and no one knows what Gen. Barker will do or if he will have the final say. Interesting? Files told me Barker has a very high regard for both DeBlois & me. So do DeBlois and I, so we are all agreed there.

> Wilber did keep track of the promotion possibilities. The battalion commander position was normally held by a lieutenant colonel. The major who filled it could expect a promotion.

Good night. I love my family. — XXXOOO Wilber

This is the next A.M. (Sept. 23) and I have taken one page of this letter out of the waste basket. After I wrote it last night, I decided you would regret it and threw it away. However since the mail will be censored soon, I have sent it along. Please know I love you....

I must stop and get to work. I love you. I love you. You are mine – mine mine. When you go to bed please pretend I'm there with you and snuggle close. I'll know and be glad. — Your lover and husband, Wilber. I'll write Hale & Valerie soon.

> Wilber may have known that he was within one short week of embarkation, but those of lower rank could only surmise its imminence from the disappearing howitzers and other signs. The activity and the emotions escalated as the date approached.

12

"There are good times and bad times"

Fort Ord, California
SEPTEMBER 1942

During the last week before embarkation, Wilber wrote a series of "goodbye" letters as he faced a distant and possibly unknown objective. Each carried overtones of his uncertain future and the possibility that he might not survive the voyage or the events beyond it. He wrote several to Norma in which sexual courtship was interspersed with descriptions of the events going on around him. The first letter was to me.

10:30 P.M., SEPT. 23, 1942

Dear Hale [son] — How are you today! There is a lovely violin piece being played on my radio here now. I decided it meant I should write to you.

We have been loading freight onto boxcars all day and the men are pretty tired. They are busy cleaning rifles in their spare time too. Did I ever tell you the Army puts melted grease all over its guns whenever they are in storage. It makes each gun a big greasy glob that must all be cleaned off. It sure is a mess but it stops rust.

Son, I am proud to have a boy like you to go to war for. I know you will do all you can to keep "the home fires burning" until I come back. I'm sorry to be away from you now but I would be sorrier and so would you if I were trying to keep from fighting for my country. When you study history you will notice that there are good times and bad times for people. Anyone who lives very long sees some of both. It isn't really so important how good or bad times are. It is really important if people are afraid or not to worship God, and are afraid [or not] to have the right to talk freely, and to be given a trial before being punished. If people are afraid like the

French were things will be really bad but if they aren't afraid to fight as the Greeks did, things will be OK again. One of my best clerks is a Greek.

Someday you will go away from your home and then you will really know that I pray everyday that you will never be afraid and that you will be waiting for the good days we will have together some day. – I love you – My Boy. — Wilber

> He was trying so hard to be a good absentee father, and I try hard to resist the tears every time I read this.

x·o·ø·o·x

SEPT. 24, 1942, 11:00 P.M.

Beloved Mate — Another glimpse into your life and thoughts came today. I was glad you slept a couple of nights instead of writing. I want to know you are resting. There will be many nights when I'll keep you awake for loving when you will be too tired. I just heard a story – A man was sun walking in the field with hat, coat and shirt and shoes on. He was lacking trousers and underclothes and was entirely exposed even above the critical area. A neighbor watched until curiosity got the best of him then asked why. He answered, "Yesterday I went out without a hat and got a stiff neck. It's an idea of my wife's." – You my wife will never have to try any such experiments on me. All you need do is make a simple symbol in a letter or send me a word that I had been welcomed to your arms.

Dearest this isn't a letter about our sex life. I just love you every possible way. You are such a sweet girl to be my wife, the memories of you are so wonderful, and the comradeship of you is so strong that I am wholly yours. Last night I dreamed of you. It ended in my covering you with kisses and caresses, which you may know is a very nice way for dreams to end and an hour with you to begin. I won't go into details but you would have liked some of the events and would have balked at some others. I was quite a rapist but in the dream you seemed to cooperate very wonderfully. When I woke I lay and recalled our first night in Hatt [Hattiesburg, Mississippi]. I'll never forget the wonder of your virginity or the flame of your passion. If it were not impossible I would take you to this Pacific Island with me and make you sleep all day and be rested and flaming with love all night.

The time draws near when mail by me will be censored and it will be "several weeks" before I'll be able to get a letter thru. So, Dear One, don't be worried and don't be bothered by the headlines. I'll have you in my thoughts and heart all the time and am not afraid so long as you are mine.

CHAPTER 12   *There are good times and bad times*

Don't drink too much and think someone else is me. You might be embarrassed 9 months later. I want you just for me when I return. White arms, soft lips, burning vagina, swelling breasts, firm bottom, strong thighs, and sweet juices – all of them are mine. Don't forget the scent of your hair and the pressure of your body snuggled in my arms or the touch of your cheek on my chest – I want them too.

Dear One – every one of my thoughts comes back to the same idea (you with me).

Major "Knight" [not his real name for reasons that will become apparent later in our story] will be C.O. [commanding officer] of the 169th [Field Artillery] and is a good officer. He and DeBlois and I were at [Fort] Sill together. — Love Love Love Love, Wilber

Wilber exhibited no outward disappointment at not being chosen to lead the battalion. As executive officer (second in command), he surely was considered carefully. Major Knight was probably senior to Wilber; that is, he had been a major for a longer time.

His mention of Norma mistaking someone else for him revealed a typical concern of departing troops. Was there reason for his concern at this time? Perhaps. Norma had made the acquaintance in New York of a certain Monte Bourjaily who had been editor of the Bangor Daily News when we had lived there. He became close to us in New York City and we to his family (his mother, Terkman, and three grown sons). I, again, sometimes caught myself referring to the local adult male as "Daddy."

x · o · ø · o · x

Since Valerie's school, P.S. 41, was new for her, Wilber wanted to hear how it was going.

SEPT. 25, 1942
Dear "Tumble Bug" [Valerie] — I have been wondering how you are getting along in school. Do you walk very far? What is the schoolroom like? Do you have some new friends? I imagine you are wearing some new clothes too. What about shoes? Are they new? Do you try to walk with your foot straight? [This was a longstanding parental nagging point Valerie had to tolerate.]

It is cold here tonight. I think I'll put more covers on my bed. That is the trouble with the Army. When I'm home and it's cold all I have to do is snuggle a little closer to Nana. She is very nice for a bed warmer. Of course I like her biscuits too and her pies. That reminds me of that cake you made. It surely was good. You aren't such a bad cook yourself, you know. You fry a mean egg too.

How about the bicycles? Did they get there? How did you get them from the station to the apartment [in NYC]? Pedaled down Broadway I suppose....

I was remembering our date today. We went to the place where they skate in winter. [Rockefeller Center in NYC]. I thought you were the cutest girl there. Did you enjoy yourself? I had a wonderful time.

Mother writes me some very good things about you. I'm glad there are no slackers in my family. If you keep our home full of love and happiness, I'll have to come back to it. No Jap will stop me.

… If you keep trying you will be a very lovely and liked woman. I am very proud of you. I love you, Darling. Really + truly I do. — Your "Pop" goes the weasel, Wilber "Goombie"

> Wilber was trying, somewhat awkwardly, to bond to a ten-year-old. He searched for topics in her world, rather than describing events in his, and warmly connected with his daughter. In future letters, he sometimes shared with her his innermost and impolitic thoughts about the killings in combat. She was a companion who would never think ill of him.

x · o · ø · o · x

> Secrecy about the battalion's departure date and destination was paramount because its ships would be vulnerable to Japanese submarines during the long voyage across the Pacific. This created an awkwardness for the spouses who were thinking of making quick last-minute trips to California.

[ABOUT SEPT. 25, 1942]
Hello Dearest [Norma] — Surprise! I'm still scuffing the good Old USA dirt off my feet. If I had the $ in reserve I sure would have had you & the offspring out here. It is sure a good climate to be in love in. Remind me to try it with you some day. Various wives are arriving, most of them breathing a bit hard after their sprint. One or two others started today without checking with Hub. They will get to see the West, but it is going to look pretty empty to them. It is too bad but they just don't "figger." I'd love to have you here but I know you are here in spirit anyway. It is sweeter to have you for a wife in NYC than anyone else in Calif. Anyway if you were here you would get pregnant and we would both be worried then....

Today we received 9 new (very new) 2nd Lts and one Capt Doctor. We now have all our officers and only lack 3 of having all our enlisted men. There is no

CHAPTER 12   *There are good times and bad times*

equipment shortage for us now. We ask and receive. [Just-promoted] "Col" Files took DeBlois and [me] to dinner at the Officers Club tonight. Steak & cauliflower & pie and no Norma across the table – not quite complete....

I've been asleep so guess I'd better stop. I love you, I adore you, I hunger for you. Tonight I'll hold your spirit close to me. You are my guiding star, My Little Princess, My Flame Girl, My sweet mother of my babies. Don't forget I love you. — XXXOOO Wilber

x · o · ø · o · x

12:05 A.M. SUNDAY, SEPT. 27 [1942]
Bedfellow of Mine [Norma] — Two of the most wonderful letters came today from you. It is so helpful to have a little of you in my day. These were so complete too. The day's news of the children; your day including one sore thumb (I'm so sorry. I could fix it, too.); some encouragement (maybe flattery but I love it) for me; a lot of love both spiritual and physical. They do go together for us you know. It was sweet and daring of you to say you would put your arms around my neck and swing against me. I can imagine it too as something pretty thrilling. I'll be expecting that. Your saying you would want my hands and lips on your breasts and "everywhere" really was wonderful. You are learning the things a husband-lover wants to hear.

I'll keep these letters down deep in my bedroll to reread when I can just be with thoughts of you. If it really causes you pain to think of being possessed by me, don't write so intimately of yourself. It was such sweet sentiments that I missed last spring. If you are repelled by the idea of mentioning some of the thrilling caresses and games you use to nearly cause me to explode with juices, don't do it. I do think that penis and vagina and Venus Volcano are perfectly honest words and nothing to be worried about.

Anyway lover, your letters were absolutely just what I need. I don't want to lose the picture of you and your love making. I want to know you just as well when I come back as I do now. You are right. My lips would be on your breasts and my hands all over you. I would caress and fondle you and hold you close in my arms. You are such a sweet seductive little bit of femininity that I am always hungry for you. Next time I catch you I'll start at your cute little toes and cover every inch of your soft body with kisses and caresses. I'll open up the springs of your love and drink until you are drained dry and are all hot and tense with passion. Then if you have been as captivating and thrilling as I know you usually are, I'll expect to feel the same way.

Wow. Could he top this? Were such explicit and well-crafted descriptions being written in the thousands of letters penned in those days by the soldiers of the 43rd Division? I am sure there were many attempts, but perhaps none so eloquent. Norma was reciprocating Wilber's long distance lovemaking in her letters. He continued the letter that evening.

Sept. 27, 1942 10:15 P.M. — ... I have made out "Safe arrival cards" for you, Father and Doug [acting head of the Chem. Dept. at U. of Maine]. These cards are held at this Post until our unit reports by wire that we have arrived safely less whoever fell off the boat. They don't stop the boat for one man overboard, so if I slip I'll grab a couple to go with me. My orderly is instructed that if I go overboard to yell, "Three men overboard." Some of my "sarcastic" friends say the splash would justify it anyway. [Wilber was on the heavy side.]

My baggage and roll goes [sic] out today so I'll sleep in my size 48 overcoat.... — Your man & Husband, Wilber

Wilber's gallows humor regarding men falling overboard was not so funny in reality, but it perhaps helped preserve his and his correspondents' sanity in those rather perilous circumstances.

x·o·ø·o·x

SEPTEMBER 28, 1942
Hello Paul and Josephine [Wilber's brother and new sister-in-law] — There is so little time left for me to write that I couldn't wait to be officially informed of your marriage before welcoming my new sister into the family. Josephine, I am very happy about you, and I hope you find a comfort in being a Bradt....

Hello Paul – many times I remember when I was a Lt. (second class), you a Sgt. and Rex [the younger brother] a Cpl. [Corporal]. When communications go bad, I have wished you were the Communications Officers in my Bn. many times. I'll be seeing each of you some day. — Love, Wilber.

Paul and Rex probably had rather deep emotional reactions to seeing their brother and former national guard comrade going off to war without them, but as noted, they—and Wilber too—were beyond the age of being liable for draft into Federal service.

x·o·ø·o·x

CHAPTER 12 *There are good times and bad times*

The vessels that were to carry the 43rd Division to New Zealand had been loaded with the division's military cargo and were ready to take on the troops. After a full day of last minute preparations, on the evening of September 30, the men of the 169th Field Artillery marched to the train at Fort Ord for the 100-mile (or more) trip to San Francisco. The train began its five-hour journey to the docks at 8:00 p.m. and arrived at 1:15 a.m., October 1. Boarding the USAT Maui began at 2:00 a.m., under cover of darkness possibly for security reasons, and the ship left dockside at 11:45 a.m., October 1. [169th FA Journal]

The final five letters written by Wilber before his departure were emotionally charged and, from their uncharacteristic brevity, quite rushed. They were written beginning at 11:00 p.m. and extended into the early morning hours; the final mail call before departure must have been imminent. The first letter, to Norma, had strong suggestions that he was already on the USAT Maui looking out over the waters of San Francisco Bay. He called it "letter number one," and then he remembered the two of them "drifting on the St. Joseph River in the evening and rowing on Twin Lakes," and he was reminded of "the moon on the Ohio River and the Island Queens [riverboats]."

Wilber dated and time-labeled these letters a full 36 hours before the Maui's departure when he would still have been at Fort Ord, which is not in accord with these observations. I suspect therefore that they were written a day later during his last hours in San Francisco, and that he had already boarded the Maui. If so, he had arrived, probably by vehicle, at the ship before his unit in order to arrange for their boarding, a likely supposition. (Also, it became clear that he was indeed confused about the date.)

If this scenario is correct, he wrote these last farewell letters on the Maui as he awaited the arrival of his troops and indeed was looking out over the moonlit waters of San Francisco Bay as he did so. He recalled many intimate moments with Norma late on this, his last night in the United States.

SEPT. 29 [30?], 1942, 11:00 P.M.
My Dear Beautiful Love — It is late again but I do so enjoy writing to you. Your thrilling and so sweet letter of the 25th came today with one from Valerie. Hers was so dear I almost cried. I do love my two girls so much. That little Sparlin touch reaches right to my heart.

Today has been quite busy with phone calls, court-martials, inspections, and the more efficient confusion, which only the army can devise. However I must say for the army that it feeds one well. Mail is now being censored as it leaves the division.

Incoming mail is not censored. One boy wrote to his girl today, "These censors are just interested in military information. They never read anything else, not even an occasional dirty joke." In the same vein, I'm not going to let the third party in this correspondence spoil my communion with you.

Your letter was really wonderful. I lived each sentence with you. You are truly a marvelous wife and mate. I'm glad I didn't leave my letter in the waste basket. If you liked sharing true thoughts, you know how I like to have yours.

Being out here has made so fresh in my mind the times we had together. Do you remember us on the beach at Taholah [Washington] and Circus Jim [?] and the car we pushed away from the high tide. I loved camping there alone with you. We lay on the beach for hours and listened to the surf and I was so content with you. In fact, I can't recall a thing you wore – maybe you didn't, for I can recall being most interested in you and having some very exciting times. It always has been more beautiful to possess you under the open sky – My Spring Queen. You are really probably a dryad-e[x]ample: your charm in the woods along the Ohio hills – your comradeship in the Indiana woods when we were nutting – your homemaking in the Washington woods – your sweet love in the woods of the Idaho (Moscow) Mts. Do you remember us beside the trail in the hot sun? You were so lovely so precious to me and so satisfying. You always are at your best in an Indiana woods. Do you remember the picnic there when we roasted corn and the drive away when we stopped beside the road and you were wearing a blue lace dress. It was so pretty on you and your arms were so dear, your skin so white. I remember the very curve of your lips and the sweetness of you is still near me.

Then I also remember us drifting on the St. Joseph River in the evening and rowing at Twin Lakes. The calm and sweetness of your spirit was a blessing on my heart.… I will never forget the joy and sense of relaxation I felt when you came to Hattiesburg. When you came off the train, the station was brighter, the harsh noises became music, and all the people seemed more friendly. Nana was there! It changed everything for me. Later when the children were in bed, and you were certainly very tired, you undressed your beauty for me and took me in your arms. I'll never forget the thrill of that night. You were so beautiful, so responsive, so thoroughly feminine. I can feel again each sweet contact. It's late at night but you were not too tired, you were wonderful and I'll be back. Save yourself for me for I'll want all of you when I come back.

There is a pretty moon tonight – just a few days past full. It reminded me of the moon on the Ohio R. and the Island Queens [steam and paddle driven riverboats]. The thing I like most about you is your sweet willingness to be loved. I do love you and do want you … Anyway for letter number one this is longer than I had expected. Goodnight pink flesh and white body. You are a woman among women

CHAPTER 12   *There are good times and bad times*

for me. I'll be looking for you when this war is over, and I won't be fooling. I do love you. — XXXOOO Wilber

What wonderful sentiments and memories! I saw here no hint that Norma was reluctant to join in outdoor activities, including lovemaking.

x · o · ø · o · x

Even later that evening, Wilber wrote his final letters to Valerie, me, and his parents.

SEPT. 29 [30?], 1942, 11:55 P.M.
Dear Daughter — Your letter was very neat. I enjoyed reading it very much. The school must be very fine. What does the little Anita look like? Is she tall and dark like a movie actress or short and dumpy and blonde? I expect she is cute and hope I can see her soon.

So you are in the 5th grade. I'm surely surprised. You have been sneaking up on me. I love you, Dear. It is good to know so many fine friends. I hope they will like you. It's too late, 12:25 A.M. Sept. 30 [Oct. 1?]. Now I am too sleepy to write any more.

Be my special girl friend while I'm gone and write to me when you can. I love you. Take care of Hale and Nana for me. — I love you. OOO XXX, Wilber

Please be the Army Nurse in my family while I'm gone and take care of all the hurts for me. — Goodbye my Little WAAC. Wilber

This was Wilber's last letter to Valerie before sailing. Valerie was his "little WAAC," that is, his imaginary member of the Women's Army Auxiliary Corps.

x · o · ø · o · x

SEPT. 30, 1942 [OCT.1, EARLY A.M.?]
Hello Big Son, [to son Hale] — This is just a note to tell you that it is a good day here. Tomorrow is the first of October. If I were home we'd plan a camping trip for next weekend. How about Mt. Katahdin?

I want you to be my Liaison Officer in the family. A Ln. O. helps keep contact between two commanding officers, Norma and Wilber. He is responsible for

185

sending messages about how things are going at the other headquarters. You can consider that I am at the forward Hq. and you are at the Main Hq. — I love you Hale, Wilber

P.S. I am enclosing an autographed photograph of George Washington [a dollar bill] for you and Valerie.

x · o · ø · o · x

SEPT. 30, 1942 [OCT.1, EARLY A.M.?]

Dear Father and Mother — I'm in a bit of a rush just now, so can only enclose the twenty I would normally try to get to you for Nov. 1.

It is beautiful here and I have enjoyed California very much. Please take care of yourselves until I finish this job. I'd like very much to know you aren't worrying. I'm very content with my surprise assignment and subordinates. — Love Wilber

> Wilber remained executive officer of the 169th Field Artillery Battalion. The "surprise assignment" is puzzling. I speculate that it might have referred to the 43rd Division going to the Pacific rather than to Europe, or possibly he was referring to his assignment with the 169th Field Artillery, which was old news (eight months) by then.

x · o · ø · o · x

> Wilber managed to get another letter off to Norma before the final mail collection. He called it #2 but dated it the day before Letter #1 above, which carried the date Sept. 29, 11 p.m. (This demonstrates his confusion about dates.) I think it likely that this letter was written after the above four letters in the early hours of his departure day, October 1.

SEPT. 28, '42 [OCT. 1, EARLY A.M.?]

Hello Beloved [Norma] — Letter No. 2 will be very short. I just want to say again that I love you more than anything else in the world. I'll come back to you just as soon as possible.

You know of course not to say anything about your guesses of the movements of the 43d in your letters. Censorship is on.

Dear Darling Mate of Mine you will be in my arms so many times in spirit even if not in fact. You must not feel alone. I will be beside you all the time. You and Hale

CHAPTER 12   *There are good times and bad times*

The last letter Wilber sent me shortly before leaving San Francisco. He probably wrote it during the early morning hours of October 1, 1942; see text of this book for explanation and for transcription. The "photograph of George Washington" referred to a one-dollar bill.

and Valerie and I will do many happy things together as soon as we can. Until then My Heart, My Interest, My Love is with all of you until I come back. Please be kind and gentle and considerate to each other so my wonderful home won't be spoiled. It's my family, you know.

Your last letter was wonderful and thrilling. It was the one with Hale's letter and the very wide V. I was so thrilled. It's wonderful to see you and talk with you. I can use that wonderful wifey letter many times during the next weeks when I can receive none. I'll keep it in my money belt.

Don't feel badly about the Frisco 48 hour leave. If you were here, you could not have spent 5 minutes with me or have seen me [because I was so busy].

I have the facts now [about where we are going] and you would have been just as sick about it as I. We'll finish this war; you and Valerie and Hale & I [will] then be together.

The children and you gave me a wonderful summer [in Mississippi, 1942]. I'll never forget the kindness and love each of you showed me every minute. Truly my cup overfloweth.

Don't be downcast or worried. I'll be armed and protected by your love and prayers, and I'm really counting on those prayers a lot.

I didn't and won't write a check [for cash]. Not needed. Thank you. — Love Love Love to each and every one of you, Wilber

x · o · ø · o · x

Wilber sailed from San Francisco Bay on the USAT Maui on October 1, 1942, for a destination (New Zealand) that was unknown to his family and probably to most of his men. His being "sick" about it is probably a reference to the great distance it would impose between him and Norma. We have seen that he had long ago mentally adjusted to fighting the Japanese in the western Pacific. After 19 months of training, he was embarking on an epic adventure with the 43rd Division that would entail 11 sea voyages interspersed with three periods of combat, two of which were intense and sustained. It would be three years and one week, or 1,103 days, before he would again be able to set foot on his homeland.

PART III

VOYAGES TO WAR

AT SEA, NEW ZEALAND AND NEW CALEDONIA
OCTOBER 1942–FEBRUARY 1943

13

"I will come back to my own, my beloved Nana"

Pacific Ocean, USAT Maui
October 1–22, 1942

At this point, as Wilber began his three-week voyage to the Southern hemisphere, I interrupt the story to reveal how I came to possess his letters to Norma.

I had been well aware since the war that Wilber had written home several times a week throughout his almost five years of military service. Did my mother (Norma) still have any of those letters? On the few occasions when I asked her, she said or implied that she no longer did. She had told my sister Valerie that she had burned them long ago, an easily believable story given the painful memories associated with them. By the time of my conversation with my sister Abigail in December 1980 (described in the Prologue to this book), Norma had suffered one or more of the small strokes that preceded her death of heart failure five years later. Nevertheless, although her piano skills had suffered greatly, she was quite coherent.

Norma and her second husband had moved to a small condominium in St. Petersburg, Florida, and he died shortly thereafter, in April 1979. In the postwar years, they had lived in large homes in Westport, Connecticut; Grafton, West Virginia; Bangor, Maine; and Spring Lake, New Jersey, as well as in two apartments in New York City. Those homes were filled with manuscripts of their writings and papers related to their newspaper interests. Any letters Norma had not burned could well have been lost in this plethora of documents or during one of the many house moves.

With faint hope, I asked Norma in one of my weekly phone calls if she might still have any of Wilber's letters, and to my surprise, she allowed that she might. On my next visit from Boston to her Florida condo sometime in 1981, she took me into her study and tentatively pointed to a tattered corrugated shoebox-sized cardboard box high on the top shelf of a bookcase. It was wrapped with several strings and ribbons. In it, indeed, were hundreds of handwritten letters from Wilber. She had carried them secretly from home to home during those 35 years after his death.

I had told her I was interested primarily in Wilber's combat stories and their historical aspects, and, as the only son, would deeply appreciate having them. When she agreed, I could not resist reading a few of the letters right then. She then became curious and asked to see a few. How she felt, rereading one or two of those letters from her former husband and lover, was hard to imagine. After leaving her home, I read those letters assiduously in random order every moment I could find. I was mesmerized. My parents' entire war experience—and an inside view of the Pacific war itself—opened up before me.

A few months later, Norma found another smaller batch of Wilber's letters hidden deep in her cedar chest and mailed them to me. During the war, when a particularly interesting letter from Wilber would arrive at our home in the States, Norma would send it to Valerie and me if we were away from home at camp or school. The letters would be marked variously with her notes such as: "Hale, send to Valerie; Valerie, return to me; this is important." And, amazingly, we preteens did that. She would sometimes cut off the last half-inch or so of the letter before mailing it because it was "too lovey-dovey." Well, those little cut-off strips of paper from the bottoms of the letters were also in the cardboard box. The irregular scissor cuts allowed easy matching to the letters, and they were not very "lovey-dovey." The torrid letters we have just read above, and will read more of again, were another matter; Valerie and I never saw those!

I have asked myself whether it would be appropriate to share the Wilber-Norma intimacies publicly. The very religious Norma, and probably Wilber as well, both from an earlier generation, would surely have objected strongly. However, from afar and with emotional detachment, they might well have been able to see the humanistic and historic value of doing so—of presenting their lives richly and fully. Norma was a performer and a writer who fervently sought recognition through her music and writings. In fact she was a key player in a much larger drama, and in my opinion would have come to relish that role—one that typifies the challenges faced by war wives

CHAPTER 13   *I will come back to my own, my beloved Nana*

even now. For Wilber's part, he was a student of the classics and was clearly writing for history. He was well equipped to record his own odyssey.

For me, their story, honestly told through their letters, honors both of them.

x·o·ø·o·x

We now return to Wilber on the U.S. Army Transport (USAT) Maui in a convoy traversing the Pacific Ocean, a three-week voyage; its destination was Auckland, New Zealand. Wilber wrote a letter every day or two for a total of 17 on the 21-day voyage. I've selected and presented here portions of nine of these letters.

Sailing as a passenger on a long voyage presented Wilber with a sudden oasis of leisure, compared to the hectic pace preceding embarkation. What occupied his mind during the voyage, and how were the 500 men in his battalion kept occupied? The Japanese then controlled large portions of the western Pacific, Indochina, the Philippines, and New Guinea, and the battle for Guadalcanal in the Solomon Islands was raging. Japanese victory there was a feared outcome, and submarine attacks on Wilber's convoy were a very real threat. The ships sailed under blackout and radio-silence conditions. No lights were to show, and incoming radio messages could not be acknowledged. Lifeboat drill was a serious matter.

(I spent two years in the U.S. Navy during the Korean conflict as a

USS (later USAT) Maui in port, 1919. The Maui transported troops in World War I and again in World War II. This ship carried Wilber from San Francisco to New Zealand in October 1942. [WIKIPEDIA COMMONS, U.S. NAVAL HISTORICAL CENTER, NEW HAMPSHIRE, 102945; PUBLIC DOMAIN]

193

young officer just out of college. I was on a cargo ship, the USS Diphda, and traversed the Pacific between Oakland, California, and Japan a dozen times. We did not sail with other ships nor did we cross the equator, nor were we liable to hostile attack. Nevertheless, Wilber's descriptions resonate with me in many ways, and also I hope with the reader.)

Wilber wrote this first letter to Norma two days after his departure from San Francisco. This was a letter that would sit un-mailed on the ship for three weeks and then would take another two or three weeks to reach Norma. He could easily have written just once at the end of the trip and been equally in touch with his family. But he found it necessary to commune with Norma day by day. He was also writing for history; he knew he was on an epochal journey of unknown outcome.

OCT. 3, 1942 [USAT MAUI]

Dearest Norma — It is the night of Oct. 3. I am in the dining room of a former Matson Line ship. It has been a wonderful experience so far. Most of the officers and men were seasick the first day out but they are mostly on their feet now. I was fortunate and had no trouble at all. Good old digestion! You would love it here. The dining room is oak paneled and has about six large tables in the center with small ones along the wall. As I sit here, the room sways with the waves and keeps you a bit dizzy. I am in stateroom 206 on the highest passenger deck and share it with Chas. Cronin, Walter Leland, and René DeB[lois].

The first night out was wonderful. Strong cross wind and waves over the side of the ship with spray blowing, and out ahead our covering protection with the convoy just dimly visible. René & I stood on the fore part of the "B" deck and wished our wives were with us. You would have loved it, and I would have wanted you and Hale & Valerie with me if there were no danger. Now I know where we are supposed to be going and wish I could tell you. There were no days spent in S[an] F[rancisco] before sailing so we were wise to plan nothing.

Our boat drill is giving us good results and if needed should be OK. Willie [Wilber] is the "For'd" [Forward] Emergency Officer and stands on the upper deck receiving reports from half his Bn. and all of a sister Bn. as they clear the holds. When the last man is out he reports that to the Capt. of the ship. All he lacks is the peanuts to eat by the peck. [Wilber was known for eating peanuts when hiking.] Of course the fact that you get this letter [which will be mailed at the ship's destination] proves that it wasn't a "burning deck" [true emergency]. It's a normal job for an Exec so [I] took it on instead of handing it to René.

We (offs & men) are really very comfortable, the food is excellent and the ship clean. All that is lacking is the girl of my travels that I miss so much and the two fine children that keep me so happy. I love you so much, Dearest. These black-outs are serious here but they could be awfully comfy if you were here. Some of these days we will be able to have our own private blackouts on Broadway in Bangor....

Dearest I love you more than I can ever tell you. Please take care of yourself and the children until I can take care of you again. — XXXOOO Wilber

x·o·ø·o·x

OCT. 4, 1942 [V-MAIL]

Dearest Wife — I should report to you officially that there are no nurses and no WAACs [female soldiers] on board this ship. A very thorough search has been made and not even one discovered. There is however a very constantly recurring memory of one very sweet Norma Sparlin who keeps her spirit aboard. Her face is in the waves, her whispers in the wind, and the touch of her hand still lies in mine. Norma, standing by! It is so good to know you are standing by.

Your first V-mail letter was delivered to me on shipboard. It had just come on board in time to sail with us.... The censor is going to read this too and all my other effusions. – I've had a bit of fun figuring how far and in what direction we have traveled. Tonight I estimate we have covered 700 miles but shouldn't give the direction. Today at evening I sat on the deck for a long time and watched the sea and sky and the convoy. It is so beautiful and majestic that one can hardly stand it. You would love it. That is the hard part – you away.

Did I tell you we have a great violinist in our Bn. now? He is a radio artist and concertmaster of considerable experience. I was inclined to suspect his record was overstated until he played for a Battery dinner. He is really accomplished and plays double stops like Eva.... — Love to N. H. V. Wilber

> Was Wilber tweaking Norma's potential for jealousy with his WAAC remark? He may well have been!
>
> During those first months after leaving the States, Wilber and Norma used "V-Mail" (V for Victory) for some of their letters. These one-page letters (on an 8.5 by 11 inch form) were photographed and sent from overseas bases as negative film. Then prints were made and delivered to the recipient at reduced size, four by five inches. They were meant to save valuable airplane space and, to encourage their use, no postage was required. They limited the writer to one page, and the reduced size and overexposures made the delivered images difficult to read. The bracketed "V-mail" label on this and later letters indicates they arrived as reduced photographic reproductions.

CITIZEN SOLDIER   PART 1II: VOYAGES TO WAR

Two different V-mail letters written and mailed to Norma the same day while Wilber was en route to New Zealand, to see which would arrive first in New York. They could not begin the trip to America until the ship reached New Zealand on October 22. We received the full-size version as he wrote it because he affixed a six-cent airmail stamp to it. The other, without stamp, arrived as the reduced photographic image shown. It is likely that the larger and more easily readable version arrived first because Wilber rarely used V-mail after several such trials.

CHAPTER 13   *I will come back to my own, my beloved Nana*

The alternative was "airmail" which required a six-cent stamp. The stamp assured airmail service once the letter arrived in the United States. It could have arrived from overseas by air or by ship. Wilber experimented with both methods, alternating them and sometimes sending one of each the same day, and he asked Norma to do the same. He found the paid airmail to be generally faster than V-mail. For a while he found the easily available V-mail forms to be convenient stationery; the form was designed to fold up so as to resemble a normal letter. If one affixed a six-cent airmail stamp to the folded sealed form, it would be delivered as written without photographic processing. Later he used ordinary stationery in a standard airmail envelope with a six-cent stamp affixed.

x · o · ø · o · x

OCT. 5, 1942 [V-MAIL]

Beloved Wife and children — It is evening again and all is well. The Pacific is living up to its name and is very quiet and peaceful. It is warm enough to justify cottons so we have packed our woolen uniforms.

Today was the Captain's 40th anniversary at sea. The crew gave him an enormous cake, one of our Lts. (Keegan) sang a parody on Barnacle Bill the Sailor changing it to Pineapple Bill which is his nickname. The Capt is a very interesting person, with a very poor regard for most of the Maine Skippers [of past centuries]. He says they robbed their crews of food and built houses.

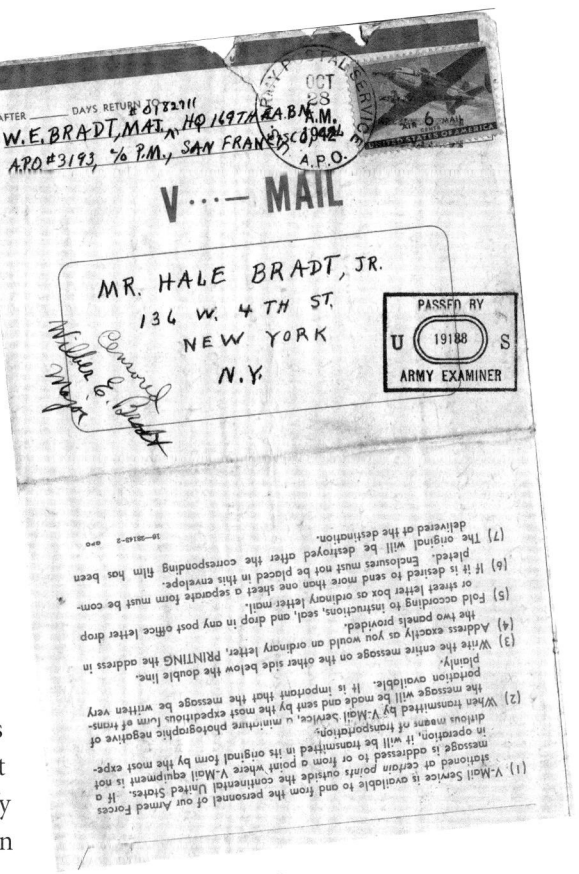

Reverse side of the October 8 letter on V-mail stationery (previous figure). This image is rotated so the long direction of the letter form would be horizontal, but blank side flaps (in this view) have been cropped. The "October 28 U.S. Army Postal Service" postmark could have been stamped in San Francisco if the letter traveled by air, but most likely it was stamped in New Zealand. The six-cent airmail stamp would hasten delivery once it reached the U.S.

The crew and our (my own) .50 caliber machine gunners had target practice today and the sea was noisy with our fire. We definitely are not sneaking across this ocean but move and act as if it belonged to us. Personally we think we do. The men are well and morale is high, training has been resumed and life is quite normal again. There are no fish in sight but numerous sea birds seem to have plenty to eat so our fishermen are still wishing they could drop a line overboard. I love you all and am hoping everything is going well with my loved ones. Please have a round and round for me. — XXXOOO Wilber

A "round and round" was a tradition in our family. We four would join hands in a circle as a symbol of togetherness.

x·o·ø·o·x

Here he reached out to me.

OCT. 8, 1942 [V-MAIL]
Dear Son — A few minutes ago I was out looking at the stars. The Big Dipper is getting very low in the northern sky so that I cannot see it in the evening. You could see it well because you are farther north than I. Overhead is Vega and in the N.W. [northwest] is Arcturus, which is a bright blue star. In the west is Spica a bright red star and in the south is Fomelhaut, which you cannot see at all. You pick out Vega and I will too so we can each look at the same star and know that star carries our greetings to each other.

Today a big turtle like you saw in the Aquarium was swimming in the sea. We soon passed him. I don't believe he was going as far as we are for he had an unambitious look on his face.

… How is your school progressing? I hope OK. I love you. — Wilber

x·o·ø·o·x

Wilber resumed his ever-so-effective long-distance courtship of Norma in a letter that, even today, chokes me up.

OCT. 8, 1942 [V-MAIL]
Dearest Wife — I have just finished a letter to Hale and still want to tell you a bit about my love for you. Last night the watches were retarded [set back] one hour for the third time on this boat. That gave me an extra hour and I spent it thinking of you. You truly have been a wonderful wife. I was thinking of you serving a

breakfast around our blue table in our yard and how casually I accepted it. Now it would be a gift from heaven to be able to do it again.

I remembered a night in a church in Portland Ore. where a lovely young bride named Norma heard the pastor say "Kiss the girl, Lad." Such a good beginning. All the later nights that Nana was kissed and hugged and mussed and tumbled are as precious to me. Your spiritual beauty has led me while your physical charms have enslaved me. You have the gift of completely satisfying my hunger in the most interesting ways. Darling never fear but that the joy of your body will keep me from any other women. You are my V girl and with the end of this war I will reclaim you and hope you will not have forgotten your wiles.

I send you my caresses. I hold you in my arms. My dark body presses against your white blonde skin. My lips are on your breasts. I am your lover. Please do not worry about my returning unchanged. I will come back to my own, my beloved Nana. — XXXOOØ Wilber

x·o·ø·o·x

> Wilber gave Valerie a piece of his world that she would appreciate. It was mostly fun, but the war did intrude.

OCT. 12, 1942 [V-MAIL]

Miss Valerie Bradt — My Darling daughter, We crossed the equator the other day and today we were all initiated by the Navy boys who had crossed before. I have a diploma, which says I am now a "shellback." King Neptune came on board [with] Mrs. Neptune to initiate us. Mrs. Neptune was definitely a mermaid. She wore a grass skirt made of rope and very rosy apples for breasts. She sprayed the hose on most all of us and kept everyone laughing except those [persons] Neptune was paddling or giving drinks of sea water to. He also specialized in daubing grease and mashed beets on people. Everyone had a fine time and got very wet.

Tonight we had an alarm and everyone went to their stations but nothing happened so we went back to dinner and I ate a lamb curry. It wasn't as good as Nana's curry dinner. The pie wasn't as good as Valerie can make either.

… Good Night Darling. It is 8:00 P.M. here now and 3:00 A.M. tomorrow for you in N.Y. — I love you Wilber XXXOOO

> Perhaps unwittingly, Wilber had given Valerie a good fix on his location with both latitude and longitude, the former with the equator crossing and the latter with the time difference. In February 1942, President Roosevelt had placed the entire U.S. on Daylight Time, known as "War Time," year

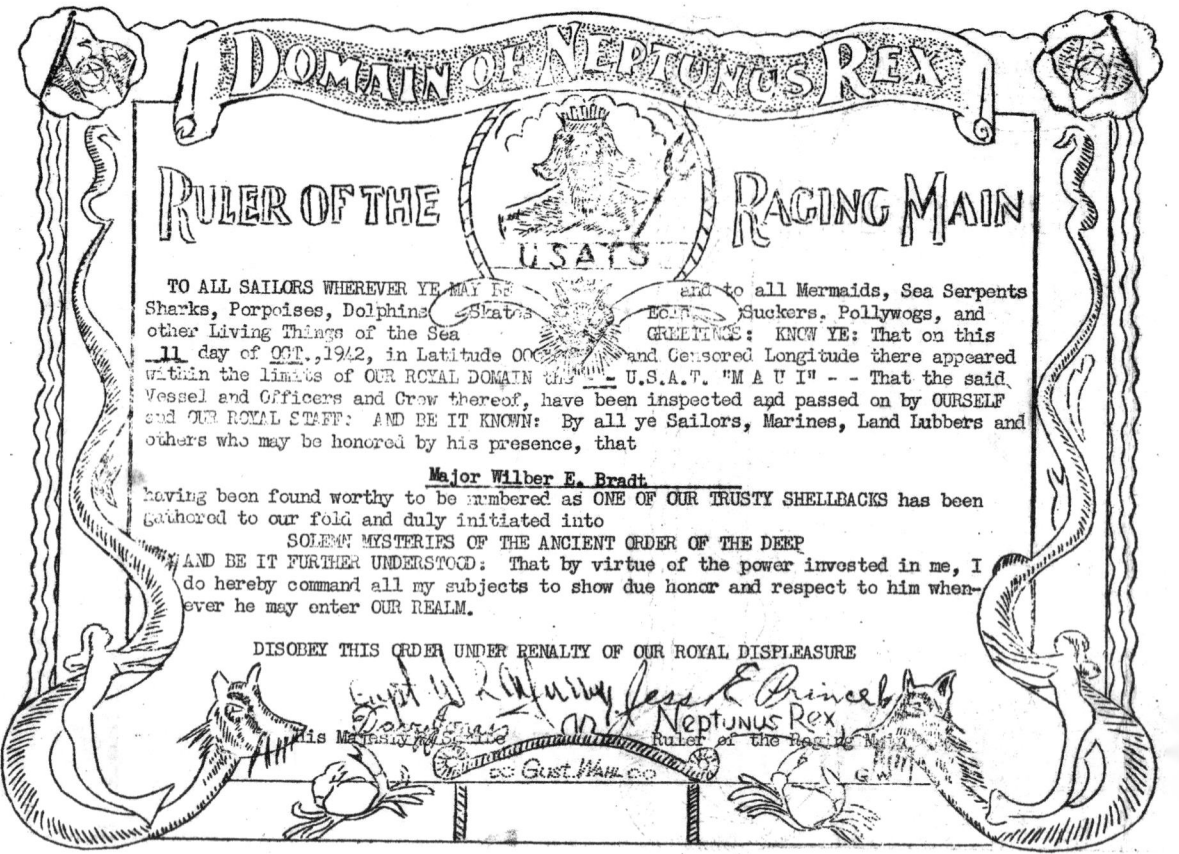

Shellback certificate awarded to Wilber for his first crossing of the equator on October 11, 1942, on the USAT Maui.

round to save energy resources; people went to bed earlier and hence used less illumination energy. This made Eastern War Time four hours later than Greenwich Mean Time. The time difference Wilber noted thus placed him seven time zones west of New York and 11 time zones west of Greenwich, England, or close to 165 degrees west longitude.

This position placed most of the Pacific behind them, with their destination ahead the Southwest Pacific, which could have meant Guadalcanal, New Caledonia, New Zealand, or Australia. The fight for Guadalcanal was still raging. The "Shellback Certificate" he received noted that the equator crossing had been on October 11.

The rough position Wilber had revealed was not moot, despite being received weeks later; the 43rd Division was clearly not going to Hawaii or Alaska, or to Europe through the Panama Canal. I have no recollection that we made these deductions at the time. In fact, other details in his letters soon revealed that he

CHAPTER 13   *I will come back to my own, my beloved Nana*

was in the South Pacific. Furthermore, we were prone to thinking that this was where he was headed anyway because the fighting was there.

The letter above was written on Columbus Day, 1942, the 450th anniversary of Columbus's 1492 landfall in the western hemisphere, though Wilber failed to comment on it. He certainly could have drawn parallels between their respective voyages, each with its highly uncertain destination.

x · o · ø · o · x

OCT. 13, 1942 [V MAIL]
Hello Again [Norma] — It is a pain in the neck to be here and not let you know everything is OK. I know how you will worry and imagine things are bad and forget that God holds all of us in his hand. Good Old Hand! Anyway, My Rose, the fact that you get this letter is some evidence that I still love you.

I am reminded daily of you and what you mean to me by one of our more foolish officers. He has a fine pair of tinted photos up in our stateroom of "a very dear friend" not the wife "who will go to almost any effort to spend an hour and a half with me." He, the sap, thinks she is most lovely and frequently so states. She has the face of a gold digger of the first water and eyes of a double crosser. So I am reminded by contrast of my own good fortune. The dear friend who spends hours and halves with me is my own darling Nana. She has lovely eyes and a face that will cheer me thru my entire life. Greetings to you my Love from the Southern Hemisphere. I caress your dear hands. How about an hour on my lap just talking and dreaming together?

What a trip this is becoming! I feel like the Flying Dutchman. I'll draw the line after the next war. Three wars ought to be enough. After that I'll stay around and guard an airport. The holds of this ship [where the men are bunked] are a lot cleaner than ever before. That is one of my jobs. The inspectors have had to increase their standards and create a new rating. Today all he could say was "Tops! Absolutely Tops!" Of such things are armies made. If I'm captured by the Japs, I'll probably have to clean up their prison camp.

Today I held another school for my staff on Security on the March. I want these boys all thinking in parallel lines. Beloved Wife I hope all is well with you. Keep the chin up. Here's my arm around you. — XXXOOØ Wilber

Wilber felt it important to emphasize his vow of fidelity to Norma and his contempt for those who acted otherwise. Later (in Book 3) we will find a softening of his attitude toward the infidelity of a fellow officer he knew well. Meanwhile, his pride in the level of cleanliness and neatness in the spaces occupied by his men would be a recurring theme in his letters. Casualties in wartime from unsanitary conditions could (and did) exceed combat losses. A sanitary force was an effective force, and inspection after inspection made that possible.

x · o · ∅ · o · x

OCT. 17, 1942
Darling Wife — As this week ends, I am thinking of my home and family....

One of our officers tossed the ship's medicine ball overboard. Probably some later ship will see [it as] a mine, and much excitement may result from reports of new enemy mining activities. I have been getting sun baths and am brown now except on the soles of my feet. Wish you were here. I reread another of your letters again today and sat for a while with the picture of N., V., & H. remembering how much joy I had with them in Miss[issippi].

You should be receiving my safe arrival card in a few days, I hope. If you don't receive this letter just keep one eye on the Hudson River, and if the fee in the Panama Canal isn't too high, I'll swim all the way home. If it's too much I'll land at Frisco and finish by train. Think of the fine practice on swimming I might get. If you do get the letter you will at least know I was protected by your prayers. Anyway to date I've slept at least ten hours every night and sometimes twelve.

I love you and wish you were with me. Goodnight. — XXXOOO Wilber

A medicine ball was essentially a weighted oversized basketball that was used for strength training. Wilber earned his letter on the swimming team at Indiana U. His bravado regarding swimming "all the way home" struck a resonant note with me at age 11.

x · o · ∅ · o · x

Five days later, the three-week voyage was nearly over. Excitement and anticipation rose.

OCT. 22, 1942
Darling Nana — We are pulling into the harbor [Auckland] now. The city is on low hills and we have sailed for hours along the shore. The hills come down to the shore

CHAPTER 13 *I will come back to my own, my beloved Nana*

and houses are scattered thru them. Little islands are sometimes rough and craggy, sometimes are pasture lands. It is cool and springtime and the fields are green.

This may be the last letter for times will be rushing for a while now. Sweet Wife I want you to know I am OK and feeling fine. Don't imagine a lot of worries. They don't help and do hurt. I hope you are doing the things I would be doing with you if I were there.

Hale and Valerie I hope you are being good soldiers and keeping things happy and cheerful at home. Are you? ... I think maybe it would be fun for me to get breakfast for the family again too. How about hot cakes and eggs? — Love, Wilber XXXOOO

As the 43rd Division approached Auckland, the U.S. Marines on Guadalcanal were desperately defending Henderson Field (airfield) there. Twice, the Japanese attacked the marine perimeter in force, no more than a mile from the airfield, on the night of September 13–14 and again on the nights of October 24–25 and 25–26. The marines (with army reinforcements in the later case) held off the Japanese at the now famous Edson's (or Bloody) Ridge. However, Japanese air raids, naval bombardments, and artillery shelling were severely limiting Allied use of the airfield.

The naval battles in and around Guadalcanal were historic. Both sides were attempting to land troops and to prevent the opponent from doing so. The Battle of Savo Island (August 9) was a major Allied defeat, and the Battle of the Eastern Solomons (August 24) indecisive. While the 43rd Division was mid-ocean, on October 11 and 12, the naval Battle of Cape Esperance was the first serious setback for the Japanese even though both sides suffered comparable losses. [Morison, vol. V]

On October 18, Admiral William F. "Bull" Halsey, Jr. relieved Admiral Robert Ghormley as commander of the South Pacific Area. He would now command all land, sea, and air forces in the area and that included Guadalcanal. His appointment injected a welcome aggressive spirit into the area during an otherwise depressing time. The evacuation of Guadalcanal to avoid a Bataan-like collapse was under consideration, but Halsey made it clear that he would do his utmost to hold the airfield with the aim of gaining the initiative and ejecting the Japanese from the island. This was a feasible plan because additional ships and aircraft were being diverted to the battle by the Joint Chiefs in Washington, D.C.

Two days later, Halsey directed that all naval officers in the South Pacific Area would no longer wear neckties with their tropical uniforms, a comforting change in tropical climates but also a highly symbolic move: "The navy is stripping for action." Army officers were already tieless.

Subsequent sea battles on October 26 (the Battle of the Santa Cruz Islands) and on November 12 through 15 (the Battle of Guadalcanal) led to capital ship losses on both sides. On balance, though, the losses were more damaging to the Japanese effort. In the latter battle, both sides were attempting to reinforce their troops in Guadalcanal, and it was the Americans who succeeded. This and the successful defense of Henderson Field marked the transition from defense to offense for the Americans. Nevertheless, the battle for Guadalcanal was far from over and one more major American naval defeat lay ahead. The shipping passage through the Solomon Islands, through which the Japanese ships approached Guadalcanal was known as the "The Slot" (Map 5). Savo Sound between Florida and Guadalcanal Islands, where the sea battles took place, became known as Ironbottom Sound for good reason. The situation was still touch-and-go in the South Pacific, and the 43rd Division was there to help tilt it in the right direction.

Two days after the 43rd Division arrived at Auckland, transports were leaving American East Coast ports with Allied troops destined for the invasion of North Africa in Operation Torch. Landings in French Morocco were to take place on November 8.

14

"I'm wearing the St. Christopher medal"

Warkworth, New Zealand
October–November, 1942

The USAT Maui arrived in Auckland, New Zealand, on October 22, and the soldiers debarked on October 24. Wilber, as a senior officer, was able to leave the ship to run errands during the interim. His unit, transported by truck, arrived at Wyngard's Camp, 50 miles north of Auckland later that same day, October 24 [Barker, p. 22; 169th FA Journal]. They would be in New Zealand for one month.

On October 26, the SS President Coolidge, a converted luxury liner of the American President Lines, arrived at Espiritu Santo in the New Hebrides (now Vanuatu) with the 43rd's 172nd Regimental Combat Team, which included the 103rd Field Artillery Battalion, one of the 43rd's four artillery battalions. The Coolidge had left San Francisco Bay six days after the rest of the division. One entrance to the harbor at Espiritu Santo had been mined by the Americans, and because orders to the ship's captain were incomplete, the ship had entered the mined entrance. It hit two mines, after which the captain drove the ship up onto the beach. All but two people were able to evacuate the ship before it slid back into deep water, where it now resides as one of the premier scuba diving sites in the world. One of those lost was a 43rd Division field artillery officer, Capt. Elwood J. Euart, who could not exit the ship in time even as he helped others escape. He was the first overseas casualty of the division.

In March 1981, I attended the 90th birthday party of Gen. Chester Files of the Rhode Island National Guard, who had been commander of the

CITIZEN SOLDIER   PART 1II: VOYAGES TO WAR

Soldiers escaping from the SS President Coolidge before it slid into deep water after mistakenly striking two Allied mines in the harbor of Espiritu Santo in the New Hebrides on October 26, 1942. [PHOTO: PROBABLY U.S. NAVY]

169th Field Artillery Battalion and later executive officer of divisional artillery of the 43rd Division during the war. At that dinner, I was seated with several former members of the artillery and learned that one was a Capt. Warren Covill whom Wilber had mentioned in his letters. Covill was one of those helping Captain Euart get the last few soldiers out of the Coolidge.

As Covill described it, the men from service battery were exiting through a door in the side of the ship. As the ship listed heavily, the horizontal passageway became nearly vertical. Euart was directing his men up a rope and would have been the last man to climb up and out. Covill and another soldier were on the side of the ship pulling Euart up by a rope tied around his waist. They had almost gotten him out as the ship was sliding back into the harbor, but ultimately failed to do so. The hatch went underwater just before Euart could emerge. Covill and the other soldier were pulled underwater but were able to resurface. [See also Barker, pp. 23, 24]

With the loss of the Coolidge, the entire 172nd Regimental Combat team of perhaps 5,000 men was stranded at Espiritu Santo with no supplies or equipment. Everything from toothbrushes to 105-mm howitzers was lost. This was a terrible setback, but not nearly what it could have been without the largely successful evacuation. Initially, the men ashore made do with clothing and other necessities provided by the U.S. Navy. The 172nd Regimental Combat team did not join the 43rd Division until the Munda campaign, eight months later.

x·o·ø·o·x

Wilber had now begun a one month stay in wartime New Zealand. It was still a peaceful island southeast of Australia, far from the raging combat on Guadalcanal, but a lot closer to it than California. Many of the New Zealand soldiers ("Kiwis") were off fighting for the British in Africa. The arrival of another division of American troops provided some hope that the Japanese advance would not extend into Australia. The 43rd Division was only the fourth U.S. Army division present in the Southwest Pacific. The 41st Division was training and on defensive duty in Queensland in the northeast of Australia; the 32nd Division had just joined the Kokoda Trail fight in New Guinea; and the Americal Division was guarding New Caledonia, a likely target of a further southeasterly Japanese advance. In addition, two marine divisions (1st and 2nd) were very busy on Guadalcanal. These few American divisions were spread thinly over a huge geographic area.

OCT. 27, 1942
Dearest Wife and Children — It is after four in the afternoon. The wind is blowing in the pines outside and I am sitting in my canvas chair in a hut about three times as large as a cot. We are pretty well settled to a routine now and it is nice to be on land in the spring. Such a spring! March weather in October. Many flowers are blooming and there are a lot of strange plants, some palms and some gigantic ferns. We saw a bit of the country, don't you know, since the camp is away from our first stop. Many things here are different. Handkerchiefs are not available, matches are scarce thereby causing the smokers worry, razor blades are not so plentiful either. I'm glad my supply is good.

My little radio is doing valiant duty on the news now. I haven't seen a newspaper for a month and don't expect to, but the radio still reaches [us]. I can't get batteries for it tho. Remember I told you I wanted one sent now and then. It's an Eveready "Minimax" 67-1/2 volts that I need. I haven't seen Jerome's friend yet, but I did visit a fellow chemist here. His name is not important but he teaches organic in the U.

here. He was a bit dazed when I walked in on him. That was before I took to the tall timber.... — Love & Hugs, XXXOOO Wilber

> Jerome Strauss was the chief research engineer of the Vanadium Corporation. He was Wilber's prime contact regarding his manganese patent. Jerome's "friend" was associated with Vanadium Corporation mining activities in New Caledonia. Was Wilber dropping hints about his location? Perhaps. He does reveal freely that he is in the southern hemisphere: springtime in October!

x·o·ø·o·x

NOV. 1, 1942

Dearest Norma and children — It's about time for me to report to my family again. It is a beautiful spring morning here with flowers in the grass, honeysuckle blooming in the thickets and birds singing in all the trees. In addition the sheep are thick on all the green hills. Except for the strange birds and trees, I could be looking out of the window of that little inn at the top of the hill near Burlington. I have just returned from communion service. The Priest could have been Father Nelson ten years ago. I wondered if Hale was also singing for an evening service at the same time....

I wonder how my family is fixed for the winter [in N.Y.C.]. Are you warm enough? What about winter coats? I hope it isn't too cold. I seem to miss all the winters. The last three have passed me by pretty lightly and I dodged this last one completely. I'll probably be discharged in a Maine midwinter. I'm very pleased about Valerie's teeth. It's good to know she is working on them. I've been doing a lot of walking and hill climbing to keep myself hard. Also I am thinking of all of you and looking forward to the days when we can be together again. I am feeling fine and love you all very, very much. I'm glad you have "round and rounds" for me. — XXXOOO Wilber

> We were getting ready for our second full winter in New York. Trucks delivering coal to apartment buildings were a common sight. Deliverymen would carry large canvas baskets of coal on their backs from the trucks into the buildings, or chutes would deliver the coal directly from the truck into a basement window. Other trucks would pick up barrels of ashes set on the sidewalks. It was a noisy, dirty business.

CHAPTER 14   *I'm wearing the St. Christopher medal*

x · o · ø · o · x

NOV. 10, 1942
Merry Christmas Darling [Norma] — It seems that I'll have to tell you about your presents so you can rewrap them for the tree. I mailed them all yesterday in one very small package, insured for $50.00 but not by airmail. This was my only chance to go to town, and the choice was poor. You of course can re-allot them as you think best.

Item #1. A piece of kauri gum [a resin] with leaves inside it for Hale, price 37 shillings. It is brittle and probably worth very little except as a novelty piece. This is a gum of the kauri tree, which is reported to grow to be 2000 years old. The gum is now dug out of the ground and polished as an ornament. It is brittle and would break easily.

> I carried that hard, yellowish translucent "gum" in my pants pocket for a long time. It was about an inch across and almost like a piece of glass, and one could see a bit of leaf or twig embedded within it.

Item #2. A second piece of kauri gum, unpolished for Father. He will know as much about where it came from as you. Please re-mail.

Item #3. A bar pin of native greenstone and sterling for Valerie. This stone is a marcasite and is famous here because the native Maori used it as ornaments. Costs of greenstone ornaments vary with the quality of the stone and the workmanship, whether by native tools or commercial tools. This is commercial. Cost 1 pound.

Item #4. A native piece of greenstone of fair quality made by native tools by (?) natives. It was worn as an ear pendant by the natives; [it] is strictly local to this place. The name of this stone is Kawakawa which is Maori for "color of green leaves." Please consider it as being hung about your neck on a chain or ribbon. All for Nana if you like it. Do not open the box until X-mas because it is especially for you. I love you. Merry X-mas to all of you.

Nov. 10, 1942 — Letter #2 for today, I didn't finish about the presents. Your special gift is in a little purple box and the stone is "Black" from Lightning Ridge, Aus[tralia]. It reminded me of the flecks deep in your eyes when the sun is shining.... — XXXOOO Wilber

> Wilber's thoughtfulness in finding, sending, and explaining the gifts was touching. The Maori references strongly suggested New Zealand. So much for censorship!

x · o · ø · o · x

NOV. 14, 1942

Dearest Nana and family — Today is nearly past and I am sitting in my canvas chair with my feet on my table (an ammunition box) with my overcoat on. The day has been very pleasant but the nights certainly do cool off. Today is also Christmas for me. A grand box of candy came today. I read the card from Nana, Valerie & Hale and decided it was too long to X-mas. Besides, where I am going the ants or some other insect may be a pest. So I am still munching. Thank all of you so much. It is hard to get candy here and this is wonderful.

I now wear a knife (stiletto type) just in case. The scabbard straps on my left arm below the elbow inside my sleeve. I had the knife made just in case things get close. Wouldn't E.O.H. [President Holland of Washington State College] be shocked if he knew I wore a knife up my sleeve and a pistol in an inside shoulder holster. I told the staff that my idea of "Defense in depth" was to use my driver's rifle while the Japs were 200–500 yds away, shift to my Tommie gun when they get to 100 yds, drop it for the pistol at 25 yards and use the knife from then on. "How big your teeth are Grandma"….

> Wilber's morbid humor was more than a little chilling; but it probably did provide a release from—or at least avoidance of—the actual implications. "Grandma" was a reference to the fairy tale, "Little Red Riding Hood."

Aren't you thrilled about the [Allied] progress in Africa [after the Nov. 8 landings]….

Nov. 15. I have just returned from communion. It seemed odd to hear the priest who lives here pray for Roosevelt. I thought of each of you all thru the service and prayed God to keep you safe. — I love you all. Wilber E. Bradt

x · o · ø · o · x

NOV. 19, 1942

Dearest Nana — Your fine box of candy is rapidly disappearing. All of us have enjoyed it so much. Thank you all again…. I'm wearing the St. Christopher medal. Will you please write to Mrs. Estes [in Bangor, Maine] and thank her. I feel so cared for by all of your love and prayers and those of your friends. I am remembering Monte [Bourjaily] and Gladys & Joe [Gingold] too. Speaking of friends I'm planning to go up to see Jerome's friend next week. Hope he'll be there for I haven't written ahead….

> This was a definite hint that he was going to New Caledonia, which I find rather shameful given the regulations forbidding such communications.

CHAPTER 14   *I'm wearing the St. Christopher medal*

This voyage would be beyond Japanese air attack range, but not beyond submarine range. Here, as well, there was the first mention of Monte in Wilber's extant letters, and it was a warm reference. He had met him on leave to New York the previous May.

I love your letters Darling. They are so cheery and such a help. I read and re-read each one. Your little daughter is a good writer too. Her letter thanking me for the bracelet was so neat and clear that I thought it was wonderful. I should write oftener but I am pretty busy. Much of my routine work is being delegated now to junior officers so my own work is much more pleasant. I love all of you. — Wilber

x·o·ø·o·x

Five days later, Wilber was on board the USS American Legion in Auckland, preparing to sail for New Caledonia. He wrote a quick note to Norma before the departure.

NOV. 24, 1942 [V-MAIL]
Lover of Mine — Day before yesterday I received three letters from you. You told me about your playing [piano] for the class [at her teacher's studio]. I am so glad you were pleased. You know I would have been sure you were the finest anyway. I don't have your letters here as my orderly put my rubber case where I keep them into my trunk, which is stored in the hold. I'll answer them in detail when I can. I am really thrilled about your playing. You really are doing things are you not? I have had no chance to tell our G-2 [divisional intelligence officer] yet of your commendation [from the FBI] but I intend to do it....

I haven't much more time if I want to mail this now. I love you and Hale + Valeric. Your letters are all so helpful. Please have a Happy Happy Birthday and you know I love you. Consider yourself spanked and spanked by your loving — Wilber

"Spanked"? He was asking us, light-heartedly, to be as well behaved for Norma as we would be if he were constantly with us.

The 43rd Division was ready to begin its first assignment in the war against the Japanese, the defense of New Caledonia. Japanese landings there would threaten the shipping routes between America and Australia. The threat was minimal, but everyone remembered Pearl Harbor and Singapore!

The Allied invasion of North Africa (Operation Torch) on the Atlantic and western Mediterranean coasts (in French Morocco and Algeria) began on November 8, 1942, and good progress was made against initially negligible resistance. Rommel's battle-weary troops were far to the east, and the local French Nazi collaborators ("Vichy French") did not contest the Allied landings. This first flush of victory was not to last long because large numbers of German troops and aircraft were pouring into Tunisia.

On November 19 and 20, the Russians attacked the flanks of the German lines at Stalingrad and, by November 23, had encircled the German Sixth Army. It would be almost three months before the trapped troops surrendered to the Soviets.

The American marines with elements of the Americal Division were beginning to expand their control beyond the Henderson Field area on Guadalcanal, and another American airfield there was under construction. The Japanese were suffering from a lack of supplies. With the arrival of the 43rd Division in New Caledonia, the Americal Division could be totally committed to Guadalcanal.

On November 30, the naval battle of Tassafaronga, off Guadalcanal, was a disaster for the American fleet; one cruiser was lost and several others badly damaged.

15

"The natives here hunt with sling-shots"

Ouenghi River, New Caledonia
NOVEMBER–DECEMBER, 1942

The convoy carrying a large contingent of the 43rd Division sailed from Auckland on November 24 for the three-day voyage to Nouméa, New Caledonia. It carried Wilber's battalion, less Battery B. Shipping resources, in great demand, were not available to transfer this and other elements of the 43rd Division until the end of December. Underway on board the venerable (built in 1919) ship, the USS American Legion, Wilber wrote to ten-year-old Valerie. He seemed to write separately to her at watershed moments in his activities. Here he described a little drama about an Italian soldier and his wife.

NOV. 25, 1942 [V-MAIL]
Dearest Daughter Valerie — How is my Tumblebug? I hope that sore throat is all gone by this time. I have two of your letters now. I saved the one you wrote before I went away. It has yellow ducklings on the top of the page. I'm glad you really are enjoying your school. It is much easier to learn if you are with friends.

I notice one of your friends is Anita who is Italian. I have an Italian friend here too. Before we sailed [from California], his new wife called him on the phone. He was in California and she was in Cleveland [Ohio]. She wanted to know if she could come see him and he couldn't tell her he was leaving in two days [due to army regulations]. So she told him she was coming out to Calif. to see what was wrong. He couldn't keep her from starting. Major DeBlois' wife sent her a telegram not to come, and after we had sailed I told him about it. He was feeling pretty bad that she would come and not find him, so he was pretty happy about our sending the

USS American Legion, AP-35 (later APA-17) operated by the Naval Transportation Service (NTS), which carried most of Wilber's battalion to New Caledonia from New Zealand in November 1942. It had previously carried marines to the August 7, 1942 landings on Guadalcanal. It was another venerable ship in the navy's service, built in 1919.
[PHOTO: NAVSOURCE ONLINE, U.S. NAVY HISTORICAL CENTER, NEW HAMPSHIRE, 92699]

wire. Just last week he had a letter from his wife asking who sent the wire. He says everything is OK now.

In a later letter, Wilber explained that the telegram to "Mrs. Italian" was signed with "Mr. Italian's" name, which caused much puzzlement. The officers could not divulge the imminent departure, but apparently, Mrs. DeBlois's telegram was sufficiently emphatic to prevent the wife's departure for California.

That pen of yours does work well. I like your letters very much. Please write + tell me your grades in school.... The people here [New Zealand] think the U.S. is wonderful because our government is so efficient and because of Gen. MacArthur. — I love you Darling. XXXOOO Wilber

x·o·ø·o·x

In this letter to Norma, Wilber clearly evoked the ambiance of being on a ship at sea in the evening in risky submarine waters.

NOV. 26, 1942 [V-MAIL]
Dearest Nana — Today is Thanksgiving and I have so much to be thankful for: My Boy, My Girl, My Sweet Nana, my own continued good health and good fortune. Soon I will have behind me two of the years away from you....

This letter is being written at 10:30 P.M. and in the dining room. Outside I hear the hum of the motors, the dull rumble of the ship's propellers and feel the roll of the ship. The wind is blowing outside. The full moon is covered, thank goodness, by clouds and rain. Our escort is busily covering us against submarines.

> The ships are less vulnerable to attack when not illuminated by moonlight.

We have been enjoying the very active belittling of the navy by the marines and vice versa. One sailor said the only reason the marines were winning on the "Canal" [Guadalcanal] was because the Japs were all worn out chasing the marines around and around the island. The marines say the Jap navy is always defeated by our navy because they get confused and sink their own ships. They both like the Army because they [we] listen well.

We are enjoying our rest again. There is nothing so restful as being on a voyage as a guest of Uncle Sam. I wish you were here too. You would love it and I would love you. For your hand in mine 50 minutes I'd give $30.00 (all I have). Here are a kiss and a hug and let's go for a nap, Lover of Mine. Happy Thanksgiving to Hale and Valerie too. — XXXOOO Wilber

x · o · ø · o · x

> The convoy arrived at Nouméa, New Caledonia, on November 27 (Map 6). This was the home harbor for the U.S. fighting ships that were participating in the Guadalcanal battles. Many were there including the cruisers that would be lost or damaged several nights later in the Battle of Tassafaronga. Nouméa was the focus of support, supply, and personnel for the Guadalcanal battle. Supplies were piling into the port much faster than they could be handled. Every aspect of the tasks there required herculean effort; crisis followed crisis. If the Japanese prevailed at Guadalcanal, or maybe even if they did not, New Caledonia was vulnerable. The aroma of war was pervasive.

NOV. 28, 1982 [V-MAIL]

Beloved Wife — This voyage is over. We are in a lovely tropic harbor [Nouméa, New Caledonia].

It is nearly completely surrounded by coral reefs and is dotted by islands. One was about 200 yards across, was oval shaped, has sandy beaches around it and was covered by palm trees. The water over the coral reefs is green like at L[ake] Louise while the other is deep blue. Ashore are hills and mountains with a little town of red roofs. I can see one church and what is probably a smelter. An occasional road leads vaguely into the interior.

CITIZEN SOLDIER   PART 1II: VOYAGES TO WAR

I cannot tell you what is in the harbor in addition to our convoy but it is the most thrilling sight I have ever seen.

It is hot here but no worse than where you were last August [in Hattiesburg]....

Dearest. I am holding [my arms] out to you. As soon as I can, I'll take you in them so tenderly, so closely and with such love you will never escape them. It's good to have arrived safely so I can still plan to hold you in my arms. — Wilber

x·o·ø·o·x

NOV. 28, 1942 [V-MAIL; SECOND OF TWO LETTERS THIS DATE]

Hello Norma — Surprise! Two letters from me today. I'm still on the ship according to the SOP [Standard Operating Procedure] of hurry up and wait. We are now at the second phase. I don't mind for I'm in undershirt and shorts on my berth [bunk] with a big electric fan doing its stuff on me. It's too hot to make love and besides you're not here so I'm just writing to you.

One of the harbors at Nouméa, New Caledonia, June 1942, early in its life as a U.S. naval base. The harbor to the left is Anse du Tir, where U.S. warships came for repairs during the Guadalcanal battles. The outer harbor in the mid and far distance would have accommodated many anchored ships. Wilber described boat rides among them [letters 1/1/43, 2/14/43]. The smoky "nickel works" are in the mid-distance to the right. [PHOTO: U.S. ARMY SIGNAL CORPS, SC 163692, CROPPED, COURTESY OF THE VILLE DE NOUMÉA, SERVICE DE LA CULTURE ET DES FÊTES]

Us [sic] field officers rate cabins that college profs could never afford. In this one are four majors and one is a division staff officer, another an engineer officer, the third is René DeBlois + the fourth is WEB [Wilber]. The division S.O. [Supply Officer] became very excited because I wasn't a CWS [chemical warfare service] officer on the staff. I told him I had made my choice [of field artillery] some time ago. He persisted and pointed out I would be a [promoted to] Lt. Col. I finally told him it was worth more to me to go into combat with real friends beside me then to be in the staff competing for promotions the way they did. That sounded pretty convincing for the next day he was commenting on the advantages of being assigned to troops....

Did I tell you that one of our officers is being recommended posthumously for a decoration. You didn't know Capt. ___ [Euart, lost on the SS Coolidge] but he was one of our very best officers and died as he lived. Love — XXXOOO Wilber

> Wilber had developed a pretty clear sense of why he had turned down an appointment in the chemical warfare service. He apparently had made the supply officer rethink his own priorities.
> Euart was awarded the Distinguish Service Cross posthumously. His loss was the first death close to Wilber in his war experience. He tended to drop such news nonchalantly, at the end of the letter, as if it did not really matter much.

x·o·ø·o·x

New Caledonia is a long slender island about 250 miles long and 30 miles wide (Map 6). It lies about a thousand miles east of northeastern Australia (Queensland) and is still a French possession. The 43rd Division, minus the 172nd Regimental Combat Team, was assigned to defend against possible Japanese landing sites northwest of Nouméa. Wilber's unit, the 169th Field Artillery Battalion, was located along the Ouenghi River flanking Highway #1, about 40 miles northwest of Nouméa on the southwest coast. Its sector included the air base at Tontouta [Barker, p. 27]. The divisional artillery headquarters was at Bouloupari (known locally as Boulouparis), ten miles to the northwest; the 152nd Field Artillery Battalion was even farther northwest, "near La Foa" [Barker, p. 27]. The 192nd Field Artillery Battalion with its large 155-mm howitzers would not arrive in New Caledonia until December 29; it would be positioned at Bouloupari. The 103rd Field Artillery Battalion, which had been on the SS Coolidge, was still in the New Hebrides. The two regimental combat teams on New Caledonia immediately went into defensive positions. Surprise Japanese attacks were still on everyone's mind. This mission would extend until mid-February.

The November 30 arrival of the 169th Field Artillery Battalion at the Ouenghi River was recorded in Wilber's "journal," a five-page list of dates of departures and arrivals, and miscellaneous events and data, such as the serial number of his pistol, the name of a ship he was on, the general order number that announced a medal he received, and so on. The journal listings were not strictly chronological; he would sometimes enter data after the fact. The pages were in a compact (6-inch by 9.5-inch) heavy, leather-bound, loose-leaf, seven-ring binder with the University of Maine seal embossed on the front cover. It was indestructible and, with seven rings, the pages would not easily tear out. It contained several other sections such as genealogical notes, chemistry notes, and 20 pages of typed names and addresses.

That indestructible notebook always seemed to be around my parents' various homes after the war. In the mid-1970s in their New Jersey home, while on a visit from Cambridge, I noticed it yet again, this time on a table beside a stairwell at the edge of the living room. Fearful that those valuable five pages of journal entries would be lost, I quietly removed them for my files. I don't think at that point Norma or any other family member placed any value on them nor would they have noticed their absence. I see this now as a poor justification!

In that same home, also in the mid-1970s, there was a large cardboard box of photographs taken by Wilber in the 1920s and 1930s. They were a priceless history of our family. The box had survived many of my parents' moves and now it lay neglected in the bottom of a third floor closet in their New Jersey home. I confess here that I also raided this without announcement, but with a modicum of responsibility: I took only the negatives and none of the prints. Sadly, in the move to Florida in 1979, that entire box was lost. I later made prints from the negatives that I shared with family. I still have those negatives and recently scanned them into my computer. Some of them are reproduced in this book. The journal and those photographs significantly enrich Wilber and Norma's story.

x · o · ø · o · x

Life on New Caledonia for the many thousands of U.S. troops of the 43rd Division was a new experience. I was as curious about the non-combat

CHAPTER 15 *The natives here hunt with sling-shots*

> WEB
>
> 145th Inf Aug. 6, 1943
> 8. WEB in Baanga I. direct support of 169th Inf. and 172d Inf. from Aug 11 to Aug. , 1943
> 9. WEB in Arundel I. direct support of 172d and 27th Inf. from Sept. 13 to Sept. 22, 1943.
> 10. 169th FABn was in Direct support of:
>   a) 169th Inf. from July 7 to July 20, 1943
>   b) 145th Inf. from July 20 to Aug. 6, 1943
>   c) 148th Inf. from July 20 to July 28, 1943
>   d) 169th Inf. in Baanga I. fr. Aug 11 to Aug 18, '43
>   e) 172d Inf. " " fr. Aug 16, to Aug. '43
>   f) 172d Inf. in Arundel I. fr. Sept 11, 1943 to 22 Sept/'43
>   g) 27th Inf. " " fr. Sept. 15, 1943 to Sept 22, '43
>   h) 161st Inf. (no combat) fr. Sept. 30 to Oct. 15, '43
> 11. WB Inducted as Capt Feb 24, 1941 Bangor, Me. Regs S-3
>   Moved (Arr) to Camp Blanding, Fla. 20 Mar, 1941 (±2) S-3, 152 FA
>   Arr Camp Shelby ca 10 Feb. 1943. Reg Exec 152d FA.
>   Trfd as Major to 169th FABn as Exec. 19 Feb 1943
>   Arr. Fort Ord. 0200 Sept. 7, 1942.
>   10/1/42 Sailed fr. S.F., Cal. 1145 Mar. on USAT "Maui."
>   Oct '42 Arr Auckland, N.Z. Oct. 22, 1943. Disembarked Oct 24, 1943
>   1942 { Arr. Warkworth, N.Z. 24 Oct. 1943 at Wynyards Camp.
>   HB { Embarked at Auckland Nov. 23, 1943 on USS "American Legion". (NPS)
>   { Sailed 24 Nov. 1942 and Arr Noumea Harbor Nov 27, 1943.
>   (Arr on Ouengi River Nov. 30, 1943 near Boulapari, N. Cal.
>   Left Noumea on USS "President Adams" 0530 Feb. 15, 1943
>   Attacked by 8 Jap planes at "Torpedo Junction" near Malaita Feb. 17, '43
>   Arr Guadalcanal on Feb 18; left Guadalcanal on "Sau Fley" Feb. 22.
>   Arr. Pavuvu I, R.I. Feb. 23, 1944.

A page of Wilber's journal written in 1943 after the Solomon actions. He recorded highlights of those actions in the upper half and some of his earlier history in the lower half where he occasionally mistakenly wrote 1943 for 1942 or 1941. The smudged ink corrections in the lower third are erroneous corrections by Norma. The pencil marks in the left margin are mine, to restore correct dates. I overlooked the last entry (arrival in the Russell Islands), which should be 1943, not 1944.

219

periods as about the combat itself. What kept the army functioning, and in particular what occupied Wilber's mind and body? It appeared that he was quick to acquaint himself with the local natural scene.

Wilber attempted to write his parents on the 28th, but was interrupted by the move to the unit's positions on the Ouenghi River. When he was settled in, he offered a description of the scene at his new home.

NOV. 28, 1942

Dear Father and Mother — Payday is just around the corner and – (resumed Dec. l). Payday came but no pay yet so I'll hold this letter until I can insert a Money Order. I am sitting on my bedroll inside a mosquito net and the net is justified. Around me are trees typical only of this island so the name must be omitted. Across a stream is a coffee and banana plantation, and a mountain range is beyond my front yard. Behind me but not visible is a very nice river of clean water, and a mile away is the ocean. Cocoanuts are ripe now and to be had for a song or a little effort. All in all it's hard to believe this is [that I am in] a tropic setting. It is quiet and beautiful and lovely in every way. The rainy season is due but has not yet arrived. Deer are plentiful and one of our Captains recently ate a steak from a sea-cow [possibly a manatee]. He said it was really good.

Dec. 2nd — It is a good day again…. There are so many mosquitos that I must stop.… — Love, Wilber

x·o·ø·o·x

DEC. 3, 1942 [V-MAIL]

Dear Hale, Valerie and Nana — Today my Christmas came. Santa came right thru the tent roof. He said he was pretty early because some people in the States were so concerned about him getting here on time. His clothes looked a bit funny. He wore a mosquito net over his face and a sun helmet and the sweat was just dripping off his face. I was sure glad to see him. He said the reason the box was busted was because some soldier jumped up + down on it a few times to get it in his sleigh. Oh! Oh! I mean his canoe.

And such wonderful presents. They weren't damaged at all. The two waterproof carriers will be just what I need here. The rainy season is supposed to come in Dec. I'll keep your letters in the little one and get in the bigger one myself on especially wet days. The tooth powder looks good but I haven't tasted it yet. I'll be sure to wash my teeth every day. The writing folder is on my trunk here and I'll use it for the letters I put things into. The slippers were just what I need for bathing for I bathe in

CHAPTER 15   *The natives here hunt with sling-shots*

Officers bathing naked in Ouenghi River, New Caledonia, January 1943. [PHOTO: CHARLES D'AVANZO]

a river near here. The radio battery is just in time. My old one is too weak to reach any stations now and there aren't any newspapers so I hope the radio works.

It was a wonderful Christmas. Thank you all. I love you all. I hope you don't mind my opening the box now. I couldn't wait. I haven't gotten any letters for a long time so maybe I'll have a lot soon. — XXXOOO Wilber E. Bradt

> It was likely that transportation was the reason for the lack of mail; they had been in New Caledonia only a week. On the other hand, Santa did arrive!

x·o·ø·o·x

> Wilber was inspired to write Valerie with a creative and touching story about bluebirds, a bird that had long been her favorite. He was really connecting to Valerie in this letter and did so by sharing events in his life with her.

Dec. 5, 1942 [V Mail]

Hello Tumblebug [Valerie] — I bet you didn't expect a letter from me today. I wonder what day of the week it is when you get it. I'll guess it comes on Wed. Dec. 30. You see if I am good at guessing.

This is the next day now [Dec. 6]. The rain has stopped and the sky is all full of white fleecy clouds. Some of them are so low they are only halfway up the mountains. They wander around between the mountains like they were too tired to climb up in the sky where they belong.

There is a bird here that sings a note like he was whistling "whew." He starts very fast and sings "whew whew whew" for about ten times and sings wheew, whe-e-e-w and about the 30th time he sounds all out of breath and sings wh—e—e—w. Some ducks came up the river this morning and quacked at each other and me. Yesterday two bluebirds stopped and spoke to me. They said a cousin of theirs used to fly up from the South Pacific Islands each spring to see a little girl named Valerie in Washington [State].

Now the cousins had just come back and said she didn't live there any more. I told them to advise their cousins to stop in N.Y. next spring and to tell Valerie her Daddy had seen them and that he loved her very much. Merry Christmas. I loved the presents. — Wilber.

I used the slippers yesterday in the river. They are great. I'm saving the coffee. Thanks. I love it too.

x·o·ø·o·x

Meanwhile, back in New York, Valerie and I were still in our lower-Manhattan schools, which were within walking distance of our West 4th Street apartment, and I continued my violin lessons with Mrs. Zacharias on 71st Street. In this school essay, I described our visit to the Rembert Wurlitzer Company on 42nd Street, the preeminent New York violin dealership and repair shop at that time. Mrs. Zacharias knew it well.

Dec. 9, 1942
Buying a Violin

Last Saturday my mother and I went to the Wurlitzer Company. Here we met my violin teacher. Mr. Wurlitzer picked out two violins. Then my teacher tried them out, and decided which one was best. She had a new chin-rest put on it, and had the bridge reshaped.

I received $10.00 on my old violin, and paid ten more for the new one. The old one is a 3/4 size, and the new one is a full size. It was made in Czechoslovakia in 1935.

CHAPTER 15   *The natives here hunt with sling-shots*

x·o·ø·o·x

DEC. 10, 1942
Dearest Nana — I have just received five letters, two from Oct. 5 and 6 and three dated Nov. __, __, and 16th.

Yesterday I went down to the town [probably Bouloupari]. It was interesting to see all the people in different dress. Some blacks, some browns, some yellow, and some white. The native black takes off his hat as we pass. Some are labor soldiers and wear fragments of uniforms. They salute with a maximum of pride. We get some salutes from very surprising individuals.

We encountered a white surveyor in connection with getting some clothes washed. The survey business is a little quiet now. My "Bon jour! Monsieur" was so successful that he exclaimed in French, "Oh you speak French." I was however a bit embarrassed because my vocabulary was about exhausted and certainly not up on laundry details. One of our officers was a bit pleased when a native said of him in French, "This one is apparently better educated than the others."

I've been looking for a sarong for you but the movies have exaggerated their quality. I'd like to see you without one anyway. I love you Dear. I'll write more later. Tell the 2 cubs Hello. — Wilber

> The movies portrayed South Pacific islands as idyllic paradises with beautiful young women wearing large colorful fabrics (sarongs) as a lower garment (skirt), with, of course, a minimal upper garment.

x·o·ø·o·x

> We gained insight into the ongoing military activities with this humorous description of an inspection by the divisional artillery commander (Barker) and his executive officer (Files), the former commander of Wilber's unit.

DEC. 12, 1942
Dearest, Dearest, Dearest Nana — Again I'm beside my river talking to my Darling wife. The tide is out and the river is a bit reduced. A bird about the size of a pigeon with yellow feet, a black head and a robin's red breast and a white tail is scolding me. He sounds like a washing machine that needed oil when he scolds. Then he stops and asks a question "Wu-Wu-Wu-Wu-Wu." This is a bird's paradise. I have never seen more anywhere. They wake me every morning.

Train taking New Caledonians to church, late 1942 or early 1943. [PHOTO: CHARLES D'AVANZO]

Today we were inspected by "Harold" [General Barker] and "Chester" [Colonel Files]. It was very comprehensive but not as thorough as the one I do nearly daily on sanitation so they couldn't find anything to criticize. "Chester" tried, but he didn't have much hope because he asked me how things would be. I answered we were coming along but very slowly. He asked what things were slow. I said "Well, you will be able to see during the inspection what I mean." He said "I probably won't see half as much as you that's wrong." He didn't. This inspection business is about 50% getting things the way you consider perfect, then 50% making sure the things the inspector looks for are the way he will think are perfect. It is a good system for inspections but I don't think it will work in battle. When I get home you will probably throw me out of your kitchen because I inquire about your methods. I'd approve your kitchen tho. I'll try not to bring back any obnoxious habits or mannerisms.

Tomorrow is Sunday and I think I'll go up into the mountains to see some of the geology....

[Dec. 13] — The army has just issued me 3 cartons of cigarettes, 1 soap, 1 toothbrush, 12 boxes matches, 1 pkg Dentyne gum and 1 pkg razor blades. The idea seems to be that I smoke more than I bathe.... There is so much happening here that I cannot write [about] that it is hard to do a good letter.... Happy New Year to you, to Valerie and to Hale. — Wilber

> Wilber was not a smoker! The unmentioned happenings were the placement and registration of the howitzers and the establishment of the

division's defensive plan. Possible air attacks and saboteurs mandated complete blackouts (no lights showing) [169th FA Journal].

x · o · ø · o · x

> In this poetic letter to Norma, we find a riverside concert scene vividly portrayed and a melding of the river scene with some explicit sexuality.

DEC. 16, 1942
Hello There Nana! — I'm sitting pretty. An airmail letter of yours left NYC Nov. 21 and I received it Dec. 13. Furthermore it was a direct answer of mine of Nov. 6. That is doing good business, isn't it? …

> He was impressed with a five-week turnaround! Can people today even imagine taking part in communications with delays of weeks? This was far from the world of texting and Skype.

Last night we had the band down for a concert for the men. They played on my river bank and half the men were on one side of the river and the other half on the other side. About five minutes after the concert started, out of the bushes came five natives. They were fascinated by the music and waded nearly across the river until they were just opposite the band. Two were perfect physical specimens. They are brown to black. The other three could probably outwork any man in our outfit. All wore cloths wrapped around their hair. These are blue or white or red patterned cloth. They were barefooted and wore short trousers or the equivalent. One wore what looked like some of your honeymoon type step-ins. They looked quite comfortable and probably would have hypnotized the feminine friends. One wore a loose flowing waist length kimono type shirt of large blue flowers on a white background. Another wore almost skin-tight shorts of a red and white pattern. Before the concert was over about 20 had collected. As it got dark they faded into the shadows until only a white (relatively only) garment or the glint of the car lights in their eyes showed. You would have been thrilled. They were all gone as soon as the music stopped.

Most of these natives are Polynesians and Melanesians. Some are Japanese. The last are frequently indentured laborers who are under contract to work here 5 or 10 years. Some are now very upset because their time is up but the war prevents their being returned to their village.…

It is getting dark by my river. The clouds are low on the mountains and the wind is sighing thru the pines (only they are not pines). It all says Nana! Nana! My Love! You are my jewel, my pearl without price. I'm thinking of you. I'll hold my Dream Girl close tonight and kiss behind those pink ears. Also I'll play with the beautiful soft breasts and the little tips that press against my chest. I'll caress the sweet curves of your thighs and the wooded mountains between. I'll enter your gates of love and push your lips apart until you are my own again. Some time I won't need to dream for I'll have you in my arms. — Wilber

x·o·ø·o·x

The next day, his letter was more family oriented; the salutation included Valerie and me, as well as Norma. Many aspects of life in New Caledonia were covered here. He was in a playful mood.

DEC. 17, 1942
Darling Nana & Children — This is another quiet afternoon and I'm again sitting by my river talking to you. This paper you sent me, Hale, is fine. It is much nicer than I can buy here. It is very easy to write on and I appreciate it a lot.…

If you were here … I could take you all swimming too. Which would you prefer the ocean or the river? You can have your choice, but in the ocean a barracuda or shark would probably take an arm or leg off you.

The natives here hunt with sling-shots. That would be good for breaking windows in N.Y.C. if there were any pebbles in the streets there. Are you interested in hunting for gold in the mountains? We could do that if you aren't too busy on New Year's Day. But then I expect you won't have time, so we could go deer hunting instead. If you see a deer, and you will see several, do you really think you would shoot it? I didn't the other day and I doubt if you will either. We could all take a sun bath, and it wouldn't take long either to get sun-burned – maybe 15 minutes.

It would be fun to go talk French too with some of the French people here. They talk very good French because many of their grandparents were prisoners sent here from Paris because they revolted against the government. Many were well educated. Others were jail birds, thieves, murderers and criminals of the worst kind. So now we aren't sure just which kind we will talk to, but they have all kinds here. A lot of them married native brown and black people so some are tanned white persons, some are pale brown, while others are pretty brown or black … If you want to go to the movies, don't go for there aren't any.

So we will stay home and Valerie will say "Oh dear. I wish I had something to do." So I'll say "OK. You bake a cake for me." And while you are baking a cake, Hale & I will get some cocoanuts for the top. We will make marks in the icing by letting my little brown lizard run around the top. He makes tracks.…

Another time some artillery were firing on some targets in the bay. Of course the bursting shells killed a lot of fish. Right in the middle of the firing, a dugout [canoe] with 2 men in it paddled out from behind a near island to where the shells were falling. We stopped firing and these 2 dopes picked up a lot of fish [that had been killed by the artillery] and rowed back. We fired for another hour and back they came again, so we stopped while they made their harvest of fish. This happened 3 times and each time we stopped. They would probably have been surprised to know just how mad we were. They probably thought we were doing it just for them. I don't know yet how they decided just when to row out....

This will be the first Christmas I ever spent swatting mosquitos. I love each of you. Let us all try to make the Bradt family a better family in 1943. I'm going to try as hard as I can to be a good Dad and Husband. I love you.   Happy New Year. Wilber

> It seemed to me that he was being as good a "Dad and Husband" as was possible given his situation. He also had to maintain the morale and combat readiness of his troops in their static assignment on the Ouenghi River.

As Christmas approached, fighting continued to rage in Eastern New Guinea as the Allies advanced on Buna. American troops were on the offensive in Guadalcanal hoping to eject the Japanese entirely from the island, but were encountering strong Japanese resistance. In North Africa also, Americans and British were on the offensive in Tunisia, but the Americans had yet to face a forthcoming German counter offensive. In Russia, the German Army had not been able to break through to its encircled Sixth Army at Stalingrad. The war was progressing in favorable directions for the Allies, but not without cost.

16

"So ended Christmas Eve with everyone pretty happy"

Ouenghi River, New Caledonia
December 1942–January, 1943

The Bradt family spent Christmas in New York City. There was to be no repeat of the 1941 Christmas visit to Florida. I was thus able to responsibly fulfill my Christmas duties with Grace Church Choir.

On New Caledonia, the river flowed on while the men of the 43rd Division defended, trained, and waited their turn to enter combat. The monotony of rain-filled days affected morale.

DEC. 18, 1942
Lover Mine — Again it is afternoon, just after the rain, and I am beside my river thinking of you....

I'm bathed and in clean underwear, same uniform, same idea (I love you). The rain is over and I'm outside again but wearing a jacket because they [the mosquitos] can't bite thru. It's amazing how much less they bother me now than at first. Maybe I'm becoming immune to them. We bought a beef and will have steak tonight and wonder of wonders a Joe Penner [a 1930s comedian] movie after. Capt. Farrell has been out working on morale problems. We are taking pretty active steps in that direction. If we are here quite a while, the rain may get monotonous....

Tomorrow [Saturday] is an off day. We don't function on a Sunday basis now. It seems the Japs might expect us to go to church on Sunday.... — XXXOOO Wilber

CITIZEN SOLDIER   PART 1I1: VOYAGES TO WAR

The Japanese attack on Pearl Harbor was on a Sunday. On this Sunday, December 20, the battalion underwent a simulated enemy attack by land and air, which forced it to move to alternate positions. Firing exercises were frequent. They were training hard.

x·o·ø·o·x

Wilber sent off the monthly letter to his parents, including news about my school grades and a humorous bit about 11-year-old Valerie.

DEC. 24, 1942 (MAILED 12/29/42)
Dear Father and Mother — I won't be able to mail this today, but anyway today I am wishing you a very merry and happy Christmas....

Note here that Wilber included his mother in the salutation.

Hale and Valerie are each doing well in school. Hale bought a new violin (full size) and paid for it out of his own earnings. Norma writes that he is very happy about it. His grades were last month, Eng. 90, Crafts, 95, Latin 95, Math 93, Social Sci. 87. Teachers' comments are "Fine work and interest" "It's a pleasure to have Hale in Class" He has made Valerie a sewing kit, which says on it 'VEB Sewing Kit'. Valerie has proudly taken it to her school and is now making herself a skirt. She woke Norma the other morning to say at 6:30 she was getting up to study. At 6:40 she woke Norma and asked for her pillow. At 6:50 she woke her again to ask about the "services" of Pennsylvania (meaning surfaces on the map). At 7:00 she woke Norma again to say it was time to get up. ...

The educational progress of the younger Hale (me) and Valerie was of interest to both Wilber and the elder Hale; both were still teachers at heart.

I've been doing a little mountain climbing lately that Paul would like.... Must stop. Am OK. I wish again that tomorrow won't be quite as hot for you as it is for me this year. — Love, Wilber

Wilber's brother Paul had developed into a first-rate and widely recognized rock climber and cave explorer. Wilber himself was a hiker who liked to become well acquainted with the terrain, to keep in shape and to study the local geology.

x·o·ø·o·x

CHAPTER 16   *So ended Christmas Eve with everyone pretty happy*

In New York City, the Bourjaily and Bradt families had become mutually supporting; both had sent members off to war. This letter is from Terkman Bourjaily, Monte's mother, to Norma. Terkman lived in New York City. Apparently she and her daughter Alice, an army nurse, were spending Christmas with relatives elsewhere, probably Connecticut. Wilber had gone overseas to the Pacific the previous October. Terkman's grandson (Monte's middle son) Vance had left for the Middle East in November to be an ambulance driver with the American Field Service. Monte's other two sons (Monte, Jr., and Paul) were in New York for the holiday.

The Christmas Eve letter is neatly written and formatted and is quite coherent. The Lebanese Terkman's English was rather limited, and even weaker on the writing side. So the letter was likely written on her behalf by a younger relative. My sister Abigail found it in one of Norma's cookbooks decades later.

Dec. 24, 1942

Dear Norma — I was happy to hear from you, and to know that you, Valerie, and Hale are well. I'm really glad that my baby [Valerie] is well now and was sorry to hear she was ill. Thank you for the dollar for Wilber and Vance [who are overseas]. I will have candles lit for both of them on Sunday, and you can be sure there will be a prayer for them also.

Thank you for the candy. It really is delicious, and Alice and I are enjoying it very much.

I do believe you will be able to give me a bit of competition on Syrian cooking, at the rate you have been going – what with cooking for the Montes and Paul.

I'm glad you are all having dinner together tomorrow and that you will be eating out. I know you have earned a day of rest.

I am now going to write you the recipe for Yubruh with hummus and oil. Here goes ….

Alice joins me in sending love to you, Hale and Valerie. — Fondly, Mother Bourjaily

There was genuine warmth here between Terkman and Norma. Terkman even saw herself, in the closing, as "Mother" to Norma. Norma was getting significant emotional support from the Bourjaily family. In return, she was providing family support in the form of meals for the three Bourjaily men remaining in New York. Norma had little support from the Bradts or from her own distant Sparlin family.

Apparently, we Bradts joined the three Bourjaily men in New York for Christmas dinner out, though restaurant dining was not our usual life style. I have no recollection of any restaurant dinners, other than one at LaGuardia Airport with Norma and Valerie after putting someone on a plane.

x·o·ø·o·x

Christmas eve on New Caledonia was beautifully portrayed by Wilber in this Christmas day letter.

CHRISTMAS DAY, 1942, PACIFIC TROPICS

Dearest Beloved Sweet; And My Darling Daughter; And My Grand Boy — This is Daddy sending from his river on Christmas afternoon. Last night was a clear warm night full of moonlight and mosquitos. The general (B) [Barker] had his field officers over for cocktails. He had achieved the miraculous and had some ice. That was more pleasant than the scotch. It was a nice party, strictly stag, and was in a hut built of niaouli bark which is much like birch bark. After all the guests who knew their etiquette had gone except about six F.A. officers, we had dinner with B. It was the first time we had all (169th FA and 152nd FA) been together since Calif. It was a pretty pleasant dinner and if the other two units [103rd FA and 192nd FA] had been here, [it] would have been a reunion. After supper we sang carols and came home.

We were invited to a nuit [a "night" celebration] by one of the French families. The C.O. [commanding officer] went later, but the three of us [instead] returned to camp. At 11:00 P.M., the Episcopal Chaplain was down here for a mass. I thought of you and our masses in Wash[ington State] and Hale probably singing in one this Christmas [at Grace Church in New York]. Our Bn. C.O. is an Episcopalian. There are about 25 of us [Episcopalians] in the Bn. and our turn-out was 27. The Romans [Catholics] had a Mass at midnight. The boys had a tree decorated with flowers and white cotton. Everyone drank coffee at 1:00 A.M. around a big bonfire and told everyone else the masses were fine which was true, that the music was fine which was not true, that the moon was wonderful which was true, that the folks at home were probably having a white Christmas which was not true because your Christmas hadn't started yet. So ended Christmas Eve with everyone pretty happy and everyone having a prayer in his heart for his people back home.

Christmas day the sun came up over the mountain like thunder and shone on me. I opened one eye, gave Old Sol an insolent look and turned my back to him and went back to sleep. Two hours later I woke again, considered going to the latrine and went back to sleep. At ten [A.M.] I woke and read a Sat. E.P. [Evening Post]

CHAPTER 16 *So ended Christmas Eve with everyone pretty happy*

from cover to cover. The Thanksgiving number [issue] came late Christmas Eve. At noon I started on the Dec. Reader's Digest, which came the same time. At 1:00 P.M. I dressed, latrined, shaved and ate turkey. Good Old Unk. Sam. He sure feeds his army....

So you were a witch [in a school play?], were you Valerie. That must have been fun. When I get back I'll expect you to fly over our Bangor house on a broom. You will be pretty handy for repairing roofs won't you? I'll give you a few shingles and send you up to fix our roof while Hale & I work in the garden.... — XXXOOO Wilber – Mailing Time.

x · o · ø · o · x

Who is this General Barker mentioned so often by Wilber? Barker was the commander of the divisional artillery, which as noted consisted of four battalions with a total of 48 howitzers as well as antiaircraft and antitank guns. He served in World War I in France and was in the Rhode Island National Guard between the wars. He was a brigadier general and commander of the artillery brigade of the 43rd Division when it was called to active duty. When the division was triangularized in January 1942, he became the divisional artillery commander. He served in that position throughout the war and thus was never advanced from his one-star brigadier-general rank. He may have been the only national guardsman commanding divisional artillery in the entire U.S. Army. That no regular army officer was appointed to his position is a tribute to his effectiveness as an artillery commander. He may also have been the only such officer to publish a history of a divisional artillery in World War II (*History of the 43rd Division Artillery*). It is a technical book with maps, orders, lists of personnel, and a good narrative. It has been invaluable to me in placing Wilber's letters in context.

Barker was a dedicated commander and exacting in what he expected of his officers and men. He would use his temper and profanity to obtain the performance he wanted. He was fearless and would freely expose himself to perilous situations. He received several medals for valor and took up flying when artillery observing became possible from small piper cub planes. Wilber admired him very much and valued his approval. He described rather humorously, as we will see later, several instances of Barker's outbursts about real or imagined poor performance.

In the course of researching this story in 1981, I spent one bitterly cold winter afternoon in the unheated "Barker room" in the basement of the Benefit Street Armory in Providence, Rhode Island. It consisted of artifacts and papers from his service days and also a small thatched-roof hut similar to one created for his command post on one of the Pacific Islands. His portable army desk still held many of his papers and I found copies of battalion and divisional journals and even Wilber's fitness reports therein! In that bitter cold room for those few hours, I was transported to the warm South Pacific.

x · o · ø · o · x

Here, Wilber described a hike up the Ouenghi River with Capt. E. Russell Davis, Jr. on which he enjoyed using his schoolboy French.

DEC. 27, 1942
Dear Hale — Yesterday I went for a hike. You would have enjoyed it. Capt. Davis and I went by car about 7 miles up the river I camp on, then walked on up farther. It was a hot day and we didn't go very fast. We were on one side and there was a native trail on the other. So over we went [to the other side] jumping from one rock to the next or wading between the rocks. This is a swift river and almost as wide as the Penobscot but usually not deep.

When we got to the trail we met 5 natives. They grinned and I said "Bon jour boys." They expect to be called boy. They couldn't talk English. I asked them where the trail went and they said up the river. That didn't help much for it was pretty obvious. I asked them if it went "au votre maison." They answered "Oui!" but that didn't help much for if I had asked them if it went to New York they would still have said, "Oui!" I asked them the name of a mountain. It was Pie de St. Vincent. They said "non-vom."

After getting all that help we went on and left them squatting on the trail grinning and saluting. This trail wound around the hills and thru the trees climbing all the time. The river below us was noisy and sometimes white, sometimes blue. Usually the bed was full of big boulders about the size of a bushel basket. Occasionally there were sand beaches. All at once the trail did this [up] a hill or mountain. [sketch of upward zigzags.] You should have seen us. About noon we were over 1000 feet above the river. From one place we could look down at 13 zigzags in the trail. If we had jumped we could have jumped over 2 or 3 before stopping. When we got to the top, the trail did this [sketch of downward zigzags] to the river again. By this time we were completely surrounded by mountains and our canteens were only 2/3 full. One canteen a day is pretty dry days.

We stopped on the rocks, undressed, and bathed in the river. It wasn't over 3 feet deep but was swift and cool. Just when we were eating one of the Army cans of breakfast, along came the natives again and squatted down to watch us chew. We

CHAPTER 16 *So ended Christmas Eve with everyone pretty happy*

gave each one a piece of candy and one surprised me quite a bit by thanking me in German. After we had Au Revoired them several times they moved on; then one came back and asked for a cigarette. Capt. Davis gave him one so they all came back for a cigarette. They next had to stop for a fumée [smoke].

Finally they left, we dressed and went on up the river for a couple of more miles. The ferns were dry from heat and had turned silver color. Some rocks were green, some nearly pure white, many were brown and a few were black. We were far enough inland so we could see both coasts from the mountain top if we were there – which we weren't by exactly one mile straight up.

We decided to go back along the river instead of going [sketch of up *and* down zigzags] again. On the way back we crossed the river 5 times. In places it was in gorges between mountains and we had to crowd along the face of the cliffs. We were certainly tired when we got back to the car. I thought of you a lot of times and wished you could be along. — Happy New Year from Wilber E. Bradt

Sketches of zig-zag trail in Wilber's letter of December 27, 1942: up, down, and up-down.

The 43rd Division remained in a defensive posture on New Caledonia. At that time, late 1942, the division was under navy command, namely that of Admiral Halsey, then commander of the South Pacific Area (Map 2), which included the forces on New Caledonia and Guadalcanal. Halsey would go on to direct the drive further northwestward in the Solomons in which the 43rd would participate. Gen. Douglas MacArthur, commanding the South*west* Pacific Area, would direct the drive westward along the northern coast of New Guinea toward the Philippines. The two commands would mutually reinforce each other, coordinating landings as well as naval and air support.

x · o · ø · o · x

As Wilber entered 1943, after almost two years of active duty, he still had not seen combat and was still on the Ouenghi River. In this letter, he brought to life the ambiance of wartime Nouméa, the capital of New Caledonia and the Allied hub of the Pacific campaign. He and his battalion commander, Lt. Colonel Knight, seemingly used the arrival of their Battery B and their sister battalion, the 192nd FA, on the USS Tryon as an excuse to visit Nouméa. The Tryon dropped anchor at 3:30 p.m. in the outer harbor on December 29. The troops debarked the next day [192nd FA Journal].

JAN. 1, 1943
Happy New Year Norma, Valerie, & Hale — This is station WEB broadcasting from the Southern Pacific. Did you know the Commanding General is called the COM-GENSOPAC? He is doing OK too in spite of the heavy title.

That acronym is for Commanding General South Pacific. The holder of that title, Maj. Gen. Millard Harmon, was the senior army officer under Admiral Halsey. He wore two stars.

Day before yesterday [actually Dec. 29], Knight & I went to the town [Nouméa] intending to stay overnight on a ship in which some of our troops had a temporary lease [USS Tryon]. We spent about three hours shuttling back and forth between the two wharves from which liberty boats left. All the MPs and Shore Patrol know us well now. By 9:00 P.M. we were about starved and plenty disgusted. We decided next time we would have our own launch and yacht. Of course we had no real reason to complain for this ship was in the outer harbor and was outside the submarine net. Maybe the net was hot for no one wanted to go thru it.

Anyway at 9:00 P.M. we decided to look for quarters ashore. First we went to Le Grand Hotel de la ___ and were told we could have a room if the COMGENSOPAC had given us an order on one. Due to a serious oversight on his part he hadn't. We inquired about dinner. Answer. So Sorry. Sneer. So we went to Le Grande et Beau Hotel de la ___ . Same answer except some other general "owned" this one. The next then could have been called Le Miserable et Mal Hotel de la ___ . In fact in Le Grande et Beau Hotel I strongly suspect we entered thru the horse stable. They had evidently served the horses to the guests. Finally we were directed to another jernt [joint] behind shutters....

After a rum and coke there, a navy commander offered them a place to stay,

... so we all repaired about 10:30 P.M. to his camp at the edge of town. Here a hitch developed on account of the fact [that] two officers were very thoughtlessly sleeping in our bunks. The "Commander" said never to mind, they had to go on duty at midnight anyway. Just not to mention to them that we expected to use their bunks. He produced some beer, the first I had seen since USA, and we five sat outside and drank 2 beers each until midnight. Promptly at midnight these two officers reluctantly got up and went on their way. It rained during the night and Knight had to go find the latrine in it. He didn't have much luck because the Navy calls it a head. I stayed in bed and chuckled – too many drinks....

The next A.M. we went back to the docks to watch the [43rd-Division] troops come in. There we ran into an old friend of Knight's who ... invited us out to his ship for lunch. Promptly at 11:45 A.M. here came the Captain's gig [boat] and the Shore Patrol [Navy police] called out "Officers for the ___ ." [name of ship] That was us. You would have been thrilled by the ride past all the ships [in the harbor]. Some of the ship's officers told us the names and where they had been recently. What stories you could write if they could be told. The dinner [on board the ship we visited] was excellent, a vegetable mixture and a fish salad and ice water and apple pie a la mode and coffee. Oh! Why didn't I get into Annapolis? Frankly I'm perfectly glad to be in the Army. Don't let me kid you. After dinner we went thru the ship and [on the return] visited them [the ships in the harbor] back the same way. The Navy makes good hosts.

During the morning, Knight had gone to get a shave, and I had 15 minutes about town. All the large buildings are taken over by [the] U.S.A. Stores are nearly empty. I looked for something to send from here and couldn't find anything you couldn't get in NYC. People on the street in the morning included many women and children. I saw one brown woman with a small child. Her hair was very black and combed back very smoothly like in pictures of Jap women. Her sarong was of a natural-like paisley cloth. She apparently was dressed for town. Another wore black silk pajama pants with a pink pajama jacket and a big straw hat. Both women were barefooted. A Chinese family, all in black, except Pop wore white pants.... All the women carry bags made of cloth and big enough for groceries. These may be plain sacks or may be made of more decorative cloth.

The native men wear ear ornaments and bands on their upper arms. One such ear ornament was gold ... Almost all the men wear hair ornaments, usually a Woolworth's style woman's head comb. They treat their hair with lime, which turns it a sad red. Usually it is red above about 2 inches of coal black so you see the treatments aren't too frequent. One dock worker who seemed to feel very well dressed wore ... a green comb carrying crystal sparkles in his hair. He wore a white undershirt like mine for a shirt, blue denim shorts for pants, and some high black rubber boots for shoes.... Most workers were barefooted.

> A principal theme in Wilber's letters was his affection for his colleagues in his former (early 1930s) Washington State National Guard unit, the 161st Infantry Regiment. He had learned that they were in his part of the world, which pleased him greatly.

Incidentally I know where Warner [Hudleson] and Donald [Downen] are now. Both are Captains. The Artillery captain [Ruhlin] I mentioned above sailed the next day for the same place [Guadalcanal]. I wrote a greeting note to them and sent it up by him. He promised as he embarked he would look them up.

... Hale and Valerie I have seen your battleship [USS Washington where we were born] and mine [USS Indiana] together. They go to fight together. Aren't you glad?....

> The USS Washington fought in the mid-November naval engagement in Guadalcanal. She destroyed the Japanese battleship Kirishima with her 16-inch guns and suffered no damage. Ironically, these same two ships (Washington and Indiana) met again—by way of a collision(!)—in the Kwajalein action a year later.

Two natives are just wading down the [Ouenghi] river after fish. One is spearing and one has a small hand net. So far I don't see any fish. One wears red shorts and the other white [and] nothing else....

Yesterday was an off duty day and I went with three of our officers for a climb. We walked about 10 miles horizontally plus another mile up then down. It was very hot and I was as warm as toast. The climb was interesting tho and the views magnificent. We crossed what was the biggest nickel ore mass I ever saw. In fact we practically skied down it for 2000 feet. When I came back, I threw away one pair shoes, 1 pants, and one shirt. This climbing for long hours is something not many of our officers have done and I am getting a bit of a reputation out of it as well as some good exposure [in the division?]. I must stop now Darlings. Happy New Year to all of you and thank you so much for the fine Christmas. I love all of you and hope you are well. — XXXOOO Wilber

> Here once again was Wilber's passion for strenuous hikes. Hiking was a quasi-solitary sport as were his other athletic interests, like swimming and handball. He was averse to, and felt incompetent at, team sports. He knew he could excel at hiking, and he did not mind a reputation to that effect.

x·o·ø·o·x

JAN. 3, 1943

Hello Darling — I hope you are feeling OK today. Probably this is the last vacation day [for the children] and you need some rest....

By the way, a lot of the Maine boys got heavy sweaters and mufflers for X-mas in the tropics. Some got coffee, which goes over fine, some got candy which was eaten hastily so the ants wouldn't get it, and cake which molded en route. However everyone had fun opening packages and bundles just because they were from home.

I've changed my work so I am outside of Hq. more now. It is good to get away from my desk (a box) a bit. After my last reconnaissance in the [mountains], a 2d Lt. who had prided himself on his ability to hike said, "I guess our Exec is no desk man. He can walk." Capt. [Dixwell] Goff said "Maj. Bradt can walk any of our battery commanders [generally younger men] off their feet. There isn't one of them that could keep up the pace he set today as long as we did." It's good to be fit again. I hope I'm fit enough when the time comes [for combat]....

The wind is blowing today and it is cloudy. Last night was so cool I pulled my [bed] roll flaps over me in addition to my blanket. What a surprise for the tropics. It's hurricane season here now. One of the navy camps had a notice up as follows "Procedure in case of hurricane. Strike tent immediately and sit on same to prevent same from blowing away." I thought I might change it to "until same blows away." However I'm not much worried for, with all the radios we have, we should have plenty of warning. The trees here don't look as windblown as those in Ind[iana].

Barker was out watching us the other day and said some very nice things about me re: my ability to see [understand] what he wanted....

> This was a giveaway that they were training intensively and also that Wilber valued Barker's compliments. And then there was Malcolm!

Jan. 5 — ... Did I tell you about our pet deer? She [He] is named Malcolm! At first all the boys were saying "Come here Malcy, Come here Sweetheart, Come have a cracker Malcolm." However, since Christmas Malcolm has discovered there are a lot of better things than crackers especially in tents. He likes figs, dates, Hershey bars, Juicy Fruit Gum, fruitcake, cookies, hard candy, mints, sweaty shirts, cashew nuts, peanuts, and sugar. He is ready and willing to sample dirty sox, field glasses, blankets, congos[?], towels, shoe polish, soap, tooth powder and Maxwell House coffee. Now "Dear Malcolm" is greeted by "Get out of there you _ _ _ _ goat." Malcolm thinks it's all a good game. He usually stays just out of kicking range and doesn't mind being tossed out of one tent when there are always 60 or 70 more with good eats in them.

Sgt. Waller got in kicking range the other day when Malcolm was engrossed in sampling a box of Whitman's [chocolates]. He, with great satisfaction, delivered an army shoe to the base of Malcolm's spine. Malcolm didn't stop to look, nor hesitate. He jumped thru Waller's mosquito bar, which made the kick cost Waller just $6.80. Result: Waller running after Malcolm with his pistol yelling "Captain, may I shoot the _ _? Let me shoot the _ _ _ _ goat." Being right in camp Malcolm won. He knew no one would be allowed to shoot in camp.

... It seems like 15 years since I took you in my arms and that is a lot of time to make up. Good–bye now.... — Wilber XXXXXX

x·o·ø·o·x

On January 5, a young soldier, Cpl. Saul Shocket, was returning to his post with the 192nd Field Artillery Battalion when he was accidentally shot and killed by a fellow soldier on sentry duty. Perhaps the sentry was overly nervous because the unit had arrived at Bouloupari only six days earlier; watching for infiltrators was taken very seriously; or perhaps Cpl. Shocket forgot the day's password.

(Shocket's now-elderly nephew and namesake had been trying to learn more about the incident. I heard of his quest and was able to learn when and how the young Shocket's unit had arrived in New Caledonia, namely on the above mentioned USS Tryon together with Battery B of Wilber's outfit. This gave me the context for Wilber's visit to Nouméa on December 30 [letter 1/1/43].)

This next letter provided insight into the distasteful aspects of the coffee industry and described Wilber's attempt to reach the Vanadium Corporation offices and mines.

CHAPTER 16   *So ended Christmas Eve with everyone pretty happy*

FRI. JAN. 15, 1943

Adorable Nana — Do you know the coffee grows in a small pod with two beans facing each other.... The pod is popped into the mouth of a native woman and cracked between her teeth. She spits the beans on one side and the cracked pod on the other. The beans lie on the ground until they are dry then are collected and sold. And now Dearest, you may have another cup. You see why I was so glad to get the G.W. [George Washington brand] coffee. At least I haven't seen the teeth that cracked the pods and besides maybe the ground is cleaner in Brazil. Poor Nana, only one cup a day. I wish you could have mine. Anyway the cups you don't drink certainly reach the Army for we have plenty....

> On November 29, 1942, the government added coffee to the list of items rationed in America. This apparently limited Norma's consumption.

[Capt.] Jim R. [Ruhlin] is back from the front [Guadalcanal]. He had a lot of valuable training data and was all full of experiences for our use....

I have the Sinclair name [at Vanadium Corporation] from you and tried to get to see him. However he is about 200 miles away which is more than I can get time for now. Davis + I took a day + a half and tried but travel was too slow. We did go up 166 miles and back and saw a lot of the country. We ate 2 meals with other outfits and cooked our own breakfast in an abandoned (or vacated) camp. That night we slept in a bark hut which had apparently been built for a B.G. [Brigadier General]. Since it rained a lot we were very glad for a roof....

Goodbye again my Dove. I love you and am hoping 1943 will bring us closer again. Here is a long kiss on the tip of each breast and a long hard hug from your Wilber. I'll take that offer for a nap but I won't waste time napping. I'll love you until you are as drunk as if you were completely bewitched. — WEB XXXOOØ

x · o · ø · o · x

JAN. 17, 1943

My Dearest Wife — The letters are coming wonderfully now. Yesterday one from you dated Dec 22 and today one dated X-mas. Both are such wonderful letters....

The wind is blowing and those bugs that I call bicycle bugs (They sound like Valerie's Bike) are clicking around and in the air in a great way. The fish are jumping. One just jumped out of the water on the bank. He sure did a fast act flopping around to get back in the water. Probably he went home + told his wife he was sober but that the bank had reached in the water and grabbed him.

Malcolm the deer has reached a new low in popularity. He is now quite valuable. I wrote you a letter in which I enclosed a M.O. for $100.00. It has just been reported to me that "That … deer" ate it.… I'm sorry about the letter you won't get.…

Later it turned out the deer had not eaten it.

Hale, I would have liked nothing better in the world than to be able to have heard + seen you in the Christmas Eve Carol Service. It must have been lovely and beautiful and holy. I'm very proud of you, My Son. You have done well in your work. I'm remembering your violin and your grades too when I say I am very glad to have you for a son.… — Wilber XXXOOØ

x·o·ø·o·x

JAN. 24, 1943

Darling Nana — It is afternoon of a warm day here and I have just finished dinner. The breeze is good and keeps the mosquitos from being too active. Again I'm very thankful for these spikes [for shoes]. I travel over the hills with the "greatest of ease" now. Thank you very much, Beloved Wife.…

The big event of the day was a lizard falling out of a tree into my shaving kit. He was sure surprised and had all the wind knocked out of him. I put a little Burma Shave on his chin and got out my razor but he didn't wait. He started running and ran off the edge of my shelf and plopped down another three feet to the ground. He sat there another minute, and as he wiped the Burma Shave off his face he said "Danged Fool thought I needed a shave." It's funny how they can talk to you. Of course I could have been mistaken about the whole thing.…

Yes, I've been getting more mail so don't feel badly. I love you. It's dark so let's go to bed. — Wilber XXXOOØ

x·o·ø·o·x

It now becomes necessary to introduce this Monte Bourjaily who had befriended Norma and her family. He was an accomplished journalist who had experienced the giddy heights of wealth, fame, and associations with famous people, and the depths of discouragement due to overwhelming debts and two divorces. He was born in 1894 in Lebanon, and emigrated at the age of six to the U.S. with his young mother, Terkman, who had purportedly left a loveless arranged marriage. Terkman was reputedly only 15 years older than her son, but possibly 18 or 19 years if a recorded birth

CHAPTER 16 *So ended Christmas Eve with everyone pretty happy*

Monte F. Bourjaily as a World War I Air Service officer and as general manager of United Features (newspaper) Syndicate in the mid-1930s. [PHOTOS: BOURJAILY FAMILY]

date is correct. They settled in Syracuse, New York. Her husband Ferris later came to America and joined his family, after which in 1907 a daughter Alice was born. Ferris died in 1910 during a gymnastic stunt gone awry. The financial needs of the family prompted young Monte, who had entered Syracuse University in 1913, to leave college a year later for full-time work on the local newspaper.

During World War I, Monte served in France in the U.S. Army Air Service. He completed ground school flight training, and was commissioned a second lieutenant on August 18, 1918. He then went on to flight training but was assigned to administrative duties before completing it, and was shipped overseas where he held staff positions in the air service. He was not at ease with things mechanical nor was he at all athletic; it is unlikely he excelled at flight training and probably was required to drop out. Nevertheless, he was always a handsome and charming man. His son Paul had understood that he flew daily back and forth from Paris to the front, and had his evenings free in Paris to enjoy the company of the Parisian ladies. If true, it is unlikely he was the pilot on those flights.

After the war he continued in the newspaper business, rising to editorships and eventually becoming the editor and general manager of United Features Syndicate in New York City in 1928. There he was instrumental in starting up such well known features and projects as Eleanor Roosevelt's column "My Day," Drew Pearson's and Robert Allen's "Washington Merry-Go-Round," Al Capp's "Lil Abner" comic strip, and *Tip Top Comics*. It was he who realized the potential of these and other projects, promoted them, and made them successful. His success at United Features stemmed from his deep knowledge of the newspaper business; he knew what editors needed, even if they did not.

Monte left United Features in 1936 a rich man and then proceeded to lose money to unsuccessful ventures: a pictorial magazine (*MidWeek Pictorial*) that preceded the hugely successful *Life* magazine to the news stands; *Judge*, a Republican humor magazine; one of the early comic books (*Circus, The Comic Riot*), which ran for only three issues in 1938; and theater productions. He then returned to journalism in June 1940 as editor of the *Bangor Daily News*, the major paper in Bangor, Maine. By May of 1942, he was back in New York City and pretty much down on his luck. For a time, he was actually working on the docks, helping with the daily hiring process. In early or mid-1943, he obtained a high administrative position in Washington, D.C., at the U.S. Commerce Department's Board of Economic Warfare and later was special assistant to the assistant commerce secretary for international trade.

CHAPTER 16   *So ended Christmas Eve with everyone pretty happy*

Monte had married a writer, Barbara Webb, in 1920 and they had three sons. The marriage failed in 1934, and in that same year, he married a 24-year old "beautiful [stage] actress" and Mt. Holyoke graduate, Elizabeth Horner Young (aka Jalna Young), from Pittsburg, Pennsylvania. That too failed, effective November 1941, while Monte was editor of the Bangor paper.

Monte's son Vance, a novelist, wrote a moving piece about his father during his low period in New York, which was when Monte and Norma first met. It was called "My Father's Life." The above quoted description of Elizabeth Young is from it. Here is a bit more:

…The extent of Dad's over-qualification for the jobs available in the late Depression was ridiculous.… Dad went to work on the docks in his mid forties. The game was still comic books, in a weird way, and he earned forty-four dollars a week at it.

Dad is dressing for the job. He is putting blotting paper inside his British wing tips to protect his socks in the places where the soles are worn through. The shoes were made for him in London during a honeymoon tour with the beautiful second wife and look good still, and he is still cheerful; he was always a shoeshine guy.

He is explaining to me, this morning, in his residential hotel room that his job involves bossing longshoremen, overseeing the opening of bales of unsold comic books that have been returned by the wholesalers. The books must have their covers cut off to make sure that they will be exported as bulk paper, and not resold as comic books. The irony there, given the choices my father made, is thicker than those British soles are thin.… [*Esquire*, March 1984, p. 98, permission of the Vance Bourjaily estate].

Monte had enjoyed the high life of the rich and famous. He was a hard worker, driven to succeed. He loved fancy homes, had an engaging personality along with a mercurial temper, and was known to one of his sons as quite a ladies' man, which could have been a factor in his divorces. He was not tall but stood straight and proud. He felt he had fallen short in the upbringing of his sons, and those sons remained most loyal to their mother; one changed his surname to hers. Nevertheless they all stayed in touch with him and displayed affection for him and for their grandmother Terkman. All three of Monte's sons served in World War II, two of them overseas.

Monte was very close to his mother until the end of her life in 1950, and had been her principal source of support in the decades after her husband's early death. Terkman's daughter Alice served as a nurse in the army nurse corps in World War II and died of cancer at the young age of 39 in September 1946. She had attended Wilber's military funeral service at Arlington

Cemetery the previous December and had made it known that she wished the same service. She too was buried in Arlington.

Norma had not met Monte when he and we lived in Bangor, Maine, but had corresponded with him as editor of the Daily News and had occasionally submitted pieces for publication. When we were living in New York, she had sent a piece of correspondence to him as editor of the Bangor paper, not knowing he had left; it was mistakenly forwarded to him in New York. This led to their meeting. Valerie and I came to know him well. Wilber had met him on his leave home in May 1942 and wrote warmly about him, grateful that Norma had the support of people like him and the Gingolds in New York [letter 11/19/42]. He knew that Monte liked Norma and, much later [letter 1/30/44, Book 3], he wrote: "It is a peculiar situation, but in a way I'm glad he is standing by in case I am liquidated."

We became quite close to the Bourjaily family as was evident in Terkman's warm letter to my mother, above. Monte was not around continuously, but he was a well-known acquaintance who lived a mere half-mile from us in lower Manhattan. He may have helped Norma care for Valerie and me on occasion, taking us to an occasional event, for example, although I remember none specifically.

It would have been in late January 1943 that Norma became pregnant by Monte. Around 1982, Norma told me that Monte had been disconsolate because his son Vance had just gone overseas, and in his depression he had more or less forced himself on her, and that this was a one-time event. This, of course, was the best story possible; the pregnancy made clear that there was at least "one" encounter. It most likely was a longer lasting affair. Since Vance had embarked overseas to the Middle East the previous November 23 (1942), perhaps that was when the affair began. Norma herself could well have been equally disconsolate as Wilber had shipped overseas in October and was now half a world away.

On occasion, Norma would have commitments in the evening and would leave Valerie and me on our own in the West 4th Street apartment. I recall one such instance. Valerie and I had discovered the sport of dumping a cupful of water out our fifth floor window onto passing pedestrians. The water would disperse during in the five-story fall, so the victims would experience nothing more than a few drops. One evening, Valerie dropped a small paper grocery bag filled with water and just missed a couple walking below. I shudder to this day at the possibility of one of us falling out of that unguarded window. That event ended our nighttime shenanigans. But it does bring to mind the fact that Norma had a musical and social life that

CHAPTER 16   *So ended Christmas Eve with everyone pretty happy*

took her out in the evenings and that she trusted us to care for ourselves, though we sometimes did not deserve that trust!

Norma was a very religious woman. She attended Grace Church regularly, where I sang in the choir. She recalled later how much she liked the sermons of the young assistant minister, John Coburn, who many years later became bishop of the Episcopal Diocese of Massachusetts. Discovering her pregnancy, possibly in early February 1943, in the face of Wilber's consistently romantic letters, must have thrown her into despair. I, as a naive 12-year old, had no hint of this. Norma soldiered on through the rest of the spring, managing her children's lives as well as supporting Wilber with her letters. She clearly was planning, with Monte but no others—not even her closest sister Evelyn—how to cope with a pregnancy she would not terminate. In the social climate of the 1940s, few would have been sympathetic to her plight.

Knowing nothing of this, Wilber directed his efforts to preparations for the 43rd Division's approaching move to the front lines. Wilber and Norma were each moving toward their respective fronts with outward assurance and inward misgivings.

On Guadalcanal, the campaign was winding down; the last organized resistance ended with the final Japanese evacuation on February 7 and 8. The Japanese drive toward the U.S.-Australia line of communications had been stopped, and the Japanese were now on the defensive. But a significant price had been paid: 5,845 casualties (killed and wounded) of about 60,000 army and marine corps troops committed. The Japanese lost (killed, wounded, and disease) a full two-thirds of its 36,000 troops in the conflict [Miller, *Guadalcanal*, p. 350].

In New Guinea, the Japanese in the Buna-Gona area on the northeast coast of New Guinea had finally been defeated by January 22, 1943, with huge cumulative losses on both sides. Overall American and Australian casualties (killed and wounded) in the entire Papua, New Guinea, campaign were 8,550 out of 33,000 participating. The losses in New Guinea, with only half as many troops involved, exceeded those of the (much publicized) Guadalcanal battle. Losses due to sickness—malaria, dysentery, dengue fever, typhus—were even larger; regiments were reduced to company strength, or 1/12 their normal manpower! Again, the Japanese losses greatly exceeded those of the Allies: of some 16,000 troops committed in New Guinea, 12,000 were lost. Toward the end, Japanese supply lines had been cut off and starvation was rampant. The Japanese remained in defensive positions northwest of Buna at Salamaua (small circle on Map 4). [Miller, *Papua*, p. 371–2]

In Russia, at Stalingrad, the final resistance of the entrapped German Sixth Army would end on February 2, 1943, with the surrender of 90,000 unwounded and 20,000 wounded men. Only about 5,000 of these men survived Russian captivity.

17

"The silver thread tying all your souls together"

Ouenghi, River, New Caledonia
January–February, 1943

The next American objective beyond Guadalcanal was to occupy the Russell Islands 35 miles northwest of Guadalcanal (Map 5). An American airfield there would materially shorten the distance to a Japanese airfield (Munda) that had been built further northwest on New Georgia Island. Although the Russells were lightly occupied, the Japanese reaction to this move was uncertain. Japan's large contingents of troops and strong naval forces in the area could respond violently, especially if they hoped to recapture Guadalcanal. On January 29, Admiral Halsey received permission to proceed with the occupation of the Russells. A week later, on February 7, Halsey ordered the 43rd Division to Guadalcanal for transfer to the invasion craft. Intense preparations for this move were underway, but Wilber could not refer to them, at least not directly in this missive to Valerie.

JAN. 28, 1943
Darling Daughter Valerie — It is just 6:50 P.M. and will be dark pretty soon, so all I can do is start this letter....

[Jan. 29] — It is the next evening now and I can see the three mountains across my river. I wish I could tell you their names....

My river forks and goes around each side of the center one. There are clouds hanging around their tops right now and the air is soft as it is before a rain. It probably is raining on the other side of the mountains now. These mountains are different from others because they can move. At least a lot of people say, "The mountains are coming closer," when they are pretty disgusted with not being home. Whenever anyone complains about anything the rest of us all sing, "The mountains are getting closer" to him. Sounds silly but it's fun.…

There are a lot of ants here and they have a highway (I think it is U.S. 2) right past one leg of my cot. About one out of every 20 ants runs up my cot leg to see how I am. If I have killed any mosquitos they grab the corpse and rush excitedly down to the Highway and yell "Food! Food!" All the others on the road yell "Pass on the word, Food on Bradt's bunk." Then they all start up the cot leg marching 8 abreast singing "Happy days are here again." and "Beer! Beer! Beer for the privates!" When they get up on top, they look around and run along the sides [of my bunk] on the canvas. They don't like to walk on a blanket so they stay on the sides where the canvas of my roll is folded back. Pretty soon the situation looks like this: [sketch: ants surrounding blanket on cot]. They catch a few more dead [mosquitos]; then all of them look at me and look and look.

Finally one 1st Sargent says "Hey You Back there, go out and see how tough he is." The Buck Private says "Who! Me? No Siree. I'se jist goin by. My Cap'm sent me for some sugar." Off he goes. But some braver ant is sent out and he takes a bite out

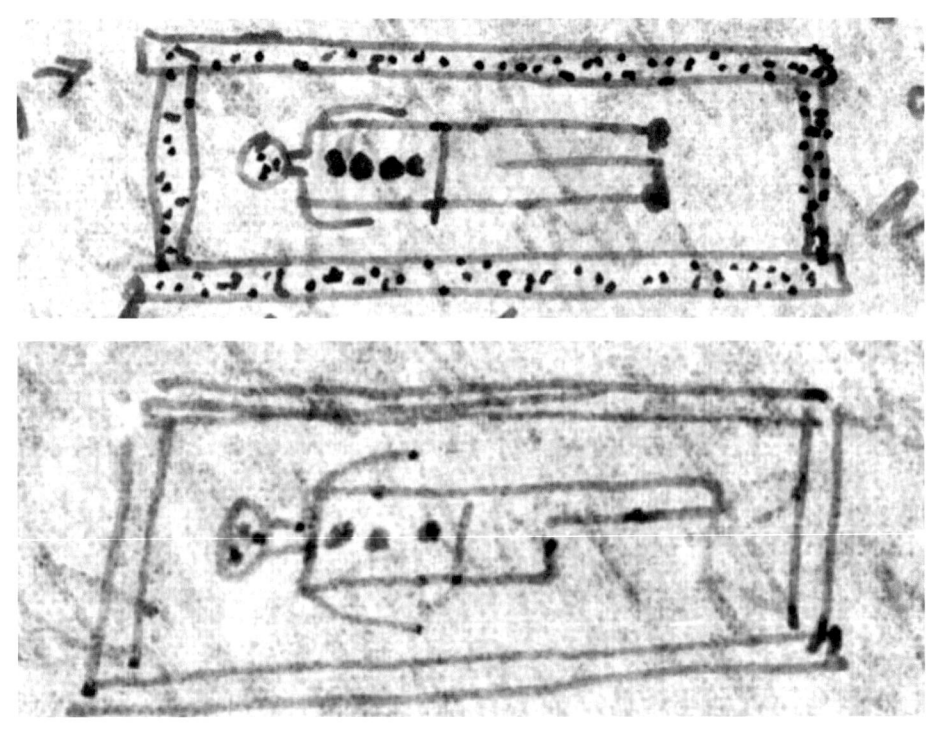

Sketches for Wilber's whimsical story of the ants on his cot in a letter to Valerie, January 28, 1943. The ants in the top panel, he implied here, departed after chewing off his right leg, bottom panel.

of my leg. I swat him and another one tries it. I swat him. Some ants go down the leg of the cot muttering about some groceries the wife wanted. Another one or two take a hunk of me and I swat them. Some more ants go down all six cot legs, talking about how late it is and when does the meat market close and besides the queen prefers hamburger. After a while the cot looks like this [sketch: no ants but Wilber has only one leg] and I go to sleep.

P.S. I captured some ant lions and put them around under my cot. They are doing well as watch dogs.…

Happy Birthday to me! [on Feb 1, age 43] This is Pop signing off and off and off and off and off and off . . . . — XXX OOO

> "The mountains are coming closer" illustrates the likely mental states of the soldiers situated there on the Ouenghi River during those long two months.
>
> Note the subconscious racism in the ant story. We liberal northerners, in those days, did not fully realize how much our own prejudices underpinned such stories: the demeaning of blacks with humorous stories built around their caricatured accent and their putative cowardice and subservience. It was everywhere; blackface comedy routines were the norm then. In fact, I still consider the ant story to be quite funny, but at what cost?

x · o · ø · o · x

FEB. 5, 1943
Hello Dearest — I'd love to have that nice white and clean face of yours in my two hands now. I'd look + look and look at each sweet feature and kiss all the shadows away. I'd hold it against my cheek and drink of the tenderness and love I know you have for me. You are my Darling, My Lovely Jewel and my Sweet Madonna. Here is a big hug and up you go in my arms and I'll carry you off to a quiet spot where I can love you and just enjoy your spirit and beauty.…

> What "shadows" did Wilber refer to? Did a letter from Norma express some despondency that reflected her now deeply conflicted life, or was he simply acknowledging that her role during his absence was a difficult one? Her letters would have taken two to three weeks to arrive; her latest would probably have been sent in mid-January or earlier, perhaps before the conception but possibly after the affair began. Wilber, though, did not have a lot of time for reflection given the increasing tempo of the training and field exercises in the endless rain.

Yesterday we went into the field for an exercise. I was an umpire. Late in the P.M., I was sent up the road about two hours drive. It had rained a little before and the roads were slippery, and, as we left the area, it started to pour. We drove thru the rain, picked up the people we were to meet, and drove again thru a woods and mountain road. The road by this time was frequently under water and Swan [Wilber's orderly and driver] was a pretty busy boy. When we were about a mile from our final destination, the car slipped off the road and mired [got stuck in the mud]. I left Swan to put chains on and, with the others, walked on to the top of our hill. It was dusk and still pouring. The bay was full of fog and the woods were wet as all get out. We did our job [as umpires] which included running around in the bushes awhile then walked back to the car. By this time it was pitch dark and raining even harder. The chains were on, but the car was even deeper in the mud, and a very mad Corp[oral] Swan was putting branches under the wheels.

We worked for another hour and got the car back on the road and ourselves even wetter if possible and mud to our ears. We drove to the main??? road??? and took off our chains, waded into a ditch and washed the worst of the mud off our clothes. It runs into your shoes if you do it the wrong way and started home. About 1/4 way back the ___ River was over the bridge and over waist deep. That was near the hospital where Paul Pooler is recovering from some gasoline burns so I decided we would go there for a late visit and maybe beg a bunk (without nurse). The road to the hospital was also pretty much under water and we again came to some too deep for the car to get thru, so we didn't see Paul. It was then about 10:00 P.M. and still raining.

You know the next move because you have driven thru the rain with me so many wonderful times. We drove to the top of a hill and went to sleep to the roar of many brooks and rivers. I slept in my roll, which you know keeps me dry and Swan slept in the car seat. The rain stopped and the frogs started to croak and the mosquito symphony opened the march of the stars across the sky as I lay and dreamed of you.

So now [it] is the next morning. The rivers have subsided and we have returned to camp. I've eaten, shaved, bathed, sun-bathed, laid all my wet things in the sun and am sitting in my chair wearing my shoes + shorts. In the tree over my head is one of those quacking crows, and he is looking at me and trying to say something. Oh yes! I get it now. He's saying "Nevermore" [after the Poe poem]. I've never been any wetter but it is warm and no one minds except for papers and equipment.

… Give the offspring a hug for me. Love to all of you. — Wilber XXXOOØ

The departure for Guadalcanal and the Russells was only nine days away.

CHAPTER 17   *The silver thread tying all your souls together*

x · o · ⌀ · o · x

Wilber's next letter was quite long and spanned four days, although I present only a few brief excerpts here. He kept being interrupted by the intense preparations.

FEB. 7, 1943

Dearest Nana — It's evening now and cool and I am thinking of you again. I still haven't mailed the box for the children because of a delay for two more pounds of coffee beans for you....

Feb. 9, 1943 — It's morning and I'm sitting in a niaouli grove. The sun has just come over a mountain and I have a few moments to talk to my family. I've been umpiring an[other] exercise and my job is just finished. Numerous people are probably relieved for I've had a grand time asking questions and making suggestions on survey and marching and occupation of [artillery] positions etc. We have been out overnight on this exercise, which sounds queer since we are really out all the time....

This may be the last letter for a week or so for our schedule is getting into the longer period exercises when there is less chance to mail letters. Please don't worry if gaps do get into my mail sequence. I'll still be OK and still be thinking of all of you and loving you. Must stop again.

Feb. 10 — I will mail this letter today before it gets any longer. I'm back on my river again.... I am so glad you are in a warm apartment [in NYC, and not in Maine]. It [February] must be pretty tough in Maine. I haven't seen cold weather for so long I'd probably freeze in a snow bank if I were in Maine. I TANK I STOP [I think I will stop]. — Love Wilber XXXOOØ

x · o · ⌀ · o · x

FEB. 11, 1943

Hello Sweet and Lovely — It's noon and I've just had a swim in the river. The hot sun is at its "scorchingest" now and I have added a few shades of tan to what is almost a coffee brown now. Maybe I should say cafe au lait to avoid too great a concentration of color in your mind....

I'm rereading your Jan 5 letter now. You are so flattering I'm afraid DeBlois will see me blush. The diary idea might be interesting but I'm afraid it would be too dull. I'd much rather write to my darling.... I love you. Must stop. Love Lots. — Wilber. XXXOOØ

We are fortunate indeed that Wilber continued to write candidly to his various family members, rather than into a journal written with a mind to publication and hence possibly less candid.

x · o · ø · o · x

On February 11 and 12, the men and equipment of the three howitzer batteries of the 169th Field Artillery Battalion moved to Nouméa and loaded onto three different attack transport ships: the USS President Hayes, the USS President Jackson, and the USS President Adams. Service and headquarters batteries boarded the Adams on the 13th. These were modern ships well equipped with defensive armament (guns), unlike the World-War-I era ships of Wilber's previous two voyages. Although one ship could hold more than two complete battalions, each consisting of four batteries, Wilber's battalion and presumably others were split up. They were embarking on the dangerous run to Guadalcanal, and the loss of a single ship would still leave intact two-thirds of the battalion. The Japanese still had submarines and aircraft within striking distance. Wilber was on the President Adams. The ship was at anchor in the harbor on the 14th, and sailed at 5:45 a.m. the 15th. [169th FA Journal]

This letter, written on board the Adams, described Wilber's nocturnal activities in Nouméa just before their departure.

FEB. 14, 43

Beloved Wife — Yesterday and today have been good days. The weather is lovely, the mosquitos are no bother at all. I have just reread your last letter dated Jan 25 and know everything is OK at home. Your letters are so interesting and I cherish each word. It's grand to be able to recall them during quiet times.

Joe's [Gingold's violin] recital must have been wonderful. I can reconstruct the whole thing. Joe, the stage, lights, people enchanted, you and so proud and worried for fear everything wouldn't be quite perfect, and above and thru everything the silver thread tying all your souls together. I can see people applauding and remember how it spoils the music, and can [see] your worry changing to a great pride + joy for Joe. The only thing I didn't like was you going home alone at 1:00 A.M. I'll take care of that some of these days too.

Wilber captured beautifully the anticipation, tension, and later the relived joy of an important musical recital. The souls of the soloist's family and friends truly were joined with a "silver thread."

CHAPTER 17   *The silver thread tying all your souls together*

I'm glad Mrs. Z. [Zacharias, Hale's violin teacher] was pleased with my acknowledging her generosity [to Hale] and had not forgotten my promise.

Wilber sent Mrs. Z. a thank-you letter, which declared he would send an artillery salvo off in her honor. She often and proudly showed that letter to visitors when I was in a lesson and talked of it for many years thereafter, until at least 1955. The story got better as time progressed: Wilber would "send the whole battalion (or more) into battle" in her name!

Today, no yesterday [Feb. 14th if it is now after midnight], I had an experience you would have loved. I was on one of our luxury liners [President Adams in the harbor at Nouméa] and had to go ashore at night. The boat's orders were to "Take the Major ashore + obey his orders afterward." I'm not trying to be mysterious. There wasn't any mystery, but the moon was in and out of the clouds so it was bright then dark several times. The waves were not big but there was a definite swell. We had no lights on our boat, and a sailor rode the bow as lookout. Big ships would loom up in the dark and disappear. Little boats would splash + sputter by, and if they passed in front of us would be efficiently and pleasantly cursed by my lookout. They would answer back with even more efficient oaths always ending with comments about our lack of lights. My lookout would be silenced but would hopefully go thru the same routine next time. I got the impression he was just practicing his swearing. Some ships were dark, some not, some quiet some busy, the air was soft, the hills lovely when the moon was out. Nearby on shore a smelter was doing its stuff in its usual noxious manner; in another cove the leper colony was dark and quiet, while a blinker station busily cut the night into dots and dashes from a [geologically] young mountain in the distance.

Thru all this cheery, solemn and wonderful night, we rolled and splashed and rolled and cursed our way to shore where I efficiently stole a car out from [under] the nose of a guard and went about my nocturnal business. About midnight I returned to another dock and placed my(?) car in the care of the guard there with strict instructions not to let it get away and came back to my ship.

This morning I went back after the car which was still there but when it developed someone else had stolen the key out of it, I was really burned up. Even at the time I was giving the navy guard a going over, it seemed to me there was a little lack of sincerity in my comments.

However I pursued my life of crime by short circuiting the switch and continuing to use the car without a key. Incidentally the mission was a success. I do wish you could have shared that [boat] ride but doubt if you would have enjoyed the way we left that motor park in the dark.

CITIZEN SOLDIER PART 1II: VOYAGES TO WAR

What was the "mysterious mission" that led to this boyish-sounding adventure? It may have been purely administrative, perhaps involving picking up orders, which became available only shortly before departure to increase security. Wilber's nighttime ride through the harbor reminded me of similar rides I had taken returning from liberty in Sasebo, Japan, to our ship, which hung on a buoy a mile or more out in the harbor. We would pass fighting ships that had been and would be operational off the Korean coast. It was indeed mysterious and beautiful.

Yesterday afternoon we were waiting near the Ni smelter for a while so I went thru it with one of our Lts. who is a Dow Ch. Co. chemist. — [no closing]

His chemistry interest found an outlet here. This letter stopped with no closing; perhaps the last mail collection before sailing took him by surprise.

x·o·⌀·o·x

The convoy bound for "Cactus" (the code name for Guadalcanal) departed Nouméa, New Caledonia, at 5:30 A.M. on February 15, 1943. It was 2:30 p.m. on February 14, in New York City, and Norma was attending the wedding of Monte's son, Monte Jr., to the attractive brunette, Marietta ("Billy") Dake, at St. Thomas Church on Fifth Avenue. It was surely an anguished time for the religious Norma as she contemplated her own marriage vows against her familial and sexual relationship to the Bourjailys.

Valerie and I were not invited but I, at least, was fascinated by this important event. I remember telling Valerie that evening, as we lay in our beds in our shared bedroom, how nice it must be to touch a woman's smooth skin in the marriage bed. The thought really intrigued and appealed to me, but my imagination went no further. Did I, a 12-year-old, know more of marital intimacies? Probably yes, but not in all the details. It wasn't real to me and had no appeal, whereas simple skin-to-skin contact did. As I went on and on about it, Valerie, at ten not being the least bit interested in the topic, told me to pipe down so she could sleep. That ended that discussion. Such was life in New York City as Wilber headed off to the front lines.

In North Africa, American forces had moved eastward into the mountainous terrain of Tunisia. There, in mid-February, disaster struck. German forces drove through and routed American forces at Kasserine Pass. It was not until February 25 that the Americans, with the aid of British and French troops, were able to regain the pass. Command practices that led to the rout were rapidly revised and several senior commanders were relieved. This setback and the subsequent adjustments went far toward maturing the U.S. Army forces in Europe. Gradually, the Allies regained the initiative, but not without additional setbacks. The Americans from the west and southwest, and the British from the east and southeast, began the drive that would force the Italians and Germans into northern Tunisia with their backs to the Mediterranean Sea.

In Russia, on January 12, the Russians initiated a westward drive toward Kharkov. By February 20, they had created a large salient into the German lines that included Kharkov and Kursk. The Germans mounted a counterattack on February 20, driving to the Donetz River by March 18, and trapping and destroying a Soviet tank army. Both armies, quite depleted, lay low during the muddy spring season, awaiting the battles sure to come in the summer.

PART IV

HOLDING THE FRONT

RUSSELL ISLANDS, SOLOMON ISLANDS
FEBRUARY–JULY, 1943

USS President Adams (AP-38; later APA-19), August 1942 at Nouméa, New Caledonia. She was a "modern" ship, built in 1940–41 and carried defensive armament (guns): eight 20-mm, four three-inch, and one five-inch. It carried Wilber with other 43rd Division troops from New Caledonia to Guadalcanal. On February 17, the convoy was attacked by Japanese torpedo planes as it approached Guadalcanal. [U.S. NAVY PHOTO #80-G-K-556]

18

"You can't tame a machine gun by looking it squarely in the eye"

At sea, Guadalcanal
February 1943

The 43rd Division was moving to the front lines! The move of the 43rd Division from New Caledonia to the Russell Islands in the Solomon Islands was carried out in two stages. Large ships carried the division to Guadalcanal, a three-day voyage. After four days on Guadalcanal, they would embark on smaller craft for the overnight trip to the nearby Russell Islands (Maps 4 and 5).

The trip to Guadalcanal was Wilber's third voyage since leaving California. His ship, the USS President Adams (APA-19), was initially intended for commercial service with the American President Lines but was taken over by the navy in 1941 while still under construction. It was outfitted to support amphibious landings and could carry 1,400 troops and 35 landing craft. Its armament was light by warship standards, but not trivial: one five-inch cannon, four three-inch guns, and eight 20-mm rapid-fire guns. It traveled with other similar ships and escorts grouped in a convoy for mutual protection. These ships, chock-full of American troops, were tempting targets for Japanese submarines and aircraft.

The convoy passed through the Coral Sea, location of the famed Battle of the Coral Sea of the previous May (1942), when the Allies thwarted a Japanese attempt to capture Port Moresby on New Guinea at the cost of the carrier USS Lexington. They did not pass over its resting place, but must have been very aware of its nearby ghostly presence.

Wilber wrote to Norma shortly after the troops' early-morning departure from Nouméa. He included bits for Valerie and me; we were in the spring terms of our schools in lower Manhattan.

FEB. 15, 1943

Hello Sweet and Lovely — I wish I were able to have you with me tonight. You would have loved today. A little work and a few inspections in the morning, then just watching the mountains slide by on the horizon. The water is blue and calm with white foam all alongside. This is a fast convoy and we really move along. If you get this letter you will know we went thru the submarines all right. Hale, one of the guns on this ship has three Jap flags painted on it. That means that gun shot down that many planes.

Last night, Nana, I stood on the deck and thought of you and the children and how much I love all of you. It seems so long to be away and I miss you so much. Anyway we are now making another step toward the end. I expect to see Don [Downen] and Hud [Hugh Warner Hudleson] this week [on Guadalcanal].

You would love this ship. Our stateroom is one I could never afford. It is equipped with lovely furniture, beautiful bath, a davenport, built in buss lights, closets and is one of the two farthest forward on the highest deck. The cocktail lounge has been converted into an officers mess equipped with silver + linen and lovely murals and Venetian blinds. The sea is fairly smooth and in spite of the fact we are nearing the equator it is not too hot.

The boys on the machine guns got a thrill last night from a sub off the port bow. They were all very disappointed that the destroyers took over before anyone even saw it. However they probably will re-tell it quite differently after the war. One unseen sub will probably grow into swarms of subs and the fact that they took off their gun covers will probably grow into the firing of thousands of rounds. Anyway that obstacle has been hurdled and we go merrily on.

The officers (Navy) on this ship are treating us royally. We were cargo on our last voyage but now we are privileged passengers. I eat at the #2 table with the Lt. Commanders and enjoy them a great deal. Valerie, did you get the seeds? — XXXOOØ Wilber

x·o·ø·o·x

FEB. 16, 1943

Darling — It's a Lovely Morning and I wish I had you by my side. We'd take my canvas chair, which I carried on board, and set you by the rail on the bridge (on top of all the decks) and I'd stand beside you with one hand on your shoulder. We'd talk and dream and watch the sky and the foam and the flying fish and the horizon for other ships. And we'd be glad for the haughty air about the American Flag as She flies over each ship and plows thru Her Ocean. And you'd love the neatness and agility of the escort vessels and know "Uncle S[am]" was taking care of you and the ships and those flags. You wouldn't worry about subs for you have confidence in that escort and the reserves it can call forward....

> Oh, such romance! Did Wilber court Norma so poetically when in her presence, or did he develop this only through his writing? I do not remember him as particularly flowery or poetic; he was, after all, a somewhat overweight pragmatic scientist from an Indiana farm. However, to have captured the popular Norma back in 1927, his romanticism must have been evident to her.

I had figs and fried eggs + bacon for breakfast and it reminded me of our days in Hattiesburg, Miss. Lover you went behind [financially] for me on that summer, but I appreciate it. I hope some of the M.O.s [money orders I sent] will help. I'll send more if I can or will buy bonds for us [for] when we need to retire. I'm glad you are comfortable and that you like the place you live in.

Tell Valerie I want that "I wish I were in Maine" stuff stopped. She'll be there long enough to get all she wants before long. This is a war against all complainers too.

Goodbye I love all of you. — Wilber Bradt

> U.S. War Bonds could be bought for as little as $18.75 ($280 today). They would mature in ten years when they could be redeemed for $25, an effective interest rate of 3%, compounded annually. They supported the war effort and gave citizens a sense of participation. They were advertised by the government with great fanfare, and purchasing them was considered a patriotic duty. Almost $200 billion worth of them were sold during the war.
>
> The complaining by 10-year-old Valerie might have been more than simple pre-teen exasperation with her mother; she remembered Maine as a place where she had a "normal" family with a father present.

x · o · ø · o · x

FEB. 16, 1943
Dear Father — ... Today is again my second day at sea ... I just watched a flying fish stay in the air for at least a minute. It sailed along between waves for over 200

yards. – Now a storm (squall) has come up. The wind is blowing harder and it is pouring rain. Less than 10 minutes ago, I first noticed a cloud, which I thought looked wet. The sun was shining brightly. Now I cannot see our escort at all. Now we are out of the storm, but the rest of the convoy is still covered by the rain. The boat pitches a little more now.…

This is nearly two years since I was inducted. It was Feb. 24, 1941 when we were officially ordered into U.S. service. The next two years will undoubtedly be a lot harder, but the first two have kept me busy. I want you to know I have never regretted even one day of it. This is the war I wanted to fight ever since the Japs went into Shanghai [in 1932]. I was afraid we would go to the European front and this is my war over here. It's not one of maneuver and strategy. It's one where the enemy is either killed or you are killed. There is a definiteness about that that is very satisfying. These men aren't over here to play. They know it's either-or and they act accordingly. I may regret the finality of such a scrap sometime but until that time comes, here is where I want to be. Island to island warfare is supposedly the hardest kind but it has a variety too and we may get that too.

… I'm on the way to see my old Infantry Company, which is on the island to which we are going. Two of my old sergeants are now Captains there. Goodbye and Love to you and Mother. — Wilber

> Wilber's view of the Pacific combat had some truth to it: shooting rather than taking prisoners was more likely in the close confines of the jungle, because after sighting the enemy, one had little time to think about what to do. Also, neither side believed it would be well treated in captivity by its enemy. And, finally, the Japanese soldier was taught that surrender was the ultimate shame. Of course, Wilber did not intend to imply that the war against the Germans was solely one of "maneuver and strategy." Soldiers there also faced the kill-or-be-killed choice. This monologue with his father about his own death was disturbingly cool and detached. Wilber's views were largely theoretical because he had not yet been exposed to combat against a real enemy, but the next day would rectify that!

x·o·ø·o·x

FEB. 17, 1943

Greetings Glory of my life — It is 9:30 A.M. and I have taken my chair up on the Captain's Promenade, which is the aft part of the bridge. I'm in my canvas chair facing the stern. We have just passed thru a squall and I can see the edge of the rain-

CHAPTER 18   *You can't tame a machine gun by looking it squarely in the eye*

beaten area plainly. It appears to move the horizon in nearer to one and makes a white line on the water. We have just changed course, which will probably occasion 20 soldiers to ask 20 sailors whether this is the "zig" or the "zag." Someday a sailor is going to lose control of himself and kill a soldier just for that reason....

> To frustrate submarine attacks, ships in a convoy would all change course every 10 to 30 minutes by preplanned but unpredictable amounts, making a "zig-zag" track that averaged to the desired course. Such maneuvers by a convoy could lead to ship collisions if one ship failed to turn in the proper direction at the designated time.

Last night was quiet but just now a warning came over the speaker system to gun crews to be especially on lookout for enemy "flying boats." The transports are shifting their positions probably for best anti-aircraft protection. [This] convoy has made seven of these trips, and, altho ships have been torpedoed on two occasions, no ship has ever failed to get there and back. After one of the trips, the Tokyo radio announced that the "machine-gun transports" had been up [to Guadalcanal] again. They have shot down a lot of planes, and on this ship I can see from here six Jap flags on gun turrets.

Gun crews are all very busy oiling and checking their guns. This alarm of course will likely be like most, just a precautionary measure. However the sub night before last was really there and caused a little show. A destroyer went thru the ceremony and came up with us later looking satisfied but saying nothing. All we saw were some flashes.

... You are my Nana whom I love above all else. 'Cept Hale + Valerie too. — XXXOOØ Wilber

x · o · ø · o · x

> The ship had reached Guadalcanal. There was no harbor; dock facilities were built out from the beaches. Wilber made a note at the top of the letter to assure the censor that his description of a night attack was allowed.

FEB. 18, 1943, 9:30 A.M.
Not to be mailed until action is officially announced. WB
Sweet and Lovely Wife. — This is the end of our voyage and we are now in process of unloading ship. Our men are ashore and cargo is going overside now. I have slipped back to my stateroom to talk a few minutes to you. The island is palm covered plains and mountainous interior. We are landing on a narrow white beach and moving under cover of the palms. The sea is smooth, the sun already is very hot

and no breeze is blowing. This has been a real rest and a most pleasant interlude. You have no idea how good it has been to be really clean and rested. I find I think of you more when I'm well bathed than when I'm all grimy.

Last night was interesting because the Jps. took a real try at us with subs and planes. It was a night affair, beginning about 8:00 P.M. They dropped flares over us then came in against us with 12 or 18 torpedo planes. At the same time, our escort detected submarines. The moon was bright and the night clear. What with tracer bullets, shells bursting overhead and depth charges below and burning flares + planes it was quite a show. There were seven Jp. planes downed and pretty soon there were none staying. Our ship brought down three.

… Please take the children to a show for me when you next can and play me a little Beethoven just for fun. — Love Love Love XXXOOØØ

x·o·ø·o·x

The 43rd Division had arrived in Guadalcanal on February 16 and 18, shortly after the cessation of organized resistance on February 9, though there were still isolated Japanese on the island; Wilber wrote of sniper fire. Although the 43rd Division was not involved in the organized fighting, its members were awarded a battle star on the Asiatic-Pacific campaign ribbon for the Guadalcanal battle because they were there prior to the officially declared end of the action. The attack on their convoy the night of February 17 certainly justified it. Here was the view of the world-famous Guadalcanal through Wilber's eyes.

FEB. 19, 1943 [GUADALCANAL]

Beloved — It is just getting dark and this letter will be short. We are bivouacked now in a cocoanut grove. On one side is the jungle and on the other is an open area of very tall grass. It is quite hot and sultry. The grass is full of crickets and the trees full of birds. I saw two pure white parrots that apparently were talking Japanese. There are monkeys here too who talk the same language. The mosquitos are definitely Anti-U.S. The jungle is lovely with green vines and shrubs and many colored flowers. – Too dark now [to continue writing]. Am OK + love you. Wish I could send Valerie the 6-inch butterfly that I saw.

Feb. 20, 1943, 9:30 A.M. — These are planted cocoanut palms and belong to a company in US [Lever Brothers] for which many of my students work. The harvest of cocoanuts seems a bit neglected just now. The trees are loaded and last year's crop is still on the ground. I suppose that makes the price of soap a little higher for you. My chair is set under a tropical palm-like plant that the

CHAPTER 18   *You can't tame a machine gun by looking it squarely in the eye*

Davenport Hotel [in Spokane, Washington] would like to have. In front of me is a Canna-like red flowered plant that would be an ornament to any flower garden. The cocoanuts of last year and the year before are sprouting young trees now that look a lot like the palms of the 1900 parlors. The parrots are snow white and beautiful. Lizards are all lengths up to two feet and snakes have been seen up to five feet. – In general our boys have been showing up well and are as comfortable as we could expect.

It apparently rains daily or rather nightly here and that makes the latter part of the night quite comfortable. This A.M. I got up and bathed and it was necessary not because of the tropics but because I had had a particularly vivid dream of my wife. What you were doing to me completely and very effectively lifted me to the heights. You used all your old wiles and added several new ones. I partially woke once and thought you were with me in Columbia doing some of the things I wouldn't let you do then. I grabbed you to me and woke up to find you gone and myself needing a bath very badly. Even dreaming of your love is more thrilling than I can resist. You really should have been here for you missed a very enthusiastic session. Some day, My Darling, I won't dream of you. I'll hold you in my two hands and then I'll really make love to you....

Goodbye now. Must get on the job again. Please give the children a big hug for me and send me a kiss. — XXXOOØØ Wilber

> Wilber's fantasies were right out in the open. There was no doubt that he and Norma had a rich sex life; he was focused on her and apparently no one else, not even in his fantasies. By this date, roughly a month after conception, Norma would likely have lost all hope that she was not pregnant. Wilber's long-distance courting must surely have cut deep into the core of her being.

x · o · ø · o · x

After just four days in Guadalcanal, the division was preparing to move into the Russell Islands, 35 miles northwest of Guadalcanal and arguably the most forward position of U.S. troops in the Southwest Pacific. It had not been clear whether the Japanese still occupied the Russell Islands but recent reconnaissance had shown it to be unoccupied. Nevertheless, it was still possible that the Japanese would react strongly to the arrival of the Americans.

FEB. 21, 1943

Hello There Norma — You certainly sent me three fine letters and the children each one fine letter. All these came today and today is a very special day for us. I can't mail this letter until the news is officially announced but today we [the 43rd Division] are moving up on the next island, and tomorrow, if all goes well, [we] will be the farthest front of the troops in this general area. It isn't the first time we have been under attack but it is our first attack. Your receipt of this letter will mean it went well and that I mailed it after its completion. In half an hour, I go four miles to see Cris [Lt. Louis Christian], + Don [Downen], + Hud [Warner Hudleson] + Lt. [Robert] McCalder of Pullman [friends from the Washington State National Guard]. They are all veterans now and the old regiment has a reputation as a good outfit. Imagine them right alongside just as we used to plan it. It was sure good news to me.

… Your ways of love making improve each time we meet and I can hardly wait to see what new talents you have developed for me. Such eyes, such fingers, such lips! I'll always say "Nana, look at me." — [no closing]

x · o · ø · o · x

> The first echelon of the 43rd Division to occupy the Russells was loaded onto its craft on February 20 at Koli Point on the central north coast of Guadalcanal (Map 5). The troops went ashore in the Russells early on February 21. From Koli Point, it was a voyage of about 75 miles, which would have taken about eight hours for the flotilla of small ships: landing craft, destroyers, mine sweepers and destroyer-transports. Some landing craft were towed by the larger ships. The flotilla returned to Guadalcanal to pick up the 169th Regimental Combat Team, which included Wilber's battalion (169th Field Artillery Battalion). He wrote this letter awaiting his ship on the beach at Koli Point.

FEB. 22, 1943

I'm in love with Norma — Have you ever received a love letter from a guy on a pile of 105[-mm] howitzer ammunition? Yes. Today you have one. The lover is at his ease on some Smoke. Not Smoke in his eyes but smoke under + all around him.

> The smoke shells he was lying on were 105-mm shells, which released smoke on impact for use in adjusting aim. The shells would have been in hard cylindrical metal cans about five inches in diameter and perhaps 30 inches long. Wilber's reference was to the popular Jerome Kern song (1933), "Smoke Gets in Your Eyes."

CHAPTER 18   *You can't tame a machine gun by looking it squarely in the eye*

Your dear letters came yesterday and had to be packed for this job, but I certainly recall some of the high spots. Imagine my lovely wife having an orgasm on account of me. Dearest you grow more precious to me each day. You were [a] darling to tell me. Isn't it odd that on the same day I got your letter I had mailed one describing an identical experience? Tis true "stone walls do not a prison make." Having known you and having been loved by you has permanently destroyed those prison walls. I much prefer dreams of you to the fact of another woman. Lover mine, I'll hold you so close and caress you so lovingly and possess you so completely when I return I want to be tender and brutal too and to be passionate and lascivious too. I know I'll really want to be just what you desire, so think carefully and be prepared. When this war is over, my big problem is going to be how to make a living and stay close to you. Please help me solve that one for I know now you must always be near me. In the meantime my arm is around your waist and my lips in your hair.

> Norma was writing of having an orgasm too "on account of Wilber"! Was it real, alone, or with Monte, or was it only a literary creation to match Wilber's passionate writing? She may have been seeking to convince herself that her "sinful" sexual involvement with Monte was, on an emotional level, actually with Wilber. Her strong religious convictions and general societal conventions might have impelled her to take this view to ward off guilt and despair. At the same time, she was doing her duty and penance by being Wilber's dedicated correspondent, helpmate, and attentive mother to their children. Her letter with this revelation would have been written around the time of her first missed period, and she may not yet have known the eventual outcome.
> Wilber goes on to tell about his reunion with his former Washington State colleagues of Company E, 161st Infantry. The visit was not without risk.

All the old Co[mpany] E. crowd was asking about you. They certainly all talked about Norma and what was she doing now and things they remembered. You seemed almost present. All sent their greetings, even a Lt. Patterson who remembered you playing [piano]. Lt Col. Morris of Spokane Paper asked particularly to be remembered and Hud + Don seemed definitely to feel you were part of the firm of We, Us + Co. Cris grinned from ear to ear and says "Housa Mrs?" [How's the Mrs.] The boys tell me that out of the Co E. we knew, over thirty men are now officers. Hud has the same mustache + is only a little more bald.
We recalled the nights [after National Guard drill] we sat in Charlie's place [the Chinese restaurant in Pullman, Washington] + talked of fighting the Japs in 1932 and how glad we were to be here now together. Don said when I left "Are you able

to march? Can you march 12 miles in 2 hrs + 20 minutes?" I answered, "yes I did once." They all laughed and we clapped each others' shoulders for we had all been there together. I showed their Lt. Cols. Greenough + Morris the pistol they had given me and told how I won a bet with it against Choate by qualifying as expert [marksman] last year. And they all wanted me to stay for supper, but I had to get back for supper and before dark as there are still parties of Japs in the jungle. We have a date [to meet again] for each island and each continent until the one in Pullman [Washington]. Will you come to that one?

> The marching Wilber mentioned referred to the maneuvers they had been on in Washington State. A small group of them, by covering the 12 miles rapidly, were able to gain some tactical advantage for their unit. In the early 1980s, I corresponded with and met Donald Downen in Pullman, Washington. He told me that Wilber had been kidded a lot on that hike because his extra weight had made it more difficult for him.

By the way this Smoke isn't as soft as one might infer. It doesn't give the effect of a cherubim [cherub] lounging on a cloud. I'm waiting for another ship and we are doing our waiting beside + on a lovely sand beach. The ocean waves swish + wash on the sand and make me remember so many sweet hours with you. Last night I was waked by some bombing [probably of Henderson airfield by the Japanese] and watched the show; then [I] just lay + listened to the sea and thought of my Darling.

Do you remember the days on Pacific Beach [Washington]? Here I would soon have you tanned from nose to toe with nothing spared. You could wear either a loin cloth or a pair of sea shells for breast cups during the meals, but the rest of the day you would dress informally.... — Wilber

> It was from this letter that I learned the name of the beach (Pacific Beach) where we had stayed during Wilber's Tacoma, Washington, strike duty in 1935. It is 80 miles west of Tacoma.
>
> Many years later in May 1981, Donald Downen wrote me the following assessment of Wilber: "I thought of him as always considerate of others, happy, jolly chuckle, never autocratic or overbearing. Never hurried or flustered. Always seemed to have time for the occasion."

x · o · ø · o · x

> Wilber was still on the same beach at Koli Point when he wrote to Valerie and me. In this letter, after some inspiring words about enjoying beauty in life, he told the story of the Japanese attack on his convoy. It was typical for

CHAPTER 18   *You can't tame a machine gun by looking it squarely in the eye*

him to write the details of combat episodes days or even weeks later when he was in a more relaxed mood.

FEBRUARY 22, 1943 [GUADALCANAL]
Dear Hale and Valerie — I just got your very nice letters yesterday. It is hard to find time to write when you are going to school. That makes me appreciate your letters a lot more because you gave up playtime to write me.… .

Hale, I appreciated getting your letter about Xmas and the program. I never sang anything pppp [*double* pianissimo, a notation for extreme softness rarely used]. It must have been beautiful. You are getting a fine chance to learn the wonderful beauty of music, and I hope you keep all your life the ability to see and hear and find the beautiful and fine things in this world. Some people just see the sad and dirty and mean things and they certainly live a dreary and nasty little life. Other people never learn to see at all. They just exist and eat and work and sleep and never see the sky, or flowers, or the beauty in a building or a lake or a person. They don't appreciate kind acts, or a quiet hour or a good meal. Norma is giving you a great chance to see, and I know you are learning. Valerie is already seeing some things especially well and I know you are too. The next step is to be able in your life to create beauty that will make the world better. That can be a picture or music or a better car or a new medicine or a better dishwasher or a better and more friendly spirit or writing a letter to someone who needs a letter.

In a little while now I'll have to stop and get on a ship again. This will be a fairly short trip and will be my fourth island [to Pavuvu Island in the Russells]. We certainly didn't stay on this one very long.

The attack on our convoy on the way up here was one of the prettiest sights I have seen. There were Jap flares in the air to help their planes find us. The moon was calmly watching the whole fight, and its light danced on the waves just like in Maine. The planes would come scooting in toward us from the dark, and then the tracer bullets would start reaching out from the ships. When they hit the plane, a little fire would start to spread and maybe the plane would begin to go crooked. One big gun hit one plane right square in the middle before the pilot dropped his torpedoes at [toward] the ship. The shell burst in the plane and so did his torpedo. There was a great flash and thunderous report and that plane was completely gone. All this time the ships were zig-zagging calmly just as if they were on a drill. Some torpedoes went close to the ships, one close to mine, but all missed and exploded away from us. One pilot tried to drop his burning plane on one of our ships, but he missed. Two or three planes landed on the water and burned there. Several pilots apparently took to the water for we saw flash[ing] lights winking in different places. Lights on a nearby island blinked and waved and signaled. We figured the pilots were sending a message to Hirohito saying "So Sorry."

All this time, our escort ships were running around us dropping depth charges that went whamo so it sounded as if a thousand tons of pig iron had fallen on a hundred big steel boilers. At the same time all their antiaircraft guns were busy. All this lasted only about 20 minutes and the thing was all quiet and people began to count how many planes had been shot down by each ship. Our colored [black] gunner shot down two and helped on a third. He certainly was a popular nigger. One major admitted later that he had taken about two looks and gotten down on his hands and knees and crawled off the bridge in the best doughboy style. He suddenly decided he wasn't needed there at all. Your Pop went down behind a steel gun shield a couple of times when things seemed to be coming his way. You know you can't tame a machine gun by looking it squarely in the eye....

> There was that "n" word again. Wilber rarely used it; he knew it was derogatory, even in 1943. Note his use of "colored," the polite word of the 1940s. He slipped into the vernacular when portraying others' descriptions of the popular gunner.

My boat is in sight now so I must stop. Children I like to write to you about the things I see but would rather have you and Nana along so we could see them together (except the Japs).

Don't worry about the famous Jap snipers. All our friends say they never hit a moving target, and one took three shots at me yesterday and missed badly. If they don't hit me I don't mind being shot at. Warner [Hudleson] says they let them shoot at them; then if the Jap just keeps on, they go around under all the trees until they find where he is. Then they shoot at and hit Mr. Togo. He probably exaggerated a little.

> The American press often used "Tojo" as a caricature of a traitorous Japanese person. The name referred to Hideki Tojo, a general of the Japanese Army and Prime Minister of Japan from 1941 to 1944. He was primarily responsible for the attack on Pearl Harbor. Wilber seems to have confused Prime Minister Tojo with Shigenori Togo the Japanese foreign minister at the time of Pearl Harbor who was adamantly opposed to war with the United States, but reluctantly signed the Declaration of War when diplomacy failed. The most famous Togo was the Admiral who defeated the Russian fleet in the Russo-Japanese war of 1905.

The ship is out here now and so goodbye now. I'll mail this letter from the next island so if you get it at all you'll know everything is OK with me. I love you dearly,

CHAPTER 18   *You can't tame a machine gun by looking it squarely in the eye*

Hale and Valerie. You are helping me a lot when you study and practice and avoid quarrels. I know you are doing as well as you can. Give Nana a big kiss for me. — Your Daddy

Consider "I don't mind being shot at" and "can't tame a machine gun by looking it in the eye." Was he taming inner fears with light-hearted banter or was he truly enjoying the risk-taking? I think a bit of both. His standing in the open during the convoy attack when all enlisted and non-essential personnel would have been ordered below decks was revealing; he was not about to miss that show. But later, he came to eschew thoughtless risk-taking; one takes risks, he said, only when the potential gains are of more value. Apparently, he saw some value in satisfying his own curiosity.

Wilber boarded the destroyer USS Saufley DD-465 on February 22 and arrived at Pavuvu with his battalion on February 23 [WB Journal]. This was a second phase of the division's first assault landing.

19

"Hail to you, My Nana"

Pavuvu Island, Russell Islands
February–April, 1943

The landings at Pavuvu and Banika Islands in the Russells on February 21 and 23 were unopposed and the Japanese made no attempt to drive the Americans from them. The landings were a learning experience according to one of Wilber's officers, Robert Patenge, who contacted me in 1996 and whom I visited late in his life. He told me his boat coxswain first landed him on the wrong island, Banika. Eleven months after the landings, Wilber made similar comments that were prompted when Norma sent him "bulletins" about the very first Allied landings on the "toe" of mainland Italy in September 1943.

JANUARY 15, 1944
… I enjoyed the "bulletins" from Italy. They were certainly interesting. The landing scene was good too where they were met by children selling things. That [It] …was a little like our landing on the Russells – nobody home! Probably it was just as well as there were some definitely amateur aspects to that landing. For example Rainey's pilot confessed during the night that he had never been in "these parts" before. I don't know why he should ever [have] been there, but Rainey was certainly disappointed in his pilot, especially after he spent the night on a reef.…

The 169th Field Artillery Battalion spent four months on Pavuvu "guarding the front" and training for future combat (Map 7). It was bivouacked in a palm tree grove planted by Lever Brothers, the international soap manufacturer. There they awaited the next advance up the Solomons, to attack the newly constructed Japanese airfield at Munda Point on New Georgia Island, about 120 miles to the northwest (Map 5). Their mission was to protect the Russells and in particular an American airfield that was to be constructed on Banika. Japanese bombers and fighters from Munda airfield did attack the 43rd Division encampments and later the Banika airfield. They also flew beyond the Russells to attack the American-held Henderson field on Guadalcanal. In turn, American fighters and bombers from Guadalcanal and the Russells hammered Munda airfield and others beyond it. Encounters between the two forces would lead to air battles over the Russells for which Wilber had a ringside seat.

FEB 24, 1943 [PAVUVU ISLAND, RUSSELL ISLANDS]

Dearest Wife of Mine — It's just two years ago today that the Army separated us [from each other] officially. I still don't like it. Just as soon as this war is over, I'm for a fine civilian suit any color just so it's not OD [olive drab] and a Stetson Hat to lose when I please and low shoes and a high quality belt with a rich but quiet buckle. Also I will want white shirts and sox to match the tie you select. It looks now as if you might have to meet me in Seattle or Frisco to do my shopping [when the war is over].

Today is hot and sultry. It is cloudy and has rained twice. I'm under another palm tree on another island now and just at present have a few minutes. We celebrated yesterday in a downpour and a lot of the men found out that trucks aren't the only way to move equipment + supplies. [They were carried by hand.] It was a rude awakening for some of them and tough work for all of them....

Today I saw a lovely marble topped dresser, which was in an abandoned plantation house. The drawers were half full of Japanese articles. It had apparently been used by some officer who had left hurriedly. There were fittings for belts, cartridge cases, shoes, [and] a decorative paper umbrella....

Feb 27 — Darling I'm back again. It's 2:30 P.M. and the past two days have been hectic and hot. We have been rushing all things artillery and furnishing transportation to other troops at the same time. Everything is quiet and peaceful. The beach is a lovely palm-lined shore until you find the coral is sharp as a knife and the water full of sharks. I've been organizing the area for defense and getting the details of food, shelter + water in order. The Japs very thoughtlessly did not leave things in the best of conditions.

You would enjoy this magnificent cocoanut palm grove. As I sit here they are making long corridors in all directions as far as I can see. They were planted in 1905 + 1906 + 1908 by Lever Bros. to whom I send students each year ... I also can see from here last year's crop on the ground. The current crop is falling now and helmets are definitely in style.

Sweetheart, Everything is OK with me. I hope it is with you too. Anyway I love you dearly and am waiting for the day we can be together again. — Love. XXXOOØ Wilber

x·o·ø·o·x

Norma was prompted to write old friends in Washington State to express her concern about Wilber's move to the front lines and possibly dangerous combat. Her knowledge of his exposure to danger could only be surmised from newscasts.

136 W. 4th St., N.Y.C., Mar. 1 [1943]
Dear Eileen, Carroll — Just a note to say we have just now heard that Wilber has gone up to the front to join Hud + Donald. Isn't it amazing they should get together in this way after separating so widely! Wilber's been in touch with Hud + Donald by personal messenger for some time but wrote from the boat on Feb. 16 [en route to Guadalcanal], he was on the way to see them.

Thank you for the wonderful letter to Wilber and the message to us.… My "babies" are just about as tall as I am, but still the same Hale and Valerie.

I had to send you the news about Wilber. I find my knees are weak today but know he'll be all right. Especially with Don + Hud around! — Love + best wishes, Norma Bradt

Norma's "my knees are weak today" expressed a genuine worry for Wilber as he went "up to the front."

x·o·ø·o·x

MAR. 2, 1943
Hello again [to Norma] — … Your letter written Jan 30 answering mine of Jan 17 came yesterday. Dearest, it is useless to send air mail now. It all comes about the same way, either by boat or by air. You undoubtedly know now that Malcolm [the deer on New Caledonia] didn't eat the M.O. He just chewed at the letter a bit.…
— Wilber

x·o·ø·o·x

> Wilber provided a rich description of Pavuvu Island and used a brilliant star as a segue into some romance.

MAR. 4, 1943

My Darling — It's noon now and I'm taking a little time off to be with you. It is hot but not too uncomfortable here. For three days it hasn't rained and the ground has lost its musty odor. The long rows of cocoanut palms look like cathedral aisles and at the end is oftentimes the very blue of the sea or the pure white of a cloud or the pale blue of the sky. In the evening just before sunset, I sit leaning against a palm, and in the west the sky is fiery red and orange thru the aisles. It is so bright thru the then dark palms that it nearly seems to be flames.

An hour later a great brilliant evening star [probably Capella] hangs above the horizon in that particular corridor in which I like to sit. It is beautiful, heavenly, and so lovely it cannot be looked at too long at a time. I imagine how the shepherds felt about the Star of B[ethlehem]. They must have felt it was too holy to be stared at, that rather it should be a symbol to be worshipped. You would never forget this Star if you could see it. I know my picture of it is poor but maybe you will have a glimmering of what I see.

> Capella would be low in the late evening; it would have set at about 1:30 AM. The brighter Sirius would be higher in the sky; setting at about 4 AM

Last night as the Star was setting, I turned on my radio and got an a cappella choir in Aus[tralia] which was singing one of the numbers you + I heard the St. Olaf's choir sing in Spokane. I don't know the name of the song + don't care, but it brought us together again. I remembered each second there with you, the beauty of the music, the realization that I must never never let you sit away from me, the feeling of having achieved a goal in my life I had needed for so long. All this came to me so vividly yesterday and was further made complete + consummated by my knowledge that you do still sit only with me, that your love is even greater than I had dreamed. Beloved, this war has made us nearer + dearer in many ways. Your chemist husband might never have seen the Star and never have remembered so much of our first time together. Hail to you, My Nana!

In this dark of the night, everything is quiet (sometimes) then, KLUNK! goes a cocoanut. Last night it seemed to happen every 15 minutes. I was awake most of the night so heard most of them. It's funny sometimes for maybe a voice in the dark will say "Missed me" and then more silence. We have seen some amazing things lately. Men wear helmets voluntarily, and dig slit trenches without instructions, watch for planes and do similar duties with enthusiasm.

I went into the jungle a couple of miles yesterday to get acquainted with it.

CHAPTER 19   *Hail to you, My Nana*

From left, Admiral William Halsey, Jr. 4-star area commander, and Major General (2-star) John Hester, commander of the 43rd Division in Russell Islands. It is doubtful that Hester really drove that jeep; he would always have had a driver. [NATIONAL ARCHIVES PHOTO: 208-AA-88B 1A]

So far it has been a long ways from being "impenetrable." My experience in the Olympics, at [Fort] Lewis [both in Washington], and in Maine are a big help. The jungle on this island is supposed to be pretty tough but you can write Culver that he + I have done worse. It is fascinating too. There are enormous trees with great gnarled roots, others with roots that make walls out from the tree trunk, so there are small rooms around the tree. Some are as white as birch, some stand on ten or twenty legs.... Others are the banyan with its limbs dropping roots to the ground. In nearly every tree are vines + vines. Many are enormous. Papaya is common and many trees have nuts + fruits in them. Breadfruit is here but so far I have seen none. Limes grow wild. I have a book on tropical fruits + flowers and try to read a little every day.... I love you. I want you, and I'll be wanting you when you read this too. — Wilber

x·o·ø·o·x

MAR. 10, 1943

Lovely one — … Did I tell you that we call the Jap planes that come over Washing Machine Charlie or Maytag Charlie because their motors are not synchronized and they make a rhythmic beat, RRRRRRrr RRRRRrrr RRRRRRrr.…

Oh yes. How about naming the baby Russell after your uncle. I think he would appreciate it, and I like the old gent. The S.E.P. [Saturday Evening Post] has dropped out since our last activities and I'm expecting soon to have the ideal situation where installment I to VII of the last murder mystery are all available at once.…

I love you. I love you. Must stop now. Here is a kiss for each lovely breast. — XXXOOO Wilber

> The reference to "naming the baby Russell" was clearly a hint about his location in the Russell Islands. He was certainly unaware of any real baby, and Norma had no uncle named Russell. But upon reading of "the baby" Norma could only have been engulfed by a cold fear that he had somehow learned of her pregnancy.

x·o·ø·o·x

MAR. 13, 1943

Flower of Mine — Two more letters came, yours of Feb. 2 + Hale's of Feb. 8… Imagine my children big enough to put out incendiary bombs! [This referred to air-raid drills in school.] I'm impressed. Won't they be good at sprinkling the garden when we go back to Maine? All I'll have to do is put an incendiary bomb out where I want sprinkling and yell "Bomb."

It was nice of F. [Wilber's father] to give Hale a copy of Mark Twain. I know how he must enjoy it. Don't worry about Father not writing. He tries to keep the peace in his own home, and I know [he] is really interested in the children. His letters often mention them. You have done a good job on Mn [Manganese patent]. When you can, thank Burgess for me too.…

> Wilber's mother Elizabeth would not have favored her husband writing to Norma.

I spent an hour this morning putting spikes in another pair of shoes. In the jungle they go [bad] pretty fast (shoes), and one pair is good for just one more long climb, then I'll take out the spikes + save them. In the jungle I wear them near the toe and instep … and when I step, those in the toe dig in and no slipping back occurs. When I'm jumping from root to root or limb to limb of trees I step in the instep and stick like a cat. When sliding down rocks or jumping from one to another, I land flat footed and hold my ankles stiff and do I slow down! I do. A hundred times a day I thank you for a firm footing. With these spikes I think I can wear any Jap in the jungle right down to a frazzle and don't ever forget I've two wicked weapons more. If I ever kick anyone's teeth in with these shoes, even the "near misses" will really make marks. You know how handy Paw is at kicking door lintels and chandeliers in peace time.... Love to Hale, to Valerie + to Nana. — XXXOOØ, Wilber

> Norma was writing Wilber assiduously and sending him things he needed. The spikes she sent him for his shoes were essential for getting around in the jungle. It is surprising they were not standard army equipment for all the men in this terrain. Army planning was not perfect, and improvisation by the individual soldier was essential.
>
> (And just to eliminate any doubt in the reader's mind, Wilber never kicked in lintels or chandeliers or anything else. He was not a violent person!)

x·o·ø·o·x

MAR 27, 1943

Maid O'Mine [Norma] — We have been here over a month now and are practically at home. Life has been pretty quiet. For example I don't even get down to the local movie (There isn't any.) Neither have I been to a single dance. (Thank Goodness.) Of course we go skiing quite often (in the mud) and have picnics in the woods (canned rations for lunch)....

Our neighbors [Japanese] on the next island come over [in airplanes] frequently (nearly every night) and we all get up + stay by our slit trenches until the All Clear comes along. We aren't quite in his favorite target area so are usually spectators. Whenever I see the anti-aircraft shells bursting high in the air, I think of the Star Spangled Banner and get a thrill for I know the flag is still there. Incidentally we now are the farthest forward troops in this part of the war. The boys are quite proud of that fact. It's about time they had something to their credit except enduring monotony....

... The word I have is that I have been recommended by Files and Knight [executive officer of the divisional artillery and C.O. of 169th FA Bn. respectively] to the Gen. [Barker] for the next vacancy for battalion commander. Since there is no vacancy in sight and since my standing might change before one occurs, I am not particularly excited. It looks to me as if I were in my rut and probably my next opportunity will be to put on civilian clothes.

Anyway it's good to know I am in good standing here; I'll try to stay that way. Another reason I would not request transfer now is that it could be said I decided after and because of enemy action. Anyway I have Hud + Cris + Don just one island back of me [on Guadalcanal]. That is a cheering thought.…

Your account of the wedding + reception [for Monte Jr.] was interesting. However there is one Bourjaily wedding I don't want you to attend [Monte Sr. and Norma!] so beware of your irresistible charm. I'm figuring on a silver wedding trip [25th anniversary in 1952] to Lake Louise for you, and the plans can't be changed at this late date.…

> Wilber might have passed this off lightly as a kind of joke, but the mere thought seemed to reveal an underlying uneasiness about the situation at home. This comment did not go unnoticed, as we shall see. He certainly was not consciously concerned, because, after discussing routine business, he turned absolutely poetic about Norma with no hint of concern.

What a shame to waste time in writing business to you. What I want to talk about is my Norma and her lovely eyes and the perfume of her hair and the softness of her lips. I want to plan hours with her and to recall wonderful days shared with her. She must be told that my love for her is like a golden waterfall in a snowcapped mountain, irresistible, flooding and a rushing power, which is above the strength of man. I'd like to go with my Love to Cinci [Cincinnati] and live in a little apartment [as they had from 1927 to 1930] and eat macaroni and walk the sidewalks and sit in Eden Park and steal a kiss on a streetcar. We could go to Lexington [Kentucky] again and to the Ohio hills and to the shows and out to funny little restaurants.

But always we would come home together and I'd love you and take you for mine. Maybe it would be better to go to Ponte Vedra [recalling our Florida vacation in 1941] for after all we have two children you know, and we would swim + walk the beach and sit in the hotel and loaf in our cottage. We could dance at night or just look at the sea + sky and know we were together. Also don't forget about night. Then is when we won't be sleeping. We'll do that in the afternoons. — Love Love Love. Wilber E. Bradt

> What memories and dreams he had!

x·o·ø·o·x

> Wilber chose this day to send me a morning snapshot of his world on Pavuvu Island; he was doing his fatherly duty.

CHAPTER 19   *Hail to you, My Nana*

MARCH 29, 1943

Dear Son — The planes are going "Zoom, Zoom, Zoom," overhead. It is morning before breakfast and the air is very quiet and cool. The palm trees are full of birds and cocoanuts. The birds are waiting to see the sun come up, and the cocoanuts are waiting for someone to walk under their tree without a helmet. Since they are as high as our house they land with quite a whomp. One of the planes is just now coming back in a hurry. We always wonder what he saw or did to make him hurry so. Maybe he thinks, "Gee Whiz, I left the coffee on the stove." or "Holy Smokes, forty Jap planes! I'd better go get the boys!" or "Oh Boy, Oh Boy, hotcakes for breakfast," or "I sure ruined that ship, I'll hurry home and tell the Skipper and ask for ten days leave," or "Come on Jessie, let's go home, maybe I got a letter." Anyway, this time he must have come after "the boys" for "the boys" are sure going back up front now.

The sun is coming up now and a whole row of varicolored dragon flies have lined up on each tent rope to get the first rays. They are bright red with black bodies, and some with transparent wings and bodies except for a yellow spot at their tail and a yellow head. Others are like that except the spots are red. They look like just two spots of color sailing thru the air always the same distance apart. Others are brown or green or yellow winged with striped bodies. However, they all line up on the tent rope together … When they are tired their wings fold forward around their head.…

There are natives here too.… [They] kept sending up a lot of signal flares at night probably to Japs. However we told Chief Tom that if it happened anymore, there would be some big explosions right in his village. The flares stopped right then.

It's nearly noon now and I have been interrupted by the morning work. I also did some digging on my trench both for the exercise and to get a little more room. There still isn't room in it both for me and a bomb. If one falls right in with me, I expect to get out in a hurry. However if one just falls nearby I expect to be as comfortable as a bug in the mud.…

Please write me again when you have time. I enjoy your letters a lot. Mother writes me some very fine things about your conduct and I am glad she can. Please give Mother and Valerie a hug for me. — I Love you, Wilber

> Wilber injected a bit of humor, "room … for me and a bomb," probably to shield us from the realities of his own vulnerability. He would become much more serious in his letters when he entered close-in combat. In the midst of all this, he was still able to focus on the beauty around him, whether it was "palm trees full of birds" or "varicolored dragon flies."

x·o·ø·o·x

Norma by now surely knew she was pregnant and had, we can infer, decided against an abortion. An abortion would have been very tempting because of the great shame attached to an out-of-wedlock pregnancy. It was a taboo subject; girls in high school would disappear to "visit Aunt Millie" for a few months. And it was expensive to have a safe and legal abortion, say, by going to Canada. Monte had run through his resources and had little to contribute. Nevertheless, between the two, they probably could have managed a discreet abortion. The likely scenario was that Norma decided to see the pregnancy through for moral and religious reasons. It was also possible that Monte, at age 49, wanted another child to whom he could pay more attention than he had paid to his own boys. More likely, though, Monte was acceding to Norma's strong feelings.

Did they have a plan? First and foremost it was to keep the pregnancy a secret from family and friends and even from Valerie and me because of the disgrace it represented. Furthermore, it was conventional wisdom reinforced by government announcements that bad news written to overseas soldiers would damage their morale and thus endanger their lives. Keeping the secret from Wilber was essential to his well-being, and it was their patriotic duty!

In this letter, Wilber responded to Norma's laying the first seeds of her grand deception. She was, she had said, considering doing some sort of "war work."

MAR. 31, 1943

Dearest — Today ends my first six months of foreign service [since leaving San Francisco]. If the next six is as interesting as the past I will have no complaints. One thing I want to make definite is the fact that I am more sure than ever you are the sweetest girl in the world. So here's to a happy six months from Wilber....

We were visited and inspected by our corps commander the other day and received an official and written commendation. It is being read to the men today.

It's April 1st now and I'm sitting naked in my canvas chair. The occasion is that I have been digging my trench deeper and larger....

[April 2, 1943] ... You ask about Mobilization of Women. I don't know the answer. If you think you should go and can arrange for the care of the children, go ahead.... I could say I want you to stay home but I also want this war to end the right way and as soon as possible. One thing, please remember that you are inclined to take on too much. If you do go into the service of our country in any way, go in all over and don't try to keep up the home work and the other too. What about [working for] the F.B.I.?

The children are old enough to understand, and they would be old enough to realize their responsibility too. Remember boys Hale's age work in factories in Europe and girls Valerie's age gather scraps of garbage for food. Whatever you do, I'll not worry....

I love you, My Darling. Whatever you do will be OK with me anytime. Just keep well for me. — XXXOOØ Wilber

> Wilber's acceptance of Norma doing war work and giving up home-making was impressively progressive. At that time, women were moving into previously male jobs due to shortages of male workers; "Rosie the Riveter" was the prototypical factory worker. Most of these workers were lower-class and minority women who had moved from lower paying traditional women's jobs, but many middle class women were also entering the workforce. Most men with sufficient means preferred that their wives stay at home, and mothers of children were urged to stay at home to care for them. Wilber's adequate salary, his overseas service, and their two children certainly exempted Norma from any financial or moral pressure to do war work. Wilber's easy acquiescence to her "plan" is thus quite surprising to me. He probably attributed this to her strong patriotism and typical enthusiasm for taking on new projects. He still warned her not to "take on too much."

x · o · ø · o · x

APRIL 8, 1943
Hello Snow White [Norma] — This is one of the dwarfs, Grouchy. Do you remember how Snow White used to manage him and make him grin? Well I'd like you to love me and play with me until I forget all the worries and duties and work I'm supposed to do and just know you are with me. Yesterday was another general's day and you can imagine all the touring and escorting and explaining that went on. Today we are recovering from the strain. Everything is officially "Fine! Fine! Just Fine!" We continually have showers and thunderstorms so I suspect the rainy season approaches. That isn't too bad because it is much cooler and breezes are common.

... In about an hour I leave for our most historical island [Guadalcanal] to take a short orientation course – a study of the battlefields on the battlefields....

Yesterday we had another air show except that we were below the clouds and the planes above ... We saw one U.S. plane thru a hole in the clouds [going] after a Zero [Japanese fighter plane] with three Zeros right after him. We heard "control" tell him there were some behind him. Our pilot was apparently named Winfield for he was called by that. There was a lot of wild sound of firing and flying coming out of that cloud for a few minutes. "Control" kept asking Winfield if he was there and no answer. We didn't know whether he was too busy to talk or down until everything was over and "control" asked, "Did Winfield and D— return to the field?" When we heard the field answer that they were back OK we felt like cheering. Those boys of ours sure are doing a great job up there. I don't think there is a soldier who doesn't realize that the Air Corps is saving them a lot of punishment and thank them for it.

I must stop and tell you just once more that I love you more than anything in the world. Kiss the children + give them a big hug for me. I love you — Wilber XXXOOØ

> Control of the air in a combat region was all-important. The Americans were working to establish it in the Solomons.

x · o · ø · o · x

Nighttime in a boat on the water was always a magical experience for Wilber. Here he described a trip partway to Guadalcanal on a PT boat of the kind Jack Kennedy commanded. This was a fast ride in waters subject to Japanese attacks; but it too had poetic aspects. Back on land, he wrote about his very mobile command post.

APR. 10, 1943

It's Pop again [to Norma] — … It's a good day to write for I am back under my palm trees and it's nearly noon. Noon is a good time to be in the shade. About each ten minutes the phone rings for me so I feel a bit interrupted so far as this letter is concerned. The trip to the next island back [Guadalcanal] didn't materialize. Rather I got halfway and my orders were cancelled, so after a nice ride on a PT boat during the night I'm on the job again.

The ride was a thrilling experience. You know it was these boats that took MacArthur out of Bataan [actually Corregidor]. They travel fast and altho we weren't rushing I would guess we were doing more than 35 miles per hour. The night was cloudy for the first half of the trip and as dark as I ever saw it. The sea was more phosphorescent than I had ever seen. As we (two boats) speeded along, the wake seemed all afire with greenish yellow fire. In the general glow, were many little whirlpools and swirls of brilliant glowing spots that danced and brightened to an almost flame-like intensity. The spray beside our bow often came above the rail (if it had been a rail). It looked like a spray of molten silver and the waves out from the bow looked like living essence of moonlight.

CHAPTER 19   *Hail to you, My Nana*

I sat beside [Capt. Ed] Keegan and [Capt. Dixwell] Goff astride a torpedo tube and was practically speechless with the beauty of the whole picture. One could imagine that Elijah saw something like that when he was taken up to heaven. I wish you could have been with me for you would have appreciated the glory and delicacy of the sea. Later the clouds cleared and the stars came out and added the beauty of the sky to that of the sea. Dearest there is so much that is lovely and fine and unforgettable even in war. Don't ever forget.

Incidentally Hale + Valerie will be interested to know there were three Jap flags painted on this boat. That means official credit for sinking three of their ships. It's raining now, so you see how often and quickly the rain can come.

I'm in the tent now. My phone is on a long wire so the phone moves with me, in the tent, out of the tent, under one palm, then another wherever the shade is best. Where[ever] I sit is the C.P. [Command Post]. Sometimes the C.P. moves into my slit trench, which now is quite to my satisfaction. I'm down below the surface about three feet on to clean coral rock (no mud) with a roof of sheet iron and logs to stop fragments and stray bullets from planes. The logs are reinforced by sand bags and the whole thing [is] camouflaged.… I love you and Hale + Valerie. — Wilber XXXOOØ

Wilber was very well prepared for bombing raids.

20

"We have ourselves a general now"

Pavuvu, The Russell Islands
April–May, 1943

The 169th Field Artillery Battalion was still on Pavuvu in the Russell Islands. Wilber wrote Valerie, about to turn 11, more vivid descriptions of air raids and nighttime sounds.

APRIL 12, 1943

Darling Valerie — Your very neat and interesting letter that you wrote on Lincoln's Birthday came a few days ago. I enjoyed it immensely. Since this is April 12th and practically your birthday (Apr. 18), it is just the day to write to you.…

Last night the Japs sent a plane over us to look around. It was pretty dark but the moon gave some light. All our lights were out and the men put out their cigarettes and got into their trenches. The first thing, a little light started in one of the tents, I yelled, "Put out that light." The fire got bigger and ten men yelled, "Put out that light." All the time this plane was going around and around up in the air. Zoom, zoom, zoom trying to decide where to drop his bombs. Zoom Zoom Zoom. The fire got still bigger and about fifty men yelled, "Put out that fire." Finally the corporal in charge of that tent looked up out of his hole and saw it was his fire. He let out a bellow and six men popped out of his hole like Jumping Jacks and grabbed this waste basket of burning paper and rushed over + dumped it into a hole wrong side up and sat on it.

The plane kept going around up there in the sky Zoom Zoom Zoom, then all at once over on a hill in the jungle away from everybody there was a big "WHOOMP," and in a minute another "WHAUMP" and the Jap plane started off toward his island Zoom Zoom Zoom Zoom Zoom Zoom … saying, "Boy I just put them in the exact spot. Maybe I'll get a medal, well anyway an extra dish of rice for this." In a little while all our soldiers came out of their trenches and went back to bed.

Thirty minutes later all one could hear was the guards moving now and then and the telephone operator on night duty answering the phone and a lot of good comfortable and noisy snores. Everyone settled down for a good night's sleep except for two other times later in the night when the Japs came back probably to see if they could see any damage.

Between times the wild dogs in the mountains howl and howl and howl, and there are heads of cattle loose on the island. They graze thru our camps and bawl and snuffle and chew their cuds. One night the general slept up here and he claimed they spent the night right outside his tent belching and blowing and pulling grass and bellowing and bawling. There are some with bass voices, some altos, tenors, sopranos and a few falsetto cows so he had a good chorus especially when the wild dogs joined in with their devil's chorus. The general hasn't been here at night since....

I love you Sweetheart and am thinking about you everyday. Take good care of Nana and Hale for me. — Your Father, Wilber

x·o·ø·o·x

On April 15, the first of two airstrips on Banika Island, the island adjacent to Pavuvu, was completed.

APRIL 15, 1943

What a Day! [to Norma] — Letters and letters and letters all at once. We had received no mail for quite a while then WHAM you break thru from the 4th dimension with mail galore. Dearest you are so faithful and loyal and dear. They were such wonderful letters, so full of love and inspiration and news and cheer. The dates were Mar 1, 4, 6, 7, 8, 13, 14, 15, 21, 23, 24. I had already received Mar 5, 10, 9 and cleaned Feb. [have answered all your February letters.]

> Norma was saturating Wilber with letters, perhaps driven in part by a sense of guilt. Her contribution to the war effort was to be supportive of her overseas soldier and above all to protect him from disconcerting news that could distract him in combat. Did those letters arise from a need to remain close to Wilber and to keep their love alive?

... Your church letter was one of the nicest yet. I wish I could have walked in and sat beside you while you wrote....

> Norma often sat in Grace Episcopal Church before and after services waiting for me to finish my choir duties. She was a deeply religious woman. Her prayers in that church at that time must have been intense and anguished.

The enclosed piece of aluminum is to be a bracelet for Valerie. Hale can take it to his shop and have it bent into a circle so it will just slip over her hand. It is made from a plane flown by a Jap who thought we couldn't shoot straight. I hope that Valerie likes it....

Here is a kiss and a hug and an hour before the fireplace with my arms about you. All from me and no one else. — XXXOOØ Wilber

> Clearly, Wilber was totally unaware of Norma's situation. His awareness of his vulnerability, though, was evident in his "you are so faithful and loyal and dear" and in the pointed closing of the letter, which would have gone straight to Norma's heart. I doubt though that Norma was miserable every hour of every day. She would have accepted her lot in life and conscientiously continued her mothering, music, and writing, and of course, the letters to her man overseas. The arrival of one of Wilber's poetic courting letters would likely have momentarily pierced whatever equanimity she had managed to build after the previous such letter. For his part, Wilber was effectively keeping himself in the game.

x · o · ø · o · x

It was Easter on Pavuvu, and there was the reality of military life on Pavuvu overlaid with Wilber's imaginative visions of the scenes around him.

EASTER MORNING [APRIL 25, 1943]
The Top of the morning to ye' [to Norma] — Hello smiling eyes. Happy Easter. Today you should be opening a pair of ear-rings for Nana but I timed things for Valerie's birthday and missed that too. So today you must remember that this morning I wanted you to have a little extra joy. This Easter morning is cool and fresh. The sun is just up peeping between clouds that showered us last night. The air smells clean and a quiet breeze is drifting thru the palms. A few hundred yards away, at our homemade chapel, the R. Catholics are holding high mass. The singing sounds fine probably because the portable organ has given up the ghost. The chants + songs are all a cappella.

In the south, the bluest sky I have ever seen symbolizes the hope of peace that is in every soldier's heart today. Farther to the west, great mountainous heaps of pure white clouds form fairylands with coves and castles and cliffs and gorges in which invisible giants live who probably battle all the little fairies. To the north, the sea glints thru the corridors of palms like a band of silver thru green lace. Overhead the white and red and blue birds all [are] a bit less raucous and make bright jewels of color in the green trees. Even Lizzie the Lizard our neighborly two-foot lizard came out of my trench to greet the Easter Sun. Of course the poor cooks are as always laboring around their kitchens with a thin column of smoke coming up even from their practical altars [stoves].…

Good Bye now. I love you this Easter Day and am praying that God will care for you and for Hale + for Valerie. I am your most devoted and adoring husband. — XXXOOØ Wilber

x·o·ø·o·x

Norma offered a few glimpses of our life in New York City in a letter to Prof. Irwin Douglass, Wilber's replacement as department head of the University of Maine.

Apr. 26, 1943 [Monday]
Dear Doug — A message from Wilber says that the first shipment of Indalone [mosquito repellant] has arrived and been put into use. "It is very effective and has a not unpleasant odor."

He wanted me to thank you, as on a night when the mosquitoes were very bad, he had been forced, by orders, to leave his mosquito bar and sleeping bag. He applied the Skat twice during the night. Thanks from me, too.

I hope this finds you all well. Valerie has mumps on both sides and Hale has gone alone to visit his Uncle Paul in Washington, D.C.

Best Easter season greetings to you and Grace and children. — Norma B.

Norma had planned for all three of us to visit Washington, D.C., during the spring school breaks. Because Valerie was sick, I took the train alone. Previous family trips to Florida and Mississippi had made me quite familiar with Pennsylvania Station and train travel. I was 12 at the time.

Paul Bradt was an expert rock climber and a founding member of the rock climbing section of the Washington, D.C., Appalachian Trail Club. On that visit, I was first exposed to rock climbing on Old Rag Mountain in the Blue Ridge, a favorite of that group. I remember walking with Paul at night in Washington, seeing lit-up factories we were not permitted to approach because of war security. Paul looked so much like Wilber that I could not conjure up how my dad's face was different.

x·o·ø·o·x

CHAPTER 20 We have ourselves a general now

Norma's intense letter writing campaign continued into April. How to conceal her pregnancy, now at three months, from Valerie and me was a problem she needed to face. Sending us to summer camp would be part of the solution.

APRIL 30, 1943
Darling Norma — Last night two letters came from that little Blonde again. I must have made quite a hit with her for she writes me faithfully nearly every day....

Your ideas for the children's summer camp sound very practical and interesting. I am only worried about you while they are away. Will you be too lonesome? I don't remember your being completely abandoned by your family before. Of course that might be just the rest you need. Please plan something really nice for yourself and don't just work harder or be a little orphan Norma at home....

Did you know that Griswold has re-entered my life. He was the commanding Gen. of the IV Corps who asked after me by name in Miss[issippi]. That created quite a bit of consternation in the Bn. then. He is now our Corps commander again, which is good news. There is no tendency on his part to be fooled by eye wash [b—s—]. He inspected us today and it was a pleasure to hear questions asked about essentials. Some, by the way, will force a very active reconsideration of some views I have proposed [on operating in the jungle]. When I made them, they were smiled away, but now it seems he too does not consider the jungle [to be] impenetrable. It seems now too that a lot of those special reconnaissances of mine [into the jungle] are right down the groove. Of course, he doesn't know anything of that but it was reassuring to see him force the same ideas on some of my colleagues. Incidentally he considers ordinary division and island generals in about the same light as I do Second Lts. Once he said "where is that general? No not you. That other general here. Oh there you are. What about —?"

This was vindication for Wilber. He had continued his habit of hiking into the jungled and mountainous interior. The value of this had not been appreciated by his colleagues and seniors. Whether or not elements of the division had received adequate jungle training would become a vital issue several months later in their first combat.

A corps consisted of two or more divisions and its commander was nominally a lieutenant (three-star) general. Maj. Gen. Oscar Griswold, West Point class of 1910, was still a two-star general when he took over the XIV Corps, of which the 43rd Division was a part, in April 1943; he was 58. His knowing Wilber, a lowly major, by name was no small tribute. They would meet again later under combat conditions. Wilber's attitude toward his senior officers was worth watching. He exhibited modesty about his own position mixed with some cynicism about the bureaucracy emanating from above. This prompted him to steer clear of his seniors so he was free to do his job as he saw it. On the other hand, he exhibited frank admiration of officers he respected and was proud when they complimented his work. How all this would play out under the pressure of combat was not yet clear.

May 1 — Don't worry about me getting into my dugout on time. I'm trying to do this war with my head [intelligently]. If it is time to take cover, I do. We are not yet undergoing any hardships, nor are we staging any epochal battles. So don't let your imagination get you all worried. Remember, I told you that the news items always play up the spectacular items and create an impression that all the front is strenuous, hazardous and glory ridden. As I have said so often, it is more commonly a battle against boredom, disease and little annoyances. That is still true most of the time. You must always remember this because the other course will give you needless worry.

> This captured well the difference between the presentation of the war in the news and the reality of the war. But then, suddenly, Wilber adopted a whole new persona.

Your dream of us is still just a little bit in error. If I'm ever in bed with you where people who are coming and going can see us, they will see a lot of activity. Don't ever worry. When we are in bed together from now on, you are going to be a very busy girl. It is going to be pretty hard to get an uninterrupted night's sleep too. Those little annoyed "No!s" of the middle of the night are going to be changed to some very pained "Oh!s" Don't count either on my spending much time playing with your breasts and body to "get you ready."

You can plan on keeping yourself ready whenever I'm around. And furthermore, right now you want to start training the muscles of your stomach and those that hold up your breasts. When I get home I plan to burn all your girdles, corsets and brassieres and I want those two luscious breasts to raise right up and beg whenever I am near them. You won't be mad Dear about my not taking you. You will be scared about what I'll do to you while I am taking you. Also you had better take advantage of the opportunities of the N.Y.C. libraries to study up on the methods of the great seductresses such as Mme Pompadour, Cleopatra, Helen of Troy and some of your own Norman ancestresses. I expect to be a willing pupil but demand the best.

So My Lover, times a flitting, and you have a lot to do beside practice piano and write about love and take care of the children. Your big job is to be ready for the return of your man. After that you can close your professional careers and concentrate on how to keep a man busy in bed, on davenports, on the floor by the fire, in the tall grass, among the trees. There isn't going to be one inch on this lovely little body that you can call your own after this war ends. Anyway your dream was a start in the right direction but was a rather weak start.

I can see you expect the picture to be like the past. Do you know what happened to you on your first night in Miss. [Mississippi]? That was a very small and mild sample of what is to come. I could give you a few advance tips but it would only break down the censor's (me) morale now. So prepare yourself. I have no intention of coming home a tired worn out old man. It's only fair to warn you I'm more fit now than I have been since you have known me. Also the recollection of my joy in you coupled with an accumulated desire for your body of over two years gives me a lot of incentive for a bit of violent high-grade love making and you're it.

> From where did all this tough talk come? It approached a threat of rape! It was so unlike the Wilber of earlier letters. He was putting on a "tough-guy" persona that, in my experience, was typical of military talk, but it did not fit him. He could have been primed for it by the long deployment without women and the attendant frustration and repression. Perhaps Norma had set him off by suggesting that he needed to take time to help her "get ready" so she could readapt to him. She much later told me that she needed that kind of attention when he returned from overseas and that he had not adequately provided it. This outburst clearly reflected the not uncommon view then, and perhaps now for some, that a woman's role was to serve her man and that aggressive lovemaking was OK and could be exciting for a woman. "No means No" was not yet on the scene in 1943.

… For the past few weeks, Davis + I have been "forbidden" the jungle so I have made little [geology] progress. However I have prepared a map for the [Geology] Soc. but of course can only hold it until after the war …. Now that Griswold is back with us, the interest in the jungle is increasing by leaps and bounds, and I expect soon to be encouraged to continue my expeditions. Just now Davis [his frequent companion on hikes] is under the weather, apparently nothing serious, maybe a touch of sun.

… You + Monte surely put me in the pot. Why don't I ever learn to keep my big mouth shut?

> This line referred to their (Norma and Monte's) response to Wilber's comment in an earlier letter [3/27/43] that he did not want to hear of Norma attending "another Bourjaily wedding" i.e., one between her and Monte, Sr. It appears that not only Norma wrote in protest, but Monte himself also did to reassure Wilber there was only friendship between him and Norma. Wilber could not see through their disingenuous protests. The

long delay for round-trip communications played a role here. Wilber was reminded of the potential of another man in her life a full month after he "misspoke." It could only have reinforced any subconscious doubt he might have had. However, he successfully put them aside, closing on a gentle note:

… Goodbye now, my sweet Dove.… Love Love Kiss Kiss. Why Dear don't we go up the stairs together again. — Wilber XXXOOØ

x·o·ø·o·x

The monthly letters to his father continued as did his concern for his parents' well being.

MAY 1, 1943

Dear Father — Mother's [68th] birthday should be a good day for a letter. I hope it is a good day for her and for you. It seems queer to find the days getting shorter and temperatures dropping (to 85–90°F) here as May approaches. We do notice a definite easing of the heat. Each month is divided into two parts: the light of the moon or air raid season, and the dark of the moon when we expect shore landings. The days are divided into three conditions: Green (or secure), Yellow (unidentified planes in the distance) and Red (or enemy planes overhead). Of course "overhead" is used pretty loosely so frequently we only watch the show. At other times we take to the ground with some enthusiasm. So you see we are having a quiet time just now.…

I'm glad you didn't take the probation job because of the extra work. How about your living costs? Is the $25.00 enough to keep you going? I don't see now where I can get more, but if the need is urgent I'll do what I can. Don't hesitate to write me anyway. — I love you, Wilber

x·o·ø·o·x

MAY 4, 1943

Good Afternoon Nana — This is Dopey speaking from a very wet jungle island. No I didn't go somewhere. The rain came today. First it was a cloud burst and now just a good steady rain. I set my two canvas buckets under the tent edge and have both filled with fine soft water. Baths coming up.

Yesterday I … made an inspection of some of our barbed wire defenses. Ask Hale if he knows what a "cheval de frise" is. It's a gate of barbed wire, which can be put in or taken out of a wire defense. My infantry experience [in the Washington State National Guard] is helpful every once in a while.…

CHAPTER 20   *We have ourselves a general now*

It's still raining, and I'm reminded of your hard efforts to give me a good vacation on the Oregon coast once. I'm ashamed of my persistent despondence now. It must have been quite a trial. I ought to be able to enjoy a vacation after this war. There is certainly plenty of time spent just letting time pass. I'm pretty good at it except I find myself grinding my teeth sometimes. That is probably a subconscious desire for a good pre-war steak....

... It's mail time, so here is my arm about you until the next time. — XXXOOO Wilber

> The reference to "persistent despondence" might have been his first admission in extant letters of such a problem. We first heard of it from Norma in her 1941 (February 3) letter to his parents. This letter implied that it might have gone on for some time during that vacation. There was another occasion "on a trip into Yellowstone [National Park]" mentioned in his letter of January 27, 1944 (Book 2). Vacations can be a challenge for some, in that the driving force of an occupation is missing. I never knew or heard of depression incapacitating Wilber in his occupation or home life. This suggests to me that it was only an occasional problem for him, but perhaps it was more. It was a positive sign, though, that he was able to acknowledge it.

x · o · ø · o · x

General Griswold's interest in jungle training was having practical consequences, to Wilber's satisfaction.

MAY 9, 1943
Hello Golden Girl — I hope today is a fine warm spring day with gentle breezes and clean sunshine just for my family. School will be nearly over by the time you get this letter and I can just imagine all the plans and ideas that are in ferment as to what happens then....

In my last letter [actually that of April 30], I spoke of the inspiration and encouragement I had gotten from Gen Griswold's visit and inspection. It is beginning to have some very specific consequences. I am now ordered to do that which I have been unable to obtain permission to do before. A lot of wishful thinking [that jungle training was not necessary] on the part of several high officers has been re-evaluated. You have no idea how much better I feel because of having him at the helm again. You will recall that it was Griswold and the IV Corps, which then included us, that ran the entire First Army ragged in the Carolina maneuvers in '41. We have ourselves a general now.

My CO [Knight], not being enthused about hiking in jungles and as he said, because of my demonstrated liking for that sort of thing, gave me that end of things. Because it is not my normal duty, I could have declined but I'm glad of the experience so took it on. My previous work had really saved his face anyway because he could say we had already started what is now required. There is no additional hazard, so you need not be concerned. We will just get a little mountain and jungle experience.… — XXXOOO Wilber

> Wilber was beginning to lose confidence in his commanding officer.

x · o · ø · o · x

> Meanwhile, Wilber's reputation for hiking was getting a lot of play, and he was obviously proud of it.

MAY 12, 1943
Beloved Wife — Here I am again with a lot of love for my Darling. It's a nice clear and hot afternoon with the sunshine making gleaming emerald patterns across the grass in the aisles between the palms.…

This boy Davis would talk your arm off in one hour, and I find [he] has been giving me a lot of publicity in the infantry. I was checking with them [the infantry] on going into an area where they were firing day before yesterday and discovered their chief concern was that I would overtake their men who had six hours start and get in front of them during the firing. I laughed that off but Col. Fowler said "Oh No. They knew about my hiking abilities" and "They understood I really covered the ground." Now I'll have to be very careful that I don't get involved in one of their marches and disillusion them. If they ever saw me going up these mountains in super low gear, I'm sure the speed wouldn't impress them. Anyway the reputation seems a bit widespread.

Yesterday another aspect of the same thing cropped up. [General] Barker + Lt. Col. Knight had been going around + around over some position possibilities [i.e., where to place artillery howitzers] with no progress. Eventually B. blew up and ordered me down to his Hq. It is a two hour boat trip [to Banika Island; Map 7]. So down I went expecting I might get blasted for [in place of] Knight. No such luck. B. told me what he wanted. I told him what was unreasonable including a reference to King Canute who you recall ordered the tide not to come in. He got the point and asked what I recommended which was fine. "Fine!" "Fine!" "FINE!" It seems I'm one of the only two officers [in division artillery?] who have gone to see what's in the jungle.

CHAPTER 20   *We have ourselves a general now*

This probably referred to plans for emplacing artillery for the forthcoming Munda operation beginning June 30. The 169th Field Artillery Battalion would be stationed on a jungle island (Sasavele) just off the "mainland." Wilber may have assured Barker that it was feasible to so place the battalion there and for it to function well. General Barker was commander of the divisional artillery and thus was Knight's boss, and Knight as battalion commander was Wilber's boss. Barker's frustration with Knight in their discussions (arguments?) about "position possibilities" must have been enormous, given that he called upon Knight's subordinate (Wilber) for his opinions. The army way was to follow the chain of command, and this definitely was not it.

… I really + truly am most happy about my family + I love each of you with all my heart. — Wilber XXXOOØ

x · o · ø · o · x

MAY 14, 1943
Dearest Girl [Norma] — My sun is shining again because I have three letters from you; Apr. 6, 7, and 19. It's always so nice to hear from you, to know your thoughts and know you are still all right. One letter had a paper by HVDB [Hale] (87%). Very interesting and well done.…

Your report on Hale's ability with a violin is certainly fine. I hope he really gets pleasure out of it. Mrs. Z. [Irma Zacharias, my violin teacher] is certainly nice to be interested in Hale, but Hale is a pretty nice boy to be interested in too. If you stop his choir activities next year to get him outdoors more, won't finances become a problem again? I had thought the choir experience was the most worthwhile of his activities. Your comments about gym and baseball and other impromptu games had made me feel that Hale was getting a well balanced life. Why don't you discuss him with some of his teachers? Of course, there is no need to point out to you the problems [that] will develop from too much free time.

It would be good for both children to have work out of doors in the summer. A farm would be ideal, but the one in Indiana is out of the question. I don't want them to be where there is a critical attitude toward you. If you went west for a summer with them that might be possible. In another year, that might be a solution. For this year I think your plan for camps will be best.

… May 16 — This letter is getting to be a serial. Anyway you get all the installments at once. Dearest, I love you this peaceful Sunday morning. There is never

a day that I don't wonder at the miracle of my having you for a wife and mate....
— XXXOOØ Wilber

Norma's pregnancy was surely dominating her thinking. The school year would end soon and she needed to be ready for it. Camps would cover the summer, and she was exploring her options beyond that.

On April 22, the Allies in Tunisia had launched a final offensive on the isolated Axis troops in Northern Tunisia, which were suffering a severe lack of supplies due to increasing Allied control of the air and the Mediterranean. On May 13, the Axis troops in Tunisia surrendered with some 250,000 German and Italian troops passing into captivity; North Africa was in Allied hands.

In the North Pacific, a small American force moved to eject the Japanese from the two western Aleutian Islands they had occupied since June 1942. On May 11, U.S. troops landed on Attu, the westernmost Aleutian island. Fighting continued there through May. On June 8, the Japanese ordered the evacuation of nearby Kiska Island, which was accomplished under cover of fog on July 28. Unaware of this, an American force "invaded" and occupied the island in mid-August.

21

"Oh! There go 5000 rings"

Pavuvu, Russell Islands
May–July, 1943

The 43rd Division was still holding the front on Pavuvu Island at the end of May 1943, but was preparing for the attack on Munda airfield on New Georgia Island. Wilber's unit would land on July 4, five weeks later. Each of the past moves had carried a heightened sense of risk, but this would be the real deal. Munda was a well defended airfield; the Japanese would not give it up easily.

At the same time, Norma was in her own countdown toward the end of the school year, the breakup of the family, and the anticipated October birth of her baby. The letters between Norma and Wilber continued to flow.

MAY 29, 1943

How'r'ya Toots! [to Norma] — Your encyclopedic letter of Apr. 23 came with a series up to includ[ing] Apr 27….

Knight found the flesh was too weak and is off for recuperation, rejuvenation and communion, relaxation and inspiration. He "discovered" that he had high blood pressure and the temptation was too great. Do not quote [this]. Anyway he has lost a lot of weight, not by exercise, and looked pretty bad, so he is on the way to a rear hospital. On the other hand Ol' Man Bradt is still … free wheeling, so [Gen.] Barker says it looks as if I had a job. Of course, you understand this is a temporary arrangement for reasons I have explained before.…

You must have made quite a social event of Valerie's mumps on Easter. I suppose that supper afterward cut into the ration cards too. — [no closing]

Wilber displayed some contempt for Knight's leaving just before the Munda landings, but grudgingly allowed that he could be truly sick. In subsequent letters, he vented further criticisms, probably with some justification, which is why I suppress Knight's real name in this work. As executive officer (second in command) of the 169th Field Artillery Battalion, Wilber, on May 28, assumed command of the battalion. Barker had apparently already decided that Wilber was the man who would receive the permanent appointment. The formalities would take a couple of months and the associated promotion to lieutenant colonel even longer. He had thus risen to a significant position of substantial responsibility in the two and a quarter years since induction when he had been merely a captain on the regimental staff. Wilber would be commanding officer of the 169th Field Artillery Battalion when it entered its first ground combat in a mere five weeks.

Due to wartime scarcities, a ration card was issued to everyone in the United States so they could purchase approved amounts of rationed goods, such as sugar and meat. Gasoline was also strictly rationed. Each car had a priority sticker on it, A, B, or C, depending on the owner's profession and needs. The stickers indicated how much gasoline could be bought: three to four gallons per week for A, eight gallons per week for B, and more for C.

x·o·ø·o·x

In this monthly letter to his father, Wilber revealed more about the politics of his explorations into the jungle and mountains. The son was discussing manly military issues with the father.

MAY 30, 1943

Dear Father — I can imagine that the spring is well along in Indiana now. It certainly is a much more desirable climate than I have seen in the last two years and you should appreciate it as such.

Things here have been on a routine basis since I last wrote. Out of the other duties, I have stolen quite a lot of time in the jungle. This has been possible only by my assuming duties normally assigned to officers of lower rank, such as liaison and reconnaissance officers. My Bn. C.O. expressed himself by granting permission, but saying I was crazy to do it. However I have learned a lot of things about rates of travel, road building, tactics and artillery possibilities in the jungle that are not in books....

It has amazed me how the men have become acclimated to this area. They have unusually good health, look good, and are very fit. A few have been returned to rear stations but very few. We, as a battalion, have consistently stood high [in ranking] on the medical reports on hospital admissions [the fewer the better]. Last month our admissions were next to the lowest in the Division.... — [no closing]

In camp, Wilber had constantly pressed hard on cleanliness to keep diseases at bay.

x · o · ∅ · o · x

Wilber soon took hold of his command and things began to change.

MAY 31, 1943
Darling Wife of Mine — I'm so far behind in answering your letters that I have before me Apr. 27, May 3, 9, and 13.... Today I took the battery commanders into the jungle on reconnaissance. It was the first time they had been in there. One of them commented that it was the first real hike he had had since we came here. They are going to get around on foot as long as I'm in command until they can hike....

I'm sitting in our (DeBlois' + my) tent with a gasoline lantern on. The situation is now such that lights are legal provided none goes out from under the tent. We hang a large tin can over and around it for a shade so the light can only go straight down. Members of the Staff come over and study and read until 8:00 P.M. when I get the radio out and we listen to the news and maybe a half hour of music. Then I carefully put the radio away wrapped in clothes to protect it if we are bombed and Ray says to the Staff, "Why the Hell don't you fellows go home?" And so to bed....

A Rhode Islander, René DeBlois had been the 169th Field Artillery Battalion S-3 (training and plans) officer. When Wilber vacated the executive officer position, DeBlois filled it while also remaining for a time the S-3. As the executive, he was responsible for the normal operations of the battalion so the C.O. could deal with strategic issues. He and Wilber would work together, hand in glove, during the forthcoming combat.

June 1 — I love you and Hale the mountain climber and Valerie the girl scout. — Wilber E. Bradt XXXOOØ

x · o · ∅ · o · x

The rescue of American aviators with an overlay of wry Indiana humor started this letter, before it turned to serious matters.

JUNE 3, 1943

Hello Fun Girl, [Norma] — I wish I were having fun with you now. There are so many things we could do together that would be fun. My arm around your waist would be fun for me. Then again I'd like to sit on a mountainside with you and dream. Your letters of May 11 and 13 haven't been answered yet so here goes. First I enclose a letter from Don with news of Hud and some of the others.

It's good to know the "Zero" ring and bracelet arrived and that they were liked. The "ring" industry here is becoming quite a pastime for some of the men. It was quite funny the other day during a rather sad moment when as one of our planes landed on and sank in the ocean near us to hear one voice say "Oh! there go 5000 rings." All the rest of us were holding our breath as we watched the personnel in the plane scramble out into their rubber boat. They were all saved. You have to admit these boys see the most serious aspects of any situation....

Your letter about sending the children to other schools was quite a surprise to me. The decision rests entirely with you, Dearest. I have all the confidence in the world in your judgment and know I am not able to see the whole picture from here.... I approve heartily of your desire to do something, and I want it to be what you most prefer to do, i.e., music. However remember if I would have been an enlisted man in this war, I would not have been able to enlist for financial reasons. This does not mean I would object to your serving in Europe or Africa, providing your release could be relied on in case you were needed at home. I do not know what are the regulations for WAACs [Women's Auxiliary Army Corps] in such cases.

The schools sound wonderful. I'd like to go myself. I also think the children would gain in self-reliance in such situations, particularly if they do not have the worry that they are abandoned. I'm sorry they will be separated but that too may be a good thing. I like the idea about their being out of the city for a while. Country environment will be a good variation....

You certainly are a go-getter Mrs. B. I'm very impressed that you would have even applied for a $5000.00 [annual salary] position. You are just the girl who might have gotten it too. I'm sorry you didn't get it. Better luck next time. There doesn't seem to be any need for me to caution you about selling your services too cheaply. I understand about the F.B.I., Dear.

> Norma had decided how to maintain the secret of her pregnancy after our summer camps were over: she would place us in boarding schools she had carefully selected. For me, it was St. Bernard's School in Gladstone, New Jersey, 40 miles west of New York City, and for Valerie, St. John the Baptist School in Mendham, six miles from St. Bernard's. They both had Episcopalian underpinnings. This would free Norma to participate, she said, in the war effort. In fact, however, she would instead be nurturing

her pregnancy and later her baby and would be unable to work. She was using her novelistic talents to create stories for Wilber about her work possibilities. She had no support from other family members (who did not know about the pregnancy), though Monte and his mother were there for her. These arrangements were taking a heavy toll on her, as suggested in Wilber's reply:

Please don't cry Lover about the broadcasts [of the war]. Keep them turned up at the corners. Remember? It sounds like nerves to me. Relax and have a little fun. You can't carry all the weight of this war yourself. Look at me having the time of my life right on the front lines. One day at a time, says I. I'll want my same cheery comrade when I get back, so take good care of her.

Don't worry about telling me of Valerie's remark re. your application [for a position]. I know the little imp. She will say too when you get it that you're "sposed" to take care of her. She means she loves you....

> Valerie could really get to the heart of the matter, and Norma clearly took it to heart. Norma was by now deeply isolated by a combination of societal strictures, Valerie's comments, and Wilber's lack of knowledge of her situation.

... It is during peace times that the artillery takes a back seat. As I see it, the marines get the publicity, the air corps get the girls, the infantry claims all the credit, but the artillery gets the credit for turning the tide of battles. We aren't modest about it either.

I've just been down to the beach to see what goes on there. It does. I must close, Darling.

You are my girl and what you decide goes for me. Keep that sweet chin up and remember my arm is about your waist and my steps always go with you.... Here is my love 'til next time. — XXXOOØ Wilber

x · o · ø · o · x

JUNE 8, 1943
Dearest Wife of Mine — On May 5 you wrote all in favor of my getting physical exercise. Today you would have been very well pleased for I took a party into the jungle this A.M. It was very warm and I must have lost five pounds by perspiration alone. Goff + I had no trouble but one of the young Lts. was pretty well fagged before we got back....

June 9 — It's another day and I'm really going to mail this today. Swan has been specializing on catching rats lately. To date he has totaled about ten. They were pretty thick and we have been working on them a bit. You would be surprised at the variety of traps that appear thru the battalion. Some are teeter-totters [seesaws] over a can of water. Some are box traps, some shoot a sharpened nail with a bow at the rat, some let a heavy weight fall on him and some catch him in a noose and choke him. It all pays dividends for we stand second on the good health records this week for this area.... — Wilber. XXXOOØ

x·o·ø·o·x

JUNE 13, 1943
Hello Dearest Wife of Mine — I'm sorry about the Lee [payments for the Washington State house] checks. However I'm pretty sure you can get pretty quick action because I think it is a pretty serious offense in Wash. State to write checks that bounce.

You have been in quite a rush, I'm afraid, over all the requests I've sent you. You are sweet to go to all that trouble and I know I'm being very badly spoiled. By the way I got some tooth powder so don't need any for another six months. It will be good to have the books especially the Grabau [geology textbook]. I know there is much in there on this area.

> Wilber continued to bombard Norma with requests for items he needed, such as the spikes for his shoes, books, batteries, razor blades, and other items, and she dutifully found and mailed them. The military had Post Exchanges (PXs) in combat areas that provided such essentials for soldiers, though they may not have been conveniently located near smaller units, and they may not have carried the items Wilber needed. This reminded me of World War I when Wilber's father had provided such items to the front line troops in YMCA "huts." Norma was Wilber's "hut."

Since I've been C.O., I've been sending my officers into the jungles and getting them wised up and toughened up a bit. They seem to like it. Things seem all settled down now after Knight's leaving. [General] Barker was up day before yesterday and said he was well pleased. The officers did do well. I've stopped the formal schools and given the officers priorities in their own training and study. It puts the responsibility on each individual and they are smoothing out the rough spots pretty rapidly. I have said I want this to be the best firing battalion in this theater and there is a chance they can make that a fact. Anyway they will have something to work for.

CHAPTER 21   *Oh! There go 5000 rings*

Wilber aimed high: "the best firing battalion in this theater." He wanted intensely to be first in artillery and first with Norma.

The children's [boarding] schools [for next year] sound pretty fine. I don't know about the finances but of course you do. I can appreciate just why Hale thought the fields were "pretty." He probably has been able to see the dirt and sordidness of the city streets. I can never quite forget it.

Norma had taken us to New Jersey that spring to see our schools in an effort to make us more comfortable with the transition from summer camp to school in September, when she would not be with us. As a 12 year old, I recall no anxiety on my part, nor do I remember being given a rationale for the change. It may well have been that we were told what Wilber was being told, namely that Norma was going to do war work. Valerie, being younger and more sensitive, may have sensed the family difficulties more than I did. Wilber's worries surfaced again with a light-hearted joke:

… So you may be a WAAC! … With your looks and your form, there are going to be a lot of soldiers very, very interested like I'm interested in you. Did you see the quip in the Readers Digest where the long kiss at the wedding was interrupted by the small voice asking, "Mama, Is he spreading the pollen on her now?"

You need have no concern about Hale working on the farm [at his boarding school]. I don't know any better way to spend a summer. I started at eight and it didn't hurt me. His "tiredness" is nothing to be concerned about. It is likely largely mental or habit and not a physical weariness. Fresh air + sun and work is what he should have now.… Happy Summertime to all of you. — XXXOOØ Wilber

Wilber was a bit confused. I would not go to the (farm) school until the fall.

x · o · ø · o · x

Wilber continued driving the 169th Field Artillery Battalion to the high level of effectiveness required for the forthcoming combat while trying to provide leadership on the home front.

JUNE 18, 1943
Dearest — … we are getting into the groove again and the Bn. is beginning to click. DeBlois "complained" yesterday that he wanted Knight back because he missed the quiet afternoons with nothing to do. He said it was getting as bad now as [it was]

307

back in Shelby [Mississippi] where officers never had any rest. You should see these officers fire [artillery] now. They get it [the shells] where it is supposed to go and in a hurry. They are going to give some Japs some very sudden surprises. Barker was, so he said, well pleased and had no suggestions.

… The other evening I came back from a conference by boat and saw the most beautiful sunset. The sea was dotted with little palm covered white-rimmed islands toward the west. In the east was our larger jungle covered island [Banika] over which a marvelous moon was rising. In that direction the sea was all silver while toward the west it was rose colored. The horizon was spotted by great white piles of clouds, one of which cast a shadow across the sky making a huge cross rising out of the sunset. DeBlois + I watched it and wished for our wives (one each). — I love you all, Wilber.

x·o·ø·o·x

These were the final days before the 43rd Division's move against the Japanese Munda airfield. There was a sense of growing rush and tension, and Wilber's letters began again to exhibit the "goodbye" messages. At the same time in New York, Norma was in the final stages of dispersing her family and of giving up the West 4th Street apartment on June 30.

JUNE 24, 1943
Darling Daughter Valerie — … I do want you to know, tho, Valerie, that I am not sorry I'm in the army. The Germans and Japs are doing such terrible things to good people that I wouldn't want to be alive if they win this war. So you see I am proud that I can help stop them and I am very lucky to not to have to fight knowing, as the Belgians, Norwegians and Poles and Greeks did, that they couldn't win. I know we are going to win and I am proud and happy to help us win. I am proud too that you and Hale & Nana are helping by taking care of yourselves. Please write me again soon. — I love you, Wilber

On the next night, June 25, a Japanese air raid destroyed several fuel tanks on Banika Island. A second airfield on Banika was completed about this time.

x·o·ø·o·x

And to Norma, he made his best pitch, and what a beautiful one it was. If this was to be one of his last letters, as it could well have been, it would do him everlasting credit. He started by recalling their first meeting in his chemistry class.

JUNE 26, 1943

Dear Norma Sparlin — Today in 1927 you walked into my heart. I can remember yet how fresh and clean and dear you looked. The room [Wilber's lab] had been dingy and dull and it was suddenly a wonderful place to me. Your eyes and lips had a sweetness in them that seemed to be shadowed by something. I wanted then to know how to replace that shadow by a consciousness that someone who mattered loved you. I wanted to matter to you and soon. I still do. Do you remember the little black satin pleated skirt? I do Dearest. I remember how it used to lie along your lap and fan way down on one side of your chair. Yes Lover, on June 26 I was very, very interested in Norma Sparlin.

> That pleated skirt appeared in a photo of their July 4 picnic. Wilber's memory of visual details was considerable. The "shadow" he saw on Norma's face could well have been a reflection of her difficult family background and her struggles to get through college, mostly on her own two feet. It was probably enhanced by worry about her first college class in a hard science.

It was only a few days later that I discovered you were going to the Baptist Church. Do you recall the walk home? It was a beautiful evening, quiet and peaceful and you made it perfect for me. I don't recall what we talked about but I do remember the joy of our talk. It has always been a gift from God to talk with you. I knew that night you were very important to me. That was the evening I answered H. S.'s [unidentified person] letter saying she was lonesome for me and thought of matrimony favorably. Because of you, My Dear, I wrote assuring her she had been right to say, when she left, that we should make a clean break. I said I had met you and knew I loved you. It seemed a long time for me to get an answer but it finally came. In the mean time I kept falling in love with you. Our date in Spokane, on the Snake River, dinner in Lewiston, and a picnic one evening, each was as perfect as an evening can be. I knew you were the only girl I could ever love. You are.

So it has gone all thru the years. So many wonderful days, so many times I have thanked God for your comradeship, comfort, and love. Thru the dreary times, the hard times, the discouraging times, you have always been in my life and all those times have become sacred to me. This year is the same. Amid all my worries, fatigue, isolation, and responsibilities, you have been my guiding light, my guardian angel.

Today I am telling you again as ever the same old story. "I love you, Nana. You are my own adored wife. The one woman for me and the mother of my two grand children."

Here My Beloved is courage for our next year. We are still one. My world is your love, my arm is about you. Please Dear let me carry your load during this next wonderful year. — Wilber

> Norma would have received this letter after the family had dispersed and as she was beginning her seventh month of pregnancy. It surely would have been wrenching for her. Wilber could reach deep into her heart with his romantic prose.

x·o·ø·o·x

> There were also practical matters between them.

JUNE 27, 1943
Dearest — … Dearest I'm sorry the shaver didn't work out and hope you don't feel badly. I know you wanted it to be with me. It makes me happy just to know you tried. Lizzie the Lizard fell in our rat trap the other night. There was a big splash and a lot of banging against the sides of the tin can. She didn't come back for two days.

Swan is acting as my personal bodyguard now. He wears one of those spotted camouflaged jungle suits. I don't know how he likes the job but I think he feels there is a bit of distinction in my being a Bn. C.O. Don't let Valerie know I told you for I wanted her to be able to tell it first, but Barker has forwarded my promotion papers. In the normal course of events I will become a Lt. Col of F.A. That will mean roughly an additional hundred a month pay. My duties will be the same because I've been the Bn. C.O. for a month now.

When you send some little packages, if the canned lobster is available, I'd like a can or two. Don't go to a lot of trouble now for it's just an idea.…

… There will likely be a gap in my letters for a while now. We are terribly busy. It will be no reason tho for you to worry, so don't be crediting all the headlines to me. You know I just work here.… I must stop now Lover Mine. Here is a very passionate man reaching for you. How I do want you! Woman of Mine. — XXXOOØ Wilber

> The "gap in my letters" message would have been known by now to Norma as notice that his unit was moving on, presumably toward increased danger. And despite his humorous disclaimer that "I just work here," the news would indeed be about Wilber's forthcoming activities, and it would provide much justification for her worries.

x·o·ø·o·x

CHAPTER 21   *Oh! There go 5000 rings*

In the rush, Wilber found time for his monthly letter to his father, probably with an enclosed check or money order for $25. His words about getting his unit in top shape took on added meaning because of his imminent departure for combat, something he could not tell his father. His fate in the coming month would be much more uncertain than it had been during the previous nine months they had been overseas.

JUNE 27, [1943]

Dear Father — I've only time for a very short note. We have been pretty busy recently and more is still ahead. I'm well and feeling fit. Did I tell you our C.O. was sent to the rear for health reasons? I've been in command for a month now. Of course I've been acting commander before, but this time it's my job and my battalion. We have been really on the job since.

Gen. B. told me that my promotion papers have gone in for approval. That may take a month but it is good to know I have earned it this way rather than by my chemical training. I turned that down a year ago and am glad now. The thing that concerns me is whether I can do the job well enough. It's a fine artillery battalion with the repeatedly earned record of being the best in this division and I have helped to make it [so]. Now, if I can keep it at top efficiency, we will do some good for "Old High Pockets" [Uncle Sam]. I love you. Am sorry to be so rushed. — Wilber

x · o · ø · o · x

JUNE 27, 1943

Dear Son Hale — Your very good letter dated June 3 came about a week ago. It should have been answered sooner but I've been pretty busy lately. You say you are writing for Nana, that Valerie was washing dishes and Norma hemming Valerie's dress. That sounds as if everyone was doing their job back home. I don't know just what that day had me doing.

This glimpse of our home life in New York shows Norma maintaining a sense of normalcy for her children despite the imminent moves.

I wish I could have gone to Indian Point with you [on a school outing to the popular amusement park on the Hudson River]. When you were on the boat did you see any planes? Today and yesterday I was going to see Barker in a boat and some planes came at us. We wondered whose friends they were, all right. It was OK too. They knew the right people [they were American].

311

Your exams sound pretty strenuous. I'm very proud of your record at school, Son. It isn't the grades so much as the fact that you have always been fair and honest and not selfish or dishonest. I am looking forward to getting back on the job of being at home someday.… — Your loving Father, Wilber

P.S. Did you know that yesterday in 1927 was the day I met your mother. I thought she was the nicest girl I had ever seen. I still think I was right. WB

x · o · ø · o · x

JUNE 29, 1943

I'm your Man. Dearest Girl [Norma] — I love you this 29th of June. Also I like the [automatic] pencil which came yesterday. It is by far the nicest I ever owned. You should not have spent so much, Dear. Thank you so much. I appreciate having my name on it too. The leads you sent work perfectly in it. They break in the Eversharp, which I don't like.

… I'm glad to be promoted because of the salary. I don't know exactly what it will amount to but it will be a bit over $600.00 a month. … Another factor of course is that I now am responsible for a lot of people and their collective efficiency. Good or bad, efficient or inefficient, successful or unsuccessful, all is credited or blamed to or on me. However now being in command I have some control and can exercise command.… Anyway I have earned this by sticking to a job rather than by shifting to an easier one.… Now I'll try to be a good Lt. Col of F.A.…

[June 30] — I'd like to see Valerie with short hair. I'll bet she is really cute. It's good her school is over now. She can rest up and get some sun. It's June 30 now and the check for my pay hasn't come yet. If it isn't in this letter, you will know it will be along later. Anyway I'll mail this letter tomorrow. Note the date of this part of the letter. Someday I'll tell you about it.

> Elements of the 43rd Division including artillery made the first landings on Rendova Island in the New Georgia group (Solomon Islands) on June 30. Rendova was the staging area for the attack on the nearby Munda airfield. Wilber's unit would embark for Rendova on July 3 and land there July 4.

Lover Mine, don't worry about "worrying" me and giving me "wrong impressions." I want to know what you do + think. I have all the confidence in the world in your ability and judgment. I know you are right in your decisions about the children. Their difficulties are I believe a normal sex antagonism coupled with the absence of both sexes in their parents. It will pass with the adolescent stage. In the mean time you have the solution. I highly approve, especially since you will be within reach of them in emergencies.…

> Norma apparently had worried about the "wrong impressions" she might have given in her portrayal of our lives at home, not only about the changes she was effecting but smaller things like our (Valerie's and my) behavior.

The radio was wonderful tonight. We listened to the news at 0800 [2000 hours or 8 p.m.?], then to Jack Benny and to some hot music. Today Col. Eason [C.O. of 169th Infantry Regiment] had Ray [DeBlois] + me over to lunch followed by a private showing of "Who Done It?" by Abbott + Costello [comedian movie stars]. It was fun and reminded me of the last time the children took me to see A. + C.…

Answering your June 12.… By the way what will you do with your furniture? Don't get too economical and Spartan about your cheap room.…

> Norma had told Wilber that she was moving to a small apartment and would take a job of some sort, but had not provided details.

Yes I felt quite a heavy [earth]quake here about the time you mention. However they don't amount to much where there are no skyscrapers or houses. No one fell out of bed, but a tidal wave surprised a few soldiers who suddenly found themselves off the beach and back up in the trees. No one was hurt but they were a bit chagrined about their supper getting wet.… — [no closing]

> It appeared that Wilber was not aware that a large tsunami could be catastrophic for his entire battalion, which was camped in the low-lying palm groves of Pavuvu Island. Was this even a consideration in the military planning?

x · o · ø · o · x

JULY 2, 1943

Dearest Norma and children — This is the last letter I will write for about two weeks. Don't be worried if you don't hear from me for a while. It means I just won't be on speaking terms with the P.O. [Post Office] Dept. for a while.

> Wilber would write occasionally, but his letters would not get mailed until later.

Today is wonderfully cool and fresh. The palms are in the breeze and drop fronds with a swish and thud. Frequently a cocoanut will drop with a whoomp. If I had the time, I'd love to picnic with you on a day like this on an island. I'd show you how to open a cocoanut so you could have a cup to drink the milk from, without even spilling any while I opened it. Sgt. Waller says some Christmas season he is going to go into an A & P store, buy a cocoanut, crack it into a cup very nonchalantly, drink the milk and toss the pieces into the corner and walk out. Can't you just imagine the people looking?

I have always forgotten to tell you about the fish that climb trees here. They are quite common, [are] usually quite small, and climb on to rocks and stumps and branches of trees along the waters edge. When you scare them they dash for the water and swim away fast. They swim on the surface of the water by skittering along. Maybe that is where the term Australian Crawl came from. It looks a little like it.

I'm very pleased about the plans you all have for next year. You should each have a good year if you will try. I want you not to forget to watch out for each other. A little distance won't matter if you really love each other. I really love each of you. I'll write again as soon as possible. — XXXOOO. Wilber

June 1943 came to an end with major changes on both sides of the Pacific. Norma was now five months pregnant and had dispersed the family to deal with her pregnancy in secret. Wilber was about to enter his first ground combat after more than two years on active duty and nine months overseas. Norma, in one last fling of family togetherness and maternal responsibility, organized a music recital for Valerie and me in the Grace Church Assembly Hall. We opened with the national anthem. Norma then accompanied us on the piano as Valerie sang a set of three songs and I played three violin pieces. Valerie then played three piano solos, and we closed the program all together with Schubert's Cradle Song. The entire program was by our threesome; there were no other participants. It was Norma's show!

This recital began at 8 p.m. on July 1, and the very next day I was off to summer camp. I would not see Norma until Christmastime. The day after that, at 4:45 p.m. on July 3, the 169th Field Artillery Battalion embarked for Rendova Island. On July 4, Wilber was dangerously wounded by a Japanese bomb, before his battalion could fire even one round in combat.

x·o·ø·o·x

This brings to an end the first phase of Wilber and Norma's three-part saga. Although bound in marriage and in spirit, each had developed into an independent entity with an independent agenda. The Depression, the

R E C I T A L

By

HALE BRADT

and

VALERIE BRADT

Grace Church Assembly Hall, July 1, 1943, 8:00 p.m.

I

Star Spangled Banner............................Francis Scott Key

Valerie, Hale, and Audience

II

A group of Songs

The Lass with the Delicate Air.........Arne (1740) (Early English)

When the Roses Bloom..................Reichart (1790) (Early German)

Dearest, believe (Caro mio ben)........Giordani (1770) (Early Italian)

VALERIE BRADT, SOPRANO

III

Violin Solos

Allegro Moderato, from the Concerto in D........Seitz

Bourree..Handel

Berceuse Slave.................................Neruda

HALE BRADT, VIOLINIST

IV

Piano Solos

The Nightingale................................Kullak

Hungarian Carol...........................Folk Song

Scherzino....................................Thompson

VALERIE BRADT, PIANIST

Violin and Piano Duet

Cradle Song..................................Schubert

VALERIE AND HALE

Goodnight!

Hymns 205. 209. 530. 104. 120

Program of recital by Valerie and me at Grace Church, July 1, 1943, typed by Norma. Norma was the piano accompanist for the songs and violin solos. This was her last hands-on act of motherhood before we three each went off to our separate destinations.

war, and their separation had forced them to engage directly and personally in the challenges each faced. These challenges were all-encompassing and followed from freely made choices: Wilber to enter the service and Norma to continue her pregnancy. Each marched off to carry out his or her duty, Wilber as a seasoned soldier heading into combat and Norma as the commander of a dispersed family on the home front.

The entire western Pacific and most of Europe remained in Axis hands, but the Allies had begun their long slow march to recover the conquered territories. British and American forces in Africa were preparing for the July 10 invasion of Sicily in the Mediterranean. In Russia, the Germans and Russians were about to engage in an epic battle for Kursk. The next step in the South Pacific, to the New Georgia Island group, had already begun, and Wilber would soon be involved.

Acknowledgments

I have been pursuing the story of my father Wilber and mother Norma for nearly 34 years and have been aided by so many individuals and organizations that it is not possible to properly acknowledge them all, but I will do my best.

First and foremost, my sisters Abigail and Valerie deserve my utmost gratitude for letting me tell our family's story and for moral support throughout. Abigail's husband Tom has been an enthusiastic supporter, and Donald, Valerie's husband, has provided sage editorial advice.

This work could not exist but for those who husbanded my father's letters for the 35 years it took me to wake up to their existence and intrinsic value, namely my mother, my Bradt grandmother, and my cousin Alan, all of whom are now deceased. My aunt, Wilber's sister Mary Higgins, chose to give me a collection of letters between Wilber's mother and father written in the 1910s and 1920s, and between Mary and her mother in later decades. These shed important light on the familial relationships that were so influential in my father's life.

In the early 1980s, I hired students and secretaries—Trish Dobson, Pam Gibbs, Brenda Parsons, and Nancy Ferreira—to type Wilber's letters into a primitive stand-alone word processor. They were persevering, patient souls who took a serious personal interest in the story. I used those files to create the volume *World War Two Letters of Wilber E. Bradt* (by Hale Bradt, 1986), a complete compilation of Wilber's letters of which I created only 40 copies, mostly for relatives. The current work is, as described in the Prologue, a distillation of the complete letters with much more supportive material.

General Harold R. Barker, Wilber's immediate superior in the 43rd Division, wrote his *History of the 43rd Division Artillery*, which is rich in technical detail—operation orders, maps, and rosters of officers, medal winners, wounded, and killed. It pertains directly to the units Wilber commanded. This, along with other published histories and documentation in Wilber's papers, provides context for the events Wilber describes. At my request in 1981 when she was 75 and still quite alert, my mother typed an eight-page summary of her life that was a valuable view of her life as she then, perhaps somewhat wishfully, remembered it.

Conversations and correspondence with Wilber's military and civilian associates and his siblings in the 1980s materially enriched this story. Especially helpful were Howard Brown, Waldo Fish, and others of the Rhode Island National Guard; Donald Downen of the Washington State National Guard; Irwin Douglass of the University of Maine; and Robert Patenge, formerly of the 169th Field Artillery Battalion. My 1983 conversation with Japanese Colonel Seishu Kinoshita, who fought opposite Wilber on Arundel, was an emotional highlight for both of us. Howard Brown died this year (2014); the others long before. My aunt Mary Bradt Higgins was especially helpful with her wonderful memory and facility with the typewriter. Her sister Ruth and brother Rex were also generous with their recollections and so were my mother's relatives, especially her sister Evelyn and Evelyn's daughters, Jane and Julie. My Bourjaily stepbrother, Paul Webb, and the former wife of his brother Vance, Tina Bourjaily, were helpfully responsive to my queries.

My visits in 1983 and 1984 to the Pacific sites of Wilber's odyssey (Solomon Islands, Philippine Islands, New Zealand, and Japan), and my meetings with the people he encountered added important dimensions and perspective. In New Zealand, Olive Madsen, Minnie and Sidney Smith, and Dawn Jones Penney were most helpful. In the Solomons, my guide Alfred Basili got me around efficiently in his motorized canoe, Liz and Ian Warne provided hospitality on Kolombangara, and Claude Colomer took photos for me after I had immersed my camera in seawater, and so did the Warnes. In the Philippines, Mrs. José Dacquel whom Wilber had known, Emma Peralto, Boysie Florendo, and the deLeon family made my visit most fruitful. Boysie spent a day driving me to sites on the Laguna de Bay, and young Edgar José drove us to Lingayen Gulf in his 1969 Ford Mustang with the music playing loudly as we cruised down roads reminiscent of the U.S. in the 1930s. These Pacific visits were facilitated by my residence in Japan while on sabbatical leave in 1983 at the Japanese Institute of Space and Astronautical Science. I remain grateful for its generous support of my scientific endeavors.

I was fortunate to have started this project when many of my informants were still living. In recent years, I have been in contact with families of soldiers and in one case a sailor who served with Wilber, namely the families of Charles D'Avanzo, Robert Patenge, Donald Mushik, Lawrence Palmer, Saul Shocket, and Marshall Dann. Their recollections and generous sharing of memories and photographs further added to the story.

Acknowledgments

Faculty, archivists, and librarians at the universities Wilber and Norma attended or taught at (Washington State University, Indiana University, University of Cincinnati, University of Maine) helped flesh out those aspects of their lives. Staff at the National Archives in Suitland, Maryland; Washington, D.C., and College Park, Maryland, on my half dozen visits over the years were expert at finding needed documents. Also helpful were librarians and archivists in New Zealand (Auckland, Christchurch, and Wellington), and at the City of Nouméa, New Caledonia; Bancroft Library of the University of California, Berkeley; Columbia University; Tacoma Public Library, Washington; Seattle Museum of History and Industry; U.S. Army Center for Military History; Japanese Center for Military History of the National Institute of Defense Studies (IDS); and elsewhere. It was Dr. Hishashi Takahashi of IDS who put me in touch with Col. Kinoshita.

I am most grateful to Robin Bourjaily, Maura Henry, and Richard Feyl for readings and editorial comments on near-final drafts. Frances King did heroic service as editor and manager of the final phases of this work, and Lisa Carta's attention to detail and superb design sense created a most attractive set of books. Suzanne Fox, Richard Margulis, Kate Hamisian, and Michael Sperling contributed much appreciated marketing advice.

The many Bradts, Sparlins, and Bourjailys I have queried and visited over the years have helped create this story. In many respects, it is their story too. Many friends and colleagues have suffered my recounting parts of the story to them over these past decades. My daughters, Elizabeth and Dorothy, and my wife, Dorothy, have borne the burden more than most, and they did so with grace.

I, of course, take sole responsibility for errors and misrepresentations herein.

Bibliography

The following references have been particularly helpful to me in creating the Wilber's War Trilogy. They do not by any means comprise a comprehensive list of World War II Pacific Theater sources. Many of these volumes and documents are now available on the Internet.

Official military journals, histories, and operations reports of the following units during World War II, U.S. National Archives and Records Administration (NARA):

172nd, 103rd, and 169th Infantry Regiments of the 43rd Infantry Division.

152nd, 169th, 103rd, and 192nd Field Artillery Battalions of the 43rd Infantry Division.

27th, 145th, 148th, and 161st Infantry Regiments; see also Karolevitz reference below.

43rd Infantry Division Historical Report, Luzon Campaign, 1945.

History of the 103rd Infantry Regiment, 43rd Division, January 1, 1945 – May 31, 1945. [Detailed narrative history of the entire Luzon campaign for the regimental combat team that included Wilber's artillery battalion]

Logs of naval units:

LCI-65

LCI (L) Group 14

Histories sponsored by the U.S. military:

United States Army in World War II, The War in the Pacific Series. Sponsored by the U.S. Army Chief of Military History, U.S. Government Printing Office, 1949–1962:

Morton, Louis. *Strategy and Command: The First Two Years.*

Morton, Louis. *The Fall of the Philippines.* [1941–42]

Miller, John, Jr. *Guadalcanal, The First Offensive.* [Guadalcanal campaign, 1942–43]

Miller, John, Jr. *Cartwheel, the Reduction of Rabaul.* [New Georgia campaign, 1943]

Miller, Samuel. *Victory in Papua.* [Eastern New Guinea campaign, 1942]

Smith, Robert Ross. *Approach to the Philippines.* [Northern New Guinea campaign, 1944]

Cannon, M. Hamlin. *Leyte: The Return to the Philippines.* [Leyte campaign, 1944]

Smith, Robert Ross. *Triumph in the Philippines.* [Luzon campaign, 1945]

Williams, Mary. *Chronology 1941–1945.* [World War II events]

MacArthur, Gen. Douglas, *The Campaigns of MacArthur in the Pacific, Reports of General MacArthur, Volume 1,* U.S. Army Center for Military History, CMH Pub 13-3, 1994.

Morison, Samuel Eliot. *History of the U.S. Naval Operations in World War II.* New York: Atlantic, Little, Brown, 1948–60:

Vol. III, The Rising Sun in the Pacific.

Vol. V, The Struggle for Guadalcanal.

Vol. VI, Breaking the Bismarck Barrier.

Vol. VIII, New Guinea and the Marianas.

Vol. XII, Leyte.

Vol. XIII, The Liberation of the Philippines.

Memoirs and histories by participants:

Barker, Harold R. *History of the 43rd Division Artillery.* Providence RI: John F. Greene Printer, 1961.

Eichelberger, Robert L. *Our Jungle Road to Tokyo.* Rockville MD: Zenger Publishing Company, 1949.

Halsey, William F. and J. Bryan III. *Admiral Halsey's Story.* Rockville MD: Zenger, Publishing Company, 1947.

Krueger, Walter. *From Down Under to Nippon.* Rockville MD: Zenger Publishing Company, 1953.

Ockenden, Edward. *The Ghosts of Company G.* Infinity, 2011. [The TED Force in New Guinea]

Sledge, E. B. *With the Old Breed.* New York: Ballantine Books, 1981.

Zimmer, Joseph E. *History of the 43rd Infantry Division 1941–1945.* Baton Rouge, LA: The Army and Navy Publishing Company, undated, probably late 1940s.

Other histories and memoirs:

Bauer, K. Jack and Alan C. Coox. "Olympic vs. Ketsu-go," *Marine Corps Gazette,* August 1965, v. 49, No. 8.

Bourjaily, Vance. "My Father's Life," *Esquire Magazine*, March 1984, p. 98.

Donovan, Robert. *PT 10.* New York: McGraw-Hill, 1961.

Drea, Edward J. "Previews of Hell." *Quarterly Journal of Military History,* vol. 7, no. 3, p. 74. Aston, PA: Weider History, 1995. [Planned invasion of Kyushu]

Drea, Edward J. *Defending the Driniumor: Covering Force Operations in New Guinea, 1944,* Leavenworth Papers No. 9, Combat Studies Institute, 1984.

Estes, Kenneth W. *Marines Under Armor.* Annapolis MD: Naval Institute Press, 2000.

Goodwin, Doris Kearns. *No Ordinary Time.* New York: Touchstone, Simon & Schuster, 1994.

Hammel, Eric. *Munda Trail.* London: Orion Press, 1989.

Hasegawa, Tsuyoshi (Ed.) *The End of the Pacific War, Reappraisals.* Stanford, CA: Stanford University Press, 2007.

Keegan, John. *The Second World War.* New York: Viking Press, 1989.

Knox, Donald. *Death March.* New York: Harcourt, Brace, Jovanovich, 1981, pp. 181–184, 227. [The Lumban bridge story]

Karolevitz, R. F. (Ed.) *History of the 25th Infantry Division in World War II.* Nashville, TN: Battery Press, 1946, 1995. [Actions of the 27th and 161st Infantry Regiments]

Larrabee, Eric. *Commander in Chief.* New York: Simon & Schuster, 1987.

Paull, Raymond. *Retreat from Kokoda.* Australia: Wm. Heinemann Press, 1958.

Potter, E. B. *Nimitz.* Annapolis MD: Naval Institute Press, 1976.

Skates, John R. *The Invasion of Japan.* University of California Press, 1994.

The Official History of the Washington National Guard, Vol. 6, *Washington National Guard in World War II.* State of Washington: Office of the Adjutant General. [Also contains WW I and the 1935 strike duty]

Unpublished or self-published documents:

Antill, Peter, *Operation Downfall: The Planned Assault on Japan, Parts 1–4,* http://www.historyofwar.org/articles/wars_downfall1.html (1996).

Bourjaily, Monte F., "Re: Monte Ferris Bourjaily," 1936. [Résumé with references]

Bradt, Hale V. *Story of the Bradt Fund, the F. Hale Bradt Family, and their Versailles, Indiana Farm (1906–2001).* Self-published, 2004. [Early years of Wilber Bradt's life]

Bradt, Hale V. *The World War II Letters of Wilber E. Bradt.* Self-published 1986. [The nearly complete letters, transcribed and privately bound and distributed]

Bradt, Norma S. *Memoir, 1981.* [Eight page self-typed document]

Bradt, Wilber E. *Personal Journal (1941–45).* [Five handwritten notebook pages of dates, places, incidents]

Fushak, K. Graham. *The 43rd Infantry Division, Unit Cohesion and Neuropsychiatric Casualties.* Thesis, U.S. Command and General Staff College, 1999.

Higgins, John J. *A History of the First Connecticut Regiment, 169th Infantry 1672–1963.* Unpublished, 1963.

Patenge, Robert. *Memories of Wilber E. Bradt,* 1997. [Patenge was a survey officer in the 169th Field Artillery Battalion under Wilber Bradt in the Munda campaign, World War II, and later served with the 103rd Field Artillery Battalion.]

Saillant, Richard. *Journal of Richard L. Saillant.* Transcribed by Joseph Carey. [Saillant was an officer in the 118th Engineers of the 43rd Division until April 1944. The

Munda campaign is vividly described.]

Zimmer, Joseph E. *Letters from Col. Joseph E. Zimmer to his wife, Maude Files Zimmer 1942–1945*. Transcribed by Maude Zimmer. [Zimmer was an infantry officer in the 43rd Division who served in the 169th Infantry, 103rd Infantry, and other elements of the 43rd Division from 1941 until May 1945.]

Newspaper archives, 1941–45:

Bangor (Maine) *Daily News*

New York Times

Wellington (New Zealand) *Evening Post*

Washington (D.C.) *Post*

Washington (D.C.) *Star*

Notable conversations with 43rd Division participants and one Japanese officer:

Howard Brown (1981 through 2012)

Warren Covill (1981)

Seishu Kinoshita, Kyushu, Japan (1983)

Albert Merck (1984, 2009)

William Naylor (1984)

Robert Patenge (1997)

INDEX Book 1

Bold page numbers indicate a chapter or, if a page range is given, a part.
Italic page numbers indicate a photograph or map.
WB — Wilber Bradt; "Hale" is Wilber's son; "F. Hale" is Wilber's father

1st and 2nd Marine Divisions
   in Guadalcanal 1942, 207
3rd Infantry Division
   at Fort Ord, 169
   deployed to East Coast, 171
32nd Infantry Division
   Kokoda Trail, New Guinea, 207
41st Infantry Division
   in Queensland 1942, 207
43rd Infantry Division
   activated Feb. 1941, 115
   deployment decision, 165
   Guadalcanal, 265
   New Zealand, 205
   Nouméa New Caledonia, 215
   readied, fall 1940, 108
   reorganized 1942, *xxvi*, 144
   Russell Islands, 275
103rd Field Artillery Battalion
   shipped to New Hebrides, 165
   stranded at Espiritu Santo, 207
152nd Field Artillery Regiment
   Carolina maneuvers, 136
   disbanded, 144
   leaving Maine towns 1941, 116
   WB executive officer of, 143
169th Field Artillery Battalion
   formed with WB as executive, 144
   Maj. Knight commanding officer, 179
   WB commanding, 302
172nd Infantry Regiment
   shipped to New Hebrides, 165
   stranded at Espiritu Santo, 207

air raids, Pavuvu, 281
aircraft
   came at us, in boat, 311
   destroyed on ground in Luzon, 140
   dogfight, 285
   fighters overhead, 283
   landed on water, 304
Americal Division
   committed to Guadalcanal, 212
   guarding New Caledonia, 207
ants on Wilber's bunk, 250
Army camps, **119–88**
artillery in 1920s, 36
Atlantic Monthly, letter contest, xx
Aubert Hall, U. of Maine, *94*
Auckland, New Zealand
   arrival 1942, 202
   departure 1942, 213
auction of farm debris, 22
automobiles
   Chevrolet 1927 roadster, 59
   Chrysler 1930 sedan, 62
   Ford 1930 (Model A) roadster, 59
   Plymouth 1936 sedan, 90
   repair in the 1920s, 33

Barker, Brig. Gen. Harold R.
   artillery planning, Sasavele, 298
   career summarized, 233
   commanded 43rd Div. artillery, 144
   entertained officers, New Caledonia, 232
   high regard for WB and DeBlois, 175
   sent WB to FA course, 150
   transferred WB to 169 FA Bn., 148
batteries for radio, 207
Battle of Britain, 104
Beethoven, Norma playing, 97
bicycle
   purchased in Hattiesburg, *158*
   rode to see minister, xvi
blitzkrieg attack May 1940, 104

Bloomington, Indiana
    description and home 1919, 30
    F. Hale taught at high school, 7
    visited by WB and Norma 1927, 50
bluebird story for Valerie, 222
boat drill, Oct. 1942, 194
bombing
    of Russell Is. by Japanese, 289
    of Tokyo 1942, 162
boredom, battle against, 294
Bourjaily, Abigail
    conversation with Hale 1980, xix
    cousin confided in, 44
    found Terkman letter, 231
Bourjaily, Alice (sister of Monte), 245
Bourjaily, Monte Ferris
    biography, 242
    conceived child, 246
    journalist, xx
    Norma met, 179
    photographs of, *243*
    son married, 256
    wedding imagined by WB, 282, 295
    Wilber first mentions, 210
Bourjaily, Terkman (mother of Monte)
    Christmas 1942, 231
    Norma close to, 179
Bourjaily, Vance, novelist (son of Monte), 245
bracelet
    5000 lost, 304
    aluminum for Valerie, 291
    gift to Valerie, 211
Bradt, Abram (great grandfather of WB)
    gravestone, *2*
Bradt, Alan (nephew of WB)
    WB letters at home of, 84
Bradt, Elizabeth P. (mother of WB)
    assessment by Mary, 19
    early life, 6
    financial dispute, 110
    keeping up appearances, 21
    photograph of
        portrait with family 1904, *9*
        with all her children 1936, *90*
        with family on lawn 1905, *11*
        with WB (baby) and mother-in-law, *8*
        with WB 1904, *12*
        with WB in SATC uniform 1919, *29*
    silver thimble, 7
Bradt, F. Hale (father of WB)
    assessment by Mary, 19

Bloomington High School, 29
early life, 5
family job losses, 1933, 72
financial dispute, 110
in Great War, 24, *25*
infant, 3
letter about smoking, 26
married, 7
portrait with family 1904, *9*
retired to Versailles, 126
superintendent of Versailles, 13
teaching jobs, prewar, 17
with his entire family 1936, *90*
Bradt, Hale V. (son of WB)
    bicycle purchased, 158
    bicycle, rode to church, xvi
    birth of, 61
    essays, life in Maine, 100
    father (WB) died, xvi
    fired pistol, 102
    Grace Church Choir, 134
    photograph of
        at Grace Church School 1942, *135*
        in Chrysler 1933, *67*
        on steps with Valerie ca. 1934, *68*
        with bicycle 1946, *xvi*
        with family outdoors ca. 1935, *75*
        with fish ca. 1938, *93*
        with great grandmother 1931, *62*
        with Norma and baby Valerie 1932, *67*
        with WB and Valerie, Maine 1937, *92*
    recital, Grace Church, 314
    shooting stars seen, 161
    train to Mississippi, 157
    U.S. Navy, 194
    violin teacher, 255
    visited SS Normandie, 155
    visited Washington, D.C. 1943, 292
Bradt, Isaac H. (grandfather of WB)
    gravestone, *2*
    portrait, *4*
Bradt, Mary Ann (aunt of WB), 20
Bradt, Mary E. (sister of WB)
    baptism, 24
    birth of, 9
    portrait as baby with family 1904, *9*
    with family on lawn 1905, *11*
Bradt, Norma Sparlin
    at Grace Church, 247
    at Washington State College, 44
    broken leg 1933, 69

Index

concert 1938, 98
considers joining WAAC, 307
family and youth, 40
financial dispute, 110
geological outing, 55
given away, 45
lonely and fatherless, 45
memoir 1981, 41
met Monte Bourjaily, 179
moved to NYC 1941, 109, 116
photograph of
    at picnic 1927, *38*
    with family outdoors ca. 1935, *75*
    with her piano ca. 1937, *91*
    with siblings 1909, *42*
    with Valerie 1937, *91*
    with Valerie and Hale 1932, *67*
    with WB at her graduation 1929, *51*
    with WB on honeymoon 1927, *49*
    with WB, engagement ring 1927, *47*
pregnant, 246
wedding announcement, *48*
Wilber first met, 39

Bradt, Paul (brother of WB)
    as baby 1905, *11*
    assessment of WB, 36
    birth of, 9
    Hale visited 1943, 292
    in silo as child, 22
    memories of father, 17
    rock climber, 230, 292
    sergeant in national guard, 182
    the day WB died, xvi
    visited by WB family 1931, 64
    WB letters at home of, 84

Bradt, Rex
    gullible as boy, 22
    in national guard, 182
    lost job 1933, 72
    sketched Versailles home, 15

Bradt, Ruth (sister of WB)
    50th reunion, Indiana University, 30
    graduation Indiana University 1937, 98
    high school graduation, 72
    to marry John Wilson, 128
    wrote "thick-lips disease", 57

Bradt, Valerie E. (daughter of WB)
    attended PS 41 in NYC, 168
    birth of, 66
    bluebirds her favorite, 221
    date with WB in NYC, 155
    dropped bag of water, 246

ear infection, 123
father (WB) died, xvii
finding letters to, 136
had mumps, 292
in love with water, 97
Norma "sposed" to take care of her, 305
note (IOU) signed for bicycle, 158
note signed for bicycle, 159
photograph of
    as baby with Norma and Hale 1932, *67*
    in Chrysler 1933, *67*
    on steps with Hale ca. 1934, *68*
    with family outdoors ca. 1935, *75*
    with Norma 1937, *91*
    with sailboat ca. 1938, *93*
    with WB and Hale, Maine 1937, *92*
recital, Grace Church, 314
waking up Norma, 230

Bradt, Wilber E.
    assessment by Downen 1981, 270
    birth, 7
    childhood sayings, 10
    commander of 169 FA Bn., 302
    died, xvi, *xix*
    executive of 169th FA Bn., 144
    financial dispute, 110
    high school years, 23
    Indiana University 1918–26, 30
    journal, personal, *219*
    letter before sailing Oct. 1942, *187*
    National Guard, Indiana, 35
    National Guard, Maine, 93
    National Guard, Washington State, 66
    photograph of
        as 2nd lieutenant ca. 1922, *34*
        bringing in striker 1935, *83*
        in rocking chair 1904, *12*
        Norma's graduation 1929, *54*
        on honeymoon 1927, *49*
        on steps in SATC uniform 1918, *28*
        on USS General Pope 1945, *xiv*
        portrait with family 1904, *9*
        professor and lieutenant 1936, *85*
        with Chrysler and family 1933, *67*
        with family on lawn 1905, *11*
        with family outdoors ca. 1935, *75*
        with Indiana U. chem. grads 1923, *31*
        with mother 1904, *12*
        with mother in SATC uniform 1919, *29*
        with mother, grandmother 1900, *8*
        with Norma, engagement ring 1927, *47*
        with siblings and parents 1936, *90*

with swim team 1923, *31*
with Valerie and Hale, Orono, Maine 1937, *92*
playing doctor, 22
promoted to major, 128
research at WSC, 74
SATC and influenza, 27
seeking job at U. of Maine, 1936, 87
tribute to, by Norma, 167
University of Cincinnati 1927–30, 52
University of Maine 1936–41, 90
Washington State College, 36
Bugbee, George, Julia's brother, 4
Burtsch, Frances, 61
bus
   Fifth Ave. in NYC, 134
   Greyhound stops at farm, 154
   ride in Hattiesburg, 157
   ride to Florida, 140

cake, decorating with lizard, 226
California, **165**
   train trip to, 169
camping in Washington State, *74*
camps, summer for children, 293
Carmichael, Hoagy, at I.U., singer, 30
Charlie's Place, Pullman, Wash., 66, 269
Chemical Warfare Service, 149, 217
cheval de frise, 296
Chevrolet roadster, 1930 trip, 59, *60*
Choate, Col. John F.
   relation to Wilber, 148
   vehicle convoy, 137
   wife dying, 149
Christian, Lt. Louis K.
   WB met on Guadalcanal, 268
Christmas
   Florida 1941, 140
   New Caledonia 1942, 232
Chrysler, WB and family 1933, *67*
Cincinnati, Ohio, 37
cleanliness
   for inspection, 137
   hospital admissions low, 303
   USAT Maui, 201
Cloke, Paul, Dean at U. of Maine
   recommendation letter to, 88
   Wilber's resignation, 115
clouds
   airplanes in, 285

form fairylands, 291
great white piles of, 308
white fleecy, New Caledonia, 222
cocoanut
   falling, 283
   missed soldier, 278
   on cake, 226
   opening, 314
cocoanut palm grove
   Guadalcanal, 266
   Pavuvu, 276
command post
   exercise, Louisiana, 134
   replica of Barker's, 234
   wherever WB sits, 287
Commonplace, Versailles home
   aerial photo ca. 1985, *17*
   photo 1952, *15*
   photo ca. 1930, *14*
   plan of interior, *16*
   sketch by Rex, *14*
Company E, 161st Inf. Rgt.
   national guard meetings, Pullman, 66
   reunion, Guadalcanal, 269
   strike duty, 77
concert on Ouenghi River, 225
corporal punishment, 102
courtship from afar
   aggressive, 294
   Cincinnati memories, 282
   intimate, 179, 225, 267, 269
   WB recalled meeting Norma, 309
Covill, Capt. Warren K.
   on SS President Coolidge, 206
cows and pond ice, 23
Crosby, Bob, in Spokane, 43
Czechoslovakia, rape of 1939, 104

Daniels, Troy, 112
Davis, Capt. E. Russell Jr.
   hike with, 234
   long drive with WB, 241
   publicizing WB hiking, 298
DeBlois, Maj. René
   executive of 169 FA Bn., 303
   letter sent by wife, 213
   S-3 of 169th FA Bn., 169
   sending staff home, 303
   wanted Knight back, 307
deer. *See* Malcolm the deer

depression
  before married, 112
  on Oregon coast, 297
Depression, Great
  1932, pay cuts, 69
  F. Hale's letter 1933, 72
diary proposed by Norma, 253
Distinguished Service Cross, to Capt. Elwood Euart, 217
dog on 25-mile march, 160
Doolittle, Col. James
  bombing of Tokyo, 162
Douglass, Irwin
  acting head, chem. dept. U. of Maine, 142
  Norma wrote to, 292
Downen, Capt. Donald
  assessment of WB, 270
  meeting on Guadalcanal, 268
  WB sent note to, 238
dragon flies, varicolored, 283
ducks eating oats, *20*

earthquake, Pavuvu, 313
Edson's Ridge, aka Bloody Ridge, 203
equator, crossing, 199
Euart, Capt. Elwood
  Distinguished Service Cross, 217
  lost with SS Coolidge, 205

family trees, *xxv*
Farm to academia, **1–116**
farm, Versailles, Indiana, bought, 13
FBI
  German spies, 150
  Norma's commendation from, 211
Field Artillery School, Fort Sill
  commendation for firing exercise, 154
  WB assigned to, 149
field glasses (binoculars), 150, 154
Files, Col. Chester
  90th birthday, 205
  inspected 169th FA, 224
  most capable, 148
financial conflict 1941, 110
fire in wastebasket, 289
fish jumped out of river, 241
fishing
  after artillery firing, 226
  deep sea, 99
  from ship not allowed, 198
  Hale's school essays on 1942, 101
  through ice, in Maine, 95
  with spear, New Caledonia, 238
flares, by Pavuvu natives, 283
Florida, Camp Blanding, **121**
Fort Ord, California
  arrival at, 166
  firing practice, 170
French, speaking, 223
Front, holding the, **259–316**

geraniums in field, 23
Ghormley, Adm. Robert, relieved, 203
Gingold, Gladys Anderson
  found apartment for us, 121
  moved to NYC, 109
  walks with son and Hale, 134
Gingold, Joseph, violinist
  quartet rehearsals, 121
  recital and silver thread, 254
Goff, Capt. Dixwell
  hiking, 305
  on PT boat, 287
  WB no desk man, 239
Grace Church Choir School, 134
Grand Coulee, Norma's novel, 98
Greenwich Village, life in, 168
Griswold, Maj. Gen. Oscar W.
  Carolina maneuvers, 137
  Corps commander 1943, 293
  encouraged jungle hiking, 293
Guadalcanal, **261**
  American and Japanese losses, 247
  jungle, tall grass, birds, 266
  marine landings, 163
  naval battles, 203
gun crew, Indiana National Guard, *35*

Halsey, Adm. William F. Jr.
  43rd Div. in his command, 236
  ordered attack on Russells, 249
  took command of SOPAC, 203
  with Gen. Hester, Russell Islands, *279*
Harmon, Maj. Gen. Millard, Commanding General South Pacific, 236
Hattiesburg, Mississippi, 156
Henderson Field, Guadalcanal, 203
Hester, Maj. Gen. John H.
  commander 43rd Division 1941, 134
  with Adm. Halsey, Russell Islands, *279*
hikes
  25 miles, Mississippi, 160

Davis publicizes, 298
Goff commends, 239
Griswold approves, 293
into Pavuvu jungle, 278
reputation for, 239
up Ouenghi River, 234
with Hale in NYC, 132
Hitler, Adolf
Chancellor of Germany 1933, 68
Munich Agreement, 103
occupied Austria, 103
occupied Rhineland, 86
Holland, President Ernest O.
letter to Indiana Bradts, *51*
of Washington State College, 44
howitzers
fired at Fort Ord, 170
loaded on ship 1942, 173
lost on SS Coolidge, 207
number in battalion, 144
placement in New Caledonia, 224
placement on Sasavele Is., 298
seeing fired shell, 161
Hudleson, Capt. Hugh Warner, 238, 268

interventionists, 105
IOU for bicycle, *158*
Ironbottom Sound, Guadalcanal, 204
isolationists, 105, 129
Italian soldier and wife, 213

journal, Wilber's
acquisition of, 218
facsimile of, *219*
not systematically kept, 254
jungle
hiked into, Pavuvu, 278
training in now favored, 297

King Neptune at equator, 199
knife up sleeve 1942, 210
Knight (pseudonym), Major
appointed C.O. 169th FA Bn., 179
artillery planning, Sasavele, 298
jungle hiking, 298
resigned command, 301
visit to Nouméa with WB, 236
Kokoda Trail, New Guinea, 162

latitude and longitude, Oct. 1942, 199
letters
facsimiles

ants on cot, *250*
final to Hale Oct. 1942, *187*
graphic postscript by Hale, *161*
IOU for bicycle, *158*
Pearl Harbor attack, *139*
V-mail, two versions, *196*
Wilber's journal, *219*
zig-zags in trail, New Caledonia, *235*
final from Fort Ord, 177
first found 1980, xx
found those to Norma, 191
found those to Valerie, 136
found those to Wilber's parents, 84
Mary-Elizabeth collection, 50
WW I Elizabeth-F. Hale collection, 50
Lever Brothers, palm grove
Guadalcanal, 266
Pavuvu, 276
lines of communication, map of, *xxxi*
Little Chick Mountain, outing to, 1937, 96
lizard
fell in rat trap, 310
in shaving kit, 242
on Guadalcanal, 267
on Pavuvu, 292
track decorating cake, 226
location, coding of
1940 plan, 107
howitzers delivered, 149
Russell Islands 1943, 280
log house, Versailles, Indiana
bought in 1906, 13
description by Mary, 21
lumber camp essay 1942, 101

MacArthur, Gen. Douglas
appreciated by New Zealanders, 214
directed New Guinea campaign, 236
escaped from Corregidor, 145
machine gun practice aboard ship, 198
magazine contest, best letters, 136
Maine, **87**
bought house in Bangor, 99
Hale's essays about, 100
left for NYC, 116
National Guard, 93
natives hopeful, 95
settled in, 90
Malcolm the deer
ate money order, 242
did not eat M.O., 277
kicked by sergeant, 239

Index

maneuvers
    captured soldiers, *132*
    convoy management, *137*
maps
    Japanese Plan for War 1941, *xxx*
    lines of communication 1942–3, *xxxi*
    New Caledonia with unit locations, *xxxiii*
    Pacific Areas with voyages, *xxix*
    Russell Islands with unit locations, *xxxiv*
    Solomon Islands with voyages, *xxxii*
    United States of America, *xxviii*
march
    Hattiesburg, 25 miles, 160
    in Wash. State Guard, 12 miles, 270
marksman, expert, with pistol, 270
McCalder, Lt. Robert W., 268
medicine ball overboard, 202
Mississippi, Camp Shelby, **147**
mistress, photo of, 201
Model A, trip by Hale 1952, 59, *60*
moon phases and threats, 296
mosquitos, 220, 229
mountains, coming closer, 250
Murrow, Edward R., broadcaster, 59

natives
    collected fish in target area, 227
    fished with spear, 238
    five on trail, New Caledonia, 234
    hunted with slingshots, New Cal., 226
    made New Zealand gifts, 209
    of Maine hopeful, 95
    sent signal flares, Pavuvu, 283
    watched concert, Ouenghi River, 225
New Caledonia, **213**
    166-mile road trip, 241
    family visit to, imagined, 226
    field exercise in rain, 252
    locations of units, *xxxiii*
    train en route to church, 224
New Guinea
    American and Japanese losses, 247
    battle of Coral Sea, 162
    Buna-Gona captured, 247
    Japanese landings on, 145
    Kokoda Trail, 162
New Marion, Indiana
    F. Hale met Elizabeth, 5
    schoolhouse, 6
New York City, **121**
    apartment at 310 W 73rd, 121
    apartment near Washington Square, 156

New Zealand, **205**
    Christmas presents from, 209
    weather and plants, 207
North Africa
    in Allied hands, 300
    Italians enter Egypt 1940, 105
    Operation Torch, 212
Nouméa, New Caledonia
    arrival, 215
    departed, *256*
    harbor, *216*
    harbor boat ride, 237, 255
    visit to meet ship, 236

O River Remember, Mary Ostenso, 32
Operation Torch, North Africa landings, 212
Orono, Maine 1936–38, 90
Ouenghi River, New Caledonia
    169th FA Bn. emplaced on, 217
    concert on bank of, 225
    hiked up, 234
    natives fished in, 238
    officers bathed in, *221*

Pacific Areas, map of, *xxix*
Panama Canal, swimming, 202
pants, man without, 178
patent, manganese, 96
Pavuvu Island, the Russells, **275**
Peak, Charles, brother of Elizabeth, 5
Pearl Harbor attack, letter during, *139*
Phi Beta Kappa
    PBK key cuts no ice, 153
    WB secretary of chapter, 62
photographs
    from National Archives, *xxi*
    taken by F. Hale 1904, *10*
    Wilber's, 1920s and 1930s, *218*
picnic 1927, 39
pistol, 0.45 caliber, civilian
    gift to WB, 93
    recalled gift of, 270
Plymouth auto, new 1936, *90*
PT boat, ride in, 286
Pullman, Washington, home ca. 1934, *61*
Pyle, Ernest, at I.U., correspondent, 30

radio
    choir music, Pavuvu, 278
    listened to, in tent, 303
rationing in USA, 301
rats, caught on Pavuvu, 306

recital by Valerie and Hale, 314, *315*
reconnaissance
    in jungle, Pavuvu, 293
    in mountains, New Caledonia, 239
    of Russell Is., 267
    with battery commanders, Pavuvu, 303
reproductive education, Hale & Valerie, 102
reunion
    Ruth's 50th, 30
    with 161st Inf., Guadalcanal, 269
Rhineland annexed by Germany 1936, 86
Ruhlin, Capt. James
    returned from Guadalcanal, 241
    sailed to visit the front, 238
Russell Islands, **258–316**
    awaited shipment to, 268
    locations of units, *xxxiv*
    shortened distance to Munda, 249
Russia attacked by Germany June 1941, 130

salary of lt. col., 312
Sandy Beach, Hale essay about, 101
Santa Claus, through tent roof, 220
Sasavele Island, howitzer positions, 299
Savo Sound as Ironbottom Sound, 204
school(s), Hale & Valerie
    Bangor, Maine, 100
    boarding, New Jersey 1943–44, 304
    Maine accent, 100
    private in NYC, 134
    PS 41 in NYC (Valerie), 168
    PS 87 in NYC 1941, 122
schoolhouse
    New Marion, Indiana, 6
    Waterloo, Versailles, *18*
Seelinger, Julia Bugbee Bradt
    held baby Hale, *62*, 63
    married Isaac Bradt, *4*
    married Philip Seelinger, 4
    visits to by WB & Norma, 53
    wagon trip, 3
Seelinger, Philip
    churchyard fight, 5
    sawmill worker, 4
segregation in South, 157
Shanghai, Japanese attack 1932, 68
shellback certificate, *200*
shells, smoke, Guadalcanal, 268
ships
    SS Normandie (USS Lafayette)
        capsized, *146*
        fire on, 147
        visit to, 155
    SS President Coolidge, 205, *206*
    USAT Maui, to New Zealand, 188, *194*
    USS American Legion to New Cal., 211, *214*
    USS Diphda, Hale on, 1953–54, 194
    USS Pres. Adams to Guadalcanal, *260*, 261
    USS Zeppelin 1919, *25*
Shocket, Saul, killed, 240
silo, WB threw stones into, 22
slingshots, used by natives, 226
smoking, dangers of, 1918, 26
snakes, seeing them first, 150
snipers, Japanese, 272
Solomon Islands, map of, *xxxii*
Southerner, The, train, 157, 168
Sparlin, Norma. See Bradt, Norma Sparlin
Sparlin, Stonewall E. "Stoney" (half brother of Norma), xvii
Sparlin, Stonewall J. (father of Norma)
    birth 1866, 40
    with siblings ca. 1897, *40*
spies, Norma reports, 150
spikes for shoes
    arrived, New Caledonia, 242
    Pavuvu, 280
Stalingrad, USSR
    German Sixth Army encircled, 212
    Germans approaching, 162
    surrender of German Sixth Army, 248
stars
    Capella brilliant, Pavuvu, 278
    seen from ship, 198
    shooting, seen by Hale, 161
Strauss, Jerome, Vanadium Corp., 208
strike duty, Tacoma 1935, 75, *80*, 83
sunset on Pavuvu, 308
swimming to New York, 202

Tassafaronga, Battle of, 212
tidal wave, Pavuvu, 313
Tokyo
    bombing of 1942, 162
    radio broadcast from, 265
Tomasov, Jan, Hale's violin teacher, xv
torpedo plane attack, 266, 271
train
    Hale to Washington, D.C. 1943, 292
    New Caledonia, 224
    Norma and children, Bangor, 116
    on honeymoon, 49
    subway IRT, Hale, 134
    the Southerner to Mississippi, 157

the Southerner to NYC, 168
through southwest (WB) 1942, 169
to Minnesota (Norma at 12), 43
trip, auto
   Cincinnati to Pullman 1930, 59
   in Model A by Hale 1952, 59
   to East Coast 1931, 62
Tunisia
   German capitulation, 300
   Kasserine Pass setback, 256
turtle in sea, 198

United States, locations in, *xxviii*

Vanadium Corporation
   attempted drive to, 241
   established graduate fellowship, 74
   Jerome Strauss, 208
   patent application, 95
   patent issuance, 96
Versailles, Indiana, 13
violin
   Evelyn and Milton played, 41
   Gladys Anderson played, 109
   Irma Zacharias, Hale's teacher, 121
   new 3/4 size at Christmas 1940, 108
   purchased full size 1942, 222
   Tomasov, Jan, Hale's teacher, xv
V-mail, 195, *196, 197*
Voyages to war, **189–257**

WAAC, Women's Army Auxiliary Corps
   none on board ship, 195
   Norma considered joining, 304
   Valerie imagined as, 185
wading in flooded Indiana field, 21
Waller, Sgt. ___
   kicked Malcom the deer, 240
   opening cocoanut, 314
War Bonds, 263
war plan, Japanese 1941, *xxx*
Washing Machine Charlie, 280
Washington, State of, **39, 57**
water dumped onto pedestrians, 246
Waterloo School, Versailles, 17
wedding
   announcement, WB and Norma, *48*
   Bourjaily, imagined by WB, 282, 295
   Monte Jr., 256
   to Norma, WB remembered, 199
   WB & Norma 1927, 46
World War II
   America enters Dec. 7 (1941), 140
   began in Europe 1939, 104
   Japan surrenders, *xii, xiii*
   Russia joins Allies, 130
worries, none except …, 173

Zacharias, Irma, violin teacher, 121, 255
zig-zag of convoy
   during torpedo plane attack, 271
   the zig or the zag?, 265

★

manfis

WILBER E. BRADT, MAJOR, HQ. 152ND F. A. 43RD DIVISION, U. S. ARMY

Dec. 7, 1941 3:00 P.M.

Dearest Wife and My Darling Children,

I am just hearing news casts of Japan attacks on Honan and Manila. We have expected war to come to us for a long time. It is here and I want you to know I love you. That seems to be all there is in my heart. This may and probably will mean "all leaves cancelled." If so I am content until I can come back to you to stay. The American people have given us a lot better chance to train than the soldiers of the last war. We are approaching a state of being well equipped. I am not worried.

Beloved, Do not be afraid. This time of trial can only hurt you if you are afraid. Bad times are ahead but we will come thru them together. I counting on you to be my reserves. Goodbye now. So sorry will say Japan. He will be sorry too. Wilber